The Good Shopping Guide

The Good Shopping Guide

Published by the Ethical Marketing Group

www.thegoodshoppingguide.co.uk

Third edition published 2004 by The Ethical Marketing Group
240 Portobello Road, London W11 1LL, UK.
www.thegoodshoppingguide.co.uk.

Publishing Director William Sankey 0044 (0) 207 229 1894
Director of advertising, marketing, accreditation – Kat Alexander 0044 (0) 207 229 2115
Designed by Deborah Barrow & Gary White & Lindsey Johns
Editor Charlotte Mulvey, copywriting Richard Synge and ECRA
Photography by 86 Ltd
Media consultancy & public relations by 86 Ltd (see 86.co.uk – 0044 (0) 207 229 1958)

ISBN 0954 2529 3 4

Printed and bound in Great Britain by Cambrian Printers Ltd
on paper certified from sustainable forests.
Distributed by Central Books (orders@centralbooks.com; 0044 (0) 845 458 9911)
Sales enquiries to Signature Books (sales@signaturebooks.co.uk; 0044 (0) 1904 631320)

Thanks to Craig Morrison, Henry Postan, Elodie Masson, Lucy May Lubrani, Marie Therese, Gareth Platt, Miranda Nash, Katie Johnstone, Sarmad Jaffar and Max Sankey at 86 for their excellent media consultancy. And at ECRA, to Rob Harrison, Bruce Bingham, Sarah Irving, Jonathan Atkinson, Hannah Berry, Scott Clouder, Matt Fawcett, Mary Rayner, Ruth Rosselson, Jane Turner, Lauren Steadman, Jane Lawson, Ben Caulfield, Jenny Edwards, Elanor Gordon and Lyndsay Whaten. Thanks to Yo Fung and EIRIS for help with the ethical investment section. And to Chris Lord-Smith at AECB for input in the sustainable building chapter. Thanks also to Tricia Barnett at Tourism Concern and Fiona King at Marine Stewardship Council.

Legal Disclaimer

The Good Shopping Guide aims to provide an independent and authoritative list of mainstream brands and companies according to research data previously published by and licensed from The Ethical Consumer Research Association. While every reasonable care is taken to ensure the accuracy of the information in *The Good Shopping Guide*, neither the publisher, the printers, nor any distributor is responsible for errors or omissions. All data is accepted by us in good faith as being correct at May 2002 unless stated otherwise on p24. Pictures and advertisements are vetted to ensure there is no conflict with this editorial policy. For further information on the editorial content, fully referenced source materials are available from ECRA on request.

Contents

Foreword by the Ethical Company Organisation

'YOUR TILL RECEIPT IS AS IMPORTANT AS YOUR VOTE'

Welcome to the third edition!

The Good Shopping Guide is the world's leading ethical reference guide listing the level of corporate social responsibility of the companies behind hundreds of everyday consumer brands.

Our objective is to encourage a universally responsible corporate attitude to animal welfare, human rights and the environment.

Companies depend entirely on their customers' goodwill, so we believe that the key to a progressive 21st century lies in the persuasive power of intelligent consumer action.

The Good Shopping Guide informs you of the simple facts about each company and provides some overall recommendations to help you channel your spending power.

Thank you for all the input for this third annual edition from Friends of the Earth, Cafédirect, Christian Aid, the World Development Movement, the Ethical Investment Research Service, the Ecology Building Society, Good Energy, AECB, Tourism Concern, Ethical Consumer Magazine, the Environmental Transport Association and Survival International.

And thank you again to the Ethical Consumer Research Association, who have pioneered this field since 1989. This book would not have been possible without their substantial expertise.

WELCOME TO THE GOOD SHOPPING GUIDE

Now, more than ever before, is the time for consumers worldwide to use their spending power pro-actively. The following information can empower us all to really make a difference to the world around us.

The Good Shopping Guide aims to help you make informed decisions about what consumer brands are best for the planet, best for animals and best for people everywhere. We hope to make a difference for the environment, for animals and we also want to improve the living standards of poor people in other countries.

Everybody can make a contribution to a better world by the simple choices we make while out shopping. By choosing to buy one kind of coffee over another we can help the farmers who grow it. And most of us know that when we buy an eco-washing-up liquid we help to reduce pollution. But who on earth knows which freezer to buy; what TV manufacturer is the most ethical; what brand of yoghurt is kindest to animals; which consumer goods companies are involved in the arms trade; and which Health and Beauty products are good? *The Good Shopping Guide* tells all – in detail.

Smart choices can and do have a direct effect on global issues

We don't have to feel powerless about the world's problems. Our till receipts are like voting slips – they can easily be used constructively. This is something that the big corporations will have to notice tomorrow even if their management seems to be unaware and uninformed today.

If you care about things like global warming, pollution, animal testing, factory farming, the arms trade and exploitation of people, you are certainly not alone. You don't have to be a political activist or even to join a campaign. If you care at all, it's really simple to do something about these difficult issues, just by making good choices while you're out shopping.

Small decisions – big effects

Our choices can support progressive companies that want to improve the way business is done. And our shopping habits can force changes in the way in which even the largest food corporations and supermarkets do their day-to-day business. It's already happening, with supermarkets displaying fair trade, GM-free and organic foods on their shelves because they know that more and more customers want and appreciate these things.

'Buying ethical products sends support directly to progressive companies working to improve the status quo, while at the same time depriving others that abuse for profit. For example, when you buy an eco-washing-up liquid you're giving its manufacturer the funds it needs to invest in clean technology and advertise its products to a wider market. At the same time, you're no longer buying your old liquid, so its manufacturer loses business and will perhaps change its ways.'

www.ethicalconsumer.org

You can make a difference in lots of ways. You can begin by looking for products carrying the Good Shopping Guide's ethical 'certification' logo. Also look for fair trade, organic and GM-free foods. Also you can choose to buy sustainably-produced or recycled products. Buying eco-cleaning fluids or washing-up liquids gives progressive manufacturers more funds to invest in clean technology and helps to persuade the other manufacturers to think of changing their ways.

Each decision like this has an impact – small in itself but huge when you know that millions of others are doing the same. This book shows that you can be part of the solution, making the world a cleaner, fairer and kinder place, rather than part of the problem.

All the information you need to make good and ethical shopping decisions is contained within this book.

What is good shopping?

Good Shopping is Ethical Shopping, and that means buying things that are made ethically and by companies that act ethically – or in other words without causing harm to or exploiting humans, animals or the environment.

Ethical shopping encourages innovative products and companies and discourages others that prefer to ignore the social and environmental consequences of their practices. It also empowers you, the consumer, and gives you a say in how the products you buy are made and how the manufacturers conduct their business.

Our choices can be both positive, by buying products that you know to be ethical, and negative, by refusing to buy products that you disapprove of.

Ethical shopping can also mean supporting actions like the Nestlé boycott, which targeted all the brands and company subsidiaries to try to force the company to change its marketing of formula baby milk in the Third World.

And you can follow what the Ethical Consumer Research Association (ECRA) calls the 'fully screened approach'. This means looking at all the companies and products together and evaluating which brand is the most ethical. This is the information that *The Good Shopping Guide* brings together in the following pages.

ECRA is part of an ever-growing network of organisations committed to making the world a better place: organisations like Oxfam, Fairtrade Foundation, Traidcraft, Friends of the Earth, Naturewatch, the Soil Association, the Vegetarian Society and the Forest Stewardship Council.

By using this book you will discover more than you ever knew about what goes into the goods you buy or are thinking of buying. You will have the information you need to make clear decisions, either to buy the products of progressive and green companies or to boycott those of unethical companies.

Rob Harrison of ECRA has seen the trend towards ethical shopping grow: 'For the last 30 years or so, multinationals have been trying to shape the decisions of elected governments to fit their vision of a global free market but the ordinary people who buy their products haven't been so convinced. The scale of opposition from a new wave of ethical consumers has taken companies aback.'

How to use this book

The Good Shopping Guide takes you through all the ethical factors you may want to consider when you are buying products for the home, health and beauty, kitchens, food and drink or financial services.

For each type of product, you will find:

- A summary table – to gain a quick overview on which brands are from the most ethical companies

- A long table – to study the detail across fourteen ethical criteria, to decide precisely which brands are for you

The book

The Guide gives you the essential environmental, animal welfare and human rights background on a wide range of products, the changes that are being made by the manufacturers and the names of the most progressive companies. It summarises the most important ethical details about the different brands that are available in the UK.

Clear ratings are given for the different brands, covering the companies' environmental reporting, pollution, animal testing, factory farming, workers' rights, involvement in armaments and genetic engineering and other ethical factors.

After a close reading and considering all the companies and products together, you will have all the information you need to make some really switched-on shopping decisions.

When you are in the shops, look out for our *Ethical Company* logo – the new badge of authority that says a brand has scored well in our ethicality test. *Ethical Company* logo is already being used as an independent mark of endorsement by several leading and progressive brands (see pages 27-32).

How to read the tables

THE SHORT TABLES – BEDTIME DRINKS EXAMPLE

- Clipper
- Cocodirect
- Green & Blacks

- Cadbury's
- Ovaltine

- Galaxy
- Horlicks
- Malteasers

The summary tables that run in each product section are designed to give readers a quick view as to the overall ethicality scores of different companies and brands.

The Good Shopping Guide methodology for these tables involved initially mathematically amalgamating the results of all the ECRA ethicality categories into three broad groups.

The Good Shopping Guide Ethical Company group contains those brands and companies which, taking every audit category into account, score well in that particular product sector. These are the companies which may apply to use the logo on packaging and marketing materials.

We apply the question mark symbol to brands and companies which score in the middle section of their individual product sector.

This symbol is applied to brands and companies which score in the lowest section of their product sector.

The long tables – Bedtime Drinks example

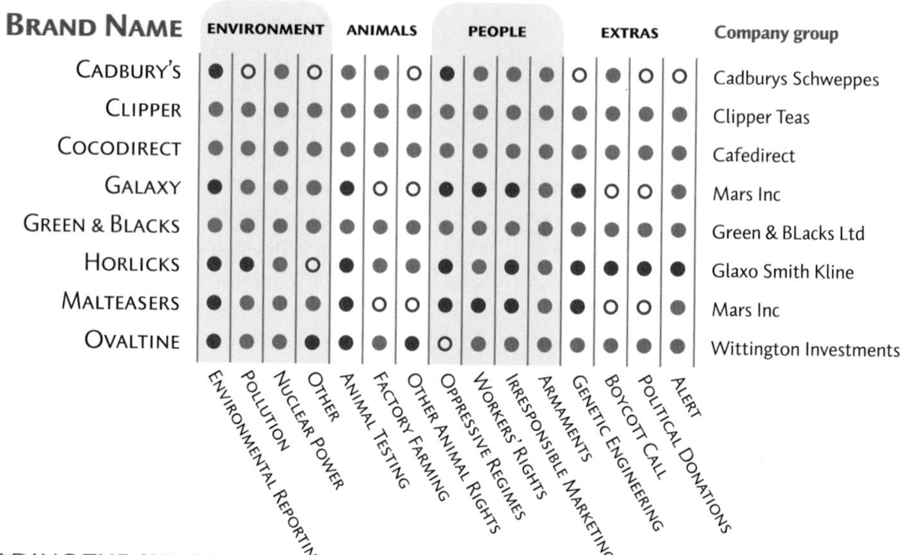

Reading the symbols

- ● **Top rating:** a green circle indicates that we have found no criticisms.
- ○ **Middle rating:** an empty red circle indicates a certain degree of involvement in that category.
- ● **Bottom rating:** a full red circle represents the worst level of involvement in that category.

(See category definitions below for clarifications of how we award these ratings).

Related companies

Amber circles refer to the performance of related companies.

- ● A related company has a bottom rating and the company itself has a middle rating.
- ○ A related company has a middle rating.
- ● A related company has a bottom rating.

So for example, if a pension company has an investment in an arms company, it will receive an amber mark in that category.

Marks on the tables represent criticism from campaign groups worldwide and are sourced from ECRA's database which contains around 45,000 references on around 25,000 companies. It has been updated for this book to at least May 2002.

The category definitions

Each table is first divided into the broad areas of Environment, Animals and People, and then sub-divided into more detailed categories. Most are self-explanatory but it is useful to understand some of the practical issues and dilemmas behind some of the categories. Fully referenced Research Supplements covering each rating are available from ECRA on request.

The Environment columns

1. Environmental reporting

The quality of a company's environmental reporting can say a lot about its ethical standards. As such reports become more commonplace it is becoming easier to rate companies on their efforts: a good report will contain fixed targets as opposed to vague statements of intent. For example, BT annually sets out new targets such as aiming to 'eliminate the use of sulphur hexaflouride for cable testing by a certain date'.

Companies who fail to produce any report get a bottom rating; companies with inadequate reports get a middle rating. The top rating in this category means a good report, however, ironically some of the corporations which have attracted most criticisms have produced exemplary environmental reports. Exception is made for small companies without the resources to publish a big annual report, and which label or market their products as eco-alternatives. (See ECRA Research Supplements for what assessment has been made for each company).

At the moment, subsidiaries are dealt with separately. When environmental reporting becomes the norm, good ratings will only be given to companies at company group level when it can be clearly seen that the same standards apply across all their operations. For further explanation as to what assessment has been made in each particular case, see the ECRA Research Supplements.

2. Pollution

Pollution inevitably affects the local environment, wildlife and human population. Its consequences may be unforeseen or even ignored. The effects of pollution can last long after the incident has been 'cleaned up'.

It makes sense for consumers to take a company's pollution record into account when choosing what to buy. In this way, consumer pressure can operate as an additional incentive to companies to take these issues seriously.

A responsible company should be minimising its likelihood of pollution incidents by following Environment Agency recommendations on emissions and safety and by minimising the use of harmful chemicals. However, responsible companies will ultimately be looking for 'closed loop' production systems. Ecover's manufacturing facility in Belgium is one of the few factories already operating to such standards.

A full red circle indicates (●) that the company has been criticised for specific instances of pollution of water, air or land; an empty red circle (○) indicates a lesser degree of involvement relative to other companies on the table. (See ECRA Research Supplements for full details).

3. Nuclear Power

Nuclear power is a target for social and environmental campaigners for two main reasons:

- Its link to the production of nuclear weapons
- The pollutant properties of radioactive waste.

The danger of the latter point is twofold: some nuclear waste materials will remain dangerous for 250,000 years; and the security problem attached to its potential for use in the manufacture of weapons of mass destruction.

The nuclear industry argues that, as an electricity generator which does not produce greenhouse gases, it should have a future role in combating climate change, however, environmental campaigners would prefer to support a sustainable future through energy conservation and the development of 'cleaner' power sources such as sun, wind and wave power.

Some nuclear industry specialists are also involved in the production of consumer goods and these are reflected in the tables. A full red circle (●) indicates the company is involved in the design, construction or operation of nuclear power stations, radioactive waste handling and/or the mining, processing or reprocessing of uranium. An empty red circle (○) indicates production of other nuclear-related equipment, for example, monitoring equipment.

4. Environment: other

A huge variety of activities can fall into this category. It is designed to cover any activity that damages the environment not covered by the categories Pollution and Nuclear Power.

A full red circle (●) indicates that the company has been criticised for:

- manufacturing products that have been highlighted as being particularly damaging to the environment such as pesticides, PVC and ozone depleting chemicals.
- lobbying against campaigns or measures intended to reduce environmental impact
- involvement in habitat destruction

An empty red circle (○) indicates a lesser degree of involvement relative to other companies on the table.

This category can be confused with the Pollution category because they both include criticisms about the release of chemicals. But while Pollution relates only to specific pollution incidents or reported releases of toxic chemicals from particular sites, this category allows us to demonstrate that a company is involved in the production of substances such as pesticides that, by their nature, can cause environmental damage.

The Animals columns

1. Animal testing

At the end of the 20th century, nearly three million animals per annum were used in experiments in the UK alone. Worldwide, over 100 million animals are tested on every year. Most tests are carried out on mice, rats, guinea pigs, birds, fish and rabbits, but other animals including dogs, cats and primates will be used.

Testing of consumer products such as lipstick and washing-up liquid account for a tiny fraction of animal tests. The vast majority are done in the name of medical research, to test new drugs. There is also the testing of pesticides and other chemicals, food additives, weapons and the use of animals in psychology experiments.

All new chemical ingredients, whether for medicines, household products, pesticides or whatever, are required by law to be animal tested for various kinds of toxicity in order to classify them as safe for the workers who make them and to minimise risk during their transport and use. The regulatory bodies list a number of animal tests that are required before an ingredient can be registered.

Alternative, non-animal tests such as tissue and cell cultures, computer production, clinical studies and the use of skin fragments do exist for all the standard toxicity and irritancy tests. But the process of 'validating' these alternative methods has been obstructed, according to BUAV, by industry and regulatory bodies' reluctance to accept these new methods.

Companies need to do two things in order to behave responsibly:

- Invest heavily in developing alternative, non-animal tests and lobby to get them validated
- Postpone the search for new ingredients and use the 8,000 established ingredients until non-animal alternatives to all animal tests have been validated

A full red circle (●) indicates that the company conducts or commissions tests on animals for non-medical products or ingredients *or* sells animal-tested cosmetics, toiletries or household products. An empty red circle (○) indicates that the company conducts or commissions tests on animals for medical products or sells medical products.

2. Factory farming

A full red circle (●) indicates that the company is: a factory farmer of meat, poultry (broiler and eggs), fish or fur *or* manufactures or supplies intensive farming equipment such as battery cages, beak trimmers, pig crates *or* sells or processes meat, poultry (broiler and eggs), or fur that is not labelled as free range or organic. An empty red circle (○) represents a lessser degree of involvement relative to the other companies on the table.

The definition for this column means that farmers, food manufacturers (such as Heinz) and retailers (such as Asda) of any meat, eggs and fish will get a lower rating. Animal breeders or 'stock suppliers' and suppliers of equipment such as battery cages, veal crates, etc are bottom rated also, along with those in the fur industry. This column specifically excludes free-range farmers/companies/ products, which are dealt with in Other Animal Rights. Dairy farmers and processors are excluded from this column because otherwise all but vegan or organic food producers would be bottom rated, and would produce a column of little practical use to consumers wishing to make a distinction.

3. Other animal rights

Philosophically speaking, there are two main types of animal campaign group – those that promote concern for animal welfare and those that believe that animals should have 'rights'. The most important 'right' is the right to live – and this category primarily helps animal rights campaigners to identify companies which are involved in the slaughter of animals or the use of animal by-products.

A full red circle (●) indicates that the company is

- a farmer of non-intensive/free range meat, poultry (broilers and eggs) or fish, or is a dairy farmer, or
- a slaughterhouse owner or user of slaughterhouse by-products such as leather and gelatin

An empty red circle (○) represents:

- supply of animal feedstuffs
- sale or processing of free range meat,

poultry (broilers and eggs) or fish
- other activities involving the exploitation of animals, e.g. zoos, circuses

The People columns

1. Oppressive regimes

Holding corporations accountable for their presence in oppressive regimes began in earnest during the campaign against South Africa's apartheid system and it has since evolved so that a 'list' of countries, as detailed below, exists. The ranking system for oppression is based on a range of indicators like use of torture, political prisoners, denial of religious freedoms and extrajudicial killings.

This list and, indeed, this column in the table is controversial, partly because many deeply unpopular governments do not appear on the list, but also because some people argue that trade is a way of engaging with and educating oppressive governments.

Companies are rated according to a point system, so middle rated for scoring up to five points, and bottom rated for six points or more under the following system:

Operations by the company or company group or related company in any of the following regimes score TWO points per country: Algeria, Burma, China, Colombia, Indonesia, Iraq, Libya, North Korea, Syria and Yugoslavia.

Operations by the company or company group or related company in any of the following score ONE point per country: Afghanistan, Bahrain, Belorus, Bosnia, Brazil, Cambodia, Croatia, Cuba, Dominican Republic, Egypt, El Salvador, Guatemala, Iran, Kenya, Kuwait, Liberia, Mexico, Nigeria, Pakistan, Peru, the Philippines, Qatar, Russia, Saudi Arabia, Sri Lanka, Sudan, Tajikistan, Tunisia, Turkey and Venezuela.

A company will not score points if all its products sourced from these regimes are marketed as fair trade.

2. Workers' rights

A full red circle (●) or empty red circle (○) represents criticism of the company or its suppliers for infringement of workers' rights, which includes: intimidation of workers by management; use of forced or slave labour; payment of wages below a level which is adequate to live on; a working week of over 48 hours; forced and/or excessive overtime; exploitative use of child labour; denial of the right to associate, form unions or bargain collectively; discrimination on the grounds of race, sex, sexuality, or creed; the provision of inadequate or dangerous working conditions.

3. Irresponsible marketing

All consumers in free-market economies learn to accept that the language of marketing accentuates the positive and plays down the negative. The point at which this becomes 'irresponsible' is difficult to define. ECRA has chosen a fairly strict definition for this category, and we only focus on practices that have direct health implications. Certain activities do avoid this definition. Coca Cola, for example, whose cans manage to find their way to the most impoverished rural settlements in the Third World, and which delivers precious little in the way of nutrition, is often criticised by development analysts. Coke, however, is not marketed as healthy or nutritious. It is simply portrayed as 'fun' so would not be bottom rated.

Four industries generate the bulk of the criticisms for this category: baby milk formula, pharmaceuticals, tobacco and pesticides.

A full red circle (●) indicates marketing of products in a way that has been criticised for causing severe physical harm.

On the tables, an empty red circle (○) indicates the marketing of products in a way that has been criticised as being detrimental to health. (See ECRA Research Supplements for more details).

4. Armaments

In the table, a full red circle (●) represents involvement in the manufacture or supply of nuclear or conventional weapons including: ships, tanks, armoured vehicles and aircraft; weapons systems components; systems aiding the launch, guidance, delivery or deployment of missiles; fuel; computing; communications services. (See ECRA Research Supplements for detail).

An empty red circle (○) represents the manufacture or supply of non-strategic parts of the military, not including food and drink.

The Extras columns

1. Genetic engineering

A full red circle (●) represents involvement in:

- the non-medical genetic modification of plants or animals, and/or
- gene-patenting, and/or
- xenotransplantation

An empty red circle (○) represents:

- the manufacture or sale of non-medical products involving or containing genetically modified organisms (GMOs), and/or
- the manufacture or sale of non-medical products likely to contain GMOs and the lack of clear company group-wide GMO free policy and/or
- public statements in favour of the use of GMOs in non-medical products.
- the development or marketing of medical procedures or products involving genetic modification, which have been criticised on ethical grounds.

2. Boycott call

This column can be problematic since a boycott may be called from groups from across the political spectrum. It is important, therefore, to be clear about the reasons why a particular boycott has been called and these are explained in the relevant ECRA Research Supplements.

Some types of campaign group have problems with boycotts. For example, development charities such as CAFOD and Oxfam have contended that boycotts of companies involved in workers' rights abuses could put workers' livelihoods at risk. However, boycotts can be a useful means of exerting economic pressure for change and cannot, therefore, be ignored.

On the table, a full red circle (●) indicates that a boycott of the brand name featured has been called somewhere in the world, or a boycott of the entire company group has been called.

A full amber circle (●) indicates that a boycott of one of the parent company's subsidiaries or other brands has been called somewhere in the world. For more information on specific ongoing UK boycotts, see *www.ethicalconsumer.org*

3. Political donations

The political donations column differs from most of the other table columns in that instead of rating companies with a mark for their involvement, we simply inform the reader where donations have been spent. We normally represent this on the table as LAB (Labour), LIB (Liberal) and CON (Conservative). Other symbols on the table have included 'CPS' referring to the Centre for Policy Studies, a Conservative think-tank, and 'BUI' another Conservative Party fund-raising mechanism. Abbreviations such as 'USA' appear where donations have been made in other countries.

We include this column because we do not believe that corporations should fund political parties. There is considerable evidence that the huge wealth of corporations can distort the political process. Elections in the USA particularly can appear to be 'bought' by the candidate with the biggest budgets, and parties with agendas critical of business can be quickly marginalised. In some countries, such as Germany, corporate funding is quite sensibly prohibited by law. Until that occurs in the UK, consumers who agree with this position can use our tables to withdraw their custom from political donors.

4. Code of Conduct

A full red circle (●) indicates that the parent company has no Code of Conduct for workers' rights at its supplier companies or did not reply to our request for a copy of one.

An empty red circle (○) indicates that the parent company has demonstrated to ECRA or other campaign groups a Code of Conduct for protection of workers' rights.

A green circle (●) indicates that the parent company has demonstrated to ECRA or other campaign groups a Code of Conduct for workers' rights AND effective procedures for independent monitoring of that code or that its products are labelled and certified as fair trade.

Very progressive brands

In two cases we have promoted a brand up a level in the short tables. This is where the brand is very ethical and progressive (Co-operative Bank and Ecover).

Previously published reports

All the long tables in this book have been previously been published by ECRA in *Ethical Consumer* magazine and /or on Corporate Critic database. ECRA has permitted *The Good Shopping Guide* to reproduce them under licence. ECRA re-checked company ratings in the Guide in May 2002 using the Corporate Critic database (see About ECRA), but please be aware that ratings or ownership of brands may have changed since then. The text of the Buyers' Guides has not been re-written by ECRA since the original publication date (see below for details), and ECRA has given *The Good Shopping Guide* a free hand to edit and re-write the text of each report.

Fully referenced abstracts detailing exactly why each mark was awarded, appear in numbered Research Supplements (see below) and/or on the Corporate Critic database itself. For more information about specific ratings contact ECRA (see page 307)

New rating definitions

In 2002 ECRA made some changes to the way it rates companies. This means that reports in this book dated after June 2002 will have been compiled according to the new criteria. The main changes were to introduce a new column entitled Political Activity to replace the Political Donations column and to require a higher standard of companies to get favourable ratings in the environmental reporting column. A new Alert column covers a range of issues like Excessive Directors Pay and operations in Tax Havens, and a new oppressive regimes list was also drafted in October 2002. The details of these new rating criteria appear below.

Minor changes were also made to the definitions addressing Nuclear Power, Environment Other and Other Animal Rights. Contact ECRA for free 'Introduction to EC' which provides details on these and other issues.

Environment

Environmental Reporting

A full red circle (●) indicates that the company or parent company:
i) did not respond to a request by ECRA for a copy of its environmental policy or report and did not display such a policy or report on its website, OR
ii) supplied to ECRA or displayed on its website an environmental policy or report which contained neither specific targets nor discussion of impacts specific to the company.

An empty red circle (○) indicates that the company or parent company supplied to ECRA or displayed on its website an environmental policy or report which contained quantified future targets but:

i) was not dated within the last two years,
OR
ii) failed to demonstrate a reasonable understanding of the company's main impacts,
OR
iii) was not independently verified.

A green circle (●) indicates that the company or parent company:
i) supplied to ECRA or displayed on its website an environmental policy or report which
(a) contained specific future performance targets, and
(b) which demonstrated a reasonable understanding of the company's main impacts, and
(c) was dated within the last two years, and
(d) was independently verified.
ii) is a small business specialising in the supply of products with low environmental impacts or which are of environmental benefit or which offer other social benefits.

People

Oppressive Regimes

A company will receive a full red circle (●) if it has operations in six or more of the following regimes, and a small circle for operations in up to five.

Afghanistan, Algeria, Belarus, Brazil,

Burma, Burundi, Central African Republic, Chad, China, Congo(DRC), Cote d'Ivoire, Egypt, Equatorial Guinea, Eritrea, Ethiopia, Fiji, Guatemala, Indonesia, Iran, Iraq, Israel, Jordan, Kazakhstan, Kenya, Kuwait, Laos, Lebanon, Liberia, Libya, Malaysia, Mexico, Nigeria, Pakistan, Qatar, Russian Federation, Rwanda, Saudi Arabia, Senegal, Somalia, Sudan, Swaziland, Tanzania, Thailand, Togo, Tunisia, Turkey, United Arab Emirates, Uzbekistan, Vietnam, Zimbabwe. A company will receive a green circle (●) in this column if all its products sourced from these regimes are marketed as fair trade.

List compiled in October 2002.

Sources: Amnesty International Report 2002, Freedom House's 'Freedom in the World' 2001-2 and the UN Human Development Report 2002

Extras

Political Activity

A full red circle (●) indicates that the company has made a donation of £50,000 or more to a political party, either direct or indirect or in 'soft money,' in the last five years, or has membership of 3 or more lobby groups, or has directly lobbied governments or supranational institutions on trade liberalisation issues.

An empty red circle (○) indicates membership of 2 or less lobby groups, or a donation of less than £50,000 to political parties in the last 5 years, or secondment of staff to political parties, governments or supranational institutions.

A lobby group is defined as a corporate lobby group which lobbies for free trade at the expense of the environment, animal welfare, human rights or health protection. A current list of such groups includes:

lAmerican Chamber of Commerce/ AMCHAM-EU l Bilderberg Group

lBusiness Action for Sustainable Development l Business Round Table l European Round Table of Industrialists l European Services Forum l International Chamber of Commerce l Transatlantic Business Dialogue l Trilateral Commission l US Coalition of Service Industries l World Business Council for Sustainable Development

lWorld Economic Forum

Alert

This column contains extra information which is not usually applicable to enough companies for it to warrant its own column A mark in this column will always be explained in the company profiles section of the product report.

A full red circle (●) will indicate involvement in one or more of the following:

i) human rights abuses, through any of the following:

a) the use of its equipment, staff or facilities in perpetrating human rights abuses

b) human rights abuses perpetrated by security forces associated with a company's operations

c) involvement in projects that have proven links with human rights abuses

d) collaboration with a government and/or military in perpetrating human rights abuses

e) allegations of human rights abuses by company staff

ii) land rights abuses; specific instances where indigenous peoples have been or may

be removed from their land, or whose livelihoods may be threatened, to facilitate corporate operations (either extant or planned)
iii) involvement in pornography: where companies produce, print, publish or distribute material classed as pornographic, including 'adult entertainment' TV stations.
Pornography is defined as material that combines sex and/or nudity with abuse or degradation in a manner that appears to endorse, condone or encourage such behaviour. This is contrasted with erotica, defined as sexually suggestive or arousing material that is free of sexism, racism and homophobia and is respectful of all human beings portrayed. It also excludes sex education and sexual health information materials of an explicit nature.
iv) involvement in Third World debt
An empty red circle (○) will indicate involvement in one or more of the following:
i) excessive directors' remuneration (where any director is paid more than £1m in any one year)
ii) subsidiaries in tax havens

Key to The Good Shopping Guide audit tables

The tables are intended to show at-a-glance which companies own which brands and what sort of activities they are involved in. They also allow people to identify those issues of most concern to them and to ignore issues of no interest.

Within the broad areas of the environment, animals and people we have a number of categories into which we place criticisms of companies. Most are self explanatory, but you can find out more about the definitions and rating system at the Ethical Consumer website (www.ethicalconsumer.org) or by obtaining 'An Introduction to Ethical Consumer' free of charge from ECRA's office.

Brand names

Within the long tables we attempt to profile the brands which together hold the majority of the market share. However, due to space limitations, short buyers' guides usually have a maximum of around 12 brands, while longer buyers' guides are limited to around 25.

Company Group

In this column we list the ultimate holding company (UHC) i.e. the top level of corporate ownership, which may often differ from the brand owner. For instance, the Umbro brand name is owned by Umbro Europe Ltd, but Umbro Europe is owned by venture capital company Doughty Hanson, which is therefore the UHC and appears in this column. It is important to note that the marks on the table represent those of the company group as a whole, so where Umbro is listed on the table the marks refer not just to Umbro but to Doughty Hanson and all companies owned by Doughty Hanson.

Definition of 'related company'

We use the expression 'related company' throughout the book and particularly on the tables. We use this term when there is a formal relationship (usually a small share holding) but not enough to be treated as a direct subsidiary or associate company.

Ethical shopping success

Over the years, and especially since the 1980s, consumers have been making an ever-increasing impact on the way governments and companies behave in all parts of the world. These are just a few examples:

- The campaign against testing cosmetics on animals changed the behaviour of nearly all the main cosmetics companies.
- A boycott in the US against Heinz forced the company to stop catching tuna with purse-seine fishing nets, which used to kill tens of thousands of dolphins each year – the tuna trade and the Whale and Tuna Conservation Society then launched a 'dolphin friendly' logo.
- In 1991, Friends of the Earth launched a campaign against the stocking of tropical timber from unsustainable sources by the six largest DIY chains – the campaign eventually became a consumer boycott and proved very successful. By 1994, all six had agreed to stop selling mahogany.
- There has been such huge growth in the spread of fair-traded goods that supermarkets such as Sainsbury's and Co-op now advertise them openly.
- Probably the most dramatic single environmental boycott was Greenpeace's campaign in 1995 against the dumping of Shell's oil platform Brent Spar – sales of Shell petrol were down by 70per cent in some German outlets and the company gave in after only a few days.
- Increasing numbers of clothing retail companies and sports shoes manufacturers have adopted codes of conduct about the conditions of the workers making their goods.
- Ethical consumerism encouraged the phasing out of the worst ozone-depleting and greenhouse gases used in fridges and freezers – in 1994, Electrolux followed manufacturers Bosch, Siemens, Liebherr and AEG in replacing ozone damaging HCFCs and HFCs with hydrocarbons.
- The UK campaign against genetically modified (GM) foods was so successful that the leading companies changed their policies – eight supermarket chains in the UK now sell their own GM-free own-brands.
- The consumer boycott of fruit and wine and other products from apartheid South Africa helped to free Nelson Mandela and to bring about democratic change.
- The *Good Shopping Guide* first edition sold out in just 3 months – showing there is real consumer demand for reliable information.
- *www.gooshing.co.uk* is set to take ethical shopping global (see page 324).

Ethical Company Organisation's accreditation scheme

The Ethical Company Organisation (E.C.O), who produce *The GOOD Shopping Guide* run an accreditation scheme, whereby companies which pass its full ethicality test can prove their independent certification by displaying the Ethical Company logo.

The logo is designed to support ethical companies' reputations and sales by clearly showing that the company is independently endorsed by *The Ethical Company Organisation*. It can be displayed on product packaging, websites, advertising, press releases, stationery etc – so that consumers can easily identify the most ethical companies.

A number of companies have already joined the scheme and are using the logo as an independent mark of endorsement. The research process takes between 4 and 8 weeks and scans over 40,000 public record documents including Court reports, criticisms from NGOs, boycott calls and environmental reports.

Listed below are some of the companies who have already joined the Ethical Company Organisation's accreditation scheme.

We can wholeheartedly recommend the following list of E.C.O accredited companies as our research team is contracted to re-test their Ethical Company status every 12 months.

Atmos Heating Systems

Atmos manufacture high efficiency air handling units, through more efficient heat exchange and better air handling. Their condensing gas boilers and water heating systems have won awards for energy efficiency, which will save you money. All of their products have many technical advantages which make them safer and more energy efficient. These advantages have been recognised by the construction industry press, and every one is designed to benefit users.

www.atmos.uk.com
Tel: 01327 871990

Brother

Brother is a world wide electronics and manufacturing company, with sales in over 100 countries. Brother feels it is their duty to do whatever they can to protect and preserve the environment and has several policies in place for protecting and preserving the environment. They have recently launched the Worlds first TCO99 Compliant Printer, which meets 50 stringent ecological, health and safety and ergonomic requirements. Brother's product ranges include: Printers; All-in-One Machines, Faxes, Labeling Systems, Laminators, Typewriters, Sewing Machines.

www.brother-uk.com
Tel: 0845 60 60 626

Caurnie Soap Company

Caurnie Soap has been providing quality Cold process hand made Vegan soaps since their founding in 1922. Cruelty free vegetarian soap, suitable for delicate skins or allergy sufferers who look to natural skin care to provide tested skin care solutions. Caurnie offers a variety of hand made cleaning products that represent the very best in Vegan personal and household cleaning.

www.caurnie.com
Tel: 0141 776 1218

Ecology Building Society

The Ecology Building Society was founded in 1981. They are a mutual organisation, dedicated to improving the environment by promoting a sustainable housing and sustainable communities. Savings placed with the Ecology fund mortgage lending on: energy efficient housing; ecological renovation; derelict and dilapidated properties; small-scale and ecological enterprise; low-impact lifestyles. Savings and mortgages are available across the U.K.

www.ecology.co.uk
Tel: 0845 674 5566

Eskimo

A visual media company, with environmental priorities, that provides photography and video services to a diverse range of clients. Eskimo specialises in natural history and social documentary and prides itself on emphasising both traditional high technical standards whilst constantly trying to create new styles and an innovative visual approach. Clients include English Nature, Secret World Animal Rescue Centre and British Waterways.

www.eskimomedia.co.uk
Tel: 0117 9656581

Good Energy

Good Energy is an independent, UK company which supplies only 100% renewable energy products to homes and businesses. Good Energy is recommended by Friends of the Earth and comes top in their league table. Good Energy sources all its renewable energy from wind power and small hydro generation stations throughout the UK. It specialises in small-scale generation helping to protecting natural habitats as well as providing a future market for British generators.

www.good-energy.co.uk
Tel: 0845 456 1640

Green Energy

Green Energy is a renewable energy supplier created to offer people who are concerned about our shared environment the chance to do something practical, positive and imaginative. Green Energy aim to grow a business that is ethical, responsible and constructive, but is also commercially sound, prudently managed and secure in the long term. Green Energy supplies electricity to domestic customers and small business customers in England and Wales.

www.greenenergy.uk.com
Tel: 0845 456 9550

Green People

Green People offer handmade health and beauty products and are committed to offering products that are 100% natural, certified organic and highly effective. None of their formulations or products are or ever have been tested on animals and most of their products are approved by the Vegan Society. All products are suitable for Vegetarians and full ingredient disclosure is given on all products. Green People support charities with related environmental concerns and each year 10% of net profit are donated to charitable causes linked to 'green' or environmental issues.

www.greenpeople.co.uk
Tel: 08702 401444

Green Stationery Company

The Green Stationery Company is the UK's premier recycled paper and green office products supplier. They select products that are environmentally benign or have environmental advantages over the standard office products. They aim to maintain business practices consistent with the goals of sustaining our fragile environment for future generations, within a culture that respects life and honours its interdependence. They are a ‘mine of information’ on all products from recycled paper to cleaning supplies.

www.greenstat.co.uk
Tel: 01225 480 556

Hemp Garden

Hemp Garden manufacture and promote a range of fine, safe and effective body-care products - seeking to make these as beautiful, beneficial and pleasurable as they can be. All products utilise hemp as a base ingredient and they have sought to enhance the properties of this phenomenal plant with botanical extracts and essential oils. Hemp Garden use only the finest natural ingredients and avoid the synthetic 'nasties' that many body-care products contain. Products include: shampoo & conditioner; soaps; hand cream; face cream; body lotion and oils.

www.hempgarden.co.uk
Tel: 01288 355572

Honesty Cosmetics

Honesty Cosmetics manufacture a wide selection of skin and hair care products suitable for vegetarians and vegans. In addition to their own range, they offer a range of complementary products from a number of other companies who adhere to compassionate policies. From everyday necessities to more luxurious products, items have been chosen to ensure quality. Honesty Cosmetics offer a fast and efficient mail order service; help and advice is available Monday to Friday 9:30am to 5pm. Products include: Bath & Shower gels; shampoo & conditioner; moisturising lotion; soap and oils.

www.honestycosmetics.co.uk
Tel: 01629 814 888

Innocent Drinks

Innocent produce delicious 100% natural drinks - made from 100% pure fruit and fresh juices – no concentrates, colourings, preservatives, water or sugar. Their range includes: smoothies (fruit in a bottle); thickies (live probiotic yoghurt, real fruit and honey); really lovely juices; super smoothies and juicy water. Innocent also funds social programmes to offset its environmental impact, including planting trees and donating money to an NGO who buy mango trees and cows for farmers in poor rural areas of southern India.

www.innocentdrinks.co.uk
Tel: 020 8600 3939

Investing Ethically Ltd

Investing Ethically are a team who offer independent financial advice with ethical expertise. The business is led by their principles and exists to provide long term, financial advice that is both technically correct and ethically based. Their service is designed for people who want to build a sustainable relationship with trusted, skilled financial professionals, who have a long term broad based knowledge of their client's situation.

www.investing-ethically.co.uk
Tel: 01603 661121

Medivac

The Medivac Company offers a unique range of allergen avoidance products which are of such clinical benefit to people with asthma, eczema, rhinitis or dust allergy, that H.M. Customs & Excise permit the Medivac range of products to be purchased entirely FREE OF VAT. Products include: bedding; vacuum cleaners & accessories and steamers.

www.medivac.co.uk
Tel: 0845 1306969

Natura Organics

Natura products are made in Provence using only organic, plant-based extracts, such as shea butter, lavender and essential oils. There is no testing on animals at any stage of the production process, even on the raw ingredients and all ingredients are natural. Natura products are made using plant-based emulsifiers and natural essential oils and are suitable for vegetarians, vegans and the ethically-minded. The Natura luxury bodycare range includes: shower gel; bath foam; body lotion; shampoo & conditioner and hand cream.

www.naturaorganics.com
Tel: 01273 685800

Naturally So

Naturally So is an online (VAT free) shop selling natural health & beauty products. They search for products that match their ethics – environmentally friendly, and free from harmful chemicals and preservatives. Products for sale have not been tested on animals and all are of 100% vegetable or mineral origin. Naturally So also check the fair trade policy of all their suppliers, so you can shop reassured that you are not damaging your body, environment or conscience.

www.naturallyso.co.uk
Tel: 014810 0263400

Organico

Organico are importers of high quality organic foods. Their origins are in the healthfood and wholefood market where they have developed a good understanding of what constitutes a healthy and nutritious diet. Organico work hard to find like-minded suppliers and the type of foods that we enjoy eating every day – "tasty foods made with natural ingredients, prepared in a manner that respects and does not destroy the earth's limited resources". Organico pledge to work ethically and openly to find high quality organic foods at fair prices, from dedicated organic farmers and suppliers.

www.organico.co.uk
Tel: 0118 951 0518

If your company would like more information on The Ethical Company Organisation's company accreditation scheme then please call us on 0207 229 2115.

Or see *www.ethical-company-organisation.org* for more details.

Or email us for an application pack on *companyaccreditation@ethical-company-organisation.org*

17 Good shopping principles

1 TRY TO ONLY BUY BRANDS FROM THE "GOOD SHOPPING" LISTS FEATURED IN THIS BOOK

Don't worry if you have some questionable brands around you today – just gradually try to replace them with *Good Shopping Guide* approved brands over the next few years.

2 LOCAL SHOPS

Look out for local, independent stores. Using them means you use your car less. They offer more personal service and they support the local community.

3 HEALTH FOOD SHOPS

These are the best places to support. They tend to stock fair trade, vegetarian and organic products as well as vitamins and herbal remedies.

4 FAIR TRADE

Look out for Fairtrade Foundation marked products, which guarantee that workers have been fairly rewarded for their labour. Organisations like Oxfam (01865 311311) and Traidcraft (0191 491 1001) also sell fair trade goods on the high street or via mail order catalogues.

5 PRODUCTS NOT TESTED ON ANIMALS

Look for 'not tested on animals' labels or contact BUAV (020 7700 4888) or Naturewatch (01242 252871) for an approved product guide.

6 VEGETARIAN AND VEGAN PRODUCTS

Look out for the Vegetarian Society symbol. It is hard to completely avoid animal products but the Vegan Society publishes the Animal Free Shopper.

7 ORGANIC PRODUCE

Organic food is free of chemical fertilisers and pesticides. Look out for the Soil Association symbol or you can contact the association (0117 929 0661) to find your nearest outlet.

8 NON-GM FOOD

Although 70% of the public oppose the use of genetically modified food, it is increasingly finding its way into our diet. Look out for GM-free labels, the Vegetarian Society symbol or the Soil Association symbols. These all guarantee GM-free.

9 ETHICAL MONEY

Choose an ethical investment fund as well as one of the more ethical banks and mortgages. These decisions are key as they involve so much money.

10 RECYCLING AND SECOND-HAND GOODS

Recycled and second-hand products save resources and reduce pressure on landfill sites. Many everyday things, and especially paper, printer cartridges and TVs, can be 'recycled'. For advice on recycling points in your area contact Wasteline (0870 243 0136).

11 Wood products
Many timber products have originated from virgin rainforests or unsustainably managed forests. The Forest Stewardship Council (01686 413916) operates independent verification of sustainable timber and paper products. Look out for the FSC logo.

12 Getting Around
Walk as much as you can and use public transport (where it's any good!) When you use a car, try to journey share as much as you can – too many of us drive solo in cars.

13 Energy
Choose energy efficient brands where you can – there are several different rating and labelling systems, including one run by the Energy Saving Trust, a non-profit organisation partly run by the government. Also make sure you switch to one of the greener electricity suppliers.

14 Support the advertisers in this book
All our advertisers are ethical brands and have been vetted. We would never accept low scoring brands. So please, support these brands. See back of book.

15 Don't Buy Bad Brands
Avoid the brands that do not score well in *The Good Shopping Guide* analysis – together we have the power to make companies change.

16 Gooshing
If you shop online, make sure you do it at *www.gooshing.co.uk*. It compares the ethics of 250,000 products and searches 350 shops to deliver you the cheapest prices on the internet.

17 Look out for The Good Shopping Guide Ethical Company logo
If you see this logo you know that brand has scored well on our ethical audit analysis. You may see this logo on selected products from January 2004.

Good Home & Office

- All-in-ones
- Batteries
- Boilers
- Cleaners
- Computers
- Cookers
- Fax machines
- Fridges & freezers
- Kettles
- Kitchen appliances
- Laundry detergents
- Paints
- Printers
- Toys
- TV & videos
- Vacuum cleaners
- Washing machines
- Washing-up liquid
- The renewable energy guide
- Sustainable building

All-in-ones

All-in-one machines consume less energy than the combined consumption of individual pieces. For example, an all-in-one printer, copier, fax and scanner will use less electricity than the four functions would as separate units. They save on raw materials by being combined as one machine. And the production process for a single unit, rather than four, is of course environmentally less damaging. They save on space and on cost. Against this background they represent an environmentally and financially excellent option.

A recent Which? report found that the quality from all-in-ones was not quite as good as the separate units. But considering the cost, space and environmental savings associated with them, they still represent a wise purchase for individual, home or small business users.

Laser or Inkjet

As with regular printers all-in-ones can use either inkjet or laser technology. Laser printers work in a similar way to a photocopier. They run at a lower overall cost per sheet. Laser printer parts use a drum and toner cartridge both of which need intermittent replacing or refilling. Ensure both are housed separately as they run out at different times. If the drum is located inside the cartridge you won't be able to replace or refill individually and waste will be high. Beware of certain c olour laser printers which can often have even more consumable parts, up to nine in total.

Inkjets produce colour and photo quality prints superior to laser printers.They are far cheaper too, but much more expensive to maintain, with cartridges running out quickly and the required glossy paper being far pricier. Whichever you choose, try to refill your empty toners and cartridges, rather than the more expensive and wasteful option of replacing them.

Efficient Use

As with all electronic goods do not leave your all-in-one switched on when not in use. Only print documents when you simply have to, preferably on both sides of the paper. And where possible use electronic fax facilities rather than paper. In fact, with the explosion of emails, fax machines are virtually redundant. If you can live without fax then buy an all-in-one without this facility and save materials and money!

Recycling

Electronic goods become obsolete, or appear to become obsolete, long before they really are. This is because technology is moving so fast in this sector. The truth is that for a normal user, an existing all-in-one with printer, scanner, copier and fax should suffice for a number of years. When it is no longer good enough for your needs there's certain to be someone for whom it would be ideal. Find these people through second hand outlets or some of the schemes available for passing on electronic equipment. See *www.wasteonline.org.uk*. The same website deals with recycling, for when the equipment is truly beyond further use.

Check *www.gooshing.co.uk* for price search comparisons on virtually every office machine available today.

- Amstrad
- Brother
- Epson
- Olivettie
- Ricoh

- Lexmark
- Minolta/QMS
- Panasonic
- Sagem
- Samsung
- Xerox

- BT
- Canon
- Hewlett Packard
- Kyocera Mita
- NEC

Brand Name	Environmental Reporting	Pollution	Nuclear Power	Other	Animal Testing	Factory Farming	Other Animal Rights	Oppressive Regimes	Workers' Rights	Code of Conduct	Irresponsible Marketing	Armaments	Genetic Engineering	Boycott Call	Political Activity	Alert	Company group
	Environment				Animals			People					Extras				
Amstrad	Bottom	Top	Top	Top	Top	Top	Top	Middle	Top	Bottom	Top	Top	Top	Top	Top	Top	Amstrad Plc
Brother	Middle	Top	Top	Middle	Top	Top	Top	Bottom	Top	Bottom	Top	Top	Top	Top	Top	Top	Brother Industries Ltd
BT	Top	Middle	Top	Top	Top	Top	Bottom	Middle	Bottom	Bottom	Top	Middle	Top	Top	Bottom	Middle	BT Group Plc
Canon	Middle	Middle	Top	Bottom	Top	Top	Middle	Bottom	Bottom	Bottom	Top	Bottom	Top	Top	Bottom	Bottom	Fuyo Group
Epson	Top	Top	Top	Top	Top	Top	Top	Bottom	Top	Bottom	Top	Top	Top	Top	Top	Top	Seiko Epson Corp
Hewlett Packard	Middle	Middle	Top	Middle	Top	Top	Top	Bottom	Middle	Middle	Top	Bottom	Top	Top	Bottom	Middle	Hewlett Packard Co Inc
Kyocera Mita	Bottom	Top	Bottom	Bottom	Top	Bottom	Top	Bottom	Bottom	Bottom	Top	Top	Top	Top	Middle	Middle	UFG Holdings
Lexmark	Bottom	Top	Top	Top	Top	Top	Top	Bottom	Top	Bottom	Top	Top	Top	Bottom	Top	Top	Lexmark Int Group
Minolta/QMS	Bottom	Top	Top	Top	Top	Top	Bottom	Middle	Top	Bottom	Top	Bottom	Top	Top	Top	Top	Konica Minolta Holdings
NEC	Middle	Bottom	Bottom	Bottom	Top	Top	Top	Bottom	Bottom	Bottom	Bottom	Bottom	Bottom	Top	Middle	Bottom	Sunitomo Group
Olivetti	Bottom	Top	Top	Top	Top	Top	Top	Bottom	Top	Bottom	Top	Top	Top	Top	Middle	Top	Pirelli Spa
Panasonic	Middle	Middle	Middle	Top	Top	Top	Top	Bottom	Middle	Bottom	Top	Bottom	Top	Top	Middle	Top	Matsushita Electric
Ricoh	Top	Top	Top	Top	Top	Top	Top	Bottom	Top	Bottom	Top	Top	Top	Top	Top	Top	Ricoh Co Ltd
Sagem	Bottom	Top	Middle	Top	Top	Top	Top	Middle	Top	Bottom	Top	Bottom	Top	Top	Top	Top	Sagem SA
Samsung	Bottom	Top	Top	Middle	Top	Top	Top	Bottom	Middle	Bottom	Top	Bottom	Top	Top	Middle	Top	Samsung Group
Xerox	Bottom	Top	Top	Middle	Top	Top	Top	Middle	Middle	Bottom	Top	Middle	Top	Top	Bottom	Middle	Xerox Group

Key
- ● Top rating (no criticisms found)
- ○ Middle rating
- ● Bottom rating
- ◎ A related company has a bottom rating and the company itself has a middle rating
- ○ A related company has a middle rating
- ● A related company has a bottom rating

Source: ECRA-See page 14 for full key to symbols.

Batteries

Much of our day-to-day equipment is battery-driven – especially those things we carry around daily like watches, mobiles and cameras – and the batteries are so small they might seem harmless. So can anyone blame us when we throw our batteries into the bin? But before we do, we need to check on the potential damage to the environment.

Toxic ingredients

Batteries inevitably contain some degree of either toxic or corrosive chemicals but the manufacturers and environmental groups have so far failed to find much common ground in their debates about production and disposal. Until these issues are fully cleared up, we should at least look for the products with the lowest impact on the environment.

Nickel Cadmium batteries, or NiCads, are the ones most often sold as 'rechargeable', a fact that rightly attracts environmentally-concerned consumers, but NiCads do contain cadmium, which is a highly toxic heavy metal. To get over this problem, the five main manufacturers – Eveready, Panasonic, Rayovac, Uniross and Varta – do have facilities to collect their own brand NiCads and to send them for recycling, if we make the effort to send them in when completely used up.

Nickel metal hydride (NiMH) batteries avoid the cadmium problem but, at the time of the EC survey, they were available only as battery packs for camcorders, computers and mobile phones. As these become more widespread, it can only be hoped that the manufacturers will put in place proper recycling arrangements that their customers will understand and want to adhere to.

Zinc and alkaline batteries are rechargeable, but far less effective than NiCads, and the real problem is that there are virtually no facilities to recycle them, at least in the UK. Although the industry maintains that the impact on landfills is negligible, environmentalists are convinced that they will leave problem chemicals in the ground for future generations to deal with.

Other types

Button cells are the small flat batteries used in watches, hearing aids and some cameras. The formulations include lithium, zinc air, silver oxide and alkaline. Previously they used mercuric oxide cells, but these have at last been phased out. If at all possible, lithium batteries should be avoided. If appropriate, silver oxide is the best option.

On the positive side, there have been considerable improvements in recent years, including the elimination of mercury and manufacturers' involvement in collecting NiCads from larger commercial users of power tools, mobile phones and emergency lighting.

What next?

The ideal situation would be the collection and recycling of all battery waste. For the industry this would mean proper labelling and establishment of recycling schemes for all batteries. For consumers, the message should be to buy rechargeable batteries from retailers that promise to accept back and recycle them, whether as single batteries or packs.

You can compare ethics and price – search for batteries and 250,000 other products at *www.gooshing.co.uk*.

Save money and help the planet!

- Energizer
- Ever Ready
- Rayovac
- Uniross

- Duracell
- Kodak
- Philips
- Varta

- Boots
- Panasonic
- Sony

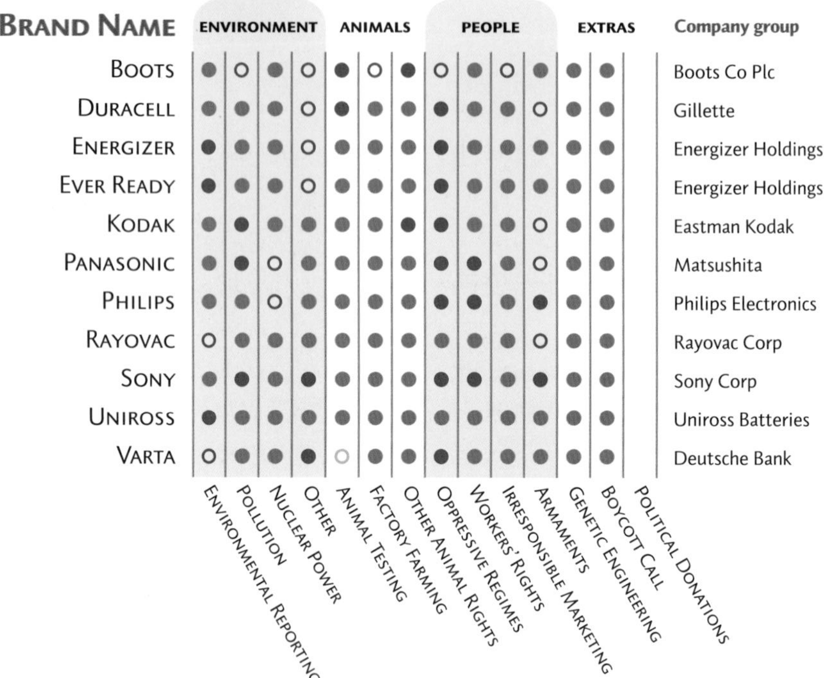

Brand Name	Environment: Environmental Reporting	Environment: Pollution	Environment: Nuclear Power	Environment: Other	Animals: Animal Testing	Animals: Factory Farming	Animals: Other Animal Rights	People: Oppressive Regimes	People: Workers' Rights	People: Irresponsible Marketing	People: Armaments	Extras: Genetic Engineering	Extras: Boycott Call	Extras: Political Donations	Company group
Boots	Top	Middle	Top	Middle	Bottom	Middle	Bottom	Middle	Top	Middle	Top	Top	Top		Boots Co Plc
Duracell	Top	Top	Top	Middle	Bottom	Top	Top	Bottom	Top	Top	Middle	Top	Top		Gillette
Energizer	Bottom	Top	Top	Middle	Top	Top	Top	Bottom	Top	Top	Top	Top	Top		Energizer Holdings
Ever Ready	Bottom	Top	Top	Middle	Top	Top	Top	Bottom	Top	Top	Top	Top	Top		Energizer Holdings
Kodak	Top	Bottom	Top	Top	Top	Top	Bottom	Bottom	Top	Top	Middle	Top	Top		Eastman Kodak
Panasonic	Top	Bottom	Middle	Top	Top	Top	Top	Bottom	Bottom	Top	Middle	Top	Top		Matsushita
Philips	Top	Top	Middle	Top	Top	Top	Top	Bottom	Bottom	Top	Bottom	Top	Top		Philips Electronics
Rayovac	Middle	Top	Top	Top	Top	Top	Top	Top	Top	Top	Middle	Top	Top		Rayovac Corp
Sony	Top	Bottom	Top	Bottom	Top	Top	Top	Bottom	Bottom	Top	Bottom	Top	Top		Sony Corp
Uniross	Bottom	Top	Top	Top	Top	Top	Top	Top	Top	Top	Top	Top	Top		Uniross Batteries
Varta	Middle	Top	Top	Bottom	Related middle	Top	Top	Bottom	Top	Top	Top	Top	Top		Deutsche Bank

Key

- Top rating (no criticisms found)
- Middle rating
- Bottom rating
- A related company has a bottom rating and the company itself has a middle rating
- A related company has a middle rating
- A related company has a bottom rating

Source: ECRA-See page 14 for full key to symbols.

Boilers

Gas bills have a habit of arriving when we least expect, and usually seem unreasonably high, especially after a long winter. But often the main reason they are so high is the inefficiency of our own equipment in the home. A better central heating boiler might cost a bit more in the first place but, once installed, it can be a lot cheaper to run.

This is a case where we can both help the environment and save ourselves some money, at least over the long term. Ideally, we should be thinking about installing gas condensing boilers or even solar-powered systems, where possible and affordable.

What is condensing?

Of the central heating boilers available, the most popular usually provide a combination of central heating and hot water for household use. Most systems are gas-fired, although there is also the option for using LPG or fuel oil. But what we really need to know is whether the boiler we're thinking of buying is a condensing or a non-condensing type.

Environmental campaigners are all agreed that gas condensing boilers (GCBs) are the best available technological choice for most people. This is because they operate at about 90 per cent energy efficiency, compared to only 70 per cent efficiency for the more common, and cheaper, non-condensing boilers.

GCBs include heat exchangers, which means that they retrieve the heat that would otherwise disappear in water vapour emissions and then return it to the system. This process helps to reduce the emissions not only of carbon dioxide but also of nitrous oxide. And this has got to be good for us all.

Of course there is a financial cost factor, because GCBs tend to cost between £700 and £1,400 – or about twice as much as non-condensing boilers. But GCBs are more efficient and their annual running costs usually turn out to be around 20 per cent lower than others – and so, if we calculate how much we spend every year on our gas or other fuel, these apparently rather expensive machines really can pay for themselves in little more than five years.

Efficiency labels

Just like fridges and several other domestic appliances, all new boilers are now required by European law to display energy efficiency labels on an A to G scale (A is best). The most extensive details of boiler models and their efficiencies are available on a British government-sponsored website at *www.sedbuk.com*. There were, at the time of this report 107 different models labelled with an A rating. Sales of GCBs have been boosted in the past by subsidies which may be available (see right).

THE PRICE FACTOR

- After installing a condensing gas boiler, the average user in a small house should recoup the extra cost in well under ten years and then make substantial savings over the 20-year life of the product
- In some local authority areas there is a £70 grant through the Big Green Boiler Scheme: *www.green-boilers.co.uk*/ Tel: 0800 028 28 55/01934 863650
- British Gas also operates a scheme whereby it sells GCBs cheaply, but not from all manufacturers
- *www.gooshing.co.uk* has a price comparison function getting you the best price from across the web

SUPPLIERS

The table features some of the main companies supplying the UK market. They all produce A-rated gas condensing boilers and were taken from the Sedbuk and Energy Saving Trust websites. Half are relatively small, privately-owned British companies, which specialise in heating systems. Several others belong to European-based heating specialists. Such companies may also make air conditioning and/or other heating systems, such as showers, for 'household' or corporate customers. One of our favourite companies is Atmos (*www.atmos.uk.com*). Atmos has joined the E.C.O Accreditation Scheme and sells a range of systems including standard and solar systems.

- Atmos
- EcoMax
- Gas 210 ECO
- Glow Worm
- Keston Boilers
- Quinta

- Arena
- Ariston
- Barcelona
- Baxi
- Eclipse ESS
- Potterton

- Bosch/British Gas
- Carfield / Geminox
- Ideal Boilers
- Worcester Greenstar

Brand Name	Environmental Reporting	Pollution	Nuclear Power	Other	Animal Testing	Factory Farming	Other Animal Rights	Oppressive Regimes	Workers' Rights	Irresponsible Marketing	Armaments	Genetic Engineering	Boycott Call	Political Activity	Alert	Company group
	ENVIRONMENT				ANIMALS			PEOPLE				EXTRAS				
Arena	Bottom	Top	Top	Top	Top	Top	Top	Middle	Top	Top	Top	Top	Top	Top	Top	Ferroli Spa
Ariston	Bottom	Top	Top	Top	Top	Top	Top	Middle	Top	Top	Top	Top	Top	Top	Top	MTS Group
Atmos	Bottom	Top	Top	Top	Top	Top	Top	Top	Top	Top	Top	Top	Top	Top	Top	House of Goodness
Barcelona	Bottom	Top	Top	Top	Top	Top	Top	Middle	Top	Top	Top	Top	Top	Top	Top	Baxi Group
Baxi	Bottom	Top	Top	Top	Top	Top	Top	Middle	Top	Top	Top	Top	Top	Top	Top	Baxi Group
Bosch/British Gas	Bottom	Top	Top	Top	Top	Top	Top	Bottom	Top	Top	Middle	Top	Top	Top	Middle	Robert Bosch
Carfield/Geminox	Bottom	Top	Top	Top	Top	Top	Top	Bottom	Top	Top	Middle	Top	Top	Top	Middle	Robert Bosch
Eclipse ESS	Bottom	Top	Top	Top	Top	Top	Top	Middle	Top	Top	Top	Top	Top	Top	Top	Vokera/Riello
EcoMax	Bottom	Top	Top	Top	Top	Top	Top	Top	Top	Top	Top	Top	Top	Top	Top	Joh. Vaillant
Gas 210 ECO	Bottom	Top	Top	Top	Top	Top	Top	Top	Top	Top	Top	Top	Top	Top	Top	Broag/Remeha Group
Glo worm	Bottom	Top	Top	Top	Top	Top	Top	Top	Top	Top	Top	Top	Top	Top	Top	Joh. Vaillant
Ideal Boilers	Bottom	Related bottom	Related bottom	Bottom	Middle	Related bottom	Related bottom	Bottom	Bottom	Related bottom	Bottom	Related bottom	Related bottom	Middle	Bottom	HSBC
Keston Boilers	Bottom	Top	Top	Top	Top	Top	Top	Top	Top	Top	Top	Top	Top	Top	Top	Stevenson Heating
Potterton	Bottom	Top	Top	Top	Top	Top	Top	Middle	Top	Top	Top	Top	Top	Top	Top	Baxi Group
Quinta	Bottom	Top	Top	Top	Top	Top	Top	Top	Top	Top	Top	Top	Top	Top	Top	Broag/Remeha Group
Worcester Greenstar	Bottom	Top	Top	Top	Top	Top	Top	Bottom	Top	Top	Middle	Top	Top	Top	Middle	Robert Bosch

Key

- Top rating (no criticisms found)
- Middle rating
- Bottom rating
- A related company has a bottom rating and the company itself has a middle rating
- A related company has a middle rating
- A related company has a bottom rating

Source: ECRA-See page 14 for full key to symbols.

Cleaners

Every year, the big detergent manufacturers come up with new brands and gimmicks for keeping our homes sparkling clean and free of bacteria. How much of the hype should we believe? And do we really need a bewildering display of sprays, liquids, creams, throw-away mops and scourers?

Try to keep things simple and use just one type of multi-surface cleaner for nearly all household jobs – kitchens and bathrooms alike. This is at least one way to reduce the unnecessary and poisonous chemicals in our homes.

Petroleum derivatives

Household cleaners are formulated from a wide range of ingredients, but they mainly contain surfactants (detergents) which help remove grease and dirt, allowing them to disperse in water. Surfactants can be naturally derived from vegetable substances, although many big brands use petroleum derivatives such as the much-criticised sodium lauryl sulphate. Petroleum-based surfactants are derived from a non-renewable resource and often biodegrade more slowly and less completely than vegetable-based ones. And, during the degradation process, they can form compounds that are even more dangerous than the original chemicals themselves.

European governments, including the UK, have been discussing a chemicals strategy that would enforce our right to know about all the chemicals present in cleaning products. But for the moment, the household cleaner manufacturers can continue to use toxic and potentially toxic chemicals in their products. There has been an increase in animal testing as companies compete to find more, different products to do essentially the same job – cleaning a surface. More and more cleaners are marketed as being 'especially formulated' for the bathroom or kitchen sink, when there is very little difference between the cleaning requirements of the two areas.

A general claim of 'biodegradable' on the labels of many products is misleading, because all such products are biodegradable; the question is how readily do the elements biodegrade? There is a big difference between products breaking down in hours or days, rather than partially over months or years. Surface active agents, cleaning agents, soil suspending agents, grease cutters and grease removers are often just clever names for petroleum-based surfactants.

Cutting down on bleach

Greater quantities of bleach and detergent are discharged directly into sewers from domestic premises than from the factories making them. Several types of bleach exist, all of which act by oxidising, and thus sterilising, organic matter. This powerful antibacterial action has been seen to persist beyond the u-bend, undermining the bacterial action that helps break down sewage. For this reason it should be used in dilute form, if at all, and never be poured neat down drains. Neither Ecover nor Bio-D produce household bleach, because they believe the action is unnecessarily powerful. Their toilet cleaners rely on acids which dislodge waste rather than sterilise it.

Water and packaging

The most common ingredient (up to 90%) of general-purpose cleaners is water. When this excess water is transported, energy and packaging is wasted and more solid waste is created for our landfills. Concentrated products in smaller bottles are a better option.

Cleaning product bottles are most often plastic. Greenpeace urges consumers to make a conscious effort not to buy things in polyvinylchloride (PVC) containers. There is usually a symbol on the bottom of the bottle indicating the type of plastic (PVC is indicated by a 3 in a recycling symbol). High and low density polyethylene (HDPE and LDPE), polypropylene (PP), polyethylene (PE) and polyethylene tetraphthalate (PET) all have fewer environmental problems associated with their manufacture and disposal than PVC.

Keep it simple; white vinegar, baking soda, salt, lemon juice and olive oil can all be handy DIY cleaners.

- Astonish
- Bio-D
- Ecover
- Orange Plus
- Stardrops

- 1001
- Dettol
- Jeyes Fluid
- Mr Muscle

- Ajax
- Cif
- Flash

GOOD HOME & OFFICE

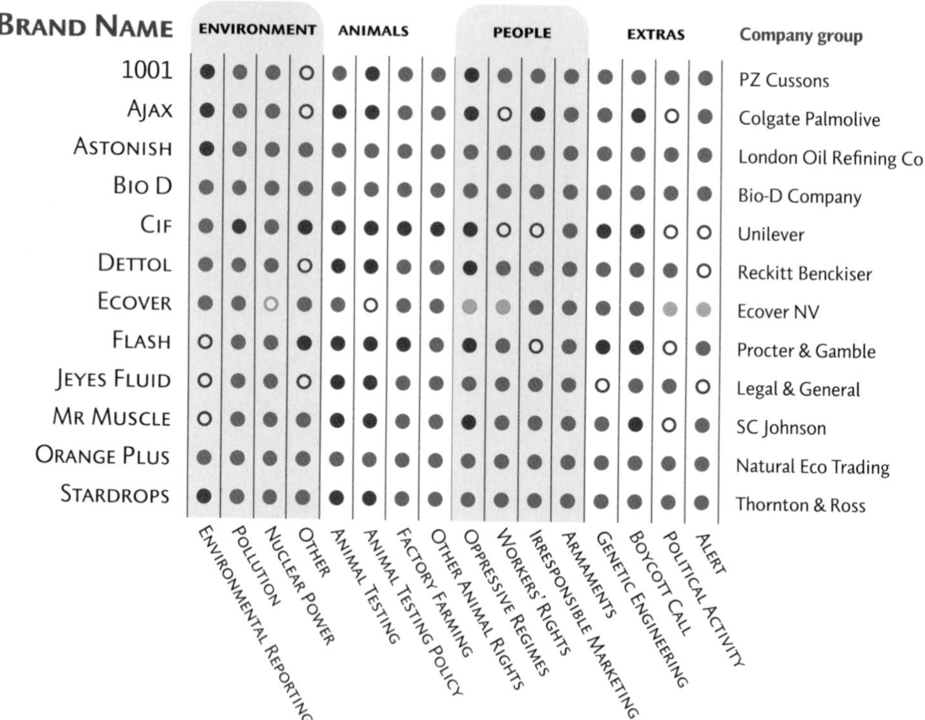

Brand Name	Environment: Environmental Reporting	Environment: Pollution	Environment: Nuclear Power	Environment: Other	Animals: Animal Testing	Animals: Animal Testing Policy	Animals: Factory Farming	Animals: Other Animal Rights	People: Oppressive Regimes	People: Workers' Rights	People: Irresponsible Marketing	People: Armaments	Extras: Genetic Engineering	Extras: Boycott Call	Extras: Political Activity	Extras: Alert	Company group
1001	Bottom	Top	Top	Middle	Top	Bottom	Top	Top	Bottom	Top	Top	Top	Top	Top	Top	Top	PZ Cussons
Ajax	Bottom	Top	Top	Middle	Bottom	Bottom	Top	Top	Bottom	Middle	Bottom	Top	Top	Bottom	Middle	Top	Colgate Palmolive
Astonish	Bottom	Top	Top	Top	Top	Top	Top	Top	Top	Top	Top	Top	Top	Top	Top	Top	London Oil Refining Co
Bio D	Top	Top	Top	Top	Top	Top	Top	Top	Top	Top	Top	Top	Top	Top	Top	Top	Bio-D Company
Cif	Top	Bottom	Top	Bottom	Bottom	Bottom	Bottom	Bottom	Bottom	Middle	Middle	Top	Bottom	Bottom	Middle	Middle	Unilever
Dettol	Top	Top	Top	Middle	Bottom	Bottom	Top	Top	Bottom	Top	Top	Top	Top	Top	Top	Middle	Reckitt Benckiser
Ecover	Top	Top	Related middle	Top	Top	Middle	Top	Top	Related bottom	Related bottom	Top	Top	Top	Top	Related bottom	Related bottom	Ecover NV
Flash	Middle	Top	Top	Bottom	Bottom	Bottom	Bottom	Top	Bottom	Top	Middle	Top	Bottom	Bottom	Middle	Top	Procter & Gamble
Jeyes Fluid	Middle	Top	Top	Middle	Bottom	Bottom	Top	Top	Top	Top	Top	Top	Middle	Top	Top	Middle	Legal & General
Mr Muscle	Middle	Top	Top	Top	Bottom	Bottom	Top	Top	Bottom	Top	Top	Top	Top	Bottom	Middle	Top	SC Johnson
Orange Plus	Top	Top	Top	Top	Top	Top	Top	Top	Top	Top	Top	Top	Top	Top	Top	Top	Natural Eco Trading
Stardrops	Bottom	Top	Top	Top	Bottom	Bottom	Top	Top	Top	Top	Top	Top	Top	Top	Top	Top	Thornton & Ross

Key
- Top rating (no criticisms found)
- Middle rating
- Bottom rating
- A related company has a bottom rating and the company itself has a middle rating
- A related company has a middle rating
- A related company has a bottom rating

Source: ECRA-See page 14 for full key to symbols.

www.THEGOODSHOPPINGGUIDE.co.uk

Computers

Computers may be revolutionising our lives in all kinds of unexpected ways but they have not turned the world into a cleaner or a less stressful place. In fact, they have created some environmental pollution problems. As they become obsolete so quickly, millions are abandoned or junked every week, but the problems start with the manufacturing process. Since the 1980s, the rush to sell the latest computers in high volumes has tempted manufacturers to cut corners both with the materials they use and with working conditions in component factories, which are located all over the world. We guide you through the key points to be aware of when considering buying a new 'whole system' computer. We also encourage you to consider upgrading your existing machine, or alternatively to buy a reconditioned machine, rather than a new one.

Fast turn-around

Computers become obsolete far quicker than any other kind of electrical equipment. Levels of waste of electrical equipment are increasing at six times that of other domestic and industrial waste, and information technology equipment makes up 39 per cent of the total, compared to televisions and audio equipment with just 8 per cent.

Studies in the US suggest that we have not even begun to deal with the serious problem of computer disposal. It is estimated that over three-quarters of all computers are stockpiled in attics, cellars and office storage cupboards. They are toxic time bombs, containing not only materials such as lead, cadmium, mercury and hexavalent chromium but also some very nasty compounds like brominated flame retardants (BFRs). Landfill sites and incinerators cannot be expected to dispose of such materials safely.

The EU's directive on Waste Electrical and Electronic Equipment has gone some way to making producers of electronic equipment responsible for disposal, with a view to reducing local councils' recycling costs. It is hoped that the directive will also persuade the manufacturers to use materials that are easier to re-use and recycle.

Making a mess

Computers are made up of modular parts, each of which contains many different components, often produced by different manufacturers around the world. Previously, much of the highly skilled work, such as silicon chip manufacture, was undertaken in the US. Semiconductor production uses more toxic gases than any other industry, with dangers for the workforce. Because of protests in the US, the computer manufacturers have been moving their most dangerous and heavily polluting stages of production to Latin America, where wages and environmental standards are lower.

IBM has made some investments in environmental design and was the first to make a computer using 100 per cent recycled plastic in all its major parts. IBM and Hewlett Packard were among the first major companies to ban the use of BFRs (see page 51) in computer casing, although they continued to rely on suppliers of components that still contained such compounds.

Upgrading and reconditioning

The most obvious sign of age in a computer is the speed of its main processor, the price of which increases the further up the scale you go. A positive step for the future would be for manufacturers to sell processor upgrades similar to that of software.

It is possible to buy a second-hand branded, out-of-the-box computer, which has been fully reconditioned with a new keyboard, mouse and software, direct from the factory and still under warranty. Second-user PCs can be bought on the internet or by mail order.

Buy your computer equipment at *www..gooshing.co.uk* to guarantee the best ethics and the best price search!

- Cyrix / C3
- Dell
- Evesham
- Time
- Tiny
- Viglen

- Acer
- AMD
- Apple
- IBM
- Intel
- Sun

- Compaq
- Fujitsu
- Hewlett-Packard
- NEC
- Packard Bell
- Siemens
- Sony
- Toshiba

GOOD HOME & OFFICE

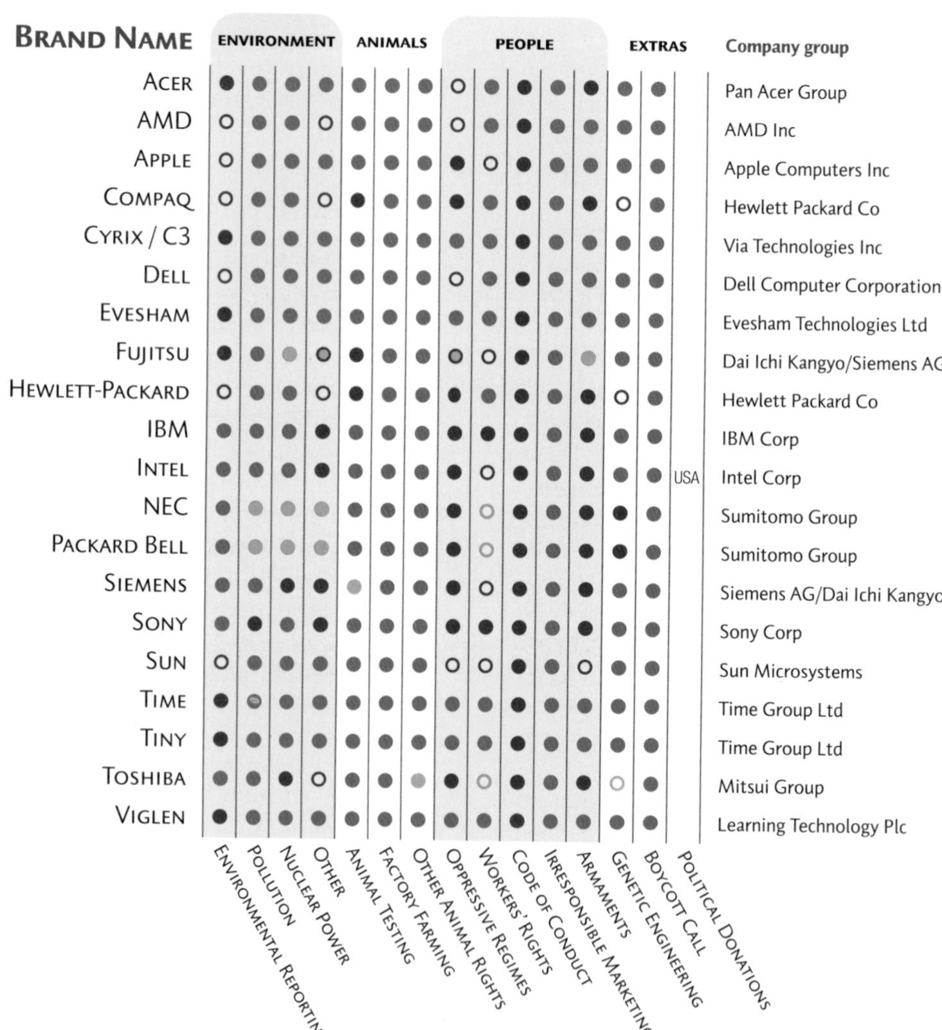

BRAND NAME
ENVIRONMENT
ANIMALS
PEOPLE
EXTRAS
Company group
ACER
AMD
APPLE
COMPAQ
CYRIX / C3
DELL
EVESHAM
FUJITSU
HEWLETT-PACKARD
IBM
INTEL
NEC
PACKARD BELL
SIEMENS
SONY
SUN
TIME
TINY
TOSHIBA
VIGLEN
Pan Acer Group
AMD Inc
Apple Computers Inc
Hewlett Packard Co
Via Technologies Inc
Dell Computer Corporation
Evesham Technologies Ltd
Dai Ichi Kangyo/Siemens AG
Hewlett Packard Co
IBM Corp
USA
Intel Corp
Sumitomo Group
Sumitomo Group
Siemens AG/Dai Ichi Kangyo
Sony Corp
Sun Microsystems
Time Group Ltd
Time Group Ltd
Mitsui Group
Learning Technology Plc
ENVIRONMENTAL REPORTING
POLLUTION
NUCLEAR POWER
OTHER
ANIMAL TESTING
FACTORY FARMING
OTHER ANIMAL RIGHTS
OPPRESSIVE REGIMES
WORKERS' RIGHTS
CODE OF CONDUCT
IRRESPONSIBLE MARKETING
ARMAMENTS
GENETIC ENGINEERING
BOYCOTT CALL
POLITICAL DONATIONS

Key

- Top rating (no criticisms found)
- Middle rating
- Bottom rating
- A related company has a bottom rating and the company itself has a middle rating
- A related company has a middle rating
- A related company has a bottom rating

Source: ECRA-See page 14 for full key to symbols.

Cookers

There is no shortage of brands to choose from, in many different shapes, sizes and combinations. Since a cooker is something so central to our lives, and something we buy only once in a while, we should really take time to think about all the important factors, including its impact on the environment.

This report looks at the main brands most widely available in the UK (but not microwave ovens).

Convenience and efficiency

Ease of use is an important consideration, and that is probably why British consumers seem to prefer electric ovens to gas ones (57 per cent to 41 per cent at the latest count) while gas hobs are marginally more popular than electric (here the balance is closer, at 54 per cent to 46 per cent). Most manufacturers acknowledge these preferences and offer dual fuel products. Overall, cooking accounts for 12 per cent of electricity used in our homes and 2.5 per cent of gas – but this is because gas is also the main fuel for heating water and central heating systems.

Unfortunately, popularity is no guide to energy efficiency. Government research shows that there is room to improve the efficiency of ovens and hobs alike.

A point to consider in making a decision between gas and electricity is the issue of carbon emissions. Here, gas is commonly accepted to be the preferable option. A study of the UK situation calculated that the 'carbon intensity' of cooking with electricity was 0.12 kgC/kWh compared to 0.05 kgC/kWh for gas. Switching to a 100% renewable electricity company will help however!

Self-cleaning oven features – in both gas and electric ovens – contribute to energy efficiency because of their extra insulation. However, as the process itself requires an extra 1.4kW of energy, if we are to save energy overall, these should not be operated more than once a month.

A fan in the oven reduces overall energy needs by cutting the heating-up time and heat loss, and thus overall cooking time. A fan also creates an even temperature throughout the oven, although if we want more heat at the top than at the bottom we should look for a model that allows for the fan to be turned off.

Induction hobs

For electric hobs, the latest 'induction hobs' use less than half the energy used by standard coils, although these are quite expensive. But aluminium and glass pans are not suitable on them, as they must be magnetic. The induction system involves a high frequency coil beneath a ceramic glass surface. Electromagnetic energy in the form of heat is transferred to the pan with the cooker surface remaining fairly cool. Nearly as good, and not as expensive, are ceramic glass units with halogen elements.

The European Commission has assessed induction hobs to be 82 per cent efficient, ceramic hobs with halogen elements at up to 70 per cent and sealed hobs at 50 per cent. Solid disc elements are the worst in terms of efficiency, using high wattages yet heating up slowly. Whatever the choice, there must be good contact between pan and element for them to work effectively.

Check *www.gooshing.co.uk* for the best prices on cookers and 250,000 other products. It searches 350 retailers to bring you the cheapest prices and shows ethical ratings too.

Whatever you cook on, enjoy your food and laugh a lot when you eat...some say it makes you live longer!

Key to opposite page

- Top rating (no criticisms found)
- Middle rating
- Bottom rating
- A related company has a bottom rating and the company itself has a middle rating
- A related company has a middle rating
- A related company has a bottom rating

Source: ECRA-See page 14 for full key to symbols.

- Aga
- Baumatic
- Belling
- Candy
- Leisure
- Miele
- New World
- Rosieres
- Stoves

- Ariston
- Bauknecht
- Bosch
- Brandt
- De Dietrich
- Gaggenau
- Indesit
- Neff
- Ocean
- Scholtes
- Siemens
- Whirlpool

- AEG
- Cannon
- Creda
- Electrolux
- GE
- Hotpoint
- Parkinson Cowan
- Tricity Bendix
- Zanussi

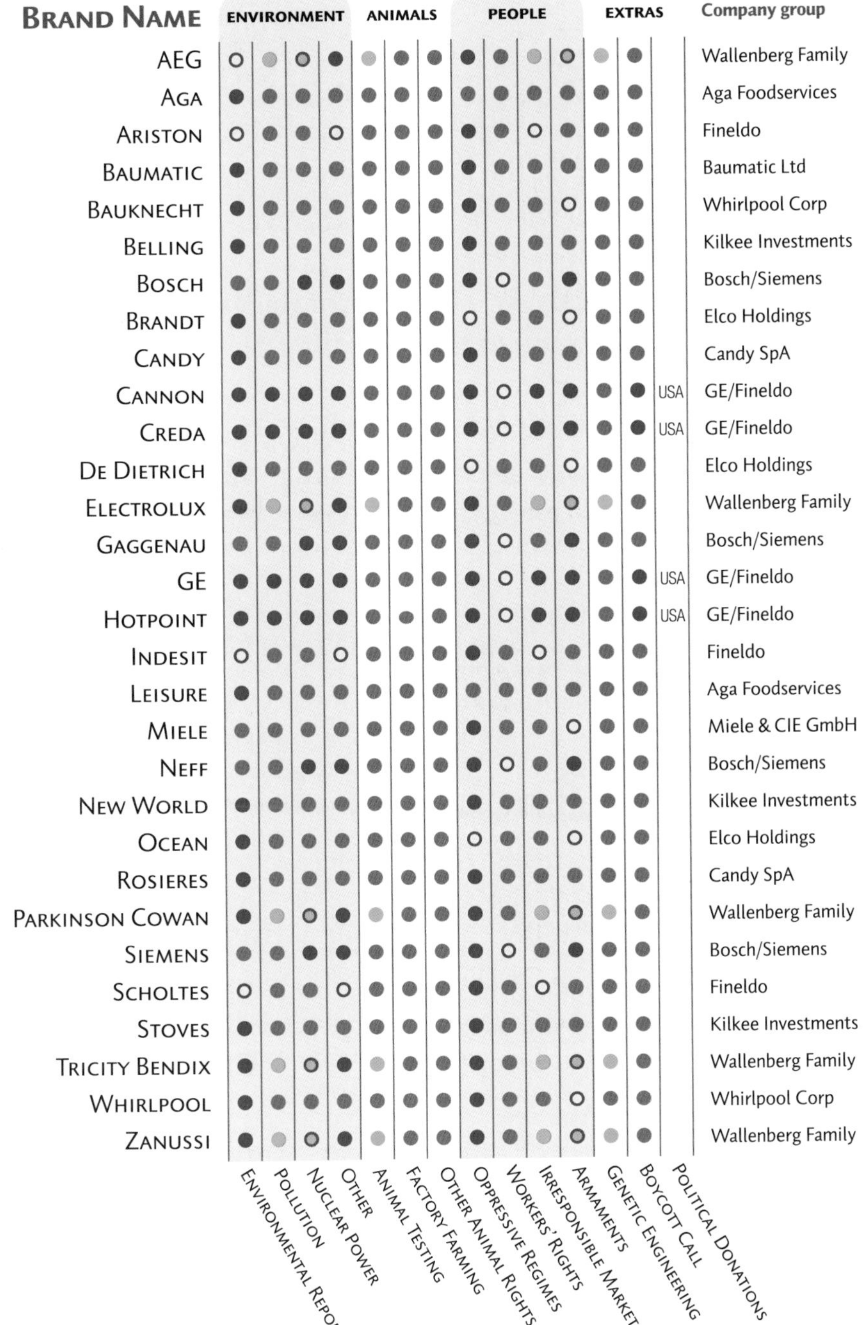
BRAND NAME
ENVIRONMENT
ANIMALS
PEOPLE
EXTRAS
Company group
AEG
Wallenberg Family
AGA
Aga Foodservices
ARISTON
Fineldo
BAUMATIC
Baumatic Ltd
BAUKNECHT
Whirlpool Corp
BELLING
Kilkee Investments
BOSCH
Bosch/Siemens
BRANDT
Elco Holdings
CANDY
Candy SpA
CANNON
USA
GE/Fineldo
CREDA
USA
GE/Fineldo
DE DIETRICH
Elco Holdings
ELECTROLUX
Wallenberg Family
GAGGENAU
Bosch/Siemens
GE
USA
GE/Fineldo
HOTPOINT
USA
GE/Fineldo
INDESIT
Fineldo
LEISURE
Aga Foodservices
MIELE
Miele & CIE GmbH
NEFF
Bosch/Siemens
NEW WORLD
Kilkee Investments
OCEAN
Elco Holdings
ROSIERES
Candy SpA
PARKINSON COWAN
Wallenberg Family
SIEMENS
Bosch/Siemens
SCHOLTES
Fineldo
STOVES
Kilkee Investments
TRICITY BENDIX
Wallenberg Family
WHIRLPOOL
Whirlpool Corp
ZANUSSI
Wallenberg Family
ENVIRONMENTAL REPORTING
POLLUTION
NUCLEAR POWER
OTHER
ANIMAL TESTING
FACTORY FARMING
OTHER ANIMAL RIGHTS
OPPRESSIVE REGIMES
WORKERS' RIGHTS
IRRESPONSIBLE MARKETING
ARMAMENTS
GENETIC ENGINEERING
BOYCOTT CALL
POLITICAL DONATIONS

Fax machines

The fax machine has been one of the few survivors from the early communications revolution of the 1980s. Even the ever-growing use of email has not taken away the usefulness of the fax as a quick way to transfer pictures, sketches, maps etc – the sorts of things that can take time to download on the internet. At the same time, plain paper fax machines which can also scan, print and copy are increasingly popular with small businesses and home offices. When considering such a machine, we need to give a thought to conservation and the other things the manufacturers get up to.

Types of paper

Plain paper machines use ordinary sheets of A4 paper while thermal fax machines use rolls of thermal paper. On the face of it, plain paper machines seem the better option, but two factors are worth thinking about: (i) a plain paper machine also requires a replaceable ink or toner cartridge or drum; (ii) a thermal fax machine cuts messages to length and thus saves on paper and energy.

Plain paper made from 100 per cent post-consumer waste is widely available. Look for the Nordic Swan symbol, a Scandinavian labelling scheme which requires the production process to have the minimum possible environmental impact. Thermal paper, contrary to popular opinion, is recyclable, although it is considered 'low-grade' waste and there are no known sources of recycled thermal paper.

The computer solution is to send and receive faxes without the use of paper, but you can only fax material which is stored in the computer and so a scanner is likely to be necessary. The drawback is that computers cannot receive faxes when they are switched off or when we are working offline.

Companies' other policies

At the time of this report, four companies – BT, Samsung, Canon and Panasonic – were selling the most fax machines in the UK. BT's machines were mainly made by the French company Sagem. The main manufacturers were international electronics and office equipment companies, half of them from Japan, with two of them – Canon and NEC – belonging to the prevailing coalitions of Japanese multinationals. It can be seen from the long table on page 52 some of the companies were involved in armaments or nuclear power.

Two environmental reports received top rating on the EC table. The BT report was accepted as a model of environmental reporting, showing progress against previous environmental targets, and reporting a 'green procurement' programme, taking into account its own suppliers' environmental objectives in its purchasing decisions. NEC similarly reported on performance against targets and operated a green procurement programme, although environmental audits were undertaken internally. However, both BT's and NEC's overall scores were brought down by other factors (see the long table).

We are pleased to recommend Brother, who have recently joined our Ethical Company accreditation scheme which allows them to demonstrate a full ethical health check. The company is making great strides in the area of energy efficiency and producing excellent machines.

The best place to buy or research fax machines is through *www.gooshing.co.uk*, where you can compare brands, ethical ratings and also price-search the best deal from 350 different retailers. It saves you maney and ensures you're buying an ethical brand!

- Amstrad
- Brother
- Ricoh

- Olivetti
- Panasonic
- Sagem
- Samsung

- BT
- Canon
- NEC

Brand Name	Environment: Environmental Reporting	Environment: Pollution	Environment: Nuclear Power	Environment: Other	Animals: Animal Testing	Animals: Factory Farming	Animals: Other Animal Rights	People: Oppressive Regimes	People: Workers' Rights	People: Code of Conduct	People: Irresponsible Marketing	People: Armaments	Extras: Genetic Engineering	Extras: Boycott Call	Extras: Political Activity	Extras: Alert	Company group
Amstrad	Bottom	Top	Top	Top	Top	Top	Top	Middle	Top	Bottom	Top	Top	Top	Top	Top	Top	Amstrad Plc
Brother	Middle	Top	Top	Middle	Top	Top	Top	Bottom	Top	Bottom	Top	Top	Top	Top	Top	Top	Brother Industries Ltd
BT	Top	Middle	Top	Top	Top	Top	Bottom	Middle	Bottom	Bottom	Top	Middle	Top	Top	Bottom	Middle	BT Group Plc
Canon	Middle	Middle	Top	Bottom	Top	Top	Middle	Bottom	Bottom	Bottom	Top	Bottom	Top	Top	Bottom	Bottom	Fuyo Group
NEC	Middle	Bottom	Bottom	Bottom	Top	Top	Top	Bottom	Bottom	Bottom	Bottom	Bottom	Bottom	Top	Middle	Bottom	Sumitomo Group
Olivetti	Bottom	Top	Top	Top	Top	Top	Top	Bottom	Top	Bottom	Top	Top	Top	Top	Middle	Top	Pirelli Spa
Panasonic	Middle	Middle	Middle	Top	Top	Top	Top	Bottom	Middle	Bottom	Top	Bottom	Top	Top	Middle	Top	Matsushita Electric
Ricoh	Top	Top	Top	Top	Top	Top	Top	Bottom	Top	Bottom	Top	Top	Top	Top	Top	Top	Ricoh Co Ltd
Sagem	Bottom	Top	Middle	Top	Top	Top	Top	Middle	Top	Bottom	Top	Bottom	Top	Top	Top	Top	Sagem SA
Samsung	Bottom	Top	Top	Middle	Top	Top	Top	Bottom	Middle	Bottom	Top	Bottom	Top	Top	Middle	Top	Samsung Group

Key

- Top rating (no criticisms found)
- Middle rating
- Bottom rating
- A related company has a bottom rating and the company itself has a middle rating
- A related company has a middle rating
- A related company has a bottom rating

Source: ECRA-See page 14 for full key to symbols.

Fridges & freezers

We can chill with a clean conscience if we bear a few things in mind when we buy a fridge or freezer unit. First and most important, we should look for the most energy-efficient models. Next, we need to be sure that the kind of coolant gas the appliance uses does as little harm to the environment as possible. And we should also ask a few questions about the manufacturing companies and their wider policies.

Energy use

Over the lifetime of each fridge and freezer, we probably spend about twice as much on powering it as we did on buying it. This is why we need to look out for the most energy-efficient machines. A less efficient one may be cheaper to buy, but it will be costing much more to run from the moment we switch it on.

Energy labelling is now compulsory for fridges and freezers. Most brands have models available that are classed as A or B. A-rated models use about half as much energy as C-rated ones. 'Energy plus' ratings are awarded to models – fridge/freezers only so far – that are even more efficient. These use as little as half the electricity of the average appliance currently on sale. The EU also awards 'eco-labels' to energy efficient models that are manufactured with minimal environmental impacts,Vestfrost of Denmark is an example of a company that has received this label.

Coolants

When CFC coolant gas went out of production because it was harming the ozone layer, manufacturers switched to HCFCs and then to HFCs (hydrofluorocarbons). There is still widespread use of HFCs in fridges even though they are known to have high global

60-SECOND GREEN GUIDE

- Buy an A-rated hydrocarbon (R600a) appliance (it will be labelled 'CFC- and HFC-free') (see *www.gooshing.co.uk*)
- When buying a fridge/freezer consider opting for a two-control model so that one of the units (for example the fridge) can be switched off when you go on holiday
- Chest freezers are more energy efficient than upright models
- Make sure your old appliance is professionally de-gassed and preferably recycled – it will probably contain CFCs or HFCs

warming potential and their production results in toxic waste.

One of the best options to look for is the 'R600a' hydrocarbon coolant (labelled 'CFC- and HFC-free'). This has a lower global warming potential, is non-toxic and is more efficient than HFCs.

Disposal

Old fridges and freezers contain a number of toxic substances, including CFC and HFC coolants and flame-retardant chemicals, so it is crucial that they are disposed of safely and correctly. Some manufacturers and retailers take back old models and may offer trade-ins, so it is worth ringing them first. Otherwise we can call our local council for advice, look in the Yellow Pages under 'Recycling'.

RUNNING FRIDGES & FREEZERS EFFICIENTLY

- Place freezers in a cool place, out of the sun and away from heaters, boilers and cookers
- Open doors for as little time as possible
- Keep fridges about three-quarters full for maximum efficiency
- Defrost regularly
- Keep the temperature right – no more than 5°C, but the colder you keep it the more energy it will use

At *www.gooshing.co.uk* you can save money on fridges and save the planet! Gooshing finds you the most ethical and the cheapest deals available.

- Brandt
- Candy
- Hoover
- Lec
- Liebherr
- Miele
- Ocean
- Proline

- Ariston
- Bauknecht
- Beko
- Ignis
- Indesit
- Merloni
- New World
- Whirlpool

- AEG
- Bosch
- Creda
- Electrolux
- Hotpoint
- Iceline
- Kyoto
- Neff
- Siemens
- Tricity Bendrix
- Zanussi

Brand Name	Environment				Animals			People				Extras			Company group
	Environmental Reporting	Pollution	Nuclear Power	Other	Animal Testing	Factory Farming	Other Animal Rights	Oppressive Regimes	Workers' Rights	Irresponsible Marketing	Armaments	Genetic Engineering	Boycott Call	Political Donations	
AEG	Middle	Rel. bottom	Rel. bottom/middle	Bottom	Rel. bottom	Top	Top	Bottom	Top	Rel. bottom	Rel. bottom/middle	Rel. bottom	Top	USA	Wallenberg Family
Ariston	Middle	Top	Top	Middle	Top	Top	Top	Bottom	Top	Middle	Top	Top	Top		Fineldo Spa
Bauknecht	Bottom	Top	Top	Top	Top	Top	Top	Bottom	Middle	Top	Middle	Top	Top		Whirlpool Corp
Beko	Middle	Top	Top	Top	Bottom	Bottom	Top	Middle	Top	Top	Middle	Top	Top		Koc Holding
Bosch	Top	Top	Bottom	Bottom	Top	Top	Top	Bottom	Middle	Top	Bottom	Top	Top		Robert Bosch/Siemens
Brandt	Bottom	Top	Top	Top	Top	Top	Top	Middle	Top	Top	Middle	Top	Top		ELCO
Candy	Bottom	Top	Top	Top	Top	Top	Top	Bottom	Top	Top	Top	Top	Top		IFEM
Creda	Bottom	Bottom	Bottom	Bottom	Top	Top	Top	Bottom	Middle	Bottom	Bottom	Top	Bottom	USA	GE/Merloni
Electrolux	Middle	Rel. bottom	Rel. bottom/middle	Bottom	Rel. bottom	Top	Top	Bottom	Top	Rel. bottom	Rel. bottom/middle	Rel. bottom	Top	USA	Wallenberg Family
Hoover	Bottom	Top	Top	Top	Top	Top	Top	Bottom	Top	Top	Top	Top	Top		IFEM
Hotpoint	Bottom	Bottom	Bottom	Bottom	Top	Top	Top	Bottom	Middle	Bottom	Bottom	Top	Bottom	USA	GE/Merloni
Iceline	Bottom	Middle	Top	Top	Bottom	Bottom	Bottom	Bottom	Middle	Middle	Top	Middle	Top		The Big Food Group
Ignis	Bottom	Top	Top	Top	Top	Top	Top	Bottom	Middle	Top	Middle	Top	Top		Whirlpool Corp
Indesit	Middle	Top	Top	Middle	Top	Top	Top	Bottom	Top	Middle	Top	Top	Top		Fineldo SpA
Kyoto	Bottom	Middle	Top	Top	Bottom	Bottom	Bottom	Bottom	Middle	Middle	Top	Middle	Top		The Big Food Group
Lec	Bottom	Top	Top	Top	Top	Top	Top	Middle	Top	Top	Middle	Top	Top		Sime Darby Bhd
Liebherr	Bottom	Top	Top	Top	Top	Top	Top	Bottom	Top	Top	Bottom	Top	Top		Liebherr International SA
Merloni	Middle	Top	Top	Middle	Top	Top	Top	Bottom	Top	Middle	Top	Top	Top		Fineldo Spa
Miele	Top	Top	Top	Top	Top	Top	Top	Bottom	Top	Top	Middle	Top	Top		Miele & Cie GmbH
Neff	Top	Top	Bottom	Bottom	Top	Top	Top	Bottom	Middle	Top	Bottom	Top	Top		Robert Bosch/Siemens
New World	Middle	Top	Top	Middle	Top	Top	Top	Bottom	Top	Middle	Top	Top	Top		Fineldo Spa
Ocean	Bottom	Top	Top	Top	Top	Top	Top	Middle	Top	Top	Middle	Top	Top		ELCO
Proline	Top	Middle	Top	Top	Top	Top	Top	Middle	Top	Top	Top	Top	Top	CON	Kingfisher Plc
Siemens	Top	Top	Bottom	Bottom	Top	Top	Top	Bottom	Middle	Top	Bottom	Top	Top		Robert Bosch/Siemens
Tricity Bendix	Middle	Rel. bottom	Rel. bottom/middle	Bottom	Rel. bottom	Top	Top	Bottom	Top	Rel. bottom	Rel. bottom/middle	Rel. bottom	Top	USA	Wallenberg Family
Whirlpool	Bottom	Top	Top	Top	Top	Top	Top	Bottom	Middle	Top	Middle	Top	Top		Whirlpool Corp
Zanussi	Middle	Rel. bottom	Rel. bottom/middle	Bottom	Rel. bottom	Top	Top	Bottom	Top	Rel. bottom	Rel. bottom/middle	Rel. bottom	Top	USA	Wallenberg Family

Key

- Top rating (no criticisms found)
- Middle rating
- Bottom rating
- A related company has a bottom rating and the company itself has a middle rating
- A related company has a middle rating
- A related company has a bottom rating

Kettles

Boiling and re-boiling unnecessary amounts of water for our tea and coffee wastes a phenomenal amount of energy every day. Luckily the efforts of efficient energy use campaigners have in recent years persuaded most manufacturers to come up with new varieties of kettles, which are much less wasteful than the traditional designs. Of those currently available, jug kettles are good, but those with concealed elements are even better.

Save water, save power

In the UK we each drink an average of 27 cups of tea and coffee each week. It has been calculated that by boiling 1.5 cups of water each time rather than the average 3.5, we could save enough electricity each week to run a TV for 26 hours.

The award-winning design of a new eco-kettle in Australia has identified consumer behaviour as the key to improving energy efficiency. Behavioural studies in the Life Cycle Analysis of the product found that the main problem was not the efficiency of the kettle but the way in which it was used. The study found that only 26 per cent of people used the water gauge even when they had one, and that the majority re-boiled the kettle when there was no need. By putting a large gauge on the top of the kettle, the designers found consumers were more likely to use it. In addition, a feature where the top of the kettle turned red at temperatures over 80°C made people less tempted to re-boil so often.

Re-boiling is not only a waste of energy but often makes a worse drink. Coffee for example should be brewed with water at between 85-90°C, so as not to damage the delicate oils in the bean, while water straight out of the kettle will be over 100°C. The 'Axis' eco-kettle is produced in Australia by MEC Kambrook, but is currently not distributed in the UK.

Stove-top kettles for gas cookers have long been an environmental favourite, as, although they use slightly more energy than a jug kettle to boil the water, the inherent inefficiency of conventional electricity production made them a better choice in terms of carbon emissions. However with the evolution of '100% green' electricity it is possible to run an electric kettle with practically zero carbon impact. Therefore electric kettles can represent the best environmental option.

Countries of origin

The production of most household appliances is now 'out-sourced,' meaning that the company which owns the brand name is only directly involved in the design and sourcing of the item, but not in the actual production. Some companies products are produced by over 25 unaffiliated manufacturers located primarily in Far East locations, such as Hong Kong, China and Taiwan. Such companies do not often maintain long-term purchase contracts with manufacturers, preferring to work on a single contract basis which is not reliant on any individual supplier.

While such practices are standard, they reflect the fundamental problems of globalisation: flexibility for a company in the North means job insecurity and a lack of long-term investment in the South. Such a multitude of suppliers also makes it very difficult for consumers to hold corporations to account for the conditions under which their goods are produced. With labour costs in Taiwan and South Korea rising, China has now become the main producer of kitchen appliances.

Good practice

- When buying a new kettle, look for one with a covered element.
- Boil only as much water as you need each time – look for a kettle with a gauge.
- If you live in a hard water area, leave the kettle empty after each use and descale it every month with a little vinegar.
- Gas kettles' efficiency can be improved by the addition of a 'heat-ring' around the base.
- If you want information on over 93 kettles, go to *www.gooshing.co.uk*. It's a free service where you can buy online, find the cheapest deals and compare ethical ratings on over 250,000 products.
- Enjoy!

- De'Longhi
- Haden
- Kenwood
- Pifco
- Russell Hobbs
- Salton

- Morphy Richards
- Moulinex
- Rowenta
- Swan
- Tefal

- Bosch
- Braun
- Breville
- Bush
- Hinari
- Philips

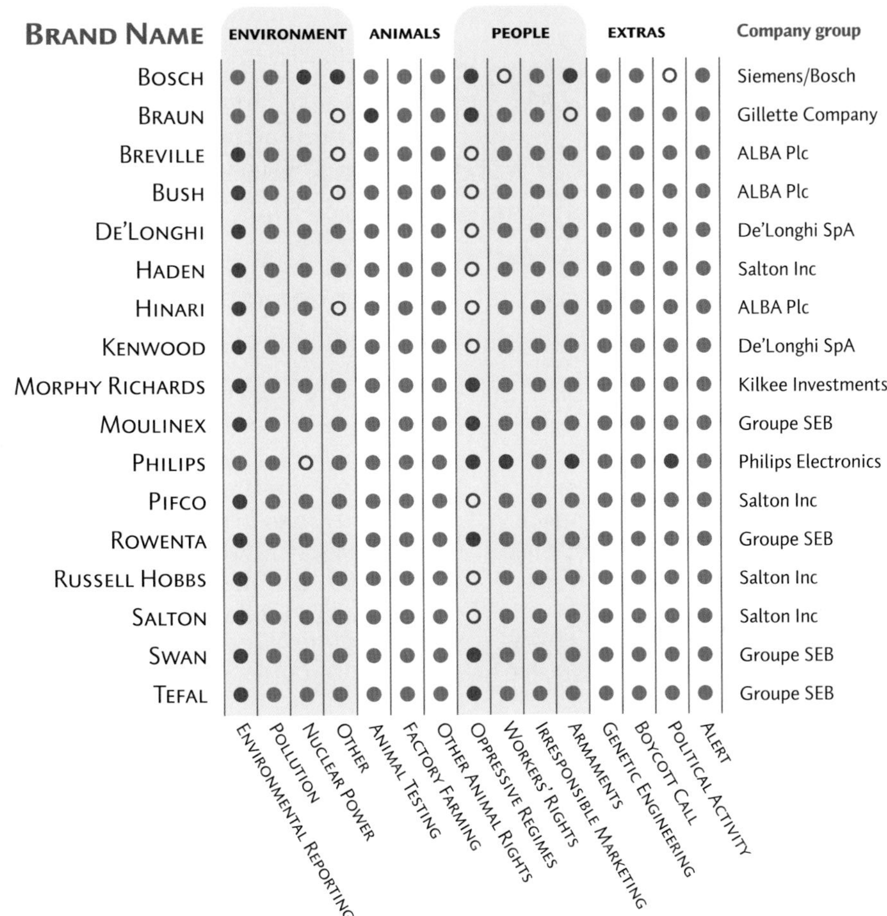

Brand Name	Environmental Reporting	Pollution	Nuclear Power	Other	Animal Testing	Factory Farming	Other Animal Rights	Oppressive Regimes	Workers' Rights	Irresponsible Marketing	Armaments	Genetic Engineering	Boycott Call	Political Activity	Alert	Company group
	Environment				Animals			People				Extras				
Bosch	Top	Top	Bottom	Bottom	Top	Top	Top	Bottom	Middle	Top	Bottom	Top	Top	Middle	Top	Siemens/Bosch
Braun	Top	Top	Top	Middle	Bottom	Top	Top	Bottom	Top	Top	Middle	Top	Top	Top	Top	Gillette Company
Breville	Bottom	Top	Top	Middle	Top	Top	Top	Middle	Top	Top	Top	Top	Top	Top	Top	ALBA Plc
Bush	Bottom	Top	Top	Middle	Top	Top	Top	Middle	Top	Top	Top	Top	Top	Top	Top	ALBA Plc
De'Longhi	Bottom	Top	Top	Top	Top	Top	Top	Middle	Top	Top	Top	Top	Top	Top	Top	De'Longhi SpA
Haden	Bottom	Top	Top	Top	Top	Top	Top	Middle	Top	Top	Top	Top	Top	Top	Top	Salton Inc
Hinari	Bottom	Top	Top	Middle	Top	Top	Top	Middle	Top	Top	Top	Top	Top	Top	Top	ALBA Plc
Kenwood	Bottom	Top	Top	Top	Top	Top	Top	Middle	Top	Top	Top	Top	Top	Top	Top	De'Longhi SpA
Morphy Richards	Bottom	Top	Top	Top	Top	Top	Top	Bottom	Top	Top	Top	Top	Top	Top	Top	Kilkee Investments
Moulinex	Bottom	Top	Top	Top	Top	Top	Top	Bottom	Top	Top	Top	Top	Top	Top	Top	Groupe SEB
Philips	Top	Top	Middle	Top	Top	Top	Top	Bottom	Bottom	Top	Bottom	Top	Top	Bottom	Top	Philips Electronics
Pifco	Bottom	Top	Top	Top	Top	Top	Top	Middle	Top	Top	Top	Top	Top	Top	Top	Salton Inc
Rowenta	Bottom	Top	Top	Top	Top	Top	Top	Bottom	Top	Top	Top	Top	Top	Top	Top	Groupe SEB
Russell Hobbs	Bottom	Top	Top	Top	Top	Top	Top	Middle	Top	Top	Top	Top	Top	Top	Top	Salton Inc
Salton	Bottom	Top	Top	Top	Top	Top	Top	Middle	Top	Top	Top	Top	Top	Top	Top	Salton Inc
Swan	Bottom	Top	Top	Top	Top	Top	Top	Bottom	Top	Top	Top	Top	Top	Top	Top	Groupe SEB
Tefal	Bottom	Top	Top	Top	Top	Top	Top	Bottom	Top	Top	Top	Top	Top	Top	Top	Groupe SEB

Key

- ● Top rating (no criticisms found)
- ○ Middle rating
- ● Bottom rating
- ◎ A related company has a bottom rating and the company itself has a middle rating
- ○ A related company has a middle rating
- ● A related company has a bottom rating

Source: ECRA-See page 14 for full key to symbols.

Kitchen appliances

Where would we be without our wonderful food? The appliances we use can wear out so fast that we often have to replace them – a good example of 'built-in obsolescence' at the heart of our lives. That's why the focus of this report is on environmental issues, energy consumption and packaging. This report covers other kitchen appliances like blenders, food processors, hand blenders, hand mixers, food mixers, juicers, deep fat fryers, kettles and toasters.

Our throw-away culture

At least six million kitchen appliances are discarded each year, mostly thrown into dustbins, with the result that proper recycling is very unlikely to happen. Friends of the Earth would like to see much higher recycling or re-use targets for waste electrical and electronic equipment; the organisation argues in favour of making products last longer, designing them for easy repair or for easy replacement of worn-out components, as well as for easy recycling for parts that cannot be re-used. FoE says that this should be the responsibility of the manufacturers, so that they carry the costs of recycling or disposal of their products.

Even if a piece of equipment seems to have reached the end of its life, that doesn't mean it's no longer usable. Second-hand shops often take our old equipment and there are schemes around the UK to recover discarded electrical equipment. Wastewatch recommends that old appliances are not dumped in the bin but taken to a civic amenity site where they can be added to other scrap for recycling. Information is available from the local authority, which will have a recycling officer, or from Wastewatch (*www.wastewatch.org.uk*).

Materials used

Various materials, such as stainless steel, iron and plastics, are used in most kitchen appliances. All the associated ills of mining and manufacturing come into play – toxic waste, pollution, energy wastage and greenhouse gas emissions. Of course these things are going to exist anyway, but a good way for us to minimise these impacts is to avoid buying new products, choosing second-hand or reconditioned items instead.

Trimming down

The new concealed-element kettles are good in that they permit the boiling of only small amounts of water, whereas old-style kettles tend to require excessive amounts of water to work.

Weighing up how often an item will be used can help us decide how necessary it is. If we're unlikely to use it really often do we really need it? It also helps to think about ease of use, as there may be another way to do a job without getting over-complicated gadgets that are often difficult to clean. For example, a blender does many of the same jobs as a food processor but uses smaller amounts of energy.

Energy use

The energy efficiency of electrical appliances varies from model to model. As there is no eco-labelling scheme for small kitchen appliances, consumers have to rely on product packaging displaying the energy usage. A kettle draws up to 3KW and when millions are turned on at about the same time, the increase in demand is massive. Compared to electricity, gas is 30 per cent more energy-efficient, which is why kettles used on gas cookers are generally a better option than electric kettles.

Hard water leaves a build-up of calcium carbonate, which reduces a kettle's energy efficiency – this can easily be cleaned off from time to time with vinegar.

Hand-operated kitchen appliances, naturally enough, are the most energy-efficient kinds you can buy – not least the whisks, forks and knives that are absolutely essential for cooking with!

www.gooshing.co.uk can save you alot of money. It searches 350 shops to find the cheapest price on your chosen brand – and gives ethical ratings.

- Dualit
- Prima

- De' Longhi
- Kenwood
- Morphy Richards
- Moulinex
- Pifco
- Rowenta
- Russell Hobbs
- Salton
- Swan
- Tefal

- Braun
- Breville
- Bush
- Goodmans
- Hinari
- Philips

GOOD HOME & OFFICE

Brand Name	Environment: Environmental Reporting	Environment: Pollution	Environment: Nuclear Power	Environment: Other	Animals: Animal Testing	Animals: Factory Farming	Animals: Other Animal Rights	People: Oppressive Regimes	People: Workers' Rights	People: Irresponsible Marketing	People: Armaments	Extras: Genetic Engineering	Extras: Boycott Call	Extras: Political Donations	Company group
Braun	Top	Top	Top	Middle	Bottom	Top	Top	Bottom	Top	Top	Middle	Top	Top		Gillette
Breville	Bottom	Top	Top	Middle	Top	Top	Top	Middle	Top	Top	Top	Top	Top		Alba Plc
Bush	Bottom	Top	Top	Middle	Top	Top	Top	Middle	Top	Top	Top	Top	Top		Alba Plc
De'Longhi	Bottom	Top	Top	Top	Top	Top	Top	Middle	Top	Top	Top	Top	Top		De'Longhi Spa
Dualit	Bottom	Top	Top	Top	Top	Top	Top	Top	Top	Top	Top	Top	Top		Dualit Ltd
Goodmans	Bottom	Top	Top	Middle	Top	Top	Top	Middle	Top	Top	Top	Top	Top		Alba Plc
Hinari	Bottom	Top	Top	Middle	Top	Top	Top	Middle	Top	Top	Top	Top	Top		Alba Plc
Kenwood	Bottom	Top	Top	Top	Top	Top	Top	Middle	Top	Top	Top	Top	Top		De'Longhi Spa
Morphy Richards	Bottom	Top	Top	Top	Top	Top	Top	Bottom	Top	Top	Top	Top	Top		Kilkee Investments
Moulinex	Middle	Top	Top	Top	Top	Top	Top	Bottom	Top	Top	Top	Top	Top		Groupe SEB
Philips	Top	Top	Middle	Top	Top	Top	Top	Bottom	Bottom	Top	Bottom	Top	Top		Philips Electronics
Pifco	Bottom	Top	Top	Top	Top	Top	Top	Middle	Top	Top	Top	Top	Top		Salton Inc
Prima	Bottom	Top	Top	Top	Top	Top	Top	Top	Top	Top	Top	Top	Top		Prima International Group
Rowenta	Middle	Top	Top	Top	Top	Top	Top	Bottom	Top	Top	Top	Top	Top		Groupe SEB
Russell Hobbs	Bottom	Top	Top	Top	Top	Top	Top	Middle	Top	Top	Top	Top	Top		Salton Inc
Salton	Bottom	Top	Top	Top	Top	Top	Top	Middle	Top	Top	Top	Top	Top		Salton Inc
Swan	Middle	Top	Top	Top	Top	Top	Top	Bottom	Top	Top	Top	Top	Top		Groupe SEB
Tefal	Middle	Top	Top	Top	Top	Top	Top	Bottom	Top	Top	Top	Top	Top		Groupe SEB

Key

- Top rating (no criticisms found)
- Middle rating
- Bottom rating
- A related company has a bottom rating and the company itself has a middle rating
- A related company has a middle rating
- A related company has a bottom rating

Source: ECRA-See page 14 for full key to symbols.

Laundry detergents

Whiter, brighter and smarter! But are we making our environment any cleaner as we endlessly chuck our scarcely-worn shirts, socks and underwear into the washing machine, throw in some liquid or powder, click the switch and forget about it? Unlikely! The very fact that every day is washing day for most families means that, collectively, we are using far more energy, water and detergents than ever before in history.

To be sure of not damaging the environment excessively, we should be thinking about the more eco-friendly products. Have a good look at the tables overleaf.

Over-performance

The research and development divisions of the mega-wash companies – Procter & Gamble and Lever Brothers churn over 84 per cent of British clothes in the wash every day – have come up with ever-more impressive-sounding formulations, leaving most of us poor consumers simply spinning with confusion. Understandably, most of us are indeed interested in performance and value for money, but we should think about whether we really need to have the highest level of performance for the simple things we put in the wash – which really only need freshening rather than a full wash that goes the whole hog with biological ingredients and all.

60-second green guide

- For mainstream brands, a washing powder is better than a liquid, and a concentrated powder better than a standard powder
- Use soap-based detergents, or ones with a high soap content
- Vegetable-based surfactants are better than petrochemical-based ones
- Use a product without phosphates, phosphonates or carboxylates
- You can make eco-products work better in hard water areas by using a water softener
- Choose a low wash temperature, or select the 'economy' cycle if your machine has one

Ingredients to watch

We should definitely watch out for the quantity of surfactants that we get through – and these are still in all the products from the mega-wash companies, together with ingredients like phosphates, phosphonates and carboxylates. For those concerned about enzymes, these are not bad for the environment, but there have been problems for workers in the factories making them – which seem largely to have been sorted out by now.

Anyone who has tried the ecological brands like Ecover and Bio-D will have noticed that they can be less efficient at removing the most stubborn stains, although they do dispense with the most environmentally damaging ingredients of the mega-wash products, especially their petrochemical-based surfactants.

AN EFFICIENT BALANCE

Having carefully considered the best trade-offs between efficiency and environmental impacts, ECRA recommends the following combination for handling the majority of our clothes:

- Ecover or Bio-D (or equivalent) for a regular detergent wash
- Biological powder for a quarterly zapping of the dirtiest items

You can buy copies of this book at *www.thegoodshoppingguide.co.uk* where you get free postage and packing.

- ACDO
- Advance (Tesco)
- Bio-D
- Clear Spring
- Co-op
- Cyclon (Safeway)
- Ecover
- Logic (ASDA)
- Novon (Sainsbury)
- Surcare

- Ariel
- Bold
- Daz
- Dreft
- Fairy

- Persil
- Surf

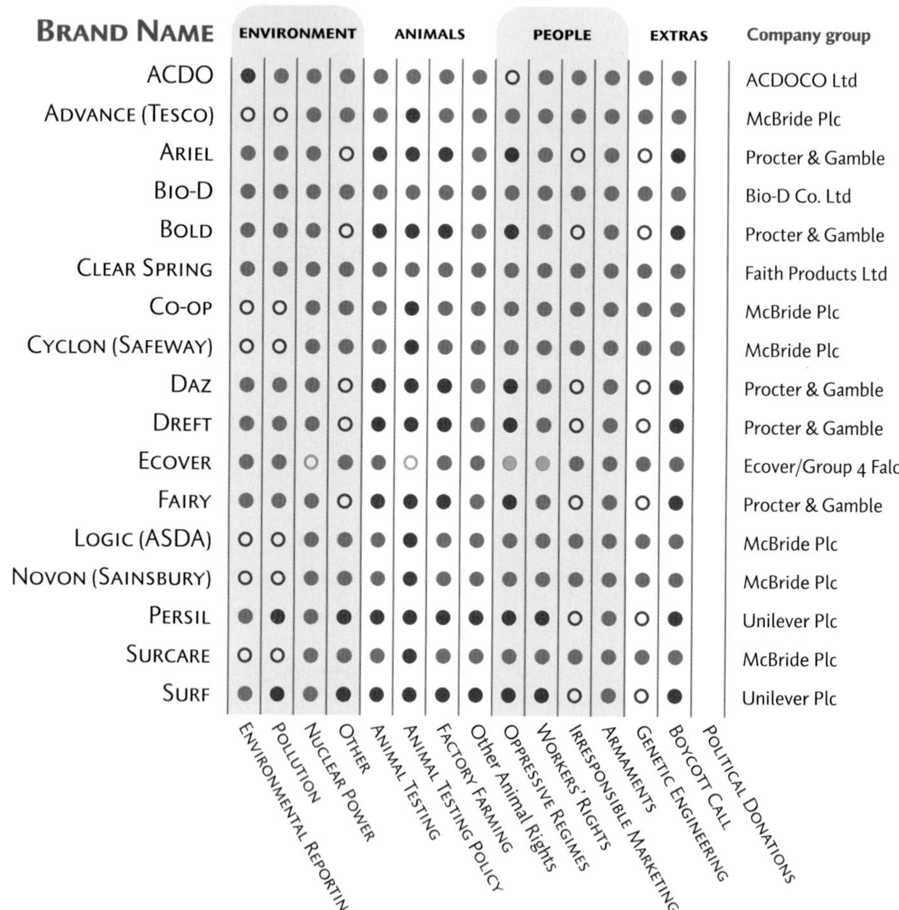

Brand Name	Environmental Reporting	Pollution	Nuclear Power	Other	Animal Testing	Animal Testing Policy	Factory Farming	Other Animal Rights	Oppressive Regimes	Workers' Rights	Irresponsible Marketing	Armaments	Genetic Engineering	Boycott Call	Political Donations	Company group
	ENVIRONMENT				ANIMALS				PEOPLE				EXTRAS			
ACDO	Bottom	Top	Top	Top	Top	Top	Top	Top	Middle	Top	Top	Top	Top	Top		ACDOCO Ltd
Advance (Tesco)	Middle	Middle	Top	Top	Top	Bottom	Top	Top	Top	Top	Top	Top	Top	Top		McBride Plc
Ariel	Top	Top	Top	Middle	Bottom	Bottom	Bottom	Top	Bottom	Top	Middle	Top	Middle	Bottom		Procter & Gamble
Bio-D	Top	Top	Top	Top	Top	Top	Top	Top	Top	Top	Top	Top	Top	Top		Bio-D Co. Ltd
Bold	Top	Top	Top	Middle	Bottom	Bottom	Bottom	Top	Bottom	Top	Middle	Top	Middle	Bottom		Procter & Gamble
Clear Spring	Top	Top	Top	Top	Top	Top	Top	Top	Top	Top	Top	Top	Top	Top		Faith Products Ltd
Co-op	Middle	Middle	Top	Top	Top	Bottom	Top	Top	Top	Top	Top	Top	Top	Top		McBride Plc
Cyclon (Safeway)	Middle	Middle	Top	Top	Top	Bottom	Top	Top	Top	Top	Top	Top	Top	Top		McBride Plc
Daz	Top	Top	Top	Middle	Bottom	Bottom	Bottom	Top	Bottom	Top	Middle	Top	Middle	Bottom		Procter & Gamble
Dreft	Top	Top	Top	Middle	Bottom	Bottom	Bottom	Top	Bottom	Top	Middle	Top	Middle	Bottom		Procter & Gamble
Ecover	Top	Top	Related middle	Top	Top	Related middle	Top	Top	Related bottom	Related bottom	Top	Top	Top	Top		Ecover/Group 4 Falck
Fairy	Top	Top	Top	Middle	Bottom	Bottom	Bottom	Top	Bottom	Top	Middle	Top	Middle	Bottom		Procter & Gamble
Logic (ASDA)	Middle	Middle	Top	Top	Top	Bottom	Top	Top	Top	Top	Top	Top	Top	Top		McBride Plc
Novon (Sainsbury)	Middle	Middle	Top	Top	Top	Bottom	Top	Top	Top	Top	Top	Top	Top	Top		McBride Plc
Persil	Top	Bottom	Top	Bottom	Bottom	Bottom	Bottom	Bottom	Bottom	Bottom	Middle	Top	Middle	Bottom		Unilever Plc
Surcare	Middle	Middle	Top	Top	Top	Bottom	Top	Top	Top	Top	Top	Top	Top	Top		McBride Plc
Surf	Top	Bottom	Top	Bottom	Bottom	Bottom	Bottom	Bottom	Bottom	Bottom	Middle	Top	Middle	Bottom		Unilever Plc

Key

- Top rating (no criticisms found)
- Middle rating
- Bottom rating
- A related company has a bottom rating and the company itself has a middle rating
- A related company has a middle rating
- A related company has a bottom rating

Source: ECRA-See page 14 for full key to symbols.

Paint

We all know that paint is a chemical concoction. What we need to know, and are never really told, is how much damage the chemicals can cause the environment and human health, whether in their manufacture and preparation, during application and cleaning of brushes, etc, or in their storage and disposal. Let's look at some of the environmental claims behind both the conventional and 'natural' paints that are used to decorate interior walls (emulsions) and woodwork (glosses).

What's in the stuff?

Modern paints are complex chemical concoctions, but most conventional paints contain petroleum-based by-products of the oil industry, a sector not renowned for its commitment to environmental protection. Indeed, three of the largest paint companies on the table, TotalFinaElf, Akzo Nobel and ICI, are thought to be amongst the most environmentally damaging in the world.

Paint production is hazardous and uses a lot of energy. Making just one tonne of paint can produce up to ten tonnes of waste, much of which is toxic. But the main issue with household paint is that of volatile organic compounds (VOCs) – these occur in gloss paint more than in emulsion paint and they evaporate during use, and can contribute to the formation of ground-level ozone. At least now several major paint brands have a voluntary labelling scheme which states the level of VOCs in their products, using five categories from 'minimal' to 'very high'. Consumers in high-street stores looking to avoid high-level VOCs are usually offered new generations of water-based gloss paints, but these contain extra chemicals so the eco-paint producers argue that it may be better to buy a solvent-based gloss paint from an environmentally aware company.

Conventional paints can emit an alarming array of noxious gases, including known carcinogens such as toluene and xylene. But the fumes given off by natural paints can also be noxious, so both types of paint may get a similar VOC rating. Other concerns are the use of synthetic alkyl phenols, alkyds and acrylics, and whether the product is biodegradable.

Titanium dioxide is used to improve the coverage or 'opacity' of the paint, and is also an important ingredient of many 'brilliant white' paints. Despite being in plentiful supply, titanium has a significant environmental impact because of the amount of energy used in its manufacture, leading some of the alternative paint companies to offer a choice of paints either with or without titanium.

15-25% of paint sold in the UK is never used! Remove paint from brushes before rinsing and don't pour it down the drain. Contact your Environmental Health Department for safe disposal or recycling.

Natural paint?

The 'natural' paints on the market claim to be both safer to use and kinder to the environment than conventional products. Not all 'natural' paints are the same; some contain only organic ingredients, and several are based on traditional formulations that have been in use for centuries, whilst others, although free from VOCs, may contain synthetic alkyds, usually in order to improve their performance. Some also contain a small percentage of white spirit, sometimes labelled as 'aliphatic hydrocarbons'.

The most common ingredients found in 'natural' paints are linseed oil, lime, turpentine, d-limonene, natural earth and mineral pigments, chalk, casein and borax. Auro, Biofa, Livos, Nutshell and OS Color will disclose ingredients on request.

Pity the poor painter

Many consumers are turning to 'eco-paints' not only for the environmental benefits but also out of concern for their own health. In 1989, the World Health Organisation's cancer research agency found that professional painters and decorators faced a 40 per cent increased chance of contracting cancer, and went so far as to deem painting and decorating to be a 'carcinogenic' activity by definition.

- Auro
- Biofa
- Casa
- Craig & Rose
- Green Paints
- Keim
- Livos
- Nutshell
- OS Color

- B&Q
- Benetton
- Crown
- Ecos
- Farrow & Ball
- Fired Earth
- Homebase

- Colour Crazy Int's
- Dulux
- Focus Do It All
- Johnstone's
- Leyland
- Manders
- Soft Sheen Inter's
- SPL
- Wickes

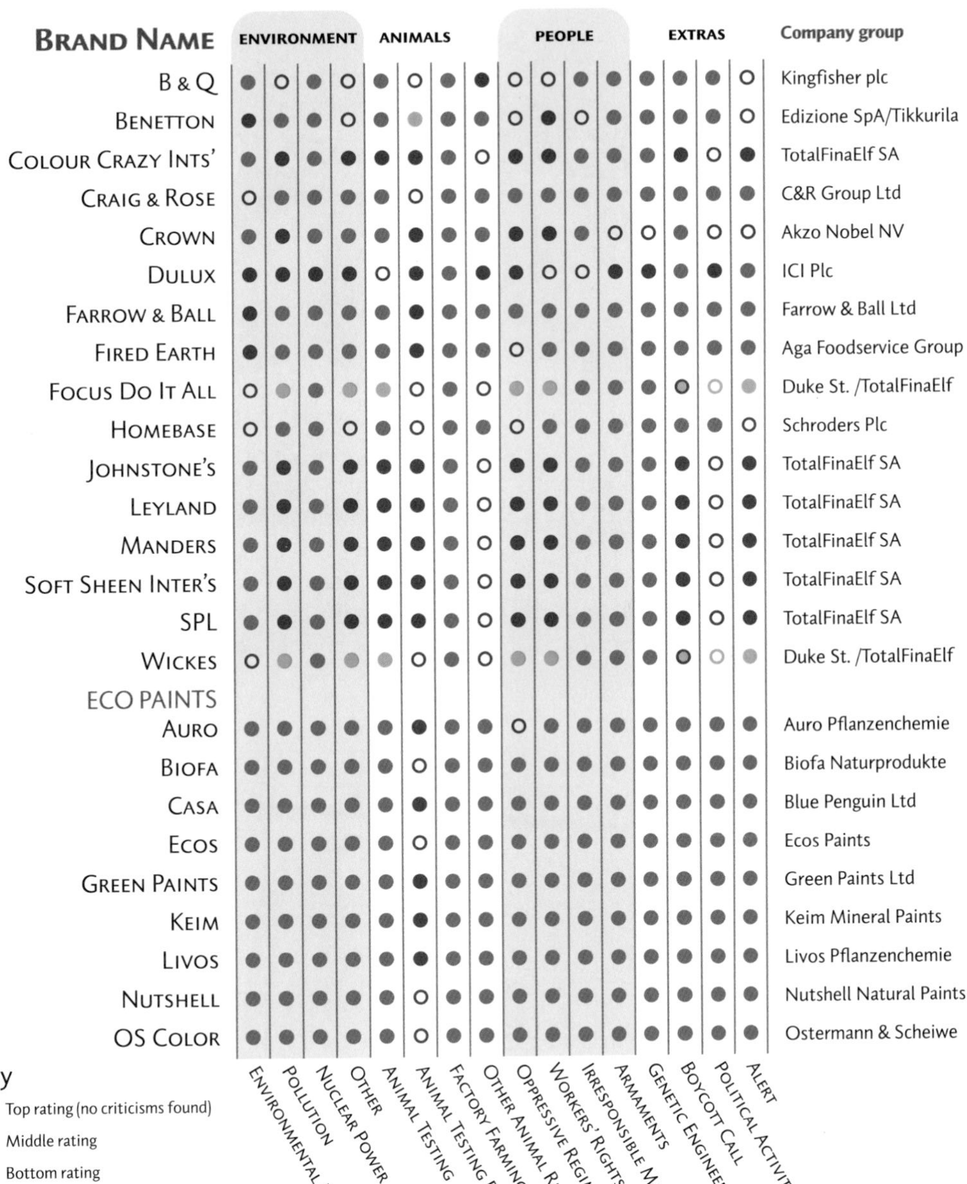

Brand Name	Environment				Animals				People				Extras				Company group
	Environmental Reporting	Pollution	Nuclear Power	Other	Animal Testing	Animal Testing Policy	Factory Farming	Other Animal Rights	Oppressive Regimes	Workers' Rights	Irresponsible Marketing	Armaments	Genetic Engineering	Boycott Call	Political Activity	Alert	
B & Q	T	M	T	M	T	M	T	B	M	M	T	T	T	T	T	M	Kingfisher plc
Benetton	B	T	T	M	T	b	T	T	M	B	M	T	T	T	T	M	Edizione SpA/Tikkurila
Colour Crazy Ints'	T	B	T	B	B	B	T	M	B	B	T	T	T	B	M	B	TotalFinaElf SA
Craig & Rose	M	T	T	T	T	M	T	T	T	T	T	T	T	T	T	T	C&R Group Ltd
Crown	T	B	T	T	T	B	T	T	B	B	T	M	M	T	M	M	Akzo Nobel NV
Dulux	B	B	B	B	M	B	T	B	B	M	M	B	B	T	B	T	ICI Plc
Farrow & Ball	B	T	T	T	T	B	T	T	T	T	T	T	T	T	T	T	Farrow & Ball Ltd
Fired Earth	B	T	T	T	T	B	T	T	M	T	T	T	T	T	T	T	Aga Foodservice Group
Focus Do It All	M	b	T	b	b	M	T	M	b	b	T	T	T	BM	m	b	Duke St. /TotalFinaElf
Homebase	M	T	T	M	T	M	T	T	M	T	T	T	T	T	T	M	Schroders Plc
Johnstone's	T	B	T	B	B	B	T	M	B	B	T	T	T	B	M	B	TotalFinaElf SA
Leyland	T	B	T	B	B	B	T	M	B	B	T	T	T	B	M	B	TotalFinaElf SA
Manders	T	B	T	B	B	B	T	M	B	B	T	T	T	B	M	B	TotalFinaElf SA
Soft Sheen Inter's	T	B	T	B	B	B	T	M	B	B	T	T	T	B	M	B	TotalFinaElf SA
SPL	T	B	T	B	B	B	T	M	B	B	T	T	T	B	M	B	TotalFinaElf SA
Wickes	M	b	T	b	b	M	T	M	b	b	T	T	T	BM	m	b	Duke St. /TotalFinaElf
ECO PAINTS																	
Auro	T	T	T	T	T	B	T	T	M	T	T	T	T	T	T	T	Auro Pflanzenchemie
Biofa	T	T	T	T	T	M	T	T	T	T	T	T	T	T	T	T	Biofa Naturprodukte
Casa	T	T	T	T	T	B	T	T	T	T	T	T	T	T	T	T	Blue Penguin Ltd
Ecos	T	T	T	T	T	M	T	T	T	T	T	T	T	T	T	T	Ecos Paints
Green Paints	T	T	T	T	T	B	T	T	T	T	T	T	T	T	T	T	Green Paints Ltd
Keim	T	T	T	T	T	B	T	T	T	T	T	T	T	T	T	T	Keim Mineral Paints
Livos	T	T	T	T	T	B	T	T	T	T	T	T	T	T	T	T	Livos Pflanzenchemie
Nutshell	T	T	T	T	T	M	T	T	T	T	T	T	T	T	T	T	Nutshell Natural Paints
OS Color	T	T	T	T	T	M	T	T	T	T	T	T	T	T	T	T	Ostermann & Scheiwe

Key

- (T) Top rating (no criticisms found)
- (M) Middle rating
- (B) Bottom rating
- (BM) The manufacturer has a bottom rating and the company itself has a middle rating
- (m) The manufacturer has a middle rating
- (b) The manufacturer has a bottom rating

Source: ECRA-See page 14 for full key to symbols.

Printers

The paperless office is efficient, pleasing to the eye and, of course, environmentally sound. For most of us though it is just a dream. Until that dream becomes reality we should choose our printers carefully. Like most computer hardware these days, printers are built in low labour-cost countries, sometimes in appalling conditions. In using them we consume a lot of energy, a lot of paper too. And in disposing of them many of us fail to extend their life by passing them on.

Labour practices

Poor practices abound. There are few codes of conduct in place. CAFOD, the Catholic Agency for Overseas Development, runs a campaign pressurising multinational computer manufacturers and exposing employment practices which contravene recognised standards.

Environmental concerns

Regulatory requirements mean that the main producers in this section are able to demonstrate surprisingly pleasing environmental concern in the manufacturing process, although as ever in the IT sector toxic chemicals require proper management. The environmental impact from printers comes mostly through their use and, ultimately, their disposal. Support those machines with the TCO and other energy efficient standards. A new Brother product release recently set the standard for the environmentally friendly printer. And on a Company level, Brother also scored highly when evaluated under the Ethical Company Organisation's company certification scheme (see *www.ethical-company-organisation.org*).

Printer use

A printer not in use should not be wasting electricity, so, don't leave it on 'standby' mode but leave it on 'sleep' mode. When printing, use the economy or saver modes, especially when printing for your own purposes and not, for example, for presentations or final documents. Print on both sides of the paper too.

Printer disposal

Unused computer hardware is an environmental time bomb. Since the boom in home electronics most consumers have upgraded their equipment once or more but few have yet disposed of their redundant machines. To find out how best to reuse, refurbish or recycle your equipment see www.wasteonline.org.uk. By the middle of 2005 all local authorities will be running collection or take back

schemes, actually funded by the producers themselves. So it will be well worth approaching your local council.

The environmental office

Until the paperless office becomes a reality we should use printers only when necessary and minimise our negative environmental impact by printing on both sides and by using economy and sleep modes. Also, we should use printers with separate drum and toner cartridges, allowing each part to be replaced separately. Look for long life drums; refill ink and toner cartridges; and change ozone filters where applicable.

Finally, look for recognised eco labels, chief amongst them the TCO Development, begun in the ever progressive Sweden in 1992. Its criteria covers labour practises, the environmental impact of production, and, interestingly, the relative health risks of using the product, including ergonomics and use of chlorinated plastics.

You can compare the live prices and also ethics on hundreds of different printers (and other office equipment) at *www.gooshing.co.uk* – once you have chosen your model, Gooshing will show you the very cheapest online purchase point for that particular model on that particular day. Saving money and the environment!

- Brother
- Epson
- Lexmark

- Minolta/QMS
- Samsung
- Xerox

- Hewlett Packard
- Kyocera Mita

brother® supports ethical shopping
At your side.

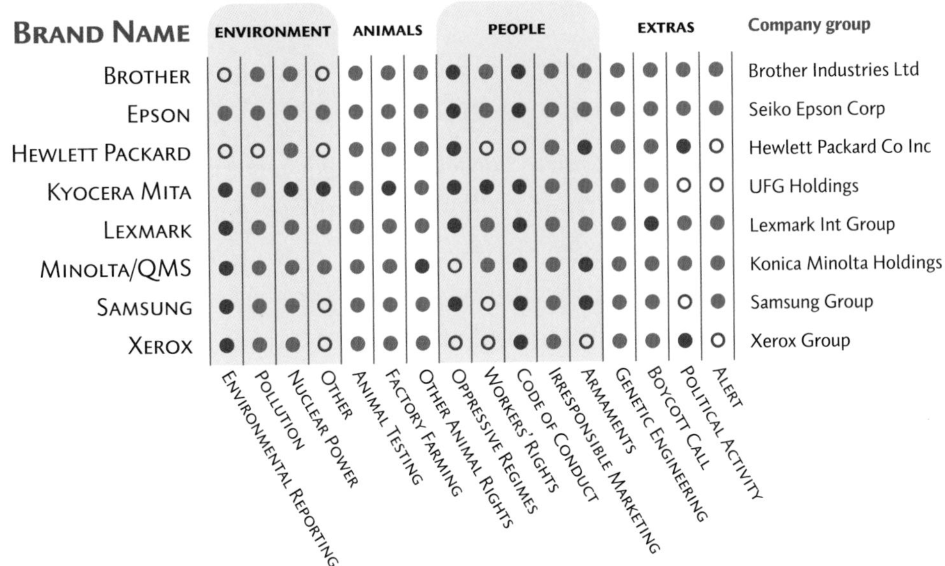

Brand Name	Environmental Reporting	Pollution	Nuclear Power	Other	Animal Testing	Factory Farming	Other Animal Rights	Oppressive Regimes	Workers' Rights	Code of Conduct	Irresponsible Marketing	Armaments	Genetic Engineering	Boycott Call	Political Activity	Alert	Company group
	ENVIRONMENT				ANIMALS			PEOPLE					EXTRAS				
Brother	Middle	Top	Top	Middle	Top	Top	Top	Bottom	Top	Bottom	Top	Top	Top	Top	Top	Top	Brother Industries Ltd
Epson	Top	Top	Top	Top	Top	Top	Top	Bottom	Top	Bottom	Top	Top	Top	Top	Top	Top	Seiko Epson Corp
Hewlett Packard	Middle	Middle	Top	Middle	Top	Top	Top	Bottom	Middle	Middle	Top	Bottom	Top	Top	Bottom	Middle	Hewlett Packard Co Inc
Kyocera Mita	Bottom	Top	Bottom	Bottom	Top	Bottom	Top	Bottom	Bottom	Bottom	Top	Top	Top	Top	Middle	Middle	UFG Holdings
Lexmark	Bottom	Top	Top	Top	Top	Top	Top	Bottom	Top	Bottom	Top	Top	Top	Bottom	Top	Top	Lexmark Int Group
Minolta/QMS	Bottom	Top	Top	Top	Top	Top	Bottom	Middle	Top	Bottom	Top	Bottom	Top	Top	Top	Top	Konica Minolta Holdings
Samsung	Bottom	Top	Top	Middle	Top	Top	Top	Bottom	Middle	Bottom	Top	Bottom	Top	Top	Middle	Top	Samsung Group
Xerox	Bottom	Top	Top	Middle	Top	Top	Top	Middle	Middle	Bottom	Top	Middle	Top	Top	Bottom	Middle	Xerox Group

Key

- ● Top rating (no criticisms found)
- ○ Middle rating
- ● Bottom rating
- ◉ A related company has a bottom rating and the company itself has a middle rating
- ○ A related company has a middle rating
- ● A related company has a bottom rating

Source: ECRA-See page 14 for full key to symbols.

Toys

As far as many children are concerned, it's a good job their parents are prepared to spend, because they're demanding more expensive and more sophisticated toys. Children are also much more media savvy, wanting toys associated with their favourite TV show or film. Younger and younger children are becoming brand-aware even before they can read.

Whose game is it anyway?

In the West we're spending more than ever on our children, but in many countries toys are still a luxury item. North American parents spent $328 on toys per child in 2000 and European parents $100, compared to $13 per child by Asian parents and $2 by African parents.

Even more staggering is the amount of money spent by the companies on advertising their toys. Pester power is apparently big business. According to the US-based National Labor Committee, the toy giant Mattel spends 30 times as much on advertising as it pays the young women who make its toys. For each £20 toy, about £3 is spent on advertising and only 10 pence on the labour of the workers making it.

Made in China

Two companies dominate the traditional toy and game market: Hasbro & Mattel. Whether or not our children's toys come from either of these companies, or one of the smaller manufacturers, the chances are that it will have been sourced from the Far East, and most probably China. An ECRA shop survey found that nine out of ten toys it looked at had been manufactured in China. Production of toys, like most consumer goods, has been shifted to China, where labour is cheaper and overall costs are low.

One report said that many Chinese workers handle toxic glues, paints and solvents without gloves or proper ventilation, and suffer dizziness, nausea, fainting, skin rashes and sore throats.

Campaigners say we should stop buying toys made in China until there are better conditions there. If everybody did this, it certainly would be a highly effective form of pressure.

Plastic fantastic?

Plastics are used in 80 per cent of new toys.

Toys aimed at the under threes which are intended to be put in the mouth should not contain any phthalates, which are the chemicals added to PVC to soften it and a potential health concern.

Most toys will have the PVC symbol on somewhere, but it's not always easy to find, especially in the shop.

Companies that have committed themselves to a PVC-free policy currently include Lego, Brio AB, Green Baby and Rubbermaid.

Other plastic toys may also contain phthalates

Toys are also becoming increasingly computerised and toy robots are always popular. These all require the use of energy of some sort, whether battery or mains operated, leading to a higher environmental impact. Batteries also require 50 times more energy in production than they will give out and are toxic when disposed of. Each year 600 million domestic batteries are consumed in the UK, contributing up to 40,000 tonnes of waste to landfill sites. Look at the section in this book on Batteries.

Interestingly, a German study in which children at a Munich nursery were 'deprived' of toys for three months, seemed to show they weren't really missed. Researchers claimed the children who took part acquired better concentration and communication skills.

- Bagpuss Soft Toy
- Betty Spaghetti
- Brio Toys
- Captain Scarlet
- Clangers Soft Toy
- David Halsall
- Galt Toys
- Green Baby
- Haba Wooden Toys
- Holz Toys
- Hornby Trains
- Lego
- Plan Wooden toys
- Playmobil

- Chicco
- Dingbots
- ELC
- Fisher Price
- Little Tykes
- Meccano
- Monopoly
- Smoby

- Barbie
- Disney
- Matchbox Toys
- Mr Potato Head
- Play-Doh
- Polly Pocket
- Tiger Electronics
- Tonka Toys

GOOD HOME & OFFICE

Brand Name	Environment: Environmental Reporting	Environment: Pollution	Environment: Nuclear Power	Environment: Other	Animals: Animal Testing	Animals: Factory Farming	Animals: Other Animal Rights	People: Oppressive Regimes	People: Workers' Rights	People: Code of Conduct	People: Irresponsible Marketing	People: Armaments	Extras: Genetic Engineering	Extras: Boycott Call	Extras: Political Activity	Extras: Alert	Company group
Bagpuss Soft Toy	Bottom	Top	Top	Top	Top	Top	Top	Middle	Top	Middle	Top	Top	Top	Top	Top	Top	Golden Bear Products
Barbie	Bottom	Middle	Top	Bottom	Top	Top	Top	Bottom	Bottom	Middle	Middle	Top	Top	Top	Middle	Top	Mattel Inc
Betty Spaghetti	Bottom	Top	Top	Top	Top	Top	Top	Middle	Top	Middle	Top	Top	Top	Top	Top	Top	Bandai
Brio Toys	Bottom	Top	Top	Top	Top	Top	Top	Middle	Top	Middle	Top	Top	Top	Top	Top	Top	Brio AB
Captain Scarlet	Bottom	Top	Top	Top	Top	Top	Top	Middle	Top	Middle	Top	Top	Top	Top	Top	Top	Vivid Imaginations
Chicco	Bottom	Top	Top	Bottom	Top	Top	Top	Bottom	Top	Middle	Bottom	Top	Top	Top	Top	Top	Artsana SpA
Clangers Soft Toy	Bottom	Top	Top	Top	Top	Top	Top	Middle	Top	Middle	Top	Top	Top	Top	Top	Top	Golden Bear Products
David Halsall	Bottom	Top	Top	Top	Top	Top	Top	Middle	Top	Middle	Top	Top	Top	Top	Top	Top	David Halsall Int
Dingbots	Bottom	Top	Top	Bottom	Top	Top	Top	Middle	Top	Middle	Top	Top	Top	Top	Top	Top	Tomy
Disney	Bottom	Bottom	Top	Bottom	Top	Top	Middle	Middle	Bottom	Middle	Middle	Top	Top	Bottom	Middle	Bottom	Walt Disney
ELC	Bottom	Top	Top	Bottom	Top	Top	Top	Middle	Top	Middle	Top	Top	Top	Top	Top	Top	Early Learning Centre
Fisher Price	Bottom	Middle	Top	Bottom	Top	Top	Top	Bottom	Bottom	Top	Middle	Top	Top	Top	Middle	Top	Mattel Inc
Galt Toys	Bottom	Top	Top	Top	Top	Top	Top	Middle	Top	Middle	Top	Top	Top	Top	Top	Top	Findel Plc
Green Baby	Top	Top	Top	Top	Top	Top	Top	Top	Top	Top	Top	Top	Top	Top	Top	Top	Green Baby

Key

- ● Top rating (no criticisms found)
- ○ Middle rating
- ● Bottom rating
- ◉ A related company has a bottom rating and the company itself has a middle rating
- ○ A related company has a middle rating
- ● A related company has a bottom rating

Source: ECRA-See page 14 for full key to symbols.

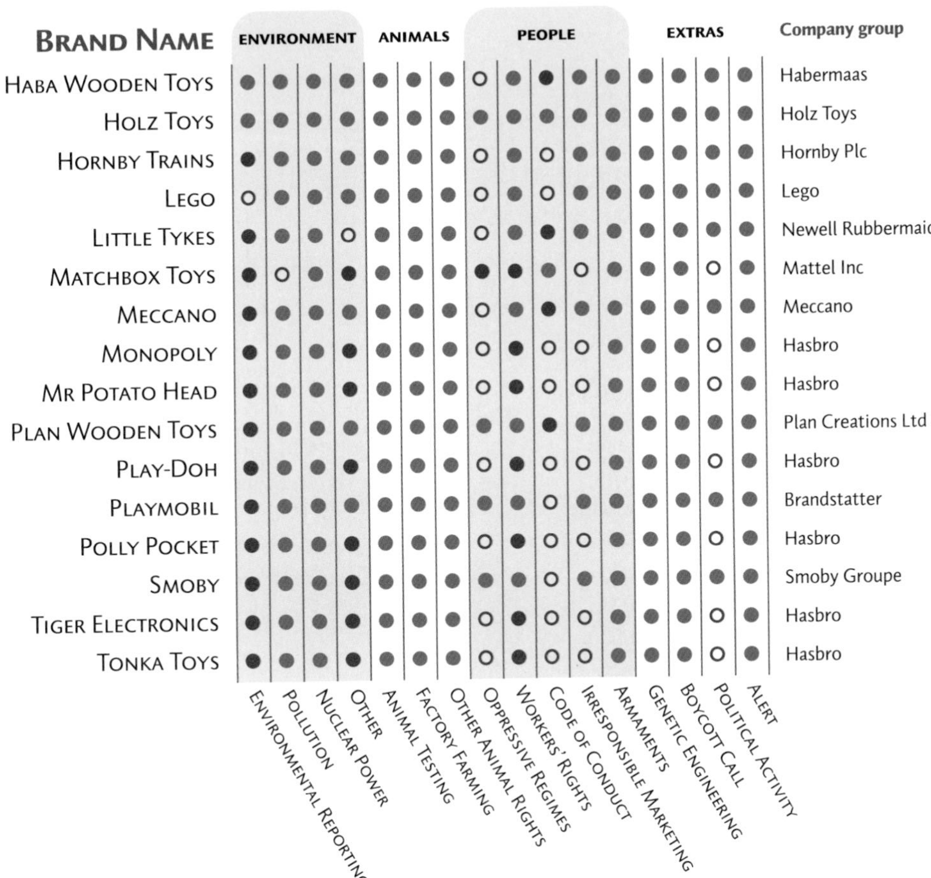

Brand Name	Environmental Reporting	Pollution	Nuclear Power	Other	Animal Testing	Factory Farming	Other Animal Rights	Oppressive Regimes	Workers' Rights	Code of Conduct	Irresponsible Marketing	Armaments	Genetic Engineering	Boycott Call	Political Activity	Alert	Company group
	Environment				Animals			People					Extras				
Haba Wooden Toys	Top	Top	Top	Top	Top	Top	Top	Middle	Top	Bottom	Top	Top	Top	Top	Top	Top	Habermaas
Holz Toys	Top	Top	Top	Top	Top	Top	Top	Top	Top	Top	Top	Top	Top	Top	Top	Top	Holz Toys
Hornby Trains	Bottom	Top	Top	Top	Top	Top	Top	Middle	Top	Middle	Top	Top	Top	Top	Top	Top	Hornby Plc
Lego	Middle	Top	Top	Top	Top	Top	Top	Middle	Top	Middle	Top	Top	Top	Top	Top	Top	Lego
Little Tykes	Bottom	Top	Top	Middle	Top	Top	Top	Middle	Top	Bottom	Top	Top	Top	Top	Top	Top	Newell Rubbermaid
Matchbox Toys	Bottom	Middle	Top	Bottom	Top	Top	Top	Bottom	Bottom	Top	Middle	Top	Top	Top	Middle	Top	Mattel Inc
Meccano	Bottom	Top	Top	Top	Top	Top	Top	Middle	Top	Bottom	Top	Top	Top	Top	Top	Top	Meccano
Monopoly	Bottom	Top	Top	Bottom	Top	Top	Top	Middle	Bottom	Middle	Middle	Top	Top	Top	Middle	Top	Hasbro
Mr Potato Head	Bottom	Top	Top	Bottom	Top	Top	Top	Middle	Bottom	Middle	Middle	Top	Top	Top	Middle	Top	Hasbro
Plan Wooden Toys	Bottom	Top	Top	Top	Top	Top	Top	Top	Top	Bottom	Top	Top	Top	Top	Top	Top	Plan Creations Ltd
Play-Doh	Bottom	Top	Top	Bottom	Top	Top	Top	Middle	Bottom	Middle	Middle	Top	Top	Top	Middle	Top	Hasbro
Playmobil	Bottom	Top	Top	Top	Top	Top	Top	Top	Top	Middle	Top	Top	Top	Top	Top	Top	Brandstatter
Polly Pocket	Bottom	Top	Top	Bottom	Top	Top	Top	Middle	Bottom	Middle	Middle	Top	Top	Top	Middle	Top	Hasbro
Smoby	Bottom	Top	Top	Bottom	Top	Top	Top	Top	Top	Middle	Top	Top	Top	Top	Top	Top	Smoby Groupe
Tiger Electronics	Bottom	Top	Top	Bottom	Top	Top	Top	Middle	Bottom	Middle	Middle	Top	Top	Top	Middle	Top	Hasbro
Tonka Toys	Bottom	Top	Top	Bottom	Top	Top	Top	Middle	Bottom	Middle	Middle	Top	Top	Top	Middle	Top	Hasbro

Key

- ● Top rating (no criticisms found)
- ○ Middle rating
- ● Bottom rating
- ◉ A related company has a bottom rating and the company itself has a middle rating
- ○ A related company has a middle rating
- ● A related company has a bottom rating

Source: ECRA-See page 14 for full key to symbols.

TV & video

If too much TV rots the brain, then we're probably all done for, but at least we can try to watch only what we really like – it's amazing how much electricity that could save, *and* it would prevent the box from wearing out so fast.

Don't dump that set

We dump around 2.5 million TV sets every year in the UK. Landfilled or incinerated sets are a loss of resources and a potential pollution hazard – plastics and cathode ray tubes can contain toxic substances. If we're getting a new set, we should look for a higher quality and more durable model that can be upgraded in future. If we want to get rid of an old one, we should take it to a second-hand or charity shop. If the old one is broken and no one will take it, it's best to take it to the civic amenity site where it can be used for scrap or recycled.

Energy efficiency

According to one scientific estimate, producing the energy necessary to power our TV viewing creates 7 million tonnes of carbon dioxide and 10,000 tonnes of sulphur dioxide per year. Manufacturers seem to have picked up on this and, as a rule, newer TVs and video recorders are more energy-efficient than earlier ones.

Even in standby mode, we waste about £12 million in electricity consumption a year, Friends of the Earth has estimated. A *Which?* study in 1998 found that Sony, Ferguson, Matsui, Samsung and Sharp came out best, using under 5 watts in standby mode – compared with more than 10 watts used by Mitsubishi, Hitachi, Toshiba and Sanyo models.

Materials

A TV set requires a surprisingly large amount of raw materials. Making the glass screen needs sand and electricity, while the glass for the cathode ray tube contains lead oxide and is coated in graphite to absorb X-rays – these impurities make the tube the hardest component to recycle and this is partly why liquid crystal displays (LCDs) are a less environmentally damaging alternative to conventional screens.

The making of circuit boards uses chemicals, water and energy and generates more hazardous waste than any other part of the TV, especially airborne particulate pollution and chemical waste. TVs and video casings often use brominated flame retardants (BFRs), the making of which can have nasty effects on animal and human health. Friends of the Earth has been campaigning for BFRs to be outlawed – there is more information on the FoE website *(www.foe.co.uk)*.

DAMAGE TO VIEWERS

TVs and videos emit non-ionising radiation over a range of frequencies. Although currently no proven adverse health links exist, the issue stimulates contentious debate and it is best to be cautious, by sitting at least six feet away from the screen and, after use, by switching off devices fully, especially in bedrooms.

60-SECOND GREEN GUIDE

- Buy second-hand TVs and videos where possible
- Switch off when you're not watching instead of leaving the TV on standby
- Don't sit too near a TV
- Favour smaller sets and/or check out LCD screens
- If the TV or video breaks, see if it can be repaired, or make sure it is recycled
- If you are buying new then do it at *www.gooshing.co.uk* – it compares ethics and prices!

- Akai
- Bang & Olufsen
- Casio
- Grundig
- LG
- Sanyo

- Bush
- Ferguson
- Goodmans
- Hinari
- Matsui
- Philips
- Samsung
- Sharp
- Thomson

- Aiwa
- Beko
- Hitachi
- JVC
- Mitsubishi
- Panasonic
- Sony
- Toshiba

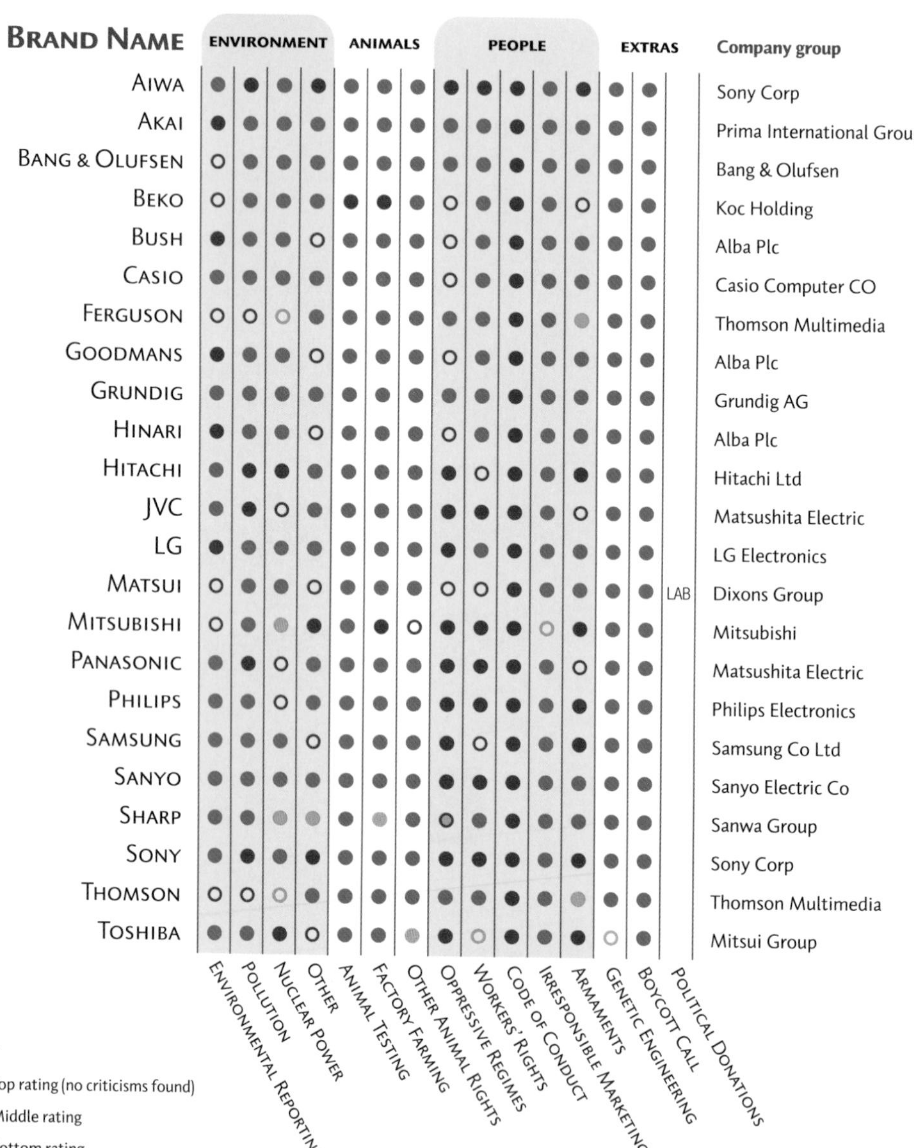

Brand Name	Environmental Reporting	Pollution	Nuclear Power	Other	Animal Testing	Factory Farming	Other Animal Rights	Oppressive Regimes	Workers' Rights	Code of Conduct	Irresponsible Marketing	Armaments	Genetic Engineering	Boycott Call	Political Donations	Company group
	ENVIRONMENT				ANIMALS			PEOPLE					EXTRAS			
Aiwa	Top	Bottom	Top	Bottom	Top	Top	Top	Bottom	Bottom	Bottom	Top	Bottom	Top	Top		Sony Corp
Akai	Bottom	Top	Top	Top	Top	Top	Top	Top	Top	Bottom	Top	Top	Top	Top		Prima International Group
Bang & Olufsen	Middle	Top	Top	Top	Top	Top	Top	Top	Top	Bottom	Top	Top	Top	Top		Bang & Olufsen
Beko	Middle	Top	Top	Top	Bottom	Bottom	Top	Middle	Top	Bottom	Top	Middle	Top	Top		Koc Holding
Bush	Bottom	Top	Top	Middle	Top	Top	Top	Middle	Top	Bottom	Top	Top	Top	Top		Alba Plc
Casio	Top	Top	Top	Top	Top	Top	Top	Middle	Top	Bottom	Top	Top	Top	Top		Casio Computer CO
Ferguson	Middle	Middle	Related middle	Top	Top	Top	Top	Top	Top	Bottom	Top	Related bottom	Top	Top		Thomson Multimedia
Goodmans	Bottom	Top	Top	Middle	Top	Top	Top	Middle	Top	Bottom	Top	Top	Top	Top		Alba Plc
Grundig	Top	Top	Top	Top	Top	Top	Top	Top	Top	Bottom	Top	Top	Top	Top		Grundig AG
Hinari	Bottom	Top	Top	Middle	Top	Top	Top	Middle	Top	Bottom	Top	Top	Top	Top		Alba Plc
Hitachi	Top	Bottom	Bottom	Top	Top	Top	Top	Bottom	Middle	Bottom	Top	Bottom	Top	Top		Hitachi Ltd
JVC	Top	Bottom	Middle	Top	Top	Top	Top	Bottom	Bottom	Bottom	Top	Middle	Top	Top		Matsushita Electric
LG	Bottom	Top	Top	Top	Top	Top	Top	Bottom	Top	Bottom	Top	Top	Top	Top		LG Electronics
Matsui	Middle	Top	Top	Middle	Top	Top	Top	Middle	Middle	Bottom	Top	Top	Top	Top	LAB	Dixons Group
Mitsubishi	Middle	Top	Related bottom	Bottom	Top	Bottom	Middle	Bottom	Bottom	Bottom	Related middle	Bottom	Top	Top		Mitsubishi
Panasonic	Top	Bottom	Middle	Top	Top	Top	Top	Bottom	Bottom	Bottom	Top	Middle	Top	Top		Matsushita Electric
Philips	Top	Top	Middle	Top	Top	Top	Top	Bottom	Bottom	Bottom	Top	Bottom	Top	Top		Philips Electronics
Samsung	Top	Top	Top	Middle	Top	Top	Top	Bottom	Middle	Bottom	Top	Bottom	Top	Top		Samsung Co Ltd
Sanyo	Top	Top	Top	Top	Top	Top	Top	Bottom	Bottom	Bottom	Top	Top	Top	Top		Sanyo Electric Co
Sharp	Top	Top	Related bottom	Related bottom	Top	Related bottom	Top	Related bottom / middle	Top	Bottom	Top	Top	Top	Top		Sanwa Group
Sony	Top	Bottom	Top	Bottom	Top	Top	Top	Bottom	Bottom	Bottom	Top	Bottom	Top	Top		Sony Corp
Thomson	Middle	Middle	Related middle	Top	Top	Top	Top	Top	Top	Bottom	Top	Related bottom	Top	Top		Thomson Multimedia
Toshiba	Top	Top	Bottom	Middle	Top	Top	Related bottom	Bottom	Related middle	Bottom	Top	Bottom	Related middle	Top		Mitsui Group

Key
- Top rating (no criticisms found)
- Middle rating
- Bottom rating
- A related company has a bottom rating and the company itself has a middle rating
- A related company has a middle rating
- A related company has a bottom rating

Source: ECRA-See page 14 for full key to symbols.

Vacuum cleaners

Beating the dust problem is not just a matter of having a powerful vacuum cleaner but of having one that is both energy-efficient and easy to handle around the home. That's why for some of us a manual carpet sweeper may be all we need. But the bigger the house the more likely it is that we will want quite a large machine with excellent reach and sucking power.

Power and noise

Vacuum cleaners are rated by manufacturers in terms of their wattage – a measure that only reveals the size of the motor. But as the average vacuum cleaner wastes most of the electricity used in heat and noise, the power rating does not necessarily provide us with any helpful information in deciding upon effectiveness.

Only about a quarter of the power output is actual suction power. Electrolux makes a SmartVac range with 450W of suction from 1500W input and this is high compared to most. Miele makes a model called Naturell with an energy-saving 800W motor. Manufacturers might be willing to disclose the suction power data upon request, but this information is not normally found on the label.

There are plans to encourage producers to make more efficient machines by way of voluntary labelling schemes. One group working on this is the Group for Efficient Appliances, a forum of representatives from national energy agencies and European governments. Most EU member states are represented but at the time of this EC report there was no UK representative – making it seem that there was no enthusiasm for recycling issues in the UK.

Bags and dust

It might be argued that Dyson machines have less of an impact on the environment because they don't use paper and resources to produce vacuum bags, but there is disagreement about whether or not a collection bag interferes with the efficiency of the suction. Dyson asserts that because its machines have no bag their efficiency is constant.

Machines with bags tend to drop in efficiency as the bag fills, and this reduces the amount that is picked up. To counter this, manufacturers such as Miele claim that the bag acts as an extra filter for dust particles and also prolongs the life of the motor.

Certain manufacturers, such as Nilfisk and Medivac, make vacuum cleaners with 'high efficiency filters' to minimise the re-emission of dust. The British Allergy Foundation (BAF) has a system of approval for vacuum cleaners which includes double-blind testing such that the testers have no idea who the individual manufacturers are.

Alternatives

If buying a vacuum cleaner, it is always possible to buy a reconditioned machine second-hand – or to repair a broken one. Handheld brushes are often more efficient than you might think and simply involve a little elbow grease, although they probably don't pick up the smaller particles which can cause allergic reactions. There are always old-style carpet sweepers, which are manual, non-electric and work a treat.

www.gooshing.co.uk can save you alot of money on vacuum cleaners. It searches 350 shops to find the cheapest place to buy your chosen brand.

60-SECOND GREEN GUIDE

- When buying a machine, look for the most efficient suction
- Get a machine with replaceable dust filters
- Dust bags should not be allowed to overfill
- Manual carpet sweepers are fine for a quick sweep-up

- Dyson
- MediVac
- Nifilsk
- Vax

- Hoover
- Miele
- Morphy Richards
- Rowenta

- AEG
- Electrolux
- Hitachi
- Panasonic
- Philips

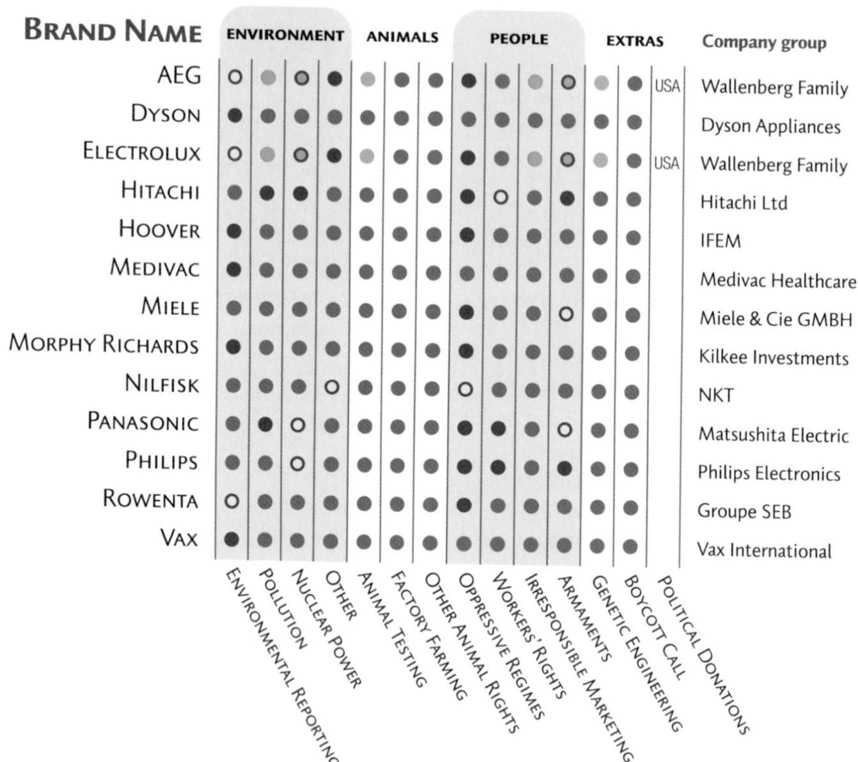

Key

- Top rating (no criticisms found)
- Middle rating
- Bottom rating
- A related company has a bottom rating and the company itself has a middle rating
- A related company has a middle rating
- A related company has a bottom rating

Source: ECRA-See page 14 for full key to symbols.

Washing machines

Washing our clothes by machine uses a lot of power and a lot of water but, gradually, the manufacturers are introducing ever-more energy-efficient machines. The way we use a machine can help cut down on wastage. We also need to be careful of how we dispose of an old one we're throwing out.

Energy labels

The European Energy Label is required by law to be displayed on many domestic appliances, including all new washing machines. Each product receives an energy efficiency rating, from A (the top rating) down to G (the lowest rating). Also rated on an A to G scale are 'washing performance' (with A giving the cleanest wash) and 'spin drying performance' (with A producing the driest clothes). A figure is also given for energy consumption per cycle (kWh) and water consumption (litres). The main rating here is the efficiency rating. Many 'AA' rated machines are now available, demonstrating that good performance and eco-efficiency can go together.

According to ECRA, two of the most energy-efficient machines are the Zanussi FLE1416W and the Indesit WE16. Apart from these, there is very little to choose between any energy efficiency 'A' class washing machines.

The water consumption for 62 different washing machines ranges from 35 to 78 litres, but averages at around 53.5. Washing machines in the table all consume less than 50 litres of water and have A class energy efficiency.

Internet information

It's worth checking the details of machines before we go out shopping for one. The main internet retailers provide the label ratings of their different models. Currys provides particularly detailed information on the technical specifications of each model, including energy and water consumption.

Reliability

Securing a reliable machine not only saves money on repairs, but it's a better environmental choice. The Consumers' Association measured the reliability of each brand and gave good marks to Miele, Candy, Bosch, AEG, Tricity Bendix, Siemens and Zanussi.

Disposal

Every year, nearly one million tonnes of used electrical and electronic goods are discarded in Britain. This includes about eight million large pieces of equipment like washing machines, cookers and fridges.

The EU has given local authorities until August 2005 to introduce 'convenient facilities' for the free take-back of waste goods by final owners, including public collection points where private households should be able to return waste 'at least free of charge'. It remains to be seen if this will really happen. All new equipment designated for collection under the scheme will in future be marked by the crossed-out wheeled bin symbol.

Next time you buy a washing machine do it at *www.gooshing.co.uk*. This website searches 350 shops to find the cheapest place to buy your chosen ethical brand.

60-SECOND GREEN GUIDE

Buying

- Choose the smallest washing machine for your needs
- Look for 'A' energy efficiency rating
- Choose one with a fast spin
- Look for an 'eco-button' that reduces temperature
- Choose one with the hot-fill option

Using

- Use a full load if possible
- Avoid the pre-wash cycle – pre soak dirty clothes
- Try to wash at 40°C or below

- Don't forget to switch to a 100% renewable energy company – that way you really are making a difference!

- Admiral
- Asko
- Bauknecht
- Brandt
- Candy
- Dyson
- Hinari
- Hoover
- Maytag
- Servis
- Whirlpool

- Ariston
- Beko
- Indesit
- LG
- Miele
- Samsung

- AEG
- Bosch
- Hotpoint
- Neff
- Siemens
- Tricity Bendix
- Zanussi

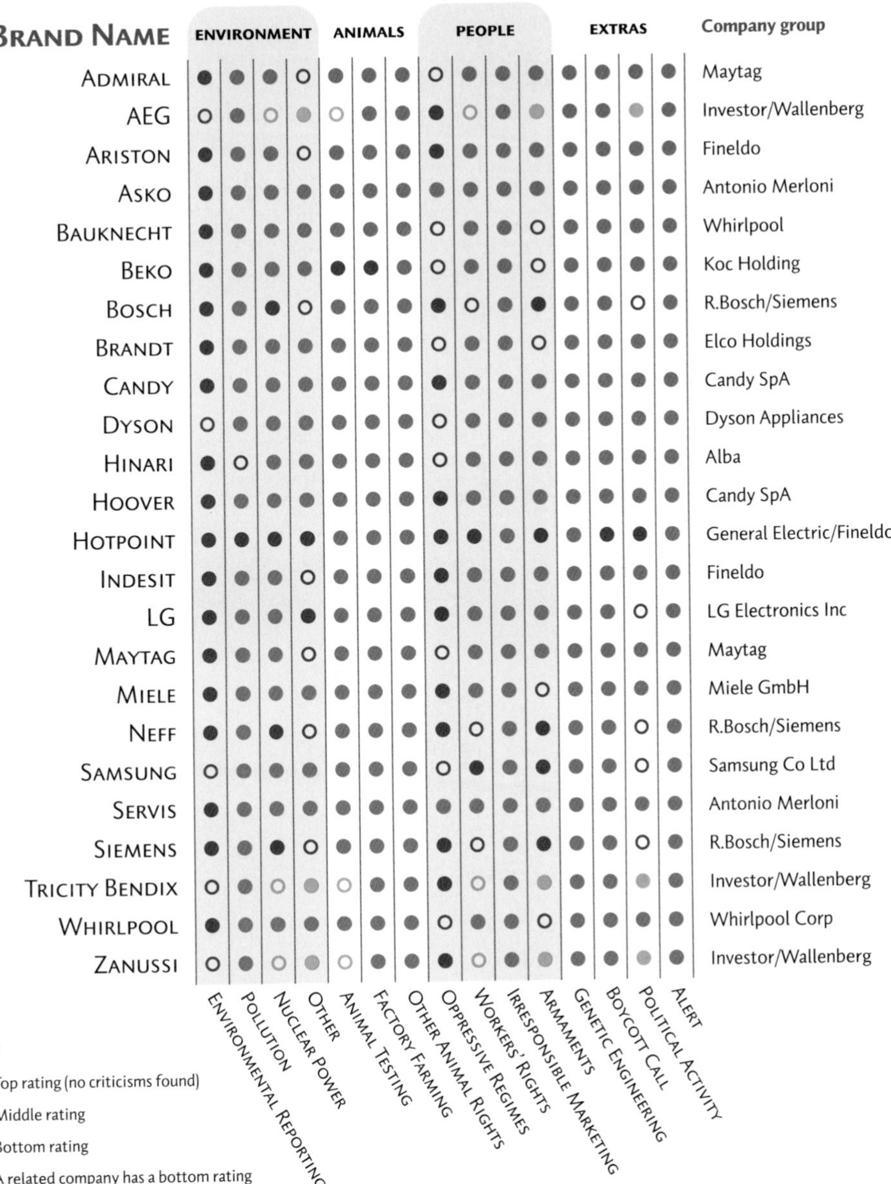

Brand Name
Environment
Animals
People
Extras
Company group
Admiral
AEG
Ariston
Asko
Bauknecht
Beko
Bosch
Brandt
Candy
Dyson
Hinari
Hoover
Hotpoint
Indesit
LG
Maytag
Miele
Neff
Samsung
Servis
Siemens
Tricity Bendix
Whirlpool
Zanussi
Maytag
Investor/Wallenberg
Fineldo
Antonio Merloni
Whirlpool
Koc Holding
R.Bosch/Siemens
Elco Holdings
Candy SpA
Dyson Appliances
Alba
Candy SpA
General Electric/Fineldo
Fineldo
LG Electronics Inc
Maytag
Miele GmbH
R.Bosch/Siemens
Samsung Co Ltd
Antonio Merloni
R.Bosch/Siemens
Investor/Wallenberg
Whirlpool Corp
Investor/Wallenberg
Environmental Reporting
Pollution
Nuclear Power
Other
Animal Testing
Factory Farming
Other Animal Rights
Oppressive Regimes
Workers' Rights
Irresponsible Marketing
Armaments
Genetic Engineering
Boycott Call
Political Activity
Alert

Key

- Top rating (no criticisms found)
- Middle rating
- Bottom rating
- A related company has a bottom rating and the company itself has a middle rating
- A related company has a middle rating
- A related company has a bottom rating

Source: ECRA-See page 14 for full key to symbols.

Washing-up liquid

When we clean our dishes effortlessly how can we be sure we're not making the planet that much dirtier? We would be well advised to look for liquids derived from vegetable sources rather than from highly-polluting petrochemical plants.

Ingredients

The active ingredient in washing-up liquid is its surfactant, which allows grease to be removed more quickly by emulsifying oils and keeping them dispersed and suspended so they don't settle back onto the surface. The most commonly found surfactants in hand dishwashing detergents are 'anionic' which usually means they create a lot of suds. Some products also list ionic or non-ionic surfactants.

All the surfactants may also be produced from vegetable oils (such as coconut) as well as from petrochemical sources, but only the eco-friendly products use the vegetable-based or 'oleo' surfactants. Faith Products, Bio-D, Little Green Shop, Down to Earth, Caurnie and Ecover are among these. In a life cycle inventory study by a German research body, the oleo surfactants were shown to be better than petrochemical surfactants in 9 of the 13 categories studied. The petrochemical surfactants were found to be slower to biodegrade and they were significantly more damaging in terms of aquatic and air eco-toxicity, global warming, depletion of water, acidification, petrochemical oxidant formation and consumption of renewable energy sources.

Synthetic perfume and colourings, also based on petrochemicals, can be slow to degrade and may cause problems for those with sensitive skin. The 'green' brands tend to be colourless and use natural fragrances such as volatile plant oils.

Antibacterial additives

Procter & Gamble launched Fairy Antibacterial in 1997, which it claims helps kill E-coli, salmonella and campylobacter. Others, including supermarket own brands, have followed with their own disinfectant formulas. Proper cooking and basic kitchen hygiene offer complete protection for everyone.

Packaging

Most washing-up liquid bottles are made of high-density polyethylene (labelled PE or HDPE). This is one of the few plastics that is beginning to be recycled in the UK, although provision of local collection schemes is patchy. Bio-D's bottles contain

55 per cent recycled material, which according to a company spokesperson is the maximum possible without the plastic becoming too brittle. Ecover and Bio-D are the only companies providing natural products suppliers with large drums that allow customers to refill their bottles regularly.

Alternatives

In a hard water area it is a good idea to use a water softener so that we can reduce the amount of suds we generate. Some people even recycle good old-fashioned soap to make a perfectly good washing-up liquid, by saving old soap scraps in a jar and mixing them up in boiling water. Try and buy *Good Shopping Guide* ethical brands when you can – it's a key area.

- Bio-D
- Caurnie
- Clear Spring
- Ecover
- Little Green Shop

- Morning Fresh
- Surcare

- Ajax
- Fairy
- Palmolive
- Persil

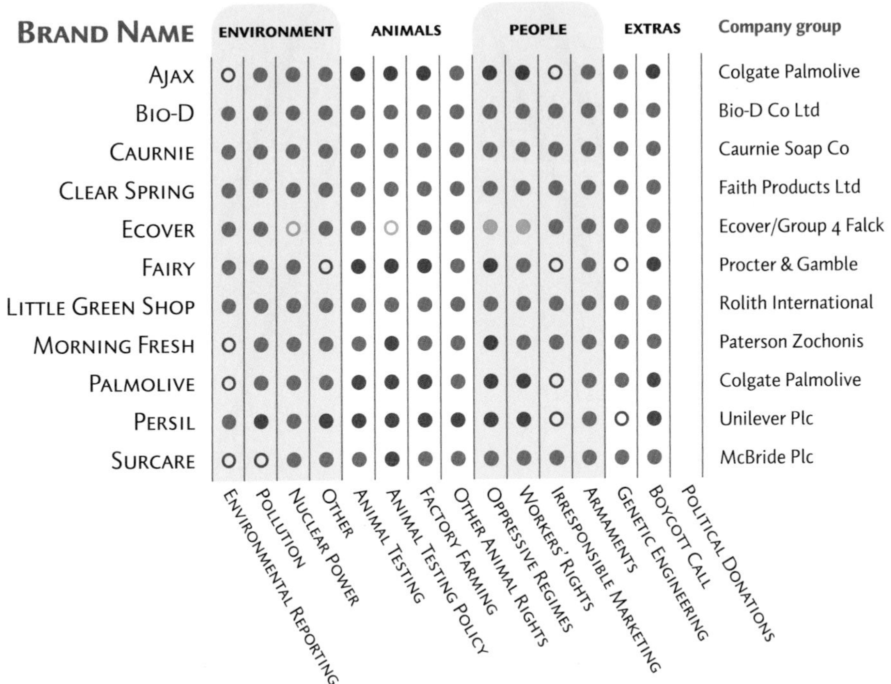

Brand Name	Environmental Reporting	Pollution	Nuclear Power	Other	Animal Testing	Animal Testing Policy	Factory Farming	Other Animal Rights	Oppressive Regimes	Workers' Rights	Irresponsible Marketing	Armaments	Genetic Engineering	Boycott Call	Political Donations	Company group
	ENVIRONMENT				ANIMALS				PEOPLE				EXTRAS			
Ajax	Middle	Top	Top	Top	Bottom	Bottom	Bottom	Top	Bottom	Bottom	Middle	Top	Top	Bottom		Colgate Palmolive
Bio-D	Top	Top	Top	Top	Top	Top	Top	Top	Top	Top	Top	Top	Top	Top		Bio-D Co Ltd
Caurnie	Top	Top	Top	Top	Top	Top	Top	Top	Top	Top	Top	Top	Top	Top		Caurnie Soap Co
Clear Spring	Top	Top	Top	Top	Top	Top	Top	Top	Top	Top	Top	Top	Top	Top		Faith Products Ltd
Ecover	Top	Top	Related middle	Top	Top	Related middle	Top	Top	Related bottom	Related bottom	Top	Top	Top	Top		Ecover/Group 4 Falck
Fairy	Top	Top	Top	Middle	Bottom	Bottom	Bottom	Top	Bottom	Top	Middle	Top	Middle	Bottom		Procter & Gamble
Little Green Shop	Top	Top	Top	Top	Top	Top	Top	Top	Top	Top	Top	Top	Top	Top		Rolith International
Morning Fresh	Middle	Top	Top	Top	Top	Bottom	Top	Top	Bottom	Top	Top	Top	Top	Top		Paterson Zochonis
Palmolive	Middle	Top	Top	Top	Bottom	Bottom	Bottom	Top	Bottom	Bottom	Middle	Top	Top	Bottom		Colgate Palmolive
Persil	Top	Bottom	Top	Bottom	Bottom	Bottom	Bottom	Bottom	Bottom	Bottom	Middle	Top	Middle	Bottom		Unilever Plc
Surcare	Middle	Middle	Top	Top	Top	Bottom	Top	Top	Top	Top	Top	Top	Top	Top		McBride Plc

Key

- Top rating (no criticisms found)
- Middle rating
- Bottom rating
- A related company has a bottom rating and the company itself has a middle rating
- A related company has a middle rating
- A related company has a bottom rating

Source: ECRA-See page 14 for full key to symbols.

Renewable energy

Welcome to *The Good Shopping Guide to Renewable Energy* which is designed to help you choose the best green electricity supplier. Although switching to a renewable energy supply is a great step in the right direction, you will find that some renewable energy companies are better and greener than others. In the following pages you can also read up on general energy saving tips that will help you save energy and money – even if you haven't yet made the switch.

GOOD ENERGY IS GREEN...

The biggest source of carbon dioxide emissions is power stations, accounting for around one third of the total. Coal power stations are the least efficient and although the increased popularity of natural gas burning has reduced our potential CO_2 emissions slightly, benefits are offset by the continued increase in overall energy usage. Our increasing electricity consumption requires more and more electricity generation, and although consumers' energy efficiency can help reduce this, the only real alternative is to source electricity from renewable resources.

CONFUSING MARKET

The domestic energy market is confusing enough – a few years ago customers knew that one gas company supplied their gas and nothing else, and another did the same with their electricity. Since 1999 all customers have been able to change their gas or electricity supplier and over 19 million customers have swapped in search of a better deal. Now homeowners have a dazzling array of tariffs and service providers, before even attempting to take the environment into account. Most of the main energy companies provide some kind of green tariff for electricity – the price and coverage depends on the area in which you live but it is generally accepted that green electricity tariffs cost the consumer either about the same or just a few pounds per bill more than conventional tariffs.

Green energy supply has been available in this country to some customers from as far back as 1997. However, it did not truly become an option for the average consumer until the energy market was completely opened up to competition in May 1999. Since then the offerings that are available to us have come a long way.

The green energy revolution has gained significant support at a commercial level. Large energy users and corporations have

taken to green energy supply in a big way. It is not only the case that large 'green'-centric companies such as The Body Shop have a green power supply, but also large institutions such as Oxford University who have 100% of their energy needs provided for by green supply.

Any company, small or large, that claims 'corporate social responsibility' that has not yet switched to a renewable energy supply should think again!

With fourteen green energy tariffs available now in the UK, there is a lot of choice available to the consumer. However, it is not the case that these tariffs all offer the same product.

The most important issue to those on a budget may be the issue of cost. For an average household, as you might expect due to economies of scale, the cost of receiving a green energy supply is fractionally more expensive, the supplement over and above a "regular" tariff is normally in the order of £20 or £30 a year. And changing your methods of payment to either Direct Debit or paying one annual fee can, in most cases, offset the entire extra cost, so there is no reason not to change your supply today.

Why switch to renewable energy?

When we read our newspapers and watch the news on TV everyday and see the environmental disasters and freak weather conditions that are attributed to Global Warming, we can see for ourselves the effects of the by-products of our traditional energy production. Electricity production is the single biggest contributor to the emissions that cause climate change. The prime gas responsible for Global Warming or 'The Greenhouse Effect' is Carbon Dioxide or CO_2. The burning of Oil, Coal and Gas, otherwise known as Fossil Fuels, in traditional power stations produces a considerable amount of this gas. The UK, with 1% of the world's population, emits 2.3% of the world's total amount of CO_2. Not only do these Fossil Fuels contribute to the degradation of the environment, but also they are finite in nature. It is only a matter of time before the planet's supply of these fuels runs out.

One alternative power source to traditional fuel burning stations is Nuclear Power. This is far from being a solution to global pollution though. Although British Nuclear Fuels Limited (BNFL) has been pushing Nuclear Power as the non-polluting solution to climate change, this is certainly not the case. During its lifetime (around 30-40 years) a nuclear reactor can produce radioactive waste that has a 'lifespan' of thousands of years. The waste needs to be disposed of safely, as it is highly dangerous. Although no CO_2 is produced there are definitely by-products to the nuclear process that potentially could do serious harm to the environment.

In contrast to these more traditional forms of energy supply, is renewable energy or 'Renewable' Energy. Not only does green energy not directly result in any by-products that may be harmful to our environment, it comes from renewable and everlasting sources such as wind and water. In fact most forms of renewable energy produce no or very little amounts of waste, and therefore have very little impact on the world around us.

'The biggest source of carbon dioxide emissions is power stations, accounting for around one third of the total.'

When you switch to a renewable energy supply, you are also supporting the future of the renewable energy industry. By showing the government and mainstream energy suppliers that you wholeheartedly support renewable energy you can help convince them to increase the support they offer to the industry as a whole.

How do you switch?

The great thing about switching to a green energy tariff is that it's incredibly EASY to do. There is no need to get electricians in, or have anything changed physically with your electricity supply. This is down to the nature of the types of green energy tariff available to the consumer, the Energy-based tariff and the Fund-based tariff and tariffs that offer a combination of the two.

Of the choices available, the Energy-based tariff is the option that actually offers you renewable energy in return for your money. Whilst there is no change in the actual electricity coming down the wires into your home when you subscribe to an Energy-based tariff, a proportion of what you pay will be matched by the equivalent amount of energy being fed into the national grid from renewable sources. Tariffs such as the one from Good Energy Ltd, (switch at *www.good-energy.co.uk)*, promise to match 100% of the units of electricity you buy from them with an equal amount from renewable sources, at the end of the year.

With Fund-based energy tariffs a proportion of money you pay the supplier is donated into a fund that supports new renewable capacity, green causes or other related initiatives. An independent body, established either by the supplier or a registered charity, normally administers these funds. In some cases the donation made from the consumer is matched in equal amounts by a donation made by the tariff supplier. A Combination tariff is usually some mixture of both Fund-based and Energy-based supply.

It is extremely easy to switch to a green energy tariff. All you need to do is register your interest with a supplier and they can sign you up over the phone or send you forms to fill out by post. It's also possible to switch your supplier with very little hassle online, at *www.gooshing.co.uk* where you can arrange to pay by Direct Debit, which will also save you money.

'Any company, small or large, that claims 'corporate social responsibility' that has not yet switched to a renewable energy supplier, should think again!'

Choosing the best supplier

Since April 1st 2004 Energy suppliers have had to make sure that at least 4.9% of all energy they provide comes from renewable energy sources. For each unit of renewable energy that they buy they receive a certificate. If companies fail to match their required 4.9% they may buy certificates from those companies that exceed their minimum.

In order to reach their minimum requirement, large energy suppliers offer a green tariff to customers. In many cases this does not exceed or match the minimum 4.9% renewable energy that the supplier is required to provide, as demand from traditional tariffs is still considerably greater. These suppliers then have to buy in certificates from smaller niche companies who only offer a green tariff, or their green tariff makes up more than 4.9% of their total energy supply. If, however, the niche company sells all its certificates other than the 4.9% it retains to meet its own government targets, it results in a net status quo in the energy market. No extra demand for renewable energy supply is generated, as total demand for renewable energy is matched across the board. Trading of certificates at this level will mean that the net average of renewable energy supply will remain at 4.9% nationwide. However if those suppliers that produce more than the minimum requirement set aside a further percentage of its certificates, above and beyond the required minimum, refusing to sell them on, additional demand for renewable energy sources is generated. At the moment only Good Energy does this.

When trying to evaluate which tariff is 'better,' it's best to look at what green tariffs are trying to achieve. Ultimately the aim is to increase the amount of renewable energy supply there is in the country. By increasing the influence of renewable energy sources, it is possible to lessen the influence of the environmentally degrading sources, Fossil Fuels and Nuclear Power. It's for this reason that purely Energy-based tariffs are the most positive choice.

Energy Companies Recommended by E.C.O

Good energy

This tariff has achieved the highest rating with Friends of the Earth for the past three years (see following pages). Good Energy is available to homes and businesses in England, Wales and Scotland. It only supplies energy from renewable sources – wind power, small-scale hydroelectric and solar power. For every unit of electricity used by a Good Energy customer, it promises to buy a unit of electricity from renewable power sources. And Good Energy is the first electricity company to publish an independent audit of its green claims.Good Energy is owned by an independent PLC, the Monkton Group, that specialises in investing in renewable energy and owns the UK's first-ever wind farm at Delabole in Cornwall. Over 1000 of the Good Energy customers are investors in Monkton Group. Good Energy has recently launched a Home Generation Scheme, which pays people for the renewable electricity they generate from small renewable generators including solar panels and wind turbines. The main reason why Good Energy continues to be recommended by FOE is that in addition to meeting government targets they set aside extra renewable energy certificates. This helps to generate extra demand for renewable energy sources and creates greater environmental benefit.

(0845 456 1640)

Green Energy 100

For every unit of electricity you buy, Green Energy 100 buys one unit of green electricity. Green Energy 100 invest 50% of profits in green electricity generation and hold on to 6.89% of the certificates of proof from these projects. Subscribers also become shareholders.

(0845 456 9550)

Ecotricity

Ecotricity is an independent energy supplier that invests in large wind-turbines. It has multiple wind-power generators already operational around the country. At Swaffham in Norfolk it built the country's first multi-megawatt wind-turbine, which alone provides enough energy for 3,000 people. The renewable energy certificates earned by Ecotricity are sold on to help other energy suppliers meet their government targets. The profits earned from the tariff and sale of certificates are then used to build further wind farms and turbines. Ecotricity have been particularly pro-active in building new power sources of renewable energy – this helps grow the amount of renewable energy available to the UK market.

(0800 032 6100)

See page 114 for contact details.

Energy Tariffs Recommended by Friends of the Earth

It is also very interesting to look at how Friends of the Earth ranks the different green electricity tariffs. The results are broadly in line with our own corporate-level analysis. It does however differ slightly as it concentrates more on the electricity tariff than the other activities that the ultimate holding company may be involved in.Friends of the Earth recommend tariffs offered by companies if they:

- Only sell green electricity or
- Produce green electricity in a large percentage of the power stations they own.
- Buy or generate one unit of green electricity for every unit you buy, and
- Hold onto at least some of the proof that they have done this.

Friends of the Earth penalise tariffs from companies that own carbon dinosaurs – ancient and inefficent fossil fuel based power stations – or if it isn't clear how their tariff would benefit the environment.

Friends of the Earth's Recommended Tariffs

(LISTED IN ALPHABETICAL ORDER):

Eco Energy

(Northern Ireland Electricity)

For every unit of electricity you buy, it supplies a unit of green electricity. No certificates necessary because in Northern Ireland, there are no laws regarding minimum amounts of green electricity so this tariff increases demand.

Green power ownership N/A

Ecotricity Old EnergyTariff

(Ecotricity)

For every unit of electricity you buy, it supplies one unit of green electricity. Hold onto 11% of the certificates of proof.

Green power ownership 100%

Good Energy

(Good Energy Ltd)

For every unit of electricity you buy, it buys one unit of green electricity – and retires an equivalent to 10% of certificates.

Green power ownership 100%

Green Energy 100

(Green Energy UK)

For every unit of electricity you buy, it buys one unit of green electricity. Invest 50% of profits in green electricity generation and hold onto 6.8% of the certificates of proof from these projects. Subscribers also become shareholders.

Green power ownership N/A

RSPB Energy

(Scottish and Southern Energy plc)

A good mixed tariff. For every unit of electricity you buy, it supplies one unit of green electricity - and hold onto 10% of the proof. For each customer, £30 in the first year and thereafter £5/year is spent on environmental schemes.

Green power ownership 26.50%

Friends of the Earth's Non-recommended Tariffs

(listed in alphabetical order):

Ecotricity New Energy

(Ecotricity)

For every unit of electricity you buy, it only supplies 0.1 unit of green electricity – increasing by 10%/year. Every new customer helps them invest in wind farms.

Green power ownership 100%

Green energy 10

(Green energy UK)

For every unit of electricity you buy, it buys only 0.1 units of green electricity. Invest 50% of profits in green electricity schemes and subscribers become shareholders.

Green power ownership N/A

Green Energy Fund

(Scottish Power)

Doesn't buy any green electricity. Invest up to £15.75/year/customer in environmental and green electricity schemes. This is matched £ for £ by Scottish Power.

Green power ownership 5.80%

Green Energy H20

(Scottish Power)

For every unit of electricity you buy, it supplies one unit of green electricity from existing hydroelectric dams. The Government doesn't regard this as new green electricity.

Green power ownership 5.80%

Green Plan

(Powergen)

For every unit of electricity you buy, it supplies one unit of green electricity. Invest £9/year/customer in green electricity schemes – and hold onto the proof from these schemes. This is matched £ for £ by Powergen. Only their carbon dinosaurs prevent us from recommending this tariff.

Green power ownership 1.35%

Green Tariff

(London Energy/SWEB)

For every unit of electricity you buy, it supplies one unit of green electricity. Invest £13.50/year/customer in green electricity schemes. Matched £ for £ by London Energy.

Green power ownership 0.09%

Juice

(RWE Innogy)

For every unit of electricity you buy, it supplies one unit of green electricity. £10/year/customer spent on research and development into wave and tidal technologies.

Green power ownership 1.36%

Green power ownership means the % of the power stations owned by a company that is renewable. N/A indicates the company is a supplier only and does not own power stations

For more detailed information about the tariffs, companies and why Friends of the Earth recommend some and not others download their indepth guide on *www.foe.co.uk*

FINAL THOUGHTS: THE FUTURE

Despite the differences in green tariffs available, and the ranking of one above another, switching to any green supply is a positive step to take. It is a win-win situation both for the environment and your peace of mind. Whether or not you choose a Fund-based tariff or an Energy-based tariff, what you are doing when you switch is registering your support for more environmental awareness from the energy suppliers. This will help encourage those suppliers who currently do not offer a green tariff to start one, which is clearly a good thing.

Your vote for cleaner energy supply also has an impact on the future of government policy. For example, in 2005 all energy suppliers will have to disclose the exact sources of their electricity and how much comes from renewables. Green energy supplier, Good Energy, have decided to spearhead this disclosure and have shown the market the way forward by making their sources publicly available already. So by supporting green energy suppliers you can also show your support for government reform.

It has never been easier to switch your energy supplier than it is now. All it takes is a simple phone call, or compare further and switch through our own Good Shopping Guide website *www.gooshing.co.uk/energy.html.* You can start helping to create a cleaner planet. So why wait!

- Ecotricity
- Good Energy
- Green Energy 100

- Eco Energy (Northern Ireland Electricity)
- Green Energy (Scottish Power)
- RSPB Energy

- Green Plan (Powergen)
- Juice (N power)
- Green Tariff (London Electricity)
- Green Fund (Seeboard)

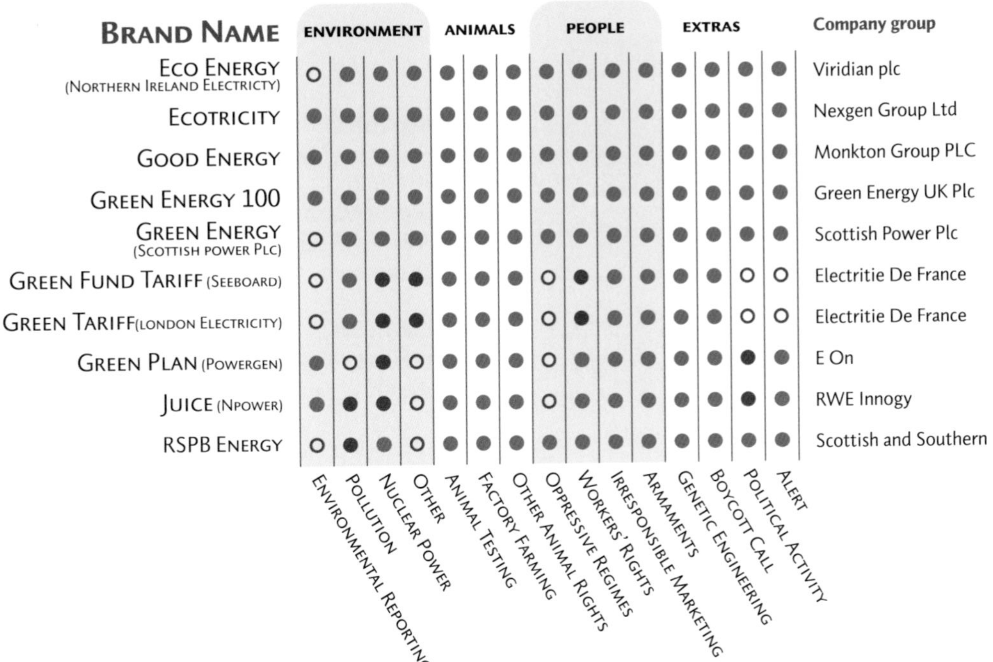

Brand Name	Environment: Environmental Reporting	Environment: Pollution	Environment: Nuclear Power	Environment: Other	Animals: Animal Testing	Animals: Factory Farming	Animals: Other Animal Rights	People: Oppressive Regimes	People: Workers' Rights	People: Irresponsible Marketing	People: Armaments	Extras: Genetic Engineering	Extras: Boycott Call	Extras: Political Activity	Extras: Alert	Company group
Eco Energy (Northern Ireland Electricty)	○	●	●	●	●	●	●	●	●	●	●	●	●	●	●	Viridian plc
Ecotricity	●	●	●	●	●	●	●	●	●	●	●	●	●	●	●	Nexgen Group Ltd
Good Energy	●	●	●	●	●	●	●	●	●	●	●	●	●	●	●	Monkton Group PLC
Green Energy 100	●	●	●	●	●	●	●	●	●	●	●	●	●	●	●	Green Energy UK Plc
Green Energy (Scottish power Plc)	○	●	●	●	●	●	●	●	●	●	●	●	●	●	●	Scottish Power Plc
Green Fund Tariff (Seeboard)	○	●	⬤	⬤	●	●	●	○	⬤	●	●	●	●	○	○	Electritie De France
Green Tariff (London Electricity)	○	●	⬤	⬤	●	●	●	○	⬤	●	●	●	●	○	○	Electritie De France
Green Plan (Powergen)	●	○	⬤	○	●	●	●	○	●	●	●	●	●	⬤	●	E On
Juice (Npower)	●	⬤	⬤	○	●	●	●	○	●	●	●	●	●	⬤	●	RWE Innogy
RSPB Energy	○	⬤	●	○	●	●	●	●	●	●	●	●	●	●	●	Scottish and Southern

Key

- ● Top rating (no criticisms found)
- ○ Middle rating
- ⬤ Bottom rating
- A related company has a bottom rating and the company itself has a middle rating
- A related company has a middle rating
- A related company has a bottom rating

Source: ECRA-See page 14 for full key to symbols.

To switch now: Contact

Good Energy
Monkton Park Offices
Chippenham
Wiltshire
SN15 1ER
Phone: 0845 456 1640
www.good-energy.co.uk

Green Energy UK: Green Energy 10/100
190 Strand, London.
WC2 8JN
Phone: 0845 456 9550
www.greenenergy.uk.com

Ecotricity
Axiom House, Station Road,
Gloucester. GL5 3AP
Phone: 0800 032 6100
www.ecotricity.co.uk

Northern Ireland Electricity: Eco Energy
120 Malone Road, Belfast.
BT9 5HT
Phone: 08457 455 455
www.nieenergy.co.uk

London Energy: Green Tariff
40 Grosvenor Place, Victoria,
London. SW1X 7EN
Phone: 0800 096 5060
www.london-energy.com

NPower: Juice
NPower Centre, Oak House,
Bridgewater Road, Warnden,
Worcester. WR4 9FP
Phone: 0800 316 2610
www.npower.com

Scottish Power: Green Energy Offer
1 Atlantic Quay, Glasgow.
G2 8SP
Phone: 0845 270 6543
www.scottishpower.co.uk

Scottish and Southern Energy plc: RSPB Energy
Southern Electric, PO Box 6009,
Basingstoke. RG21 8ZD
Phone: 0845 7444 555
www.southern-electric.co.uk

Seeboard energy: Green Fund Tariff
Phone: 0800 096 9696
www.seeboardenergy.com

To switch online, go to our own
www.gooshing.co.uk/energy.html

Our guide to energy efficiency

A standard three bedroom detached house, without any forms of insulation, can cost up to £500 a year to heat. With proper energy efficiency measure taken it is entirely possible to halve this cost. It's not only through heating that your energy efficiency in the home can be improved. Changes to your lighting and household appliances can also help reduce the amount of energy you consume.

Heating

During the cold winter months we all rely on our heating to keep us warm and cosy. However, having an energy inefficient heating system can result in you spending more than you need to on your heating costs. Here are some tips on how you can improve your heating efficiency.

Make sure you have an effective method of heating control. Boilers are unable to tell when you want heat or hot water without a form of heating control. If some form of heating control is installed you can regulate when and where you need heat. Controlling heat efficiently around the house can save you up to 17% on your heating costs.

If your boiler is more the 15 years old you should think about replacing it. New energy efficient Condensing Boilers could save you up to 32% on your fuel bills. Even without upgrading to a Condensing Boiler, modern, more efficient boilers can still save you up to 20%. In addition to this your local Council may be able to provide a grant to help you out.

If you live in a small property, you could also consider using energy efficient convection heaters or gas heaters to heat your property rather than relying on central heating.

Lighting

In the average home you can expect your lighting costs to account for 10-15% of your electricity bill. With lighting accountable for such a sizeable percentage of your costs, it seems only sensible to invest in ways in which you can improve efficiency around the house. With energy saving lightbulbs now readily available, here's some further information:

Ordinary Bulbs	Energy Saving
25W	6W
40W	8-11W
60W	13-18W
100W	20-25W

Energy saving lightbulbs only use a quarter of the energy that standard bulbs do. For this reason they are available in much lower wattages (see table). However the light from an energy saving bulb is often radiated differently to a conventional one,so you may need to choose an equivalent higher wattage bulb than you are used to achieve the same lighting effect.

At the moment energy saving lightbulbs tend to be more expensive to buy than conventional ones, at around £5 for a 20W bulb. However the cost benefit makes up for this extra initial outlay. For every conventional bulb you replace with an energy saving one it could save you up to £10 a year on your electricity bill, making back the £5 spent on the bulb and leaving you with an extra £5 in your pocket.

To complement energy saving bulbs, you could consider having energy saving fittings in which to place them. These are little transformers that fit into the base of the bulb which regulate the amount of energy that is fed into it. For the few milliseconds it takes for a bulb to light the transformer provides a surge of energy. Once a bulb is lit it requires far less power to stay alight, so the fitting maintains the electricity flow into the bulb at a very low level.

Household appliances

No matter how well you feel your household appliances are running and how few problems they have given you, they could still be extremely energy hungry and inefficient. As a general rule, the older your appliance the more it is going to cost to run. For this reason, where possible it is best to buy your fridges, cookers, dishwashers and washing machines brand new as they will be the most energy efficient. The saving you make on a second-hand purchase will soon be outweighed by the extra cost it takes to run the appliance. When buying new appliances look out for the Energy Efficiency Recommended logo. To find out more about which appliances currently available are listed as Energy Efficient, go to *www.saveenergy.co.uk* and browse the extensive database of Energy Efficient household appliances.

Insulation

Bad insulation in the home can result in a considerable heat loss. Most heat is lost through the walls and the loft space. Fully insulating these spaces can help reduce the amount of heat lost in the home by more than 50%. The walls alone can be responsible for up to 35% of the total heat wastage in the home.

Badly insulated walls can be one of the major sources of heat loss in the home. They could be costing you anywhere up to £200 extra per year. For this reason insulating the walls of your home is one of the most efficient ways to make a saving on your heating bills. If you want to find out what you can do about adding insulation to your walls, the first step is to identify what kind of walls you have in your home. Most houses built after 1930 have cavity walls. To identify whether you have cavity walls you can check by measuring their thickness at a door or window. They are normally around 30cm thick, this is comprised of an inner and outer layer, and in-between them is a small air gap. To fill your wall with insulation, small holes are drilled into the

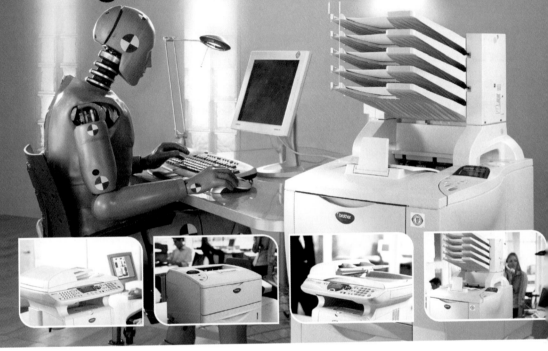

outer or inner layer and insulation material is injected into the air gap. This work has to be carried out by a professional, and will be guaranteed for 25 years by the CIGA or Cavity Insulation Guarantee Agency. The cost of the work should be recovered within five years in the savings you make on your heating costs. There are also grants and offers available to help cover the cost of the work.

As air gets hotter it becomes less dense, and as a result of this rises above cold air, which is denser. This is the reason why it is key to make sure any heat lost through the roof is minimised. Most houses have some space under the roof, normally the loft. Insulating the loft properly can save around 25% on your heating costs. You can insulate your loft easily yourself, and requires no professional work to be done. By simply adding a 250mm (10-inch) thick layer of insulation the job is done. The material that you need to insulate the roof can easily be picked up at a local DIY store or builder's merchants.

Drafts coming through the edge of the skirting board or up through the cracks in the floor can make a room feel cold and unwelcoming. Sealing up these cracks with a regular tube sealant can save you up to £10 in your heating bills. To make your floors warmer and to stop the chilly drafts coming up through them you could invest in some under floor insulation, which can help save a further £25. Remember, if you fit the insulation yourself, not to block any air bricks on the outside wall. These help maintain adequate ventilation under the floor, and without this it's likely that the floorboards will start to rot.

Heat that escapes through the space under your doors or windows also accounts for a considerable amount of heat lost in the home, as much as 20%. Draft excluders come in many different materials, from brushes to rubber strips. Without double-glazing these can be a cheap and easy way to prevent heat escaping from your home. Do remember that in some rooms ventilation is very important, especially if they have solid fuel burners, gas fires or boilers within.

Badly insulated hot water pipes and water tanks can result in 75% more energy use than those that are fully insulated. British Standard water tank "jackets" can be found at all good DIY stores and are easy to fit. The saving you make on your water heating bills means the cost can be recouped within a year. If you already have insulation on your water tank check that its at least 75mm (3 inches) thick. If it isn't it could be a good idea to replace it with a new one to make yours as energy efficient as it can be.

For further information on improving insulation you can get in touch with your local Energy Efficiency Advice Centre. If you don't know where this is you can phone 0845 727 7200 or search on the Energy Savings Trust website at *www.saveenergy.co.uk* or visit *www.gooshing.co.uk/energy.html*

Glazing

Double-glazing your windows is an ideal way to reduce heat loss in the home by up to 20%. Whilst it is an expensive option, it should definitely be considered if you are planning on renovating your window frames. Not only does double (or even triple-) glazing help prevent heat loss but can also stop condensation and reduce noise levels of sounds from outside. If you are on a tight budget you can always fit secondary glazing, which is less expensive than fitting brand new double-glazing and can still result in annual savings of around £30.

QUICK TIPS TO IMPROVE YOUR ENERGY EFFICIENCY TODAY!

- If you are too warm at home, turn down your thermostat by 1°C. This could save you up to 10% on your heating bill. If you are planning to go away over the winter for any extended period of time, turn the thermostat down to a low level. You can turn it down as far as you want, but be sure to leave it high enough so the house doesn't freeze. Your total saving could be as much as £30 a year.
- There is no need to have the hot water come out of your taps at scalding temperatures. For most people a setting of 60°C/140°F on their cylinder thermostat will be more than enough for taking baths and washing-up. Doing this can save you as much as £10 a year.
- Never leave the taps running and the plughole unblocked. If you are washing up or using hot water, try not to do it with the plughole open. The cost for hot water can soon mount up and leaving the plughole open can flush money away with the wastewater.
- Always close your curtains in the evening. Your curtains are a valuable form of insulation. If you close your curtains you can stop extra heat escaping out through the window into the cold night air.
- Try not to use electric lights when there is a good source of natural light available. Open your curtains or blinds fully rather than switch on an electric light. If you do use an electric light make sure you remember to switch it off when you leave the room.
- Electrical devices such as Television and Computers consume almost as much electricity in their standby mode as when switched on. Try to switch off all devices of this nature if you can. Obviously if this will have an effect on the appliance's memory settings then leaving it on standby can be unavoidable' so check the appliance's manual before you switch it off.
- Defrosting your fridge and freezer can help it run more efficiently; try to do this as often as possible. Also try not to leave the fridge or freezer door open for more than a few seconds as the cold air will escape, meaning the appliance will have to work harder to cool the air inside down again when you do close the door.
- It's important to try to make sure you run a full load in your washing machine and tumble dryer. If this is impossible, use the economy wash settings or run at a low heat. Modern washing powders will work just as effectively at 40°C as at 60°C. These rules can apply to dishwashers too; try to run a full load every time and use the lowest temperature setting available.
- When cooking try to use the best pot or pan available for the job, and match this with the right cooking ring. Ideally the base of the pot should just cover the edges of the ring. If you are using a gas hob the flames should only heat the bottom of the pot, any flames that

'Fossil Fuels contribute to the degradation of the environment, and are finite in nature. It is only a matter of time before the planet's supply of these fuels runs out.'

rise up the sides of the pot will be wasted heat.

- When boiling water in a kettle, there is no need to fill it all the way to the top if you are not going to use all the water. Fill the kettle with enough water to cover the element, but not more than you plan to use.
- A tap left dripping for a day can waste as much water as it would take to run a good sized bath. This is needless waste, especially if the water is hot. Make sure you firmly close all taps when you have finished with them.
- If you are used to taking baths, consider switching to a shower. An ordinary shower uses less than a half of the water that a bath does. You can easily buy devices that convert your bath taps into a shower.

Buy copies of this book and others at *www.thegoodshoppingguide.co.uk*

Buy everything else (250,000 products with price comparisonsa and ethical comparisons) at *www.gooshing.co.uk*!

You can switch to one of our recommended renewable suppliers by visiting them direct via their contact details on page 114.

Alternatively, visit *www.gooshing.co.uk/energy.html* to access a range of online comparisons and switch options

For more information see *www.ethical-company-organisation.org*

Sustainable building

All stages of building have an effect on the environment. Every stage of a building's life results in pollution of the environment to a greater or lesser extent. To minimise the effects and reduce impact, consideration should be given to careful and appropriate detailing; the choice of materials; the building process itself; how it affects the occupier and general environment and what happens to the building when it is demolished. Sustainable building should aim to lessen its impact on the environment during its whole life cycle – construction with less destruction.

Unhealthy appetite

Building and construction has an unhealthy appetite for energy and resources. 7% of UK primary energy demand is used for construction materials (9% of Co_2 production). Domestic heating, lighting and cooking is responsible for around 30% of UK energy demand and CO_2 emissions. Around 115,000 kWh of embodied energy are used in the materials, transportation and building of a typical 3 bedroom masonry house, but this is just 5% of the energy needed to power the house during its life. If we get the design right, the potential for energy and resource savings are massive. A low energy timber-frame house can halve both figures easily!

The 7.5 tonnes of CO_2 per year created by an average house could be cut by 50% if we adopted simple established energy conservation techniques. Government forecasts of climate change – higher winds, temperatures and increased flooding are already part of our experience, so CO_2 reduction must be the priority.

A sustainable balance between the reasonable requirements of people and nature lies at the heart of environment conscious building. We must take care of the natural world and use its resources wisely because we are totally dependent on it for our survival. Quality of life for people results from a sustainable, fair and healthy society, working in harmony with nature.

Sustainable building is as much a philosophy as it is an art, though the wealth of ideas and opportunities that spring from the concept can stimulate artistic talents that most of us never thought we possessed. We need to consider what materials we use, how we build, how the building affects the environment and what happens when the building is demolished.

Local design and construction to sustainable criteria will directly benefit local economies and will reduce transport and environmental costs. Since we live in a changing world, it is sensible to design buildings, which can be recycled, so that materials and foundations can easily be reused and land is not degraded or polluted.

Sustainable building criteria

- Avoid damage to people and the environment:
- Use local renewable natural materials and resources:
- Reduce emissions and non-degradable waste:
- Minimise the use of materials and energy:
- Select materials, which combine useful properties:
- Design with site and climate:
- Design for low cost, adaptability and recycling.
- Adopt holistic thinking and design principles:
- Protect and encourage biological diversity:

By following a few basic principles anyone can improve their home or building from on environmental perspective.

Energy

The facts about Co2 emissions and the greenhouse effect are well known. Vast amounts of energy are consumed in the production of building materials and during the lifetime of the building. Select materials and products that use least energy in manufacture (natural or near natural) or can be recycled, or are recycled. Ensure buildings are insulated to the highest possible standards. This will reduce fuel bills. When designing a new building take advantage of the sun's free energy. Site orientation and the use of more glazing can make the best use of passive solar energy. Where possible investigate and consider using alternative, renewable forms of energy such as active solar, bio-fuels and power from wind and water

Resources

Many materials used in buildings are from finite sources, so it is important to use those that are sustainable. Timber and bio-crops (straw etc) are generally considered to be the most renewable resource provided they are grown and harvested in a sustainable way. Timber can also be recycled and reused. Always ask for timber and wood products that bear the FSC (Forest Stewardships Council) logo, which is an independent, international and credible labelling scheme for timber and timber products.

Atmosphere

The damage to the ozone layer caused by CFCs and HCFCs has been recognized or many years. The problems associated with CFC emissions have been addressed by international intergovernmental agreements. However some insulations use HCFCs, which although having lower ozone depletion potential do have a very high global warming potential. Alternatives such as cellulose, wool, cork and foamed glass are available and should be considered.

Health

It is well known that exposure to chemicals can cause damage to human health and the environment. Hazardous chemicals are found in many products such as timber preservatives, paint and stains, etc. There is still excessive emphasis on treating timbers. For example, many banks, building societies and local authorities still insist on extensive chemical treatment of existing woodworm when providing loans or grants. Many of these chemicals approved for use in this country have been banned or restricted overseas.

Within the fabric of a new building there is generally no need to treat sound timber against infestation and rot. Insect infestation, dry and wet rot in older properties can often be dealt with by changing the environmental conditions in the building (humidity levels, temperature etc) and there are companies that offer surveys in this respect, including necessary guarantees to satisfy third parties. If treatment is considered necessary then a boron treatment should be used. Boron is considered to be the least toxic of treatments. With regard to paints and stains there are an increasing number of natural alternatives available.

Other issues related to health include the over-use of plastics in building, particularly PVC. Hazardous fumes result when PVC is burnt, but more recently it has been suggested that phthalates migrate from the plastic into the astrosphere and there is increasing scientific evidence to suggest that the exposure to some of those chemicals may cause wide-spread problems including immune system damage and cancer. Evidence suggests that some phthalates can disrupt the hormonal system. A Greenpeace campaign highlights the problems of PVC. Alternative materials to replace PVC include copper, stainless steel, iron and HDPE (for water pipes and drainage), timber (for cladding and sheeting), timber and aluminium (for windows and doors), clay (for drainage) timber and linoleum (for flooring), rubber (for electrical cable).

Water and waste

There is a greater emphasis today to avoid pollution of water supplies and to conserve water. Reed bed sewage systems are an innovative and effective way of disposing of sewerage in an ecologically sound way. WCs are available which use less water and the ultimate green loo is the composting toilet, which uses no water, evaporates the urine and turns sewage into a valuable source of nutrients for the garden. There are also urine-separating toilets which separate the urine from the faeces. The urine can then be piped onto hay or straw bales to produce nitrogen-rich compost. Rainwater harvesting systems are available which save and store rainwater from building roofs etc for flushing toilets, washing etc.

Biodiversity

As more and more land is developed it is important to conserve and encourage wildlife. Trees and hedgerows and ponds can be carefully protected during building operations and retained. Small areas of land can be set-aside as wild nature areas. New ponds can be established. Indigenous trees

and hedgerows can be planted. Dry stone walling can be used to provide habitat for animals and insects.

Design

Design buildings for life. Make the structure easily adaptable e.g. de-mountable partitions so the internal layout can be altered when necessary. Design for health and comfort; for optimum levels of daylight, sunlight, temperature and fresh air.

Costs

The costs of any building depend on the design. However, costs for sustainable building can be comparable and in the future may well be cheaper as it becomes mainstream and economies of scale come into play. Sustainable buildings give added value and avoid the hidden costs associated with conventional buildings in terms of health and pollution. Many eco products are currently manufactured on a smaller scale and can therefore be more expensive and involve high transport costs.

Selection of ecological building materials

Approximate figures for embodied energy (the energy used in their manufacture and mining etc) allow us to compare the energy costs of various materials and reveal the advantages of using easily won, natural materials and of recycling – fibreglass incorporates 15 times more energy than

PRIMARY EMBODIED ENERGY

	kWh/m3		kWh/m3
Lead	157,414	Foamed Glass Insulation	751
Copper	133,000	Concrete Tiles	630
Steel iron ore (blast furnace)	63,000-80,000	Concrete 1 : 3 : 6	600
Aluminium	55,868	Lightweight Clinker Blocks	600
Plastics	47,000	Local Slate	540
Steel recycled (electric arc furnace)	29,669	Local Stone Tiles	450
Glass	23,000	Sand Cement Render	400
Cement	2,860	Bricks (fletton)	300
Clay Tiles	1,520	Mineral Fibre Insulation	230
Bricks (non flettons)	1,462	Home Grown Green Oak	220
Plastic Insulation	1,125	Crushed Granite	150
Gypsum Plaster / Plasterboard	900	Cellulose (Recycled Paper) Insulation	133
Autoclaved Bricks	800	Home Grown Softwood (air dried)	110
Concrete 1 : 2 : 4	800	Sand and Gravel	45
Imported Softwood	754	Sheep's Wool Insulation	30

THERMAL CONDUCTIVITY OF MATERIALS

Material	W/mK
Copper	380.000
Aluminium	198.000
Steel	48.300
Granite	3.810
Limestone	1.530
Dense Brickwork	1.470
Dense Concrete	1.440
Sand / Cement Render	1.410
Very Packed Damp Soil	1.400
Sandstone	1.295
Bricks (Engineering)	1.150
Dry Soil	1.140
Clay Bricks (compressed, unfired)	0.950
Brickwork	0.840
Tile Hanging	0.840
Damp Loose Soil	0.700
Water	0.580
Adobe	0.520
Glass	0.500
Earth Blocks	0.340
Thermalite Blocks	0.140-0.190
Plaster Board	0.180
Recycled wood fibre / Gypsum Plasterboard	0.176
Hardwood	0.160

Material	W/mK
Clay Board (alternative to plasterboard)	0.140
Softwood / Plywood	0.138
Oil Tempered Hardboard	0.120
Chipboard	0.108
Strawboard	0.098
Snow (average density)	0.090
Woodwool Slab (light)	0.082
Stony Soil (normal)	0.052
Bitvent 15 Sheathing Board	0.050
Cork	0.043
Fibreglass Insulation	0.040
Flax Insulation	0.037
Sheep's Wool Insulation	0.037
Hair	0.036
Warmcell (recycled paper) Wall insulation	0.036
Warmcell (recycled paper) Roof Insulation	0.035
Expanded Polystyrene Insulation	0.033
Polyurethane Foam	0.023
Still Air	0.020

(Sources: Centre for Alternative Technology; Environmental Science Handbook; Pittsburgh Corning; Timber Trade Fed: CIRIA; A.E.C.B)

Warmcell recycled cellulose insulation.

The tables for Embodied Energy and Thermal values clearly reveal that nature has provided us with a good selection of materials with outstanding properties for high performance construction. Most materials required can be found near the bottom of each table, while a few such as glass, gypsum, plastic and steel are used only for unavoidable, small elements.

THE WAY FORWARD

Sustainable building needs to be promoted widely. It should be economical, widely accepted as the norm and supported by the government. The building regulations should ensure the relevant minimum standards are met e.g. increased insulation as we currently fall way behind our European counterparts in this area. The skill's shortage problem must be addressed.

Traditional skills (which tend to be more sustainable) must be re-taught.

Non-renewable fuels are becoming cheaper (in money terms) despite their hidden environmental costs so much more support needs to be given to the renewable energy sector and VAT reduced or removed from this area. It would be helpful if a standard design could be developed for sustainable building, which would encourage the volume builders to embrace this form of building. This would also make it easier to formulate suitable training programmes to deal with the skill's issues.

The consumer can help by being demanding, not just willing to accept the standard product on offer. We can demand higher levels of energy conservation, sure in the knowledge that the building will benefit the environment while at the same time benefiting the consumer, with lower fuel bills and higher living standards. We can also be more demanding over what type of materials are used in the building and bear in mind the high levels of environmental degradation that are involved with many standard building products and also the ethical nature of their production.

- *The Association for Environment Conscious Building (AECB) can supply more information on green architecture and sustainable building. For more information about this organisation send an A4 SAE (73p) to AECB, PO Box 32, Llandysul, Carmarthenshire SA44 5ZA, email info@aecb.net, visit our web site at www.aecb.net or phone 0845 456 9773.*

- *The Good Shopping Guide would like to thank John Shore AA Dipl for his help in compiling this article.*

- *John Shore, a long-standing member of the AECB, graduated from the Architectural Association, specialising in Ecological Design and Renewable Energy. He is responsible for designing and building the Integrated Solar Dwelling at Brighton in the 1970's – the UK's first Self-Sufficient House.*

Good Money

- Banks & building societies
- Charity credit cards
- Insurance
- Mortgages
- Ethical investment

Banks & building societies

Banks and building societies claim to have their customers' interests at heart, but are they really listening? Most of us choose our banks or building societies for reasons of convenience – simply because there's a branch around the corner or maybe because we had an account with a predecessor of one of today's conglomerates. But, as customers, we have the right to make judgements about the ways our banks behave, not least in the realm of their relationships with the developing world.

The mutual issue

Support mutual building societies like Britannia. This specifically excludes de-mutualised building societies – those that have become banks – such as the Alliance & Leicester, Halifax, Northern Rock and Bradford & Bingley. The debate over the future of mutual building societies has largely focused on their potential benefits to customers; mutual status means that there are no shareholders to pay dividends to, so profits can be ploughed back into lower loans charges and higher interest rates for savers. These claims appear to be borne out by *Which?* magazine's July 2001 study, which reported that in general, mutuals still give better deals on mortgages and savings than their de-mutualised cousins.

Some mutual building societies can also offer a better option than most banks as they don't take business customers, so they could never fund dubious business practices, like logging or oil exploration. Of those on the table, the Coventry, Yorkshire, Leeds & Holbeck and Portman do not lend commercially. Information on the benefits of mutuals, and a list of the remaining mutual building societies, can be obtained from the Building Societies Association on 020 7437 0655 or *www.bsa.org.uk*

Third World concerns

Several British banks – most notably Lloyds (now Lloyds TSB) and Midland (now HSBC) – were the focus of campaigns in the 1980s and 90s over their holdings of Third World debt. Much of this has now been written off as banks realised that they were unlikely to recoup the loans, and that they were acquiring significant bad publicity. Some, such as the Bank of Scotland, 'swapped' their poorest-country debts for commitments by national governments that they would use the money for domestic development programmes. However, EIRIS has listed some high street banks as still holding some Third World debt. See *eiris.org*.

British banks have been the targets of

other important campaigns about their holding of World Bank bonds, their involvement in the kind of currency speculation that has ruined many developing countries, and their support for the World Trade Organisation's controversial agreement on trade and services. Some of these issues are indicated in the table.

ETHICAL HEALTH CHECK

Information on the environmental and social policies and reporting standards of a range of banks can be found in an EIRIS factsheet, available from 0845 606 0324 or *www.eiris.org*.

- Abbey National
- Alliance & Leicester
- Bradford & Bingley
- Britannia BS
- Chelsea BS
- Chesire BS
- Co-op Bank
- Coventry BS
- Derbyshire BS
- Ecology BS
- Girobank
- Leeds & Holbeck
- Nationwide BS
- Northern Rock
- Norwich & Peterborough
- Portman BS
- Skipton BS
- Yorkshire BS
- Other Mutuals

- Bank of Scotland
- Barclays Bank
- Clydesdale Bank
- Egg
- Halifax
- Lloyds TSB
- National Australia Bank
- Safeway
- Woolwich
- Yorkshire Bank

- ASDA
- Bank of Ireland
- HSBC
- Morrisons
- National Westminster
- Royal Bank of Scotland
- Sainsbury's
- Tesco Plc
- Virgin Direct

Further ethical and 'best deal' financial information is available at *www.gooshing.co.uk*.

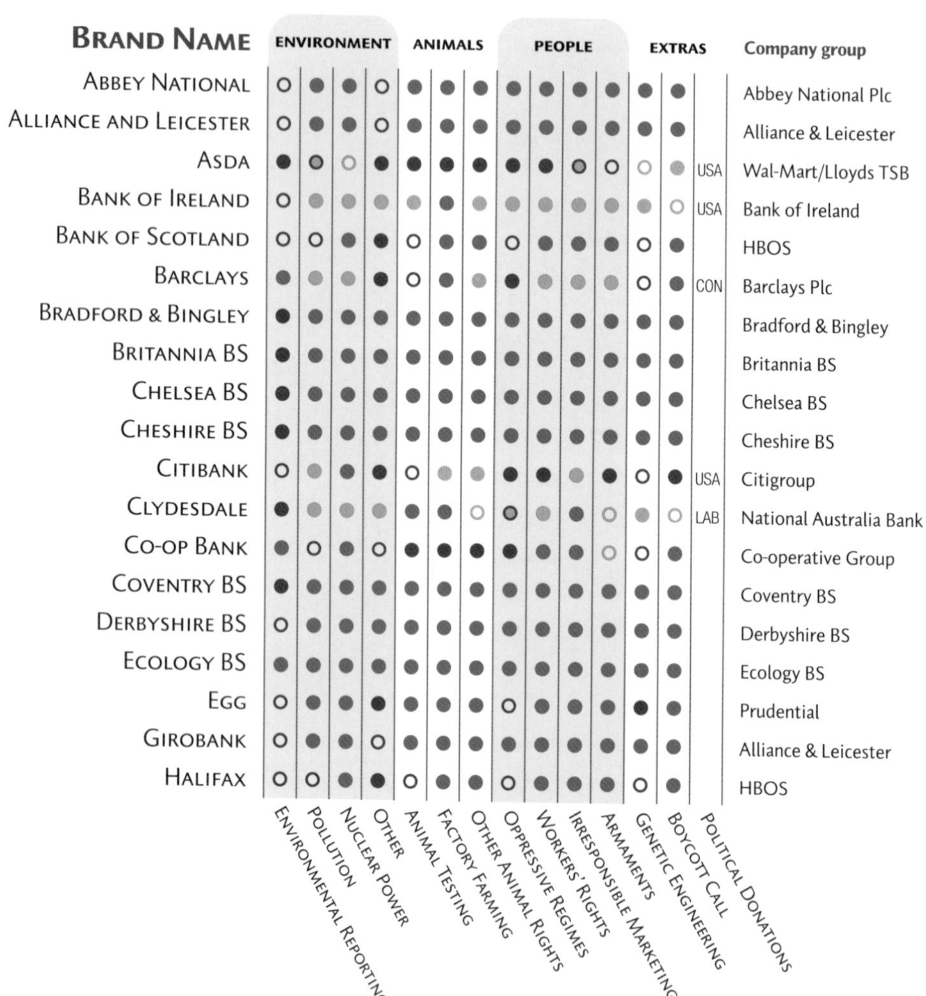

BRAND NAME
ENVIRONMENT
ANIMALS
PEOPLE
EXTRAS
Company group
ABBEY NATIONAL
ALLIANCE AND LEICESTER
ASDA
BANK OF IRELAND
BANK OF SCOTLAND
BARCLAYS
BRADFORD & BINGLEY
BRITANNIA BS
CHELSEA BS
CHESHIRE BS
CITIBANK
CLYDESDALE
CO-OP BANK
COVENTRY BS
DERBYSHIRE BS
ECOLOGY BS
EGG
GIROBANK
HALIFAX
USA
USA
CON
USA
LAB
Abbey National Plc
Alliance & Leicester
Wal-Mart/Lloyds TSB
Bank of Ireland
HBOS
Barclays Plc
Bradford & Bingley
Britannia BS
Chelsea BS
Cheshire BS
Citigroup
National Australia Bank
Co-operative Group
Coventry BS
Derbyshire BS
Ecology BS
Prudential
Alliance & Leicester
HBOS
ENVIRONMENTAL REPORTING
POLLUTION
NUCLEAR POWER
OTHER
ANIMAL TESTING
FACTORY FARMING
OTHER ANIMAL RIGHTS
OPPRESSIVE REGIMES
WORKERS' RIGHTS
IRRESPONSIBLE MARKETING
ARMAMENTS
GENETIC ENGINEERING
BOYCOTT CALL
POLITICAL DONATIONS

Key

- Top rating (no criticisms found)
- Middle rating
- Bottom rating
- A related company has a bottom rating and the company itself has a middle rating
- A related company has a middle rating
- A related company has a bottom rating

Source: ECRA-See page 14 for full key to symbols.

NB The amber, related company marks, relate to companies which are customers of the banks in question. So if a particular company has been found guilty of pollution, its bank will receive an amber mark.

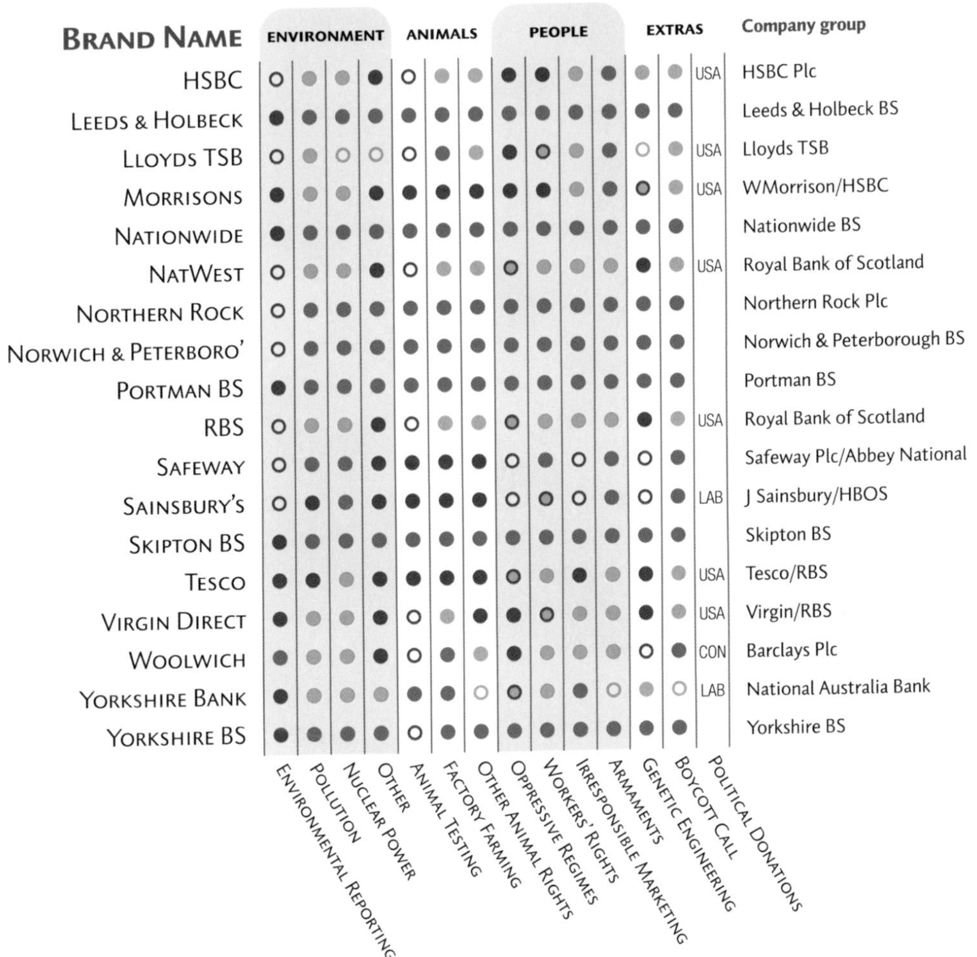

BRAND NAME
ENVIRONMENT
ANIMALS
PEOPLE
EXTRAS
Company group
HSBC
USA
HSBC Plc
LEEDS & HOLBECK
Leeds & Holbeck BS
LLOYDS TSB
USA
Lloyds TSB
MORRISONS
USA
WMorrison/HSBC
NATIONWIDE
Nationwide BS
NATWEST
USA
Royal Bank of Scotland
NORTHERN ROCK
Northern Rock Plc
NORWICH & PETERBORO'
Norwich & Peterborough BS
PORTMAN BS
Portman BS
RBS
USA
Royal Bank of Scotland
SAFEWAY
Safeway Plc/Abbey National
SAINSBURY'S
LAB
J Sainsbury/HBOS
SKIPTON BS
Skipton BS
TESCO
USA
Tesco/RBS
VIRGIN DIRECT
USA
Virgin/RBS
WOOLWICH
CON
Barclays Plc
YORKSHIRE BANK
LAB
National Australia Bank
YORKSHIRE BS
Yorkshire BS
ENVIRONMENTAL REPORTING
POLLUTION
NUCLEAR POWER
OTHER
ANIMAL TESTING
FACTORY FARMING
OTHER ANIMAL RIGHTS
OPPRESSIVE REGIMES
WORKERS' RIGHTS
IRRESPONSIBLE MARKETING
ARMAMENTS
GENETIC ENGINEERING
BOYCOTT CALL
POLITICAL DONATIONS

NB The amber, related company marks, relate to companies which are customers of the banks in question. So if a particular company has been found guilty of pollution, its bank will recieve an amber mark.

Charity credit cards

Charity affinity credit cards are excellent, because they continually raise money for good causes without serious cost to the customer. Nowadays, there are plenty on offer, most of which let us choose which charities we wish to support. Single charities issue the cards both for raising money and winning publicity. Several banks co-operate closely with them, but not all. Read here for details.

Benefits

A charity credit card raises money for a charity (or several) when the card is first taken out or first used, and from then on a small percentage, like 25p for every £100 used, goes straight to the charity. The charities benefit from the extra revenue and also because the cards and associated marketing can raise their profile and thus recruit new members.

Few affinity cards charge an annual fee, but it is worth checking on this before taking one. Some have low introductory rates of interest in the first few months, but in general the rates are close to the average available at any one time. This is irrelevant if we pay off our bill in full, as most affinity cardholders apparently do. As the donations depend on the money spent, not on the size of the outstanding balance, there is no loss to the charity if we do clear it every month.

Many banks have been happy to co-operate not only with conventional charities but also with sports clubs, hobby groups and professional organisations, seeing it as a way to gain market share. In terms of ethics, it makes little difference whether our card is Visa or Mastercard. It is more appropriate to ask which bank the charity has teamed up with to issue its credit card. Some of the banks have resisted getting involved, considering cards too costly to administer or being reluctant to pay VAT on donations.

Banks

Of the UK high street banks, Bank of Scotland, Royal Bank of Scotland, Halifax, Co-operative and HSBC all offer charity-linked cards. Three US banks, MBNA, Beneficial and People's Bank of Connecticut, jointly issue affinity cards with charities.

Co-op Bank cards support among others Amnesty International, Greenpeace, Help the Aged, Save the Children, Oxfam and the RSPB. Beneficial Bank has several cards which benefit animal welfare charities as well as the Wildlife and

Wetlands Trust, English Heritage and Unicef. Frizzell supports the Cancer Research Campaign, while People's Bank has cards for Comic Relief and the Vegetarian Society. The Bank of Scotland also has several to choose from.

The PVC issue

Co-operative Bank has been researching alternatives to PVC for its credit and debit cards and hopes to make a biodegradable plastic known as polyethylene teraphthalate, completely free of hazardous chemicals. No other UK card issuers seem to have followed their lead.

See *www.gooshing.co.uk* for the best deals on a range of ethical financial products.

- Beneficial Bank
- Co-operative Bank
- Frizzell Bank
- People's Bank

- Bank of Scotland
- Halifax
- MBNA

- HSBC
- Royal Bank of Scotland

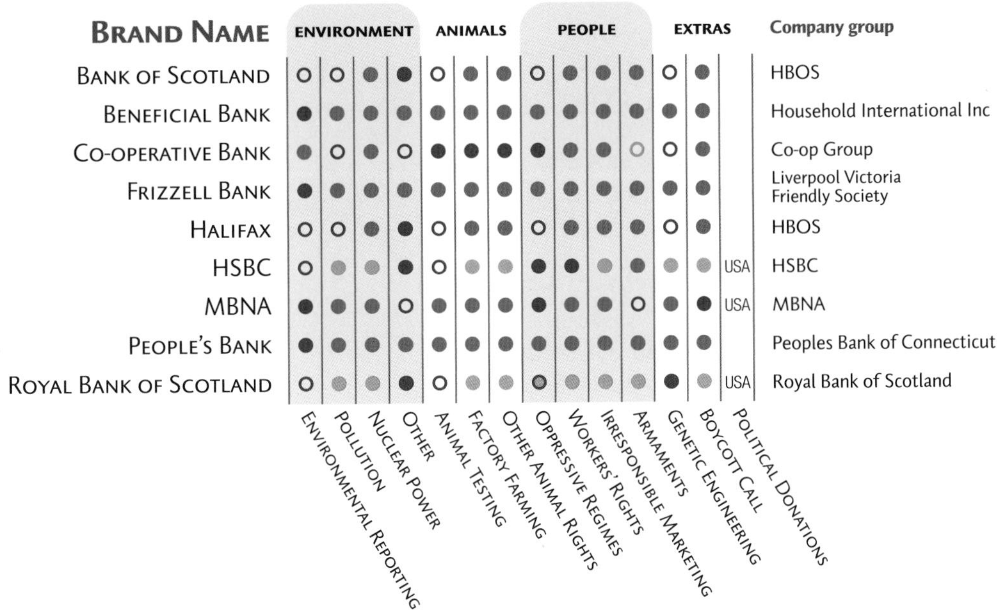

Brand Name	Environment				Animals			People				Extras			Company group
	Environmental Reporting	Pollution	Nuclear Power	Other	Animal Testing	Factory Farming	Other Animal Rights	Oppressive Regimes	Workers' Rights	Irresponsible Marketing	Armaments	Genetic Engineering	Boycott Call	Political Donations	
Bank of Scotland	Middle	Middle	Top	Bottom	Middle	Top	Top	Middle	Top	Top	Top	Middle	Top		HBOS
Beneficial Bank	Bottom	Top	Top	Top	Top	Top	Top	Top	Top	Top	Top	Top	Top		Household International Inc
Co-operative Bank	Top	Middle	Top	Middle	Bottom	Bottom	Bottom	Bottom	Top	Top	Related middle	Middle	Top		Co-op Group
Frizzell Bank	Bottom	Top	Top	Top	Top	Top	Top	Top	Top	Top	Top	Top	Top		Liverpool Victoria Friendly Society
Halifax	Middle	Middle	Top	Bottom	Middle	Top	Top	Middle	Top	Top	Top	Middle	Top		HBOS
HSBC	Middle	Related bottom	Related bottom	Bottom	Middle	Related bottom	Related bottom	Bottom	Bottom	Related bottom	Top	Related bottom	Related bottom	USA	HSBC
MBNA	Bottom	Top	Top	Middle	Top	Top	Top	Bottom	Top	Top	Middle	Top	Bottom	USA	MBNA
People's Bank	Bottom	Top	Top	Top	Top	Top	Top	Top	Top	Top	Top	Top	Top		Peoples Bank of Connecticut
Royal Bank of Scotland	Middle	Related bottom	Related bottom	Bottom	Middle	Related bottom	Related bottom	Related bottom / middle	Related bottom	Related bottom	Related bottom	Bottom	Related bottom	USA	Royal Bank of Scotland

Key

- Top rating (no criticisms found)
- Middle rating
- Bottom rating
- A related company has a bottom rating and the company itself has a middle rating
- A related company has a middle rating
- A related company has a bottom rating

Source: ECRA-See page 14 for full key to symbols.

Insurance

Choosing insurance companies is rather like a lottery. They may be offering the best deal today but who knows what will happen in the future? Companies keep merging and taking each other over and sometimes we can hardly tell their names apart. One way to keep ahead of the main companies is to look at their ethical policies and to ask questions about the companies that their managers like to invest in.

Ethical insurance

A key question for ethical consumers is: 'In which shares is the money invested?' As Friends of the Earth puts it: 'The fate of the global environment is in large part under [institutional investors'] control, and yours too – because it is your money and you are their client.' But according to the Ethical Money partnership: 'No insurer has an "ethical investment" policy whereby they avoid investing in particular types of company.'

Campaigners have become increasingly impatient over unethical corporate activities and they are learning how to put pressure on insurance companies as shareholders. One way to make this pressure work is to keep consumers aware of what their insurers are investing in. Campaigners ask the insurance companies to use their own power as shareholders to vote or create pressure for more ethical or environmentally sound behaviour by the target company.

Plummeting shares

As share prices plummeted in 2001 and 2002, many insurance companies went through a difficult time and saw their assets devalued, as their own investments in stocks, shares and property markets began to mark up losses. Premiums started to rise and companies became much more careful about the risks they were prepared to cover. In the UK, flood cover was withdrawn from a lot of homes that were deemed to be at risk.

So-called natural disasters have required insurers to make huge pay-outs, the rate of which has been doubling every decade. One report in 2002 warned that more frequent natural disasters in future could bring insurers, re-insurers and banks 'to the point of impaired viability or even insolvency.' The insurance companies usually offset their potential liabilities by trading some of the premium (like a bookie 'off-setting' a large bet with another bookie) with a re-insurance company. Many of these companies have now become involved in the UN Environment

Programme's Insurance Industry Initiative, which commits them to working together to address issues like pollution reduction, efficient use of resources and climate change – or in other words to try to work out more sustainable development policies around the world.

The UNEP finance initiatives have three working groups: environmental management and reporting (EM&R), climate change and asset management. The EM&R Working Group aims to develop international guidelines on reporting for the financial sector and its 16 members have been working with accountants PriceWaterhouseCoopers. It aims to produce guidelines on environmental management and reporting at present, with a view to expanding this to encompass social issues in the future. The Climate Change Working Group has twelve members, including Aviva and Prudential. As well as taking steps to manage the effects of climate change, the group wants to reduce 'greenhouse gas emissions now.' The Asset Management Working Group has 16 members: its purpose is to extend the understanding (which has seen renewable energy emerge as a new area for investment) 'further into the mainstream investment community'.

Choose from the greener ones and source the best insurance deals at *www.gooshing.co.uk*.

- Aegon
- Britannic
- Churchill
- Ecclesiastical
- Northern Rock
- Royal & Sun Alliance
- Royal London
- Scottish Equitable
- Standard Life

- Allied Dunbar
- Axa
- CGNU
- Cornhill
- Eagle Star
- Egg
- Legal & General
- Prudential
- Zurich

- Clerical Medical
- Direct Line
- First Direct
- Halifax
- Lloyds TSB
- Natwest
- Norwich Union
- Royal Bank of Scotland

Symbol codes used below (from the key): T = Top rating (no criticisms found); M = Middle rating; B = Bottom rating; RBM = A related company has a bottom rating and the company itself has a middle rating; RM = A related company has a middle rating; RB = A related company has a bottom rating

BRAND NAME	ENVIRONMENT				ANIMALS			PEOPLE				EXTRAS				Company group
	Environmental Reporting	Pollution	Nuclear Power	Other	Animal Testing	Factory Farming	Other Animal Rights	Oppressive Regimes	Workers' Rights	Irresponsible Marketing	Armaments	Genetic Engineering	Boycott Call	Political Activity	Alert	
Axa	B	T	T	RM	T	T	T	B	T	T	T	RM	T	M	M	Axa
Aegon	B	T	T	RM	T	T	T	M	T	T	M	RM	T	T	M	Aegon NV
Allied Dunbar	M	T	M	RM	T	T	T	M	T	T	T	RM	T	M	M	Zurich FS
Britannic	B	T	T	T	T	T	T	T	T	T	T	T	T	T	T	Britannic Assurance
CGNU	B	T	M	RM	T	T	T	B	T	T	T	RM	T	M	M	Aviva
Churchill	B	T	T	RM	RM	T	T	B	T	T	T	T	T	T	M	Credit Suisse
Clerical Medical	M	M	T	B	RM	T	T	RBM	T	RM	T	RM	T	RM	B	HBOS
Cornhill	M	T	B	T	T	T	T	B	T	T	B	T	T	M	B	Allianz AG
Direct Line	B	RB	RB	B	M	RB	RB	RBM	RBM	RB	RB	M	RB	T	M	Royal Bank of Scotland
Eagle Star	M	T	M	RM	T	T	T	M	T	T	T	RM	T	M	M	Zurich FS
Ecclesiastical	B	T	T	T	T	T	T	T	T	T	T	T	T	T	M	Allchurches Trust
Egg	B	T	T	B	T	T	T	M	M	T	T	RM	T	T	M	Prudential plc
First Direct	B	T	RBM	B	RM	T	T	B	B	T	T	T	T	M	B	HSBC
Halifax	M	M	T	B	RM	T	T	RBM	T	T	T	RM	T	RM	B	HBOS
Legal & General	M	T	T	B	T	T	M	M	T	T	T	M	T	T	M	Legal & General Group
Lloyds TSB	T	RB	RM	RB	RM	T	RB	M	M	RB	T	RM	RB	RM	M	Lloyds TSB Group
NatWest	B	RB	RB	B	M	RB	RB	RBM	RBM	RB	RB	M	RB	T	M	Royal Bank of Scotland
Norwich Union	B	T	M	RM	T	T	T	B	T	T	T	RM	T	M	M	Aviva
Northern Rock	B	T	T	T	T	T	T	T	T	T	T	T	T	T	M	Northern Rock
Prudential	B	T	T	B	T	T	T	M	M	T	T	RM	T	T	M	Prudential Plc
Royal Bank of Scotland	B	RB	RB	B	M	RB	RB	RBM	RBM	RB	RB	M	RB	T	M	Royal Bank of Scotland
Royal London	B	T	T	T	T	T	T	T	T	T	T	T	T	T	T	Royal London Mutual
Royal and Sun Alliance	B	T	T	RM	T	T	T	M	M	T	T	RM	T	T	M	Royal & Sun Alliance
Scottish Equitable	B	T	T	RM	T	T	T	M	T	T	M	RM	T	T	M	Aegon NV
Standard Life	B	T	T	RM	T	T	T	T	T	T	T	RM	T	T	T	Standard Life
Zurich	M	T	M	RM	T	T	T	M	T	T	T	RM	T	M	M	Zurich FS

Key

- Top rating (no criticisms found)
- Middle rating
- Bottom rating
- A related company has a bottom rating and the company itself has a middle rating
- A related company has a middle rating
- A related company has a bottom rating

Source: ECRA-See page 14 for full key to symbols.

Mortgages

Ten years ago, most mortgages were taken out with building societies, but since de-mutualisation about four out of five mortgages are now provided by either a bank, a life insurer or a specialist mortgage lender. This section covers a few of the remaining building societies, some of the major bank lenders and some of the ethical mortgage lenders. All of the companies in the report offer standard 'repayment' mortgages.

Why ethical?

Mortgages are likely to be one of the single biggest outlays for many people. However, monthly repayments could be contributing to loans for animal testing laboratories or investment in companies involved in other unethical activities. Consequently, the mortgage company's lending policies are as important as the kind of mortgage on offer.

Although all the banks/building societies covered in this report were asked about their approach to lending, the only ones to offer comprehensive ethical lending policies were the Ecology Building Society and the Co-operative Bank. The Ecology lends primarily to 'green' housing and the Co-op excludes companies involved in a range of activities like animal testing and arms exports to oppressive regimes.

For companies which have not offered specific information, it is probably correct to assume that building societies are less likely than banks to be involved in what ECRA describes as 'questionable' corporate lending.

Environmental issues

Homes are one of the largest sources of carbon dioxide emissions in the UK. While most mortgage lenders offer valuation surveys as part of the mortgage deal, relatively few at this stage are offering specialised environmental surveys. These environmental surveys assess how energy efficient the house we want to buy is, and give advice on energy savings measures. Currently, the Co-op Bank offers this kind of survey free with its green mortgage, as do the Norwich & Peterborough and the Ethical Mortgage Service.

All the banks and building societies in this report were asked for their latest environmental reports. Although the situation has improved since EC last covered banks, few of the companies had any environmental report that would receive ECRA's clean rating. The Co-operative Bank continues to be a leader in this sector.

Ethical & green mortgages

The Ecology Building Society currently lends only on properties that give 'ecological payback'. This translates as being houses which it considers energy-saving – such as back-to-backs, derelict houses which would otherwise have been abandoned, etc. This strict lending policy means that it won't be suitable to every person seeking a mortgage.

The Norwich & Peterborough offers a carbon-neutral mortgage. For the first five years of each of its Green Mortgages, it will plant eight trees a year. Its leaflet claims that the trees will absorb carbon dioxide to the equivalent of the estimated emissions of the property. It also offers a 'brown' mortgage scheme which aims to encourage the renovation and restoration of buildings for residential use.

The Co-operative Bank's green mortgage will 'pay Climate Care to offset around 20 per cent of an average home's carbon dioxide production for every mortgage we grant.' It claims over a 20-year mortgage, just under a fifth of an acre of forest would be planted.

The Ethical Mortgage Service is a collaboration between the Ethical Investment Co-operative (a group of Independent Financial Advisors) and consultants called Thirdwave. It offers advice on mortgages from a panel of lenders that it has ethically screened. This panel includes the Skipton, Scottish and Yorkshire Building Societies. For the purposes of this April/May 2001 report ECRA included the ratings for these building societies in the rating on the table for the Ethical Mortgage Service.

On the table, amber circles appear where the bank is an investor or service provider to companies criticised for particular activities.

- Abbey National
- Alliance & Leicester
- Co-op Bank
- Ecology BS
- Ethical Mortgage Service
- Nationwide
- Norwich & Peterborough

- Barclays
- Halifax plc
- Woolwich

- Cheltenham & Gloucester
- Lloyds TSB
- Natwest
- Royal Bank of Scotland

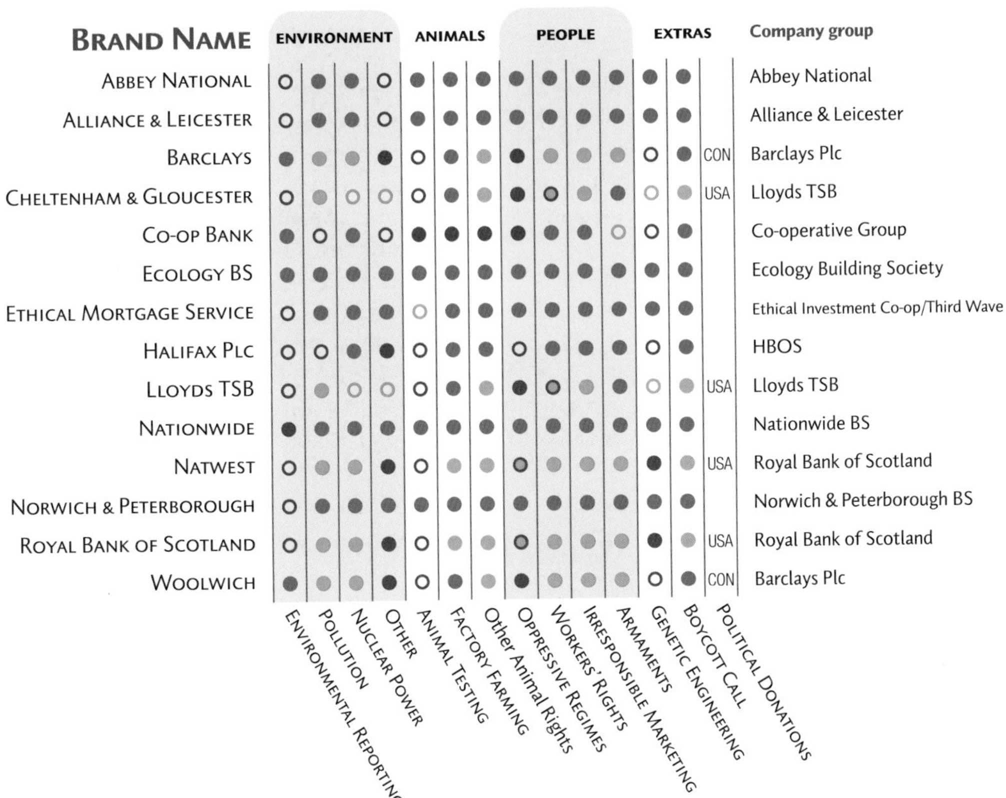

BRAND NAME
ENVIRONMENT
ANIMALS
PEOPLE
EXTRAS
Company group
ABBEY NATIONAL
Abbey National
ALLIANCE & LEICESTER
Alliance & Leicester
BARCLAYS
CON
Barclays Plc
CHELTENHAM & GLOUCESTER
USA
Lloyds TSB
CO-OP BANK
Co-operative Group
ECOLOGY BS
Ecology Building Society
ETHICAL MORTGAGE SERVICE
Ethical Investment Co-op/Third Wave
HALIFAX PLC
HBOS
LLOYDS TSB
USA
Lloyds TSB
NATIONWIDE
Nationwide BS
NATWEST
USA
Royal Bank of Scotland
NORWICH & PETERBOROUGH
Norwich & Peterborough BS
ROYAL BANK OF SCOTLAND
USA
Royal Bank of Scotland
WOOLWICH
CON
Barclays Plc
ENVIRONMENTAL REPORTING
POLLUTION
NUCLEAR POWER
OTHER
ANIMAL TESTING
FACTORY FARMING
Other Animal Rights
OPPRESSIVE REGIMES
WORKERS' RIGHTS
IRRESPONSIBLE MARKETING
ARMAMENTS
GENETIC ENGINEERING
BOYCOTT CALL
POLITICAL DONATIONS

Key

- Top rating (no criticisms found)
- Middle rating
- Bottom rating
- A related company has a bottom rating and the company itself has a middle rating
- A related company has a middle rating
- A related company has a bottom rating

Source: ECRA-See page 14 for full key to symbols.

Ethical investment

One of the most effective ways you can put ethical consumerism into practice is with your investments. With the growth in awareness on the part of companies as well as investors of the benefits of ethical investment, it is becoming easier to put your money where your mouth is...

A long history

The roots of ethical investment can be traced to the religious movements of the nineteenth century, such as the Quakers and Methodists, whose concerns included issues such as temperance and fair employment conditions. At the beginning of the 1900s, the Methodist Church began investing in the stock market, consciously avoiding companies involved in alcohol and gambling.

During the twentieth century, more churches, charities and individuals began to take account of ethical criteria when making investment choices. An ethical investment ideology began to develop in the US as controversy over American involvement in the Vietnam War led to the founding of the Pax World Fund in 1971, which aimed to avoid investments associated with the war. In the 1980s, the apartheid regime in South Africa was the focal point for ethical investment and, indeed, its success as a tool of protest there accelerated its acceptance and growth round the world.

In 1983 the Ethical Investment Research Service (EIRIS) was established as the UK's first independent research service in ethical investment, providing the underlying research into companies' social, environmental and ethical performance needed by investors to make informed and socially responsible investment decisions. The UK's first ethically screened unit trust – the Stewardship Fund – was launched by Friends Provident a year later. Now there are over 60 ethical retail funds in the UK market, with an estimated value of £3.8 billion. This growth in SRI (socially responsible investment) has been reflected globally, for example the Asia-Pacific region has seen the launch of several SRI funds in places like Japan, Australia and Singapore. In Europe there were 170 ethical funds in 1999, by the end of 2001 the number had grown to over 280.

Ethical or socially responsible investment describes any area of the financial sector where the principles of the investor inform where they place their money. Companies large and small have an increasingly large impact upon the world around them. How they conduct their business can affect all manner of things beyond the actual product or service they provide. There is a growing awareness that, alongside simply choosing to buy or not to buy their products, those of us who invest our spare money can also influence companies towards better social and environmental behaviour.

With any standard unit trust, investment trust, ISA or pension you may find your money going to companies which you would not wish to support. An ardent anti-smoker, for example would be dismayed to discover that their savings were invested in a tobacco company. Whether your investments are limited to a pension fund or if you're more involved in the stockmarket, knowing as much as you can about the ethics of the financial companies you're investing in can be as important as choosing an environmentally sound washing-up liquid. In fact, as the recent War on Want campaign to encourage the 10 million people who are occupational pension scheme members to find out where their money is invested shows, you can use your influence no matter how small your investments might seem.

How do I begin?

The first step towards positive investing is to identify what social, environmental and other ethical issues are most important to you. Areas of concern can be wide ranging, from animal testing to gambling, from human rights to nuclear power, from environmental enhancement to community involvement. Surveys by EIRIS have shown that the most prominent areas of concern were: operations in oppressive regimes, breaking environmental regulations and testing products on animals. The companies that respondents most liked their pension fund to favour over others when making investments were those with good records on environmental issues and employment conditions. Identifying these areas will reflect the type of companies you want to invest in or to avoid.

THE GOOD SHOPPING GUIDE

The Good Shopping Guide is the world's first comprehensive ethical reference guide to clearly list the behaviour of the companies behind everyday consumer brands – about 700!

Our objective is to encourage a universally responsible corporate attitude to animal welfare, human rights and the environment.

Companies depend entirely on their customers' goodwill, so we believe that the key to a progressive 21st century lies in the persuasive power of intelligent consumer action.

Nobody's perfect

It is important, however, to remember that there is no such thing as a perfect company. All are involved in activities that someone somewhere will object to and none go far enough in terms of positive social and environmental contribution to satisfy all of

the people all of the time. Ethical investment is about compromising and prioritising.

Types of funds

Once you've worked out your individual criteria, there are a diverse range of ethical funds available and different funds suit different investors. Some funds select a set of criteria which they believe will appeal to the widest range of investors. Others take a precisely focused approach, designed to appeal to a particular market. It is therefore very important to look behind the 'green' or 'ethical' label to what the fund is actually investing in before deciding to invest.

Ask:

- How the fund researches the activities of the companies in which it invests.
- Is there an ethical committee or advisory board that is independent of the investment process, to make sure the fund adheres to its published ethical policy?
- How good is the fund's communication with investors, e.g. does it have mechanisms in place to allow investors to voice their concerns?
- How active is the fund in engaging or communicating with companies? Does it encourage companies to improve their social and environmental performance?

THERE ARE THREE MAIN STRATEGIES THAT FUNDS CAN ADOPT TO IMPLEMENT THEIR ETHICAL INVESTMENT POLICIES.

- Engagement
  No companies are excluded but areas are identified in which companies can improve their environmental, social and ethical performance. The fund managers then 'engage' with the companies to encourage them to make such improvements.

- Preference
  The funds adopt social, environmental or other ethical guidelines which they prefer companies to meet. These guidelines are applied where all other things are equal (e.g. financial performance).

- Screening
  An 'acceptable list' of companies is created based on chosen positive and/or negative criteria (e.g. avoid companies involved in the arms trade, include companies with good environmental performance and so on). Funds are invested only in those companies on the list.

A TWO-PRONGED APPROACH

Ethical investing works two ways:
- by using their power as a shareholder to influence corporate behaviour;
- by choosing to invest only in companies who behave in a socially responsible manner

SHAREHOLDER POWER

One method of shareholder influence, which is as useful as much for the publicity it often receives, is the practice of posting shareholder resolutions which companies then have to consider in public at their annual general meetings. Campaigners say that the rules governing who can put forward a shareholder resolution are more restrictive in the UK than in the US. Nonetheless, a recent UK example is the resolution placed before BP's spring 2002 AGM – filed by the global environment network WWF, together with an international coalition of ethical investors – on its drilling activities in environmentally and culturally sensitive areas. This is one part of the campaign to prevent BP and others from drilling for oil in places such as the Alaskan Arctic National Wildlife Refuge, which is one of the last pristine areas left in the US and currently off-limits to oil and gas exploration and development.

VOTING FOR CHANGE

Shareholder resolutions, one of the more flamboyant ways of investing ethically, have been shown to work. Friends of the Earth used a shareholder resolution as part of its campaign against Balfour Beatty's plans to build a controversial dam in Turkey – the Ilisu dam on the Tiber River, 40 kilometres from the border of Syria and Iraq. Protest groups warned that the dam would make 78,000 local people homeless and drown dozens of towns and villages, including the world historic site of Hasankeyf.

FoE bought £30,000 worth of shares in order to submit a resolution on the dam contract at Balfour Beatty's AGM. Some months later, the company pulled out of the project, announcing that 'after a thorough evaluation of the commercial, environmental and social issues, it is not in the best interests of our stakeholders to pursue the project further.'

ALTERNATIVE INVESTMENT

Ethical investment is not confined to shares traded in stock exchanges. Many investors prefer to back individual projects or causes. Such directed investment is known by a variety of terms including, alternative investment, mission-based investment and socially directed investment. Examples of cause-based investment include regeneration projects in Birmingham (through the Aston Reinvestment Trust), and the support of projects in developing countries (through the co-operative lending society, Shared Interest). The cause-based investment sector is currently dominated by financial institutions such as Triodos Bank and the Ecology Building Society, although it also includes ethical companies who raise money directly from stakeholders by selling 'ethical shares'. Such companies include Traidcraft and the Centre for Alternative Technology.

Good for everybody

You don't need to worry that concentrating on ethical investments will make your financial performance suffer. Research by EIRIS and others indicates that investing according to ethical criteria may make little difference to overall financial performance, depending on the ethical policy applied. Five ethical indexes created by EIRIS produced financial returns roughly equivalent to the returns from the FTSE All-Share Index. For example, the total return of the Charities' Avoidance Index, which excludes the vast majority of companies involved in tobacco, gambling, alcohol, military sales and pornography, was 0.38 per cent greater than the All-Share.

And companies, too, can benefit. Over £3 billion is already invested in companies screened for good social, environmental and ethical practice by retail investors. Many churches and charities, pension schemes and local authorities are also investing according to socially responsible investment policies. That means money is being consciously diverted from companies that cannot demonstrate this good practice. And many investors are engaging with companies which they invest in or are considering investing in to persuade them to improve their policies and practices.

You can get further information by contacting the organisations listed below:

EIRIS's Guide to Ethical Funds covers the ethical retail funds (such as unit trusts, OEICs, investment trusts) available to the UK investor, giving a summary of each fund's ethical policy, top ten holdings and outlining what products (pension, ISA, etc.) are available with that fund.

EIRIS was established in 1983 by a group of churches and charities, today it is one of the leading providers of independent corporate research for socially responsible investors. EIRIS has a wealth of information for people who want to apply their principles to their investments and finances. EIRIS can provide a directory of financial advisors who have expertise in advising on ethical investments (available from *www.eiris.org*).
EIRIS, 80-84 Bondway, London SW8 1SF.
Tel: 020 7840 5700
Email: *ethics@eiris.org*

The UK Social Investment Forum is a membership network that promotes and encourages socially responsible investment in the UK including shareholder activism, social banking and community finance, *www.uksif.org* tel. 020 7749 4880)

The European Sustainable and Responsible Investment Forum (Eurosif) is a non-profit organisation promoting the concept, practice and development of responsible and sustainable investment, www.eurosif.info

Also see *www.gooshing.co.uk*

Below is a list of the ethical funds that *The Good Shopping Guide* was happy to publish and EIRIS was aware of at the time of collating this information and had been given details on by the fund provider. There may be other ethical funds that are on the market that EIRIS was not aware of or had no information on at that time. Note that by providing this list we are not making recommendations. For further information you may want to seek independent financial advice.

EIRIS defines an ethical fund as any fund which decides that shares are acceptable or not according to positive or negative ethical criteria e.g. environmental criteria, human rights criteria etc. The exception to this rule is that we do not include funds that only exclude companies involved in tobacco products.

AMP NPI Global Care Funds (Growth, Income, Pension and Pension Managed)
Type of investment: OEIC (Growth and Income), Pension Fund (Pension and Pension Managed),
Address: NPI House, 55 Calverly Road, Tunbridge Wells, Kent
Phone: 01892 515 151
Fax: n/a

AXA World Funds II – Global Portfolio Ecological Fund
Type of investment: Off-shore fund
Address: Sun Life Global Management Ltd, Royalty House, Walpole Ave, Douglas, Isle of Man IM1 2SL
Phone: 01624 643 498
Fax: 01624 643 541

AXA UK Ethical Fund
Type of investment: OEIC
Address: AXA Sun Life Fund Managers Ltd, MFD, PO Box 1810, Bristol BS99 5SN
Phone: 0117 989 0808
Fax: 0117 989 0604

Abbey Life Ethical Trust
Type of investment: Unit Trust
Address: Abbey Life Investment Services Ltd, Abbey Life Centre, 100 Holdenhurst Road, Bournemouth BH8 8AL
Phone: 01202 292 373
Fax: 01202 292 403

Aberdeen Ethical World OEIC
Type of investment: OEIC
Address: Aberdeen Unit Trust Managers Ltd, One Bow Churchyard, Cheapside, London EC4M 9HH
Phone: 0845 300 2890
Fax: 020 7463 6507

Aegon Ethical Income and Socially Responsible Funds
Type of investment: OEIC
Address: Aegon Asset Management plc, Aegon House, 3 Lochside Avenue, Edinburgh Park, Edinburgh EH12 9SE
Phone: 0800 169 5196Fax: 0131 549 4264

Allchurches Amity Fund
Type of investment: OEIC
Address: Allchurches Investment Management Services Ltd, Beaufort House, Brunswick Road, Gloucester GL1 1JZ
Phone: 01452 305 958
Fax: 01452 311 690

Barchester Best of Green Life, Pension and Offshore Funds
This fund also invests in the Jupiter Ecology Fund
Type of investment: Broker Bond
Address: Barchester Green Investment, Barchester House, 45 – 49 Catherine Street, Salisbury SP1 2DH
Phone: 01722 331 241
Fax: 01722 414191

CIS Environ Trust
Type of investment: Unit Trust
Address: CIS Unit Trust Managers Ltd, PO Box 105, Manchester M4 8BB
Phone: 0161 837 5060
Fax: 0161 837 4048

City Financial Ethical Fund
Type of investment: OEIC
Address: City Financial Investment Company Ltd, City Financial Centre, 88 Borough High Street, London SE1 1ST
Phone: 020 7556 8888
Fax: 020 7556 8889

Credit Suisse Fellowship Fund
Type of investment: OEIC
Address: Credit Suisse Asset Management Funds (UK) Ltd, Beaufort House, 15 St Botolph Street, London EC3A 7JJ
Phone: 020 7426 2929
Fax: 020 7426 2959

FRIENDS PROVIDENT STEWARDSHIP FUNDS (INCOME, INTERNATIONAL, PENSION, LIFE AND UNIT)
Type of investment: Unit Trusts and Pension Funds
Address: 72-122 Castle Street, Salisbury
Phone: 0870 600 6300
Fax: 0870 600 6366

FAMILY CHARITIES ETHICAL TRUST
Type of investment: Unit Trust
Address: 16 West St, Brighton BN1 2RE
Phone: 01273 725 272
Fax: 01273 206 026

HSBC AMANAH FUND
Type of investment: Fund based in Luxembourg (Islamic Shariah Fund)
Address: 7 Rue du Marche-aux-Herbes, Luxembourg L-1728
Phone: 00 352 47 68 12 230
Fax: 00 352 47 55 69
NB: These numbers are for dealing and administration; marketing materials should be obtained from the local HSBC Asset Management Representative

HALIFAX ETHICAL TRUST
Type of investment: OEIC
Address: CMIM Retail Funds, 33 Old Broad Street, London EC2N 1HZ
Phone: 01296 393 100
Fax: 020 7796 4824

HENDERSON ETHICAL FUND
Type of investment: OEIC
Address: Henderson Global Investors, 4 Broadgate, London EC2M 2DA
Phone: 08457 832832
Fax: 020 7956 9191

HOMEOWNERS FRIENDLY SOCIETY FTSE4GOOD UK FUND
Type of investment: Single premium bond or savings plans
Address: Homeowners Friendly Society Ltd, Hornbeam Avenue, Harrogate HG2 8XE
Phone: 0500 848 262
Fax: 01423 855 181

ISIS UK ETHICAL TRUST
Type of investment: Unit trust
Address: 15 Old Bailey, London EC4M 7AP
Phone: 020 7506 1100
Fax: 020 7236 2060

IMPAX ENVIRONMENTAL MARKETS
Type of investment: Investment Company
Address: Crusader House, 145 – 157 St John St, London. EC1V 4RU
Phone: 020 7490 4355
Fax: 020 7336 0865

INSIGHT ETHICAL AND EVERGREEN FUNDS
Type of investment: OEIC sub fund
Address: Clerical Medical Ethical Fund, Narrow Plain, Bristol BS2 0JH
Phone: 08457 772 233
Fax: 08457 772 234

JUPITER ECOLOGY AND ENVIRONMENTAL OPPORTUNITIES FUNDS
Type of investment: Unit Trusts
Address: Jupiter Asset Management, 1 Grosvenor Place, London SW1X 7JJ
Phone: 020 7412 0703
Fax: 020 7412 0705

JUPITER GLOBAL GREEN INVESTMENT TRUST PLC
Type of investment: Investment Trust
Address: Jupiter Asset Management Ltd, PO Box 14470, London SW1X 7YM
Phone: 0845 306 0100
Fax: n/a

LEGAL AND GENERAL ETHICAL TRUST
Type of investment: Unit Trust
Address: Legal and General Investments, Bucklersbury House, 3 Queen Victoria Street, London EC4N 8NH
Phone: 020 7528 6200
Fax: 020 7528 6838

LINCOLN GREEN FUND
As well as investing directly in equities, this fund invests in the Jupiter Ecology Fund.
Type of investment: Managed Life and Pension Funds
Address: Barnett Way, Barnwood, Gloucester GL4 3RZ
Phone: 01452 371 371
Fax: 01452 374 374

MERCHANT INVESTORS ASSURANCE ETHICAL CAUTIOUS MANAGED FUND
Type of investment: Managed Life and Pension Funds
Address: St Bartholomew's House, Lewins Mead, Bristol BS1 2NH
Phone: 0117 926 6366
Fax: 0117 975 2144

Continued on page 160

Continued from page 159

Minerva Green Portfolio and Green Protector Portfolio
These are funds of funds, therefore the ethical policy is derived from those funds which Minerva invests in.
Type of investment: Unit Trust
Address: Minerva Fund Managers Ltd, Kelston View, Corston, Bath BA2 9AH
Phone: 01225 872 300
Fax: 01225 872 301

Morley Sustainable Future Funds
Type of investment: OEIC
Address: Morley Fund Management, 1 Poultry, London. EC2R 8EJ
Phone: 020 7809 6000
Fax: na

Norwich Union UK Ethical Fund
Type of investment: Unit Trust
Address: Norwich Union Investment Management, PO Box 4, Surrey Street, Norwich NR1 3NG
Phone: 01603 622 200
Fax: n/a

Old Mutual Ethical Fund
Type of investment: Unit Trust
Address: 5th Floor, 80 Cheapside, London, EC2V 6LS
Phone: 020 7332 7500
Fax: 020 7332 7550

Quadris Environmental Fund
Type of investment: OEIC
Address: Regent House, 19 – 20 The Broadway, Woking, Surrey. GU21 5AP
Phone: 01483 756800
Fax: 01483 776800

St. James's Place Ethical Fund
Type of investment: Unit Trust
Address: St James's Place House, Dollar Street, Cirencester. GL7 2AQ
Phone: 01285 640302
Fax: 01285 640436

Scottish Amicable Ethical Fund
Type of investment: Unit Trust
Address: Scottish Amicable, Craigforth, PO Box 25, Stirling FK9 4UE
Phone: 01786 448 844
Fax: 01786 462 134

Scottish Life UK Ethical Fund
Type of investment: Pension Fund
Address: Scottish Life Assurance Company, 19 St Andrew's Square, Edinburgh EH12 1YE
Phone: 0131 456 7777
Fax: 0131 456 7421

Scottish Widows Environmental Investor Fund
Type of investment: Unit Trust
Address: Scottish Widows Unit Trust Managers Ltd, Charlton Place, Andover, Hants SP10 1RE
Phone: 0845 300 2244
Fax: n/a

Skandia Ethical Portfolio
Type of investment: Managed life and pension fund
Address: Skandia Life, PO Box 37, Skandia House, Portland Terrace, Southampton SO14 7AY
Phone: 023 8033 4411
Fax: 023 8072 6637

Sovereign Ethical Fund
Type of investment: Unit Trust
Address: Sovereign Unit Trust Managers Ltd, Tringham House, Wessex Fields, Deansleigh Road, Bournmouth BH7 7DT
Phone: 0800 731 1093
Fax: 01202 435 027

Standard Life UK Ethical Fund
Type of investment: OEIC
Address: Standard Life Investment Company, 1 George Street, Edinburgh EH2 2LL
Phone: 0800 333 353
Fax: 0131 245 2390

Standard Life Life Ethical and Pension Ethical Funds
Type of investment: OEIC
Address: Standard Life Assurance Company, 30 Lothian Road, Edinburgh EH1 2DH
Phone: 0845 60 60 100
Fax: 0131 245 2429

From 2005 *www.gooshing.co.uk* will feature a range of 'best deal' and 'best ethics' information concerning ethical investment.

Good Food & Drink

- Baby food
- Bananas
- Bedtime drinks
- Beer, lager & cider
- Biscuits
- Bottled water
- Bread
- Breakfast cereal
- Butter & margarine
- Cat & dog food
- Chocolate
- Cooking oil
- Crisps
- Ice cream
- Jams & spreads
- Pasta
- Soft drinks
- Soup
- Sugar
- Teas & coffee
- Whisky
- Yoghurt

Baby food

Everyone wants the 'best for baby', and that usually means the most natural available forms of care and nutrition. Luckily there has long been a high level of awareness and responsibility about the marketing of baby milk substitutes and of baby foods in general. Companies are of course eager to promote their products as the best in the market, but as always it helps to study the details. Parents not only have to consider carefully when to introduce baby to different foods but also need to have confidence in the brands they choose from the shelves.

Breast milk substitutes

The WHO/UNICEF International Code of Marketing of Breast Milk Substitutes has been developed in response to serious criticisms of the marketing practices of baby milk/food manufacturers over many years. Because of the massive amount of evidence in favour of prolonged breastfeeding, the Code lays down various guidelines, including that solid foods be labelled as only suitable from six months. In poorer countries in particular, moving from breastmilk to substitutes can have the severest consequences for babies' health. In the late 1990s there were serious breaches of the Code. (Contact Baby Milk Action for more information on this subject: 01223 464420)

Different kinds of foods

Baby food comes in three main types:

- 'wet' foods, which are pre-cooked and puréed meals packaged in jars or cans
- 'dry' foods, in boxes or sachets, which have to be rehydrated to make meals
- cereals, rusks and rice cakes, eaten plain or with milk.

The companies reviewed here produce all three types, except for Farleys, Milupa and Olvarit, which, at the time of research, only produce dry varieties.

Organic brands

Parents are increasingly looking for organic food for their babies. There are now exclusively organic companies like Baby Organix and Hipp, while Heinz and Boots also do their own organic ranges. *The Organic Baby Book* (*www.theorganicbabybook.co.uk*) lists the different brands available in the UK.

One strong argument in favour of using organic food for babies is that they are more vulnerable than adults to toxins such as pesticide residues.

Labelling & packaging

Since 1999 there has been legislation in Britain setting compulsory standards for the nutritional value and labelling of baby foods. The regulations set minimum quantities for the main vitamins, minerals and protein, and maximum quantities for fats, carbohydrate and sodium. All the baby food examined for this report did comply with these regulations.

An EC survey found that most of the packaging for baby foods is in theory recyclable but that very little attention is drawn to this fact.

Alternatives & niche brands

Baby food can of course be made at home. One good and healthy process is to liquidise or sieve cooked fruit or vegetables, preferably organic ones of course. Some good baby food recipe books are available, including *Cooking for Your Baby* (Laraine Toms, Penguin), *Complete New Guide to Preparing Babyfoods* (Sue Castle, Bantam) and *The New Vegetarian Baby* (Baird and Yntema, McBooks).

Yoghurt and fromage frais makers have entered the baby food market, with varieties labelled as being suitable from four to six months. There are also niche brands such as Mother Nature Babyfoods (which produces halal foods), Original Fresh Babyfood Co and Osska (both of these make fresh meals which are sold in the cold cabinets of health food stores and supermarkets).

- Baby Nat
- Baby Organix
- Hipp organics

- Cow & Gate
- Milupa
- Olvarit

- Boots
- Farleys
- Heinz

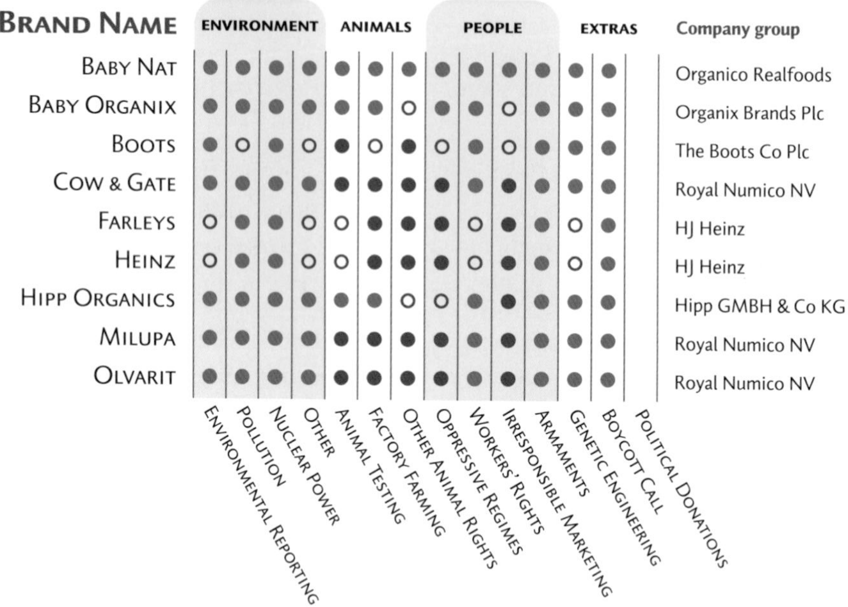

Brand Name	Environment: Environmental Reporting	Environment: Pollution	Environment: Nuclear Power	Environment: Other	Animals: Animal Testing	Animals: Factory Farming	Animals: Other Animal Rights	People: Oppressive Regimes	People: Workers' Rights	People: Irresponsible Marketing	People: Armaments	Extras: Genetic Engineering	Extras: Boycott Call	Extras: Political Donations	Company group
Baby Nat	Top	Top	Top	Top	Top	Top	Top	Top	Top	Top	Top	Top	Top		Organico Realfoods
Baby Organix	Top	Top	Top	Top	Top	Top	Middle	Top	Top	Middle	Top	Top	Top		Organix Brands Plc
Boots	Top	Middle	Top	Middle	Bottom	Middle	Bottom	Middle	Top	Middle	Top	Top	Top		The Boots Co Plc
Cow & Gate	Top	Top	Top	Top	Bottom	Bottom	Bottom	Bottom	Top	Bottom	Top	Top	Top		Royal Numico NV
Farleys	Middle	Top	Top	Middle	Middle	Bottom	Bottom	Bottom	Middle	Bottom	Top	Middle	Top		HJ Heinz
Heinz	Middle	Top	Top	Middle	Middle	Bottom	Bottom	Bottom	Middle	Bottom	Top	Middle	Top		HJ Heinz
Hipp Organics	Top	Top	Top	Top	Top	Top	Middle	Middle	Top	Bottom	Top	Top	Top		Hipp GMBH & Co KG
Milupa	Top	Top	Top	Top	Bottom	Bottom	Bottom	Bottom	Top	Bottom	Top	Top	Top		Royal Numico NV
Olvarit	Top	Top	Top	Top	Bottom	Bottom	Bottom	Bottom	Top	Bottom	Top	Top	Top		Royal Numico NV

Key

- ● Top rating (no criticisms found)
- ○ Middle rating
- ● Bottom rating
- A related company has a bottom rating and the company itself has a middle rating
- A related company has a middle rating
- A related company has a bottom rating

Source: ECRA-See page 14 for full key to symbols.

Bananas

Although British consumers have always loved bananas, it is only recently that we have really begun to notice the different kinds available or where they actually come from. As with many farmed products from tropical countries there is now a strong move towards fair trade bananas. Bananas are important in the fair trade campaign because of the threat from big plantation companies to the livelihoods of people living in the Windward islands of the Caribbean where bananas often provide the only reliable employment. There are other issues to think about as well, especially the heavy use of pesticides, and there is now a campaign for organic methods of growing the fruit.

Banana wars

The US and the EU went through a long dispute about the trading conditions for bananas during the 90s. The European countries tried to keep preferential access for bananas from the Caribbean islands, but the World Trade Organisation eventually ruled in favour of the US. This means that the 'dollar banana companies' like Chiquita, Dole and Del Monte have been able to expand their business in Europe. European companies like Fyffes and Geest import their fruit mainly, but not exclusively, from the Windward islands.

Windward bananas are grown much less intensively and more sustainably than those from other countries, especially those in Central America. Most production is done by small producers with better employment conditions and with fewer chemicals than elsewhere. Windward bananas also tend to be smaller and sweeter.

Wages & conditions

The big multinationals operating in Central and South America own sprawling plantations where workers may toil for 12 hours a day in poor conditions, as well as face intimidation by owners. Workers have been trying to organise trade unions to bargain for better wages and conditions but have encountered company harassment, especially in Costa Rica and Honduras.

A good way for us to influence the way workers are treated in these countries is to opt for fair trade bananas which, after some delay, have been accepted by a number of supermarket chains in Britain.

Pesticides & chemicals

Since the 1960s companies increasingly have been growing varieties of bananas with the highest yields. These are, however, also very susceptible to pests and diseases and so the industry uses an enormous quantity of chemicals throughout the growing process, before and after harvesting, as well as to preserve the fruit in transit. While the average usage of pesticides on farms in industrialised countries is 2.7kg per hectare, within the Costa Rican banana industry the figure is 44kg per hectare, with aerial spraying occurring up to 50 times a year. The workers are exposed to appalling health hazards and the surrounding areas can become seriously contaminated.

Organic options

Planting varieties of bananas that are more resistant to infection is the most obvious way of reducing the justification for such heavy use of pesticides. Increasing numbers of bananas are being imported from farms where they are grown without chemical assistance. This market is sure to increase as customers become more aware of the issues and observant of the different brands available.

- Fyffes
- Geest

- Del Monte
- Dole

- Chiquita

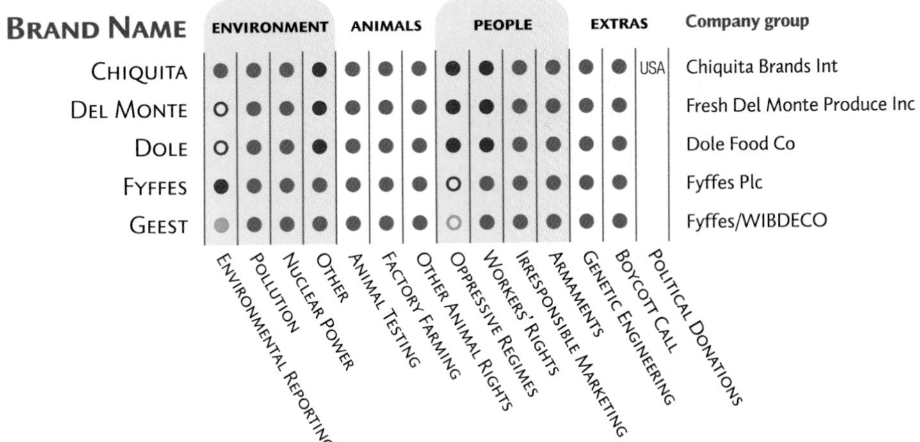

Brand Name	Environmental Reporting	Pollution	Nuclear Power	Other	Animal Testing	Factory Farming	Other Animal Rights	Oppressive Regimes	Workers' Rights	Irresponsible Marketing	Armaments	Genetic Engineering	Boycott Call	Political Donations	Company group
	ENVIRONMENT				ANIMALS			PEOPLE				EXTRAS			
Chiquita	Top	Top	Top	Bottom	Top	Top	Top	Bottom	Bottom	Top	Top	Top	Top	USA	Chiquita Brands Int
Del Monte	Middle	Top	Top	Bottom	Top	Top	Top	Bottom	Bottom	Top	Top	Top	Top		Fresh Del Monte Produce Inc
Dole	Middle	Top	Top	Bottom	Top	Top	Top	Bottom	Bottom	Top	Top	Top	Top		Dole Food Co
Fyffes	Bottom	Top	Top	Top	Top	Top	Top	Middle	Top	Top	Top	Top	Top		Fyffes Plc
Geest	Related company bottom	Top	Top	Top	Top	Top	Top	Related company middle	Top	Top	Top	Top	Top		Fyffes/WIBDECO

Key

- Top rating (no criticisms found)
- Middle rating
- Bottom rating
- A related company has a bottom rating and the company itself has a middle rating
- A related company has a middle rating
- A related company has a bottom rating

Source: ECRA-See page 14 for full key to symbols.

Bedtime drinks

Hot beverages before bed, what are the ethical issues? GM, pesticides, fair labour practices and responsible marketing all need to be considered. Many of the products are cocoa based or use cocoa to make chocolate, and despite cocoa market prices hitting a record high, many cocoa farmers are not finding themselves better off.

The farmers

The average cocoa farmer earns just £50 a year from cocoa. New varieties of cocoa have been developed, which can grow in the sun, but the trees decline quicker than traditional varieties, and require high doses of pesticides. One of these pesticides is lindane, which is banned in the EU for health reasons. Also some chocolate companies, especially those buying from suppliers in the Ivory Coast, have been unable to confirm that their cocoa is not picked under conditions of slavery [1]

So it' s crucial to choose delicious new products like Cocodirect (from Cafedirect), which is certified by the Fair Trade foundation. This means that farmers and their communities benefit from a fair price for their goods, and guarantees no child or forced labour. Cafedirect guarantee via their Gold Standard a price higher than the market price, and the Cocodirect drink contains 40% pure cocoa, which means more revenue for farmers[2] Also look out for organic brands, certified organic by the Soil Association – this helps bio-diversity and guarantees no gm and no pesticides.

Boycott calls

As the companies table demonstrates, Horlicks, Galaxy and Maltesers' are subject to boycott calls. In contrast to the drink's somewhat old-fashioned image, Horlicks's parent company is multinational pharmaceutical giant GlaxoSmithKline. It is being boycotted due to attempts to block cheaper versions of its anti-AIDS drugs,[3] unnecessary animal testing,[4] and for being one of the ten largest donors to the Republican party.[5] GlaxoSmithKline was also ruled to have made misleading health claims about its Ribena drink on three occasions, including marketing a sugar free version that contained sugar![6]

Mars, which owns Galaxy and Maltesers, is also subject to a boycott call for animal testing undertaken by its petfood division.[7] Mars has also partaken in questionable marketing when it cited confectionery as a good source of carbohydrate, in a promotional health and awareness pack.[8]

Cadbury's has also been criticised for irresponsible marketing; it launched a promotion called 'Get Active' where children were encouraged to buy cholocalte bars and save the wrappers to get free sporting equipment for schools. To get a 'free' basketball, 170 chocolate bar wrappers (representing a total 2kg of fat and over 38,000 calories) would have to be submitted – hardly a healthy way to get health-promoting sports equipment. The company has also admitted publicly that its chocolate could contain some residues of lindane.[11] Also, neither Cadbury's nor GlaxoSmithKline have publically confirmed that the drinking chocolate and Horlicks products contain no GM ingredients.[10] GM issues also crop up with a subsidiary of Ovaltine's owner Associated British Foods Plc, which has been running trials to assess commercial viability of oil seed rape for the GM giant Monsanto.[11]

So stick to *The Good Shopping Guide's* ethically certified brands – they leave a really good taste in your mouth!

- Clipper
- Cocodirect
- Green & Blacks

- Cadbury's
- Ovaltine

- Galaxy
- Horlicks
- Malteasers

1 *Ethical Consumer 79, October / November 2002;* 2 *www.cafedirect.co.uk , 31/07/03;* 3 *Utusan Konsumer, May 2001;* 4 *www.stopanimaltests.com , 07/07/03;* 5 *www.boycottbush.net, 07/07/03;* 6 *Food Magazine, July 2000;* 7 *BUAV campaign report, Spring 2002 ;* 8 *The Food Magazine, January 2003;* 9 *Ethical Consumer, August / September 2000;* 10 *www.greenpeace.org.uk , 31/7/03;* 11 *www.genewatch.org , November 2001*

café**direct**® sponsors Bedtime Drinks

www.cafedirect.co.uk

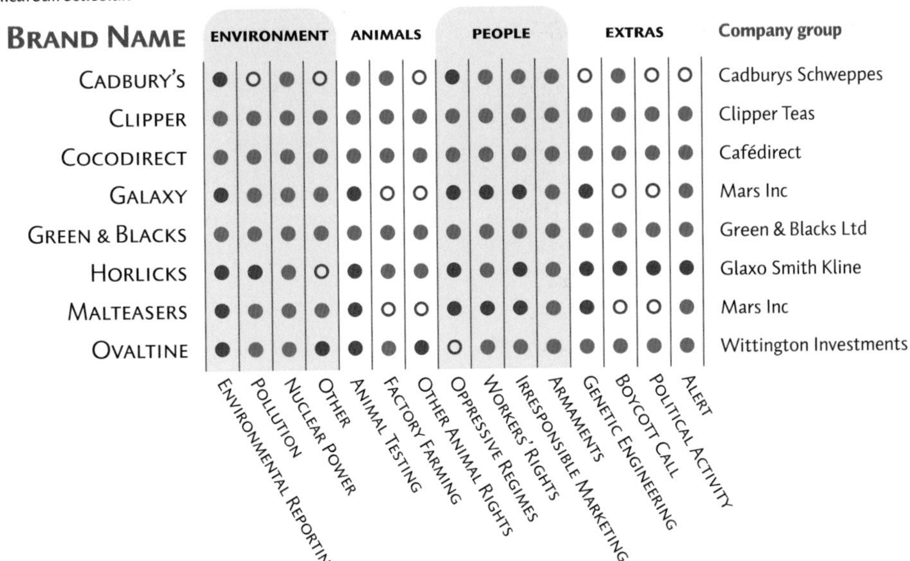

Brand Name	Environment				Animals			People				Extras				Company group
	Environmental Reporting	Pollution	Nuclear Power	Other	Animal Testing	Factory Farming	Other Animal Rights	Oppressive Regimes	Workers' Rights	Irresponsible Marketing	Armaments	Genetic Engineering	Boycott Call	Political Activity	Alert	
Cadbury's	Bottom	Middle	Top	Middle	Top	Top	Middle	Bottom	Top	Top	Top	Middle	Top	Middle	Middle	Cadburys Schweppes
Clipper	Top	Top	Top	Top	Top	Top	Top	Top	Top	Top	Top	Top	Top	Top	Top	Clipper Teas
Cocodirect	Top	Top	Top	Top	Top	Top	Top	Top	Top	Top	Top	Top	Top	Top	Top	Cafédirect
Galaxy	Bottom	Top	Top	Top	Bottom	Middle	Middle	Bottom	Bottom	Bottom	Top	Bottom	Middle	Middle	Top	Mars Inc
Green & Blacks	Top	Top	Top	Top	Top	Top	Top	Top	Top	Top	Top	Top	Top	Top	Top	Green & Blacks Ltd
Horlicks	Bottom	Bottom	Top	Middle	Bottom	Top	Top	Bottom	Top	Bottom	Top	Bottom	Bottom	Bottom	Bottom	Glaxo Smith Kline
Malteasers	Bottom	Top	Top	Top	Bottom	Middle	Middle	Bottom	Bottom	Bottom	Top	Bottom	Middle	Middle	Top	Mars Inc
Ovaltine	Bottom	Top	Top	Bottom	Bottom	Top	Bottom	Middle	Top	Top	Top	Top	Top	Top	Top	Wittington Investments

Key

- Top rating (no criticisms found)
- Middle rating
- Bottom rating
- A related company has a bottom rating and the company itself has a middle rating
- A related company has a middle rating
- A related company has a bottom rating

Source: ECRA-See page 14 for full key to symbols.

Beer, lager & cider

The big brewers may all be thinking globally these days but seasoned drinkers usually prefer their local brews when they can find them. Where the big companies often win is by persuading us that a 'local' brew from far away contains something special or unique – hence the successes of brews from Mexico, South Africa, India and Thailand.

Below we cover the big companies with nationwide brands of bitter, lager, stout or cider. The table indicates the ownership of the draught brands – which may not be the same as that of bottles and cans of the same brand.

How many miles

Our increasingly exotic tastes could be causing horrendous and fairly pointless pollution of the globe. Ingredients for a real ale from a local brewery might have travelled about 600 miles in all, which might seem far enough, but for some imported lagers produced by the multinationals the ingredients can travel as many as 24,000 miles. There may be some consolation in the fact that many of the so-called 'export' or 'continental' lagers are really brewed under licence in the UK, but there is ever more beer moving across European borders these days.

What's in the stuff?

Conventional hop farming uses a lot of pesticides – which results in what the pressure group Sustain describes as 'scorched earth' farming methods, where the ground between and beneath the hops is kept barren and dusty. Organic farming methods use mustard mixed with the hops to attract predators and combat aphid attacks.

Traditionally, the barley for malting has come from the highest-quality spring crops but recently there has been massive development of new winter barley varieties, on which farmers use almost double the number of pesticides. These changes, and the decrease in planting of summer barley, have badly damaged bird populations.

Under current UK legislation, drinks containing over 1.2 per cent alcohol are exempt from the compulsory labelling applicable to other products for consumption. This means that brewers don't tell us when they use chemical additives, as many do to increase the shelf life of the beer or to alter the colour or flavour of the brew. The lack of mandatory labelling causes problems for vegetarians, as most beers do still use animal-derived products.

Organic options

Organic beers have begun to take off although there are real problems finding organic hops – the main source of supply being far-off New Zealand! Organic production of hops in the UK is not only possible but potentially highly profitable.

BASIC DRINKING ETHICS

Don't let ethics spoil your fun...

- ....but you really should never drink then drive
- Try to support the local pubs that stock local brews
- Cans are best for drinking outdoors – and bottles are best at home
- When drinking out anywhere, always remove your empties

Brewing your own beer can potentially give you control over many elements of the brewing process. There are no UK homebrew suppliers currently stocking organic hops, however, these are available by mail order from the US (*www.Seven-bridges-cooperative.com*). While this increases beer miles, the weight of the product is only around 3lbs. Online brewing classes are now available on the web (*www.breworganic.com/index.htm*) with lots of the information you need, from the best equipment to bottling the finished product.

None for the road

The legal driving alcohol limit in the UK is 80mg%, compared with 50mg% in most of Europe and 20mg% in Sweden.

Although any alcohol affects all drivers, accident rates for young people double after only two drinks and increase tenfold after five drinks.

- Dry Blackthorn
- Holsten Pils
- Marston's
- Merrydown
- Old Speckled Hen
- Strongbow
- Wadworth's 6x

- Carling
- ESB
- Fosters
- Guinness
- John Smiths

- Beck's
- Budweiser
- Carlsberg
- Grolsch
- Heineken
- Miller
- Stella Artois

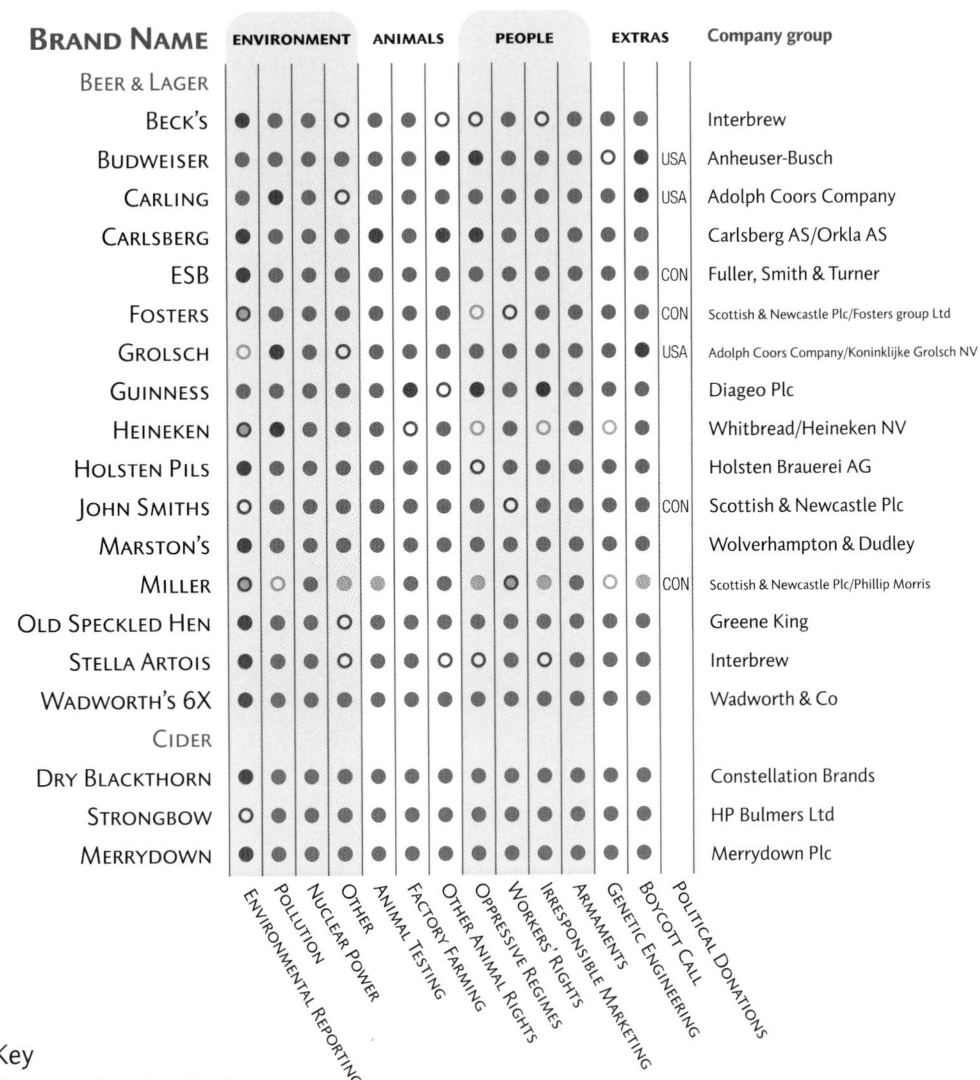

BRAND NAME
ENVIRONMENT
ANIMALS
PEOPLE
EXTRAS
Company group
BEER & LAGER
BECK'S
Interbrew
BUDWEISER
USA
Anheuser-Busch
CARLING
USA
Adolph Coors Company
CARLSBERG
Carlsberg AS/Orkla AS
ESB
CON
Fuller, Smith & Turner
FOSTERS
CON
Scottish & Newcastle Plc/Fosters group Ltd
GROLSCH
USA
Adolph Coors Company/Koninklijke Grolsch NV
GUINNESS
Diageo Plc
HEINEKEN
Whitbread/Heineken NV
HOLSTEN PILS
Holsten Brauerei AG
JOHN SMITHS
CON
Scottish & Newcastle Plc
MARSTON'S
Wolverhampton & Dudley
MILLER
CON
Scottish & Newcastle Plc/Phillip Morris
OLD SPECKLED HEN
Greene King
STELLA ARTOIS
Interbrew
WADWORTH'S 6X
Wadworth & Co
CIDER
DRY BLACKTHORN
Constellation Brands
STRONGBOW
HP Bulmers Ltd
MERRYDOWN
Merrydown Plc
ENVIRONMENTAL REPORTING
POLLUTION
NUCLEAR POWER
OTHER
ANIMAL TESTING
FACTORY FARMING
OTHER ANIMAL RIGHTS
OPPRESSIVE REGIMES
WORKERS' RIGHTS
IRRESPONSIBLE MARKETING
ARMAMENTS
GENETIC ENGINEERING
BOYCOTT CALL
POLITICAL DONATIONS

Key

- Top rating (no criticisms found)
- Middle rating
- Bottom rating
- A related company has a bottom rating and the company itself has a middle rating
- A related company has a middle rating
- A related company has a bottom rating

Source: ECRA-See page 14 for full key to symbols.

Biscuits

Children's biscuits and so-called 'healthy' biscuits are two of the fastest-growing sectors in an already saturated food market. The whole idea is hardly a healthy one – a biscuit is just a sugary, fatty treat to be enjoyed, hopefully in moderation. Meanwhile the companies make confusing claims that their biscuits are '85 per cent fat free'. Consumers tend to think these have less fat than 'low fat' ones when they have just as much as an average slice of cheesecake. Surveys have shown that more than half of consumers have no idea what these labels actually mean. The companies are happy as long as they're persuading us their bikkies are good, OK, healthy – whatever, just as long as we buy them.

Corporate crunch-up

At the time of research, the biscuit market was a perfect example of global corporate crunching. A lowly Somerfield 'basics' digestive was made by McVities – which is owned by United Biscuits, which is owned by Finalrealm, which is a consortium of Nabisco, DB Capital, Cinven and PAI. Of those in the consortium, Nabisco is owned by Kraft, which is owned by Philip Morris, the company that makes Marlboro cigarettes but has changed its name to Altria. Cinven is a leverage buy-out operation which owns companies as diverse as Odeon Cinemas, Foesco chemicals and William Hill Bookmakers. DB Capital Partners is owned by Deutsche Bank, which has been involved in financing controversial dams amongst other things. So what's new?

Ingredients

Vegetarians and vegans should be aware that many biscuits contain dairy products such as butter or whey powders. Some brands may contain non-specific animal fat. Companies are realising that consumers do often look at the labels. In the mid-1990s, Greenpeace famously persuaded McVities to stop making biscuits with fish oil from industrial fishing.

One biscuit-maker, Northern Foods, says that none of its biscuits are tainted with GM because consumers won't buy GM food. That's fine, but we should be aware that the powerful food industry lobby, the Food and Drink Federation, states: 'Biotechnology, including genetic modification, offers enormous potential to improve the quality and quantity of the food supply.' In the US, Kraft has been using untested and unlabelled genetically engineered ingredients for several years, although in Europe the company has so far been respectful of consumer pressure. Now, more than ever, is a time for vigilance against the stealthy introduction of GM technology. Try to buy Walkers, Traidcraft, Doves Farm or Bahlsen.

- Bahlsen
- Doves Farm
- Traidcraft
- Walkers

- Burton's
- Fox's
- Hill

- Jacobs
- McVities

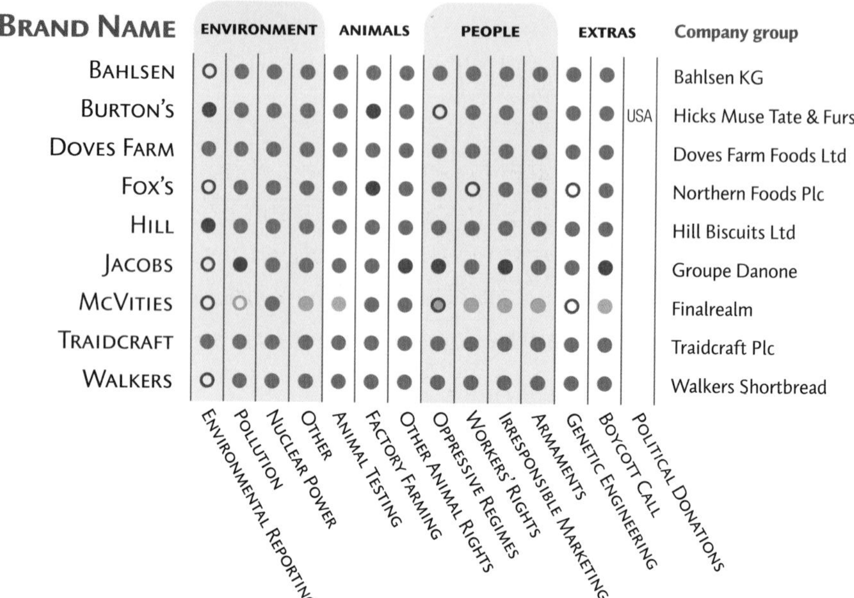

Brand Name	Environmental Reporting	Pollution	Nuclear Power	Other	Animal Testing	Factory Farming	Other Animal Rights	Oppressive Regimes	Workers' Rights	Irresponsible Marketing	Armaments	Genetic Engineering	Boycott Call	Political Donations	Company group
Bahlsen	Middle	Top	Top	Top	Top	Top	Top	Top	Top	Top	Top	Top	Top		Bahlsen KG
Burton's	Bottom	Top	Top	Top	Top	Bottom	Top	Middle	Top	Top	Top	Top	Top	USA	Hicks Muse Tate & Furst
Doves Farm	Top	Top	Top	Top	Top	Top	Top	Top	Top	Top	Top	Top	Top		Doves Farm Foods Ltd
Fox's	Middle	Top	Top	Top	Top	Bottom	Top	Top	Middle	Top	Top	Middle	Top		Northern Foods Plc
Hill	Bottom	Top	Top	Top	Top	Top	Top	Top	Top	Top	Top	Top	Top		Hill Biscuits Ltd
Jacobs	Middle	Bottom	Top	Top	Top	Top	Bottom	Bottom	Top	Bottom	Top	Top	Bottom		Groupe Danone
McVities	Middle	Related middle	Top	Related bottom	Related bottom	Top	Top	Related bottom / middle	Related bottom	Related bottom	Related bottom	Middle	Related bottom		Finalrealm
Traidcraft	Top	Top	Top	Top	Top	Top	Top	Top	Top	Top	Top	Top	Top		Traidcraft Plc
Walkers	Middle	Top	Top	Top	Top	Top	Top	Top	Top	Top	Top	Top	Top		Walkers Shortbread

Key

- Top rating (no criticisms found)
- Middle rating
- Bottom rating
- A related company has a bottom rating and the company itself has a middle rating
- A related company has a middle rating
- A related company has a bottom rating

Source: ECRA-See page 14 for full key to symbols.

Bottled water

The marketing of bottled water is largely hype but how else do we tell the difference between brands of a product that is colourless, odourless and largely tasteless? It's a business where the multinationals are in charge, even with brands like Malvern and Buxton. The worldwide market leaders are Evian, Volvic, Perrier and San Pellegrino, brands that are under the control of either Danone or Nestlé. (See the long table)

Glass mountains

Every bottle of Perrier sold around the world is bottled at source in Vergèze, France. So readers in say, Glasgow, would be drinking water that has travelled over 900 miles.

An environmental packaging solution is the re-usable glass bottle – like the milk bottle. In other European countries, higher proportions of all drinks come in returnable bottles. For example, in Germany, most mineral water is sold in a standard refillable glass bottle. The mineral water producers are members of a pool system, with their brands being distinguished by label but the bottles shared, allowing short transport distances from consumer to refiller. In the UK it seems that the big national breweries, soft drink producers and supermarkets are reluctant to use refillable glass bottles because of the extra effort (floor space and staff time) it would cause them. They prefer to encourage recycling, which hands the work over to the consumer, and they also much prefer dealing with plastics.

Pure, how pure?

Although bottled water claims a natural, pure and healthy image, all waters must meet strict quality requirements. The area surrounding a Natural Mineral Water spring requires protection against pollution and although Natural Mineral Water is legally 'pure', this is not true of all water that is sold in bottles.

Those with high blood pressure, or others who need to follow a low sodium (salt) diet should check the mineral content of their water carefully. Natural mineral waters can only claim they're suitable for a low sodium diet if they contain less than 20mg per litre. Current advice from the Food Standards Agency is that some bottled waters shouldn't be used for babies. 'Waters to avoid are those with high levels of nitrate, nitrite, sodium, fluoride and sulphate. There are limits for these in tap, spring and other bottled drinking waters, but not in natural mineral waters.'

A *Health Which?* report concluded that in terms of bottled water, price varies considerably (from 12p/litre to £1.69/litre) and the quality is hardly ever proportional to the expense. To put this in context, the price of bottled water is on average 500 to 1,000 times higher than that of tap water.

Alternatives

The simplest course of action is to drink tap water. The Drinking Water Inspectorate has warned that if opportunities are not taken to improve the public perception of tap water, consumers would never appreciate the plentiful low cost water supplied to their taps. *Health Which?* echoed these sentiments by giving both filtered and unfiltered tap water from Thames Water a five out of five score in their taste test, a result which was only replicated by seven out of the 40 bottled water types in the report.

- 1180
- Aqua Pura
- Ballygowan
- Highland Spring
- Pennine Hills
- Spa
- Strathmore

- Campsie Spring
- Evian
- Volvic

- Malvern
- Perrier
- Vittel

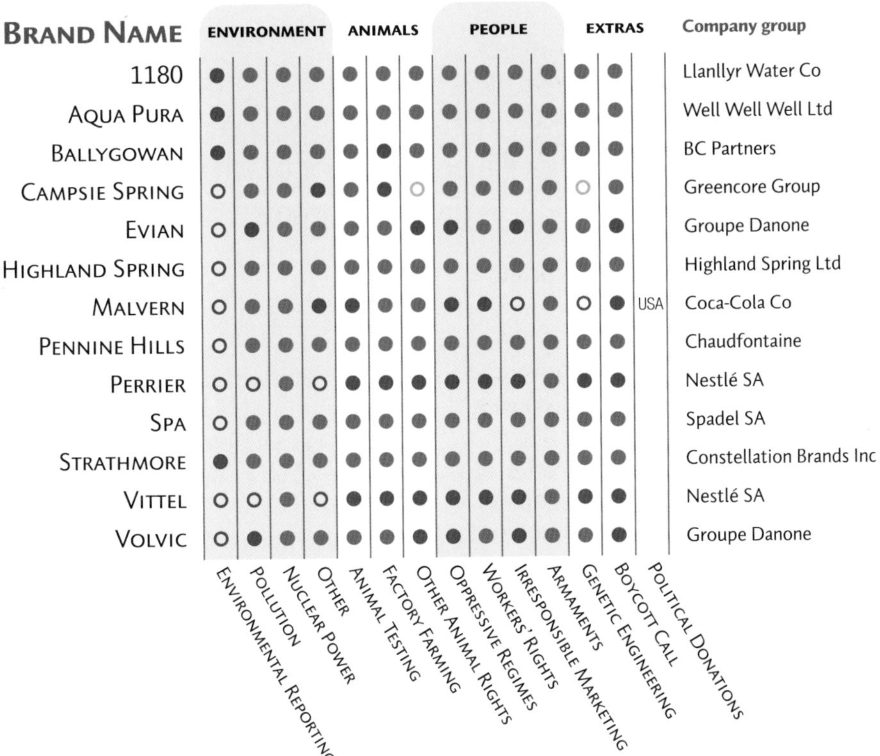

Key

- Top rating (no criticisms found)
- Middle rating
- Bottom rating
- A related company has a bottom rating and the company itself has a middle rating
- A related company has a middle rating
- A related company has a bottom rating

Source: ECRA-See page 14 for full key to symbols.

Bread

Home baking is one sure way to guarantee your bread is free from additives and plastic packaging. In the shops, wholemeal organic is the answer.

Chemicals and additives

Sliced and wrapped loaves are by far the biggest-selling kind of bread, representing 80 per cent of bread consumption. The main manufacturers are Allied Bakeries and British Bakeries, each controlling about a third of the market. Allied make Kingsmill and British Bakeries make Hovis. The biggest bakery specialist is Greggs, which controls the Bakers Oven, Olivers, Bartletts and Crawfords outlets, as well as Greggs stores.

Since 1961, plant bakeries have used a fast-track production system known as the Chorleywood Bread Process (CBP). It replaces the traditional slow fermentation with a short burst in high-speed mixers, using much greater quantities of yeast. More water is absorbed into the dough, which rises up and reaches its desired volume more quickly. There are many additives, including chemical 'improvers' which oxidise newly-milled flour. Because the bleaches used to whiten and sterilise the flour manage to strip much of the nutritional value, vitamins and minerals have to be added back in.

The drawback of conventional wholemeal bread, in which the whole of the wheatgrain is retained, is that higher levels of residues of fertilisers, pesticides and post-harvest storage treatment chemicals are present in wholemeal than in ordinary white or brown flour. This is a very good reason to choose organic bread.

Alternatives

One alternative is bread from a local bakery. However, many bakers are using technology similar to CBP, which can render the bread rather tasteless, lightweight and insubstantial.

Organic bread is catching on. In London and the South East, Goswells produces organic bread on behalf of Doves Farm and Whole Earth Foods. In the North West there's Sakers and in the Gloucestershire region there's Hobbs House.

Good bread need contain only flour, yeast, water and salt.

- Authentic Bread
- Doves Farm
- Fine Lady
- Greggs
- Village Bakery
- Warburton's
- Whole Earth

- Allinson
- Burgen
- Kingsmill
- Rathbones
- Sunblest
- William Jackson

- Enjoy Organic
- Granary
- Hovis
- Mothers Pride
- Nimble

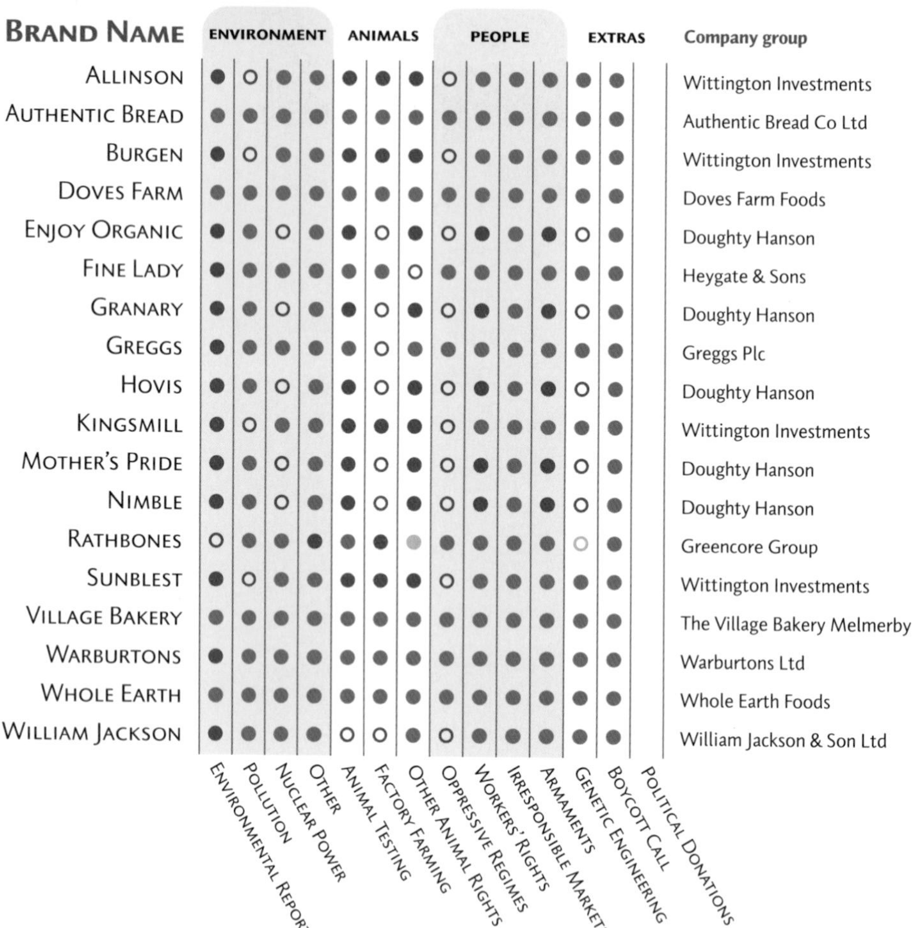

Brand Name	Environment: Environmental Reporting	Environment: Pollution	Environment: Nuclear Power	Environment: Other	Animals: Animal Testing	Animals: Factory Farming	Animals: Other Animal Rights	People: Oppressive Regimes	People: Workers' Rights	People: Irresponsible Marketing	People: Armaments	Extras: Genetic Engineering	Extras: Boycott Call	Extras: Political Donations	Company group
Allinson	Bottom	Middle	Top	Top	Bottom	Bottom	Bottom	Middle	Top	Top	Top	Top	Top		Wittington Investments
Authentic Bread	Top	Top	Top	Top	Top	Top	Top	Top	Top	Top	Top	Top	Top		Authentic Bread Co Ltd
Burgen	Bottom	Middle	Top	Top	Bottom	Bottom	Bottom	Middle	Top	Top	Top	Top	Top		Wittington Investments
Doves Farm	Top	Top	Top	Top	Top	Top	Top	Top	Top	Top	Top	Top	Top		Doves Farm Foods
Enjoy Organic	Bottom	Top	Middle	Top	Bottom	Middle	Bottom	Middle	Bottom	Top	Bottom	Middle	Top		Doughty Hanson
Fine Lady	Bottom	Top	Top	Top	Top	Top	Middle	Top	Top	Top	Top	Top	Top		Heygate & Sons
Granary	Bottom	Top	Middle	Top	Bottom	Middle	Bottom	Middle	Bottom	Top	Bottom	Middle	Top		Doughty Hanson
Greggs	Bottom	Top	Top	Top	Top	Middle	Top	Top	Top	Top	Top	Top	Top		Greggs Plc
Hovis	Bottom	Top	Middle	Top	Bottom	Middle	Bottom	Middle	Bottom	Top	Bottom	Middle	Top		Doughty Hanson
Kingsmill	Bottom	Middle	Top	Top	Bottom	Bottom	Bottom	Middle	Top	Top	Top	Top	Top		Wittington Investments
Mother's Pride	Bottom	Top	Middle	Top	Bottom	Middle	Bottom	Middle	Bottom	Top	Bottom	Middle	Top		Doughty Hanson
Nimble	Bottom	Top	Middle	Top	Bottom	Middle	Bottom	Middle	Bottom	Top	Bottom	Middle	Top		Doughty Hanson
Rathbones	Middle	Top	Top	Bottom	Top	Bottom	Related bottom	Top	Top	Top	Top	Related middle	Top		Greencore Group
Sunblest	Bottom	Middle	Top	Top	Bottom	Bottom	Bottom	Middle	Top	Top	Top	Top	Top		Wittington Investments
Village Bakery	Top	Top	Top	Top	Top	Top	Top	Top	Top	Top	Top	Top	Top		The Village Bakery Melmerby
Warburtons	Bottom	Top	Top	Top	Top	Top	Top	Top	Top	Top	Top	Top	Top		Warburtons Ltd
Whole Earth	Top	Top	Top	Top	Top	Top	Top	Top	Top	Top	Top	Top	Top		Whole Earth Foods
William Jackson	Bottom	Top	Top	Top	Middle	Middle	Top	Middle	Top	Top	Top	Top	Top		William Jackson & Son Ltd

Key

- Top rating (no criticisms found)
- Middle rating
- Bottom rating
- A related company has a bottom rating and the company itself has a middle rating
- A related company has a middle rating
- A related company has a bottom rating

Source: ECRA-See page 14 for full key to symbols.

Ethical Trade BioBiz

Breakfast Cereal

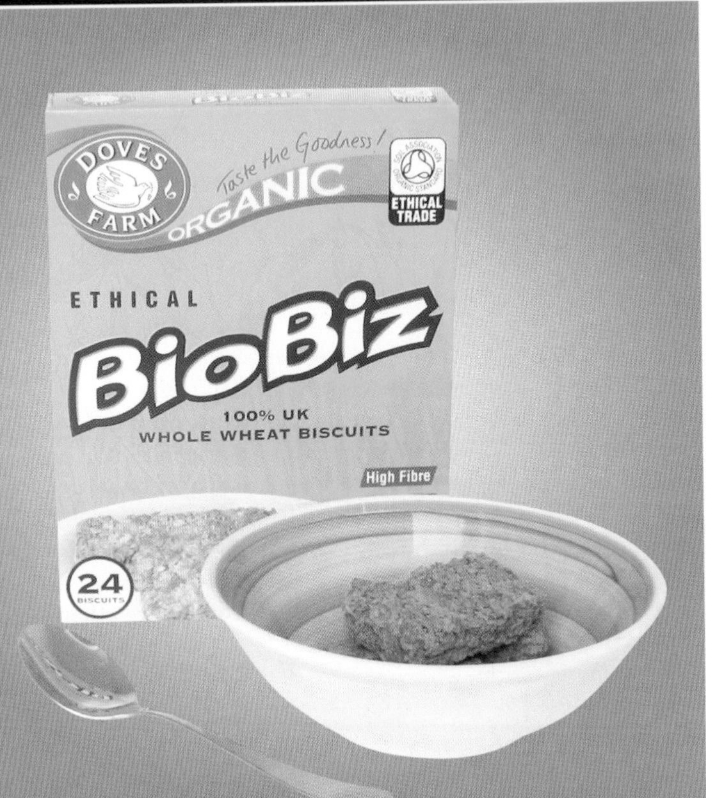

100% Organic UK Wheat
for the buzz thats the bizz
at breakfast

www.dovesfarm.co.uk 01488 684880

Our Bio Biz breakfast cereal is made with ethical organic wheat which has been finely flaked with a little malt extract, and compressed into a rectangular breakfast biscuit.

We only use wheat grown by UK organic farmers to Ethical Trade standards, which are independently certified by the Soil Association. The farmers and Doves Farm Foods are committed to;

- A fair price for the farmer
- Fair treatment of workers
- Local community support

Food quality, sustainability and the environment have been compelling forces for us since Doves Farm was established in 1978. Today our product range includes home baking flour, biscuits and snack bars and flapjacks as well as several breakfast cereals.

Breakfast cereals

There was a time, not long ago, when breakfast food manufacturers seemed to rule our lives. First thing in the morning, mums, dads and kids alike were easily persuaded that those first mouthfuls of cornflakes, sugar and milk were like manna from heaven. But the age of innocence is well and truly over.

A healthy start?

Breakfast cereals have long been a neat way for the food companies to take perfectly healthy food apart and put it back together again for profit. Inevitably these foods lose much of their nutritional benefit in the process, which is why the companies have to add all those vitamins again at the end, claiming that these make their product healthier and more special than any others.

Some companies make healthy eating claims about their products which are not, according to the Food Commission, substantiated with proper evidence. There was concern when Kellogg's claimed that they were 'serving the nation's health' while their Corn Flakes had been found to contain one of the highest salt levels on the cereals market. In 1998 the National Food Alliance found that some breakfast cereals were ten per cent saltier than sea water. (See relevent ECRA Research Supplement for details).

Sweetening the kiddies

The children's cereals sector makes up about a third of the British market for breakfast cereals, and that is why many products like Quaker's Sugar Puffs are deliberately packaged to attract children. Such products can be high in salt as well as low in fibre. One food author has complained that with sugar accounting for up to half the weight of the ingredients some products are 'twice as sweet as a jam doughnut'.

Other concerns

Pesticide residues are regularly detected in corn-based cereals even after processing, and research has shown that these residues find their way into 10-30 per cent of conventional breakfast cereals.

Until the tide turned against GM products, there was considerable doubt about the GM content of products made from soya or maize. Now Kellogg's products are reportedly free from proteins from GM crops. Weetabix Ltd stated that no GM ingredient, additive or derivatives are used in any of its processes. Quaker

Oats Ltd claimed that it does not use ingredients containing GM material in any Quaker product and that it had tested all lecithin used in its products to ensure freedom from any such material; the company also said it would only consider using ingredients derived from GM crops in the longer term if they had been fully approved by the relevant regulatory and scientific authorities.

- Doves Farm
- Infinity
- Jordans
- Mornflake
- Whole Earth

- Kallo
- Kashi
- Kellogg's
- Weetabix

- Quaker Oats
- Shredded Wheat

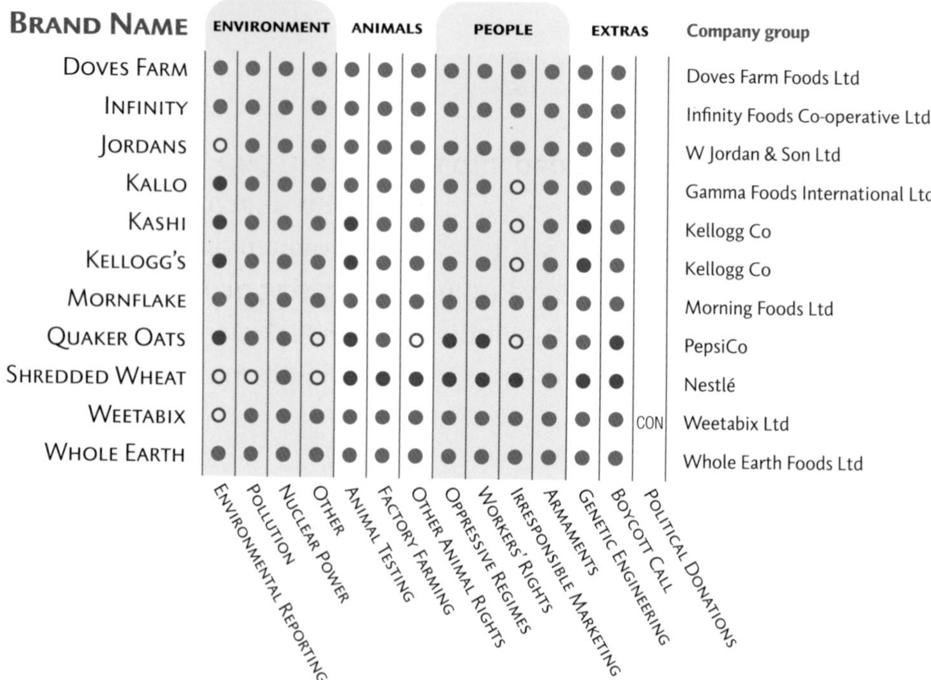

Brand Name	Environment: Environmental Reporting	Environment: Pollution	Environment: Nuclear Power	Environment: Other	Animals: Animal Testing	Animals: Factory Farming	Animals: Other Animal Rights	People: Oppressive Regimes	People: Workers' Rights	People: Irresponsible Marketing	People: Armaments	Extras: Genetic Engineering	Extras: Boycott Call	Extras: Political Donations	Company group
Doves Farm	Top	Top	Top	Top	Top	Top	Top	Top	Top	Top	Top	Top	Top		Doves Farm Foods Ltd
Infinity	Top	Top	Top	Top	Top	Top	Top	Top	Top	Top	Top	Top	Top		Infinity Foods Co-operative Ltd
Jordans	Middle	Top	Top	Top	Top	Top	Top	Top	Top	Top	Top	Top	Top		W Jordan & Son Ltd
Kallo	Bottom	Top	Top	Top	Top	Top	Top	Top	Top	Middle	Top	Top	Top		Gamma Foods International Ltd
Kashi	Bottom	Top	Top	Top	Bottom	Top	Top	Top	Top	Middle	Top	Bottom	Top		Kellogg Co
Kellogg's	Bottom	Top	Top	Top	Bottom	Top	Top	Top	Top	Middle	Top	Bottom	Top		Kellogg Co
Mornflake	Top	Top	Top	Top	Top	Top	Top	Top	Top	Top	Top	Top	Top		Morning Foods Ltd
Quaker Oats	Bottom	Top	Top	Middle	Bottom	Top	Middle	Bottom	Bottom	Middle	Top	Top	Bottom		PepsiCo
Shredded Wheat	Middle	Middle	Top	Middle	Bottom	Bottom	Bottom	Bottom	Bottom	Bottom	Top	Bottom	Bottom		Nestlé
Weetabix	Middle	Top	Top	Top	Top	Top	Top	Top	Top	Top	Top	Top	Top	CON	Weetabix Ltd
Whole Earth	Top	Top	Top	Top	Top	Top	Top	Top	Top	Top	Top	Top	Top		Whole Earth Foods Ltd

Key

- Top rating (no criticisms found)
- Middle rating
- Bottom rating
- A related company has a bottom rating and the company itself has a middle rating
- A related company has a middle rating
- A related company has a bottom rating

Source: ECRA-See page 14 for full key to symbols.

Butter & margarine

The world has long been divided into the lovers of pure butter, who defy the risks of too much cholesterol, and those who search for a palatable alternative. Although butter is still holding its own in the market, there have been huge advances in developing nice-tasting margarines, dairy spreads and vegan spreads – the drawback is that these tend to use a wide variety of different ingredients and additives, which we need to be aware of.

What's in them?

Butter is a simple product. It consists mainly of the fat found in cows' milk and it is not highly processed, beyond the churning that makes it go solid. But some of the 'spreadable' butters, the ones that stay soft in the fridge, may be blended with vegetable oil. Others are processed by breaking down the hard fats.

Margarine is usually more complex. It contains at least 80 per cent oils and fats – which can be of animal, fish or vegetable origin – as well as ingredients such as whey, vegetable colouring, flavouring and emulsifiers. Vitamins are also often added.

Any product with less than 80 per cent oils or fats has to be called a 'spread'. To be labelled as 'reduced fat' a spread may contain up to 60 per cent fat, and to be labelled as 'light' or 'low fat' it may have up to 40 per cent fat. Spreads contain at least as many added ingredients as margarine and some of the lower fat ones have gelatine and added water. The dairy spreads – the ones marketed as being 'butterlike' – contain added cream or buttermilk.

Although the major stores don't normally stock many vegan-friendly spreads, the wholefood shops usually sell a choice of products from companies like Granose, granoVita and Suma.

The search for health

During the 1980s, fears over the health risks of saturated fat convinced many people to switch from butter to margarine. But then in the 1990s it was discovered that trans fatty acids (TFAs) in margarine could raise the level of LDL, the 'bad cholesterol', by as much as saturates, while decreasing the level of HDL, the 'good cholesterol'. This is why some products, including some of the dairy spreads, are now marketed as having 'virtually no TFAs'.

Organic butter

Organic cows get better treatment than most – because they are never kept permanently indoors, which keeps them healthier, and their calves are suckled for around nine weeks.

GM issues

Many spreads and spreadable butters contain soya oils, which may be labelled simply as vegetable oil or fat. Many of these may be from GM soya beans. That's why it's better to look for products labelled as GM-free or organic.

Lecithin is a common additive derived from soya, and if it is of GM origin it need not be labelled as such on the grounds that there will be no DNA present.

Butter may not be unaffected by the GM issue, as the cows may have been given GM feed. Only organically-certified products will avoid GM entirely.

Packaging

Butter normally comes wrapped in a single piece of paper, and this is clearly better than the plastic tub packaging used for margarine and spreads. Although the tubs are marked as recyclable, how many of us actually do recycle them? If you are concerned you should contact your local authority to ask about recycling facilities.

Butter
- Anchor
- Castle Dairies
- Yeo Valley

Margarine
- GranoVita
- Pure
- Suma

Butter
- Kerrygold
- St Ivel Shirgar

Margarine
- Clover
- Utterly Butterly
- Vitalite

Butter
- Harmonie
- Lurpak

Margarine
- Benecol
- Flora
- Granose
- I Can't Believe it's Not Butter

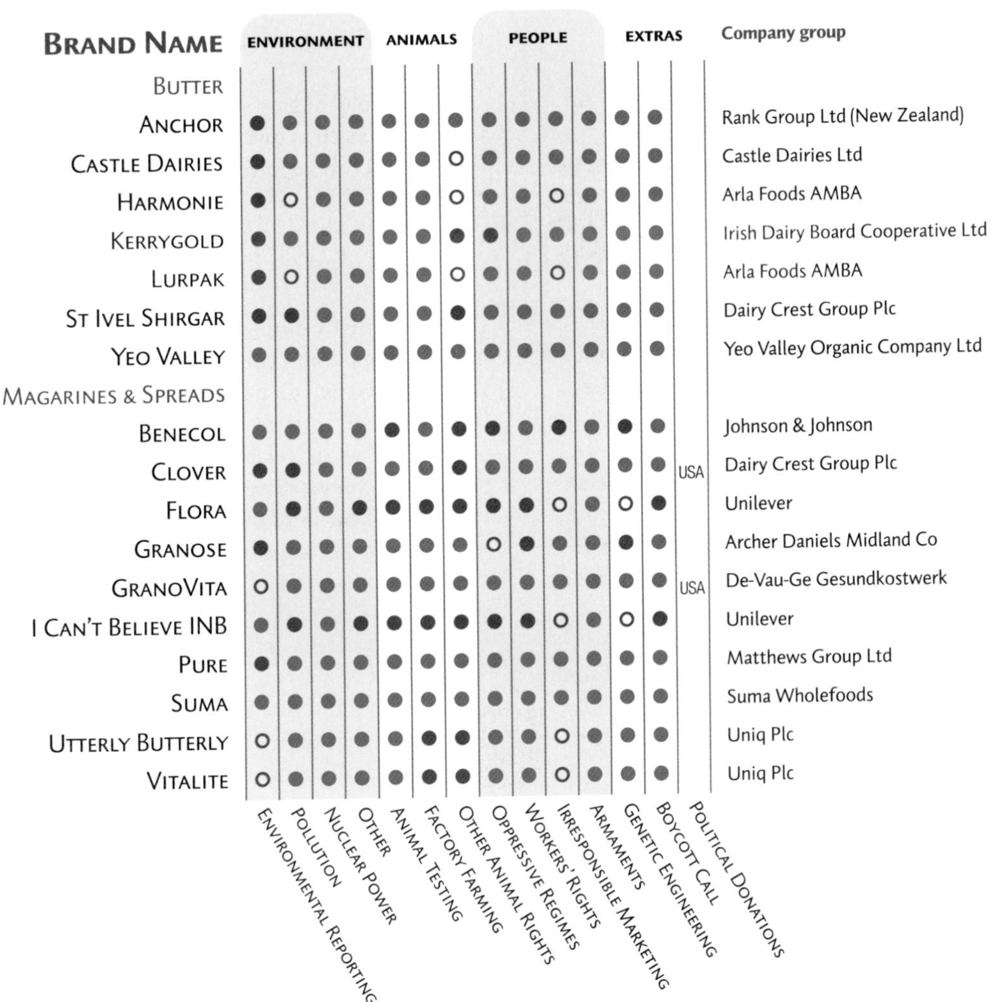

Brand Name
Environment
Animals
People
Extras
Company group
Butter
Anchor
Rank Group Ltd (New Zealand)
Castle Dairies
Castle Dairies Ltd
Harmonie
Arla Foods AMBA
Kerrygold
Irish Dairy Board Cooperative Ltd
Lurpak
Arla Foods AMBA
St Ivel Shirgar
Dairy Crest Group Plc
Yeo Valley
Yeo Valley Organic Company Ltd
Magarines & Spreads
Benecol
Johnson & Johnson
Clover
USA
Dairy Crest Group Plc
Flora
Unilever
Granose
Archer Daniels Midland Co
GranoVita
USA
De-Vau-Ge Gesundkostwerk
I Can't Believe INB
Unilever
Pure
Matthews Group Ltd
Suma
Suma Wholefoods
Utterly Butterly
Uniq Plc
Vitalite
Uniq Plc
Environmental Reporting
Pollution
Nuclear Power
Other
Animal Testing
Factory Farming
Other Animal Rights
Oppressive Regimes
Workers' Rights
Irresponsible Marketing
Armaments
Genetic Engineering
Boycott Call
Political Donations

Key

- Top rating (no criticisms found)
- Middle rating
- Bottom rating
- A related company has a bottom rating and the company itself has a middle rating
- A related company has a middle rating
- A related company has a bottom rating

Source: ECRA-See page 14 for full key to symbols.

Cat & dog food

We tend to get rather limited choice with the cat and dog food we buy in the supermarkets, because they mainly sell products from only two manufacturers – Mars and Nestlé. Apart from trying to find the healthiest and most organic alternatives, perhaps we should also be more aware of the bigger issues like animal testing and vegetarianism for pets.

Organic

Buying organic food is a way of avoiding factory-farmed meat, especially where a vegetarian diet is unsuitable. Some of the new organic brands are Yarrah and Pascoe's, both of which now sell in supermarkets.

We should always introduce new foods slowly to a pet, as they may not readily accept them at first. If it is possible feed pets home-cooked food although it is advisable to talk to a vet about this, as there is a risk of them developing imbalances in vitamins and minerals. Dogs need the right phosphorous/calcium ratio to maintain healthy bones. Without taurine, an amino acid that comes almost only from animal sources, cats can go blind. Feeding raw fish too often can cause neurological problems.

Animal testing

The British Union for the Abolition of Vivisection (BUAV) has discovered bad cases of animal testing by the pet food industry. It was found in 2000 that all the major companies had authorised tests when developing new products. These included: Alpo Pet Foods (Nestlé), Pedigree (Mars), Hills Pet Nutrition (Colgate-Palmolive), Ralston Purina and Iams (Procter & Gamble). Procedures in the UK may involve some of the following: isolation of animals for long periods, endoscopy and tissue biopsy, frequent changes of diet which may cause digestive distress, regular sedations and anaesthetics, enemas, application of skin irritants and plucking of hairs from the base of the tail. Experiments in the US are likely to be even more invasive.

Buy the dried stuff

Some dried food formulations are thought to be healthier than tinned food. Pets need to eat more tinned food than dried to gain the same amount of nutrition.

The environmental evidence is also in favour of dried food. Tinned foods are at least 60 per cent water, making the transported volume and weight much greater. Paper bags are obviously a lower environmental impact choice than tins.

Bulk-buying is preferable, whether in the form of large sacks or tins.

The new innovation of single-serve portions in plastic pouches and foil trays is utterly wasteful of resources.

VEGETARIAN PETS?

It is highly controversial but some argue that dogs can be fed a vegan diet, and three companies at least make vegan and vegetarian dog food – Top Number Feeds (Happidog), Suma (Wackidog) and Vink Sales (Yarrah). Vink also makes meat and fish-based products.

Cats do need meat because they require taurine. If they are deprived of it they will soon turn to hunting birds and mice for meat. However, the Vegan Society imports something called Vegecat from the US, designed for adding to home-cooked cat food.

- Hi-Life
- Pascoe's
- Wackidog (dog food only)
- Wagg (dog food only)
- Webbox (dog food only)
- Yarrah

- Butchers (dog food only)
- Eukanuba
- Hills Science Diet
- Iams

- Bakers Complete (dog food only)
- Friskies
- Omega Complete (cat food only)
- Pedigree (dog food only)
- Spillers
- Whiskas (cat food only)

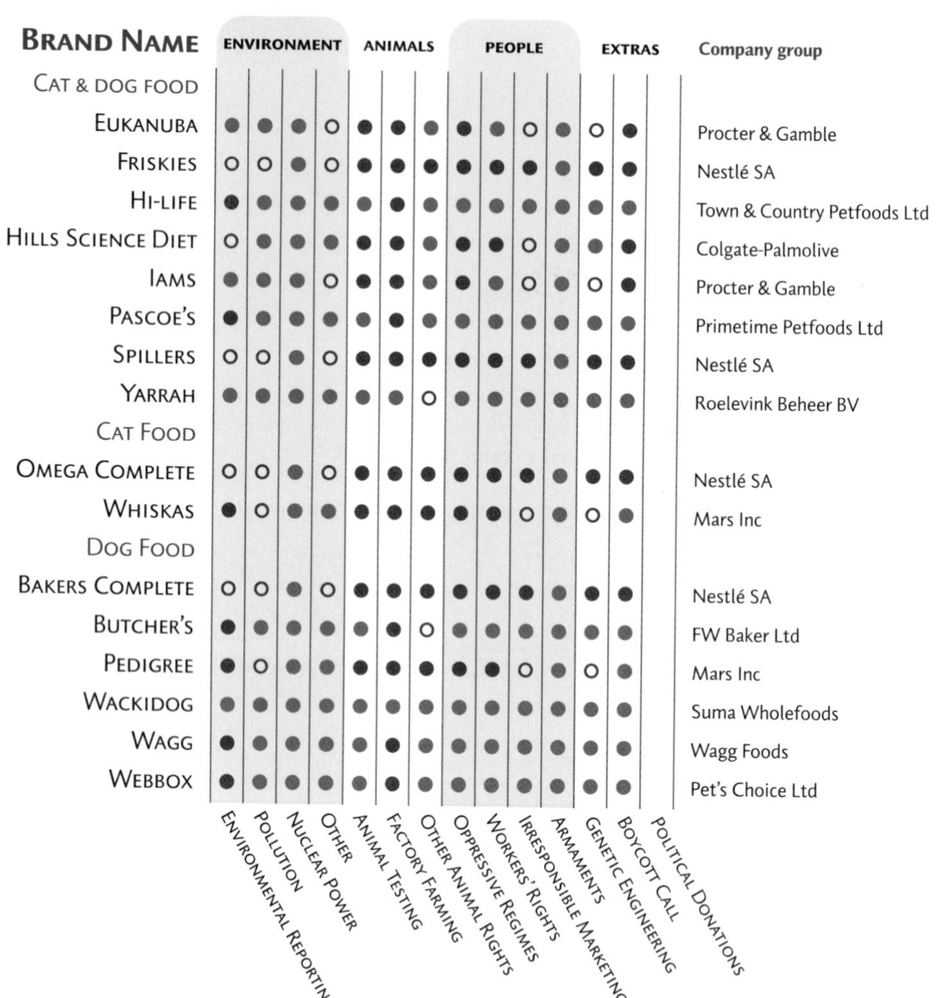

Key

- ● Top rating (no criticisms found)
- ○ Middle rating
- ● Bottom rating
- ● A related company has a bottom rating and the company itself has a middle rating
- ○ A related company has a middle rating
- ● A related company has a bottom rating

Source: ECRA-See page 14 for full key to symbols.

Chocolate

Consumers in the Western world are much more interested than they used to be in where their favourite foods come from and how they are grown. They need to be. The processes behind the trading of the most important commodities can be very ugly indeed, even leading to war in some countries. In Ivory Coast in 2002, for example, most of the foreign workers in the cocoa plantations were driven away by thugs encouraged by the ruling party. But such is the importance of the country to the cocoa trade that powerful foreign interests have up to now made sure that the country has not descended into civil war. Hopefully, normality will return and some of the abuses of the past, including child labour, can be eliminated too.

Child labour

Thanks to press investigations and television documentaries, the issue of child labour has been highlighted as a problem in several countries. The chocolate industry has been developing a Global Industry Protocol and has promised that a method of certifying that cocoa has been grown 'under appropriate labour conditions' will be in place by July 2005. Part of this process is a survey into child labour carried out by the International Institute of Tropical Agriculture in Ivory Coast, Cameroon, Ghana and Nigeria and published in July 2002. It found that the majority of children working on cocoa farms were under 14, and that approximately one-third of school-age children living in cocoa-producing households had never been to school.

In normal times, Ivory Coast produces nearly half of the world's cocoa and, according to a report published in the Earth Island Journal, it is hard to ensure that Ivory Coast cocoa is 'slavery-free'. Mars and Nestlé have tended to buy large amounts of cocoa from Ivory Coast, whereas Cadbury's has said that it buys 90 per cent of its cocoa from Ghana, which is a signatory to a tough code of conduct against trafficking child workers.

Fair Trade

Buying Fair Trade marked chocolate is currently the best way to avoid support for child labour and commodity traders. All of Traidcraft and Day Chocolate Company's chocolate is Fair Trade marked, as is Green & Black's Maya Gold. Traidcraft's organic chocolate contains fair trade sugar as well as cocoa and so has the highest proportion of fairly traded ingredients. Day Chocolate Company has taken the fair trade ethos furthest, being part-owned by the Kuapa Kokoo Co-operative in Ghana.

Plamil, a vegan company, doesn't use the Fair Trade mark on the grounds that it only protects humans from exploitation and not animals, but it says that its cocoa is all sourced from the Dominican Republic and fulfils the social standards set out by the Fairtrade Labelling Organisation.

Cadbury's has a supplier code which, it says, 'measures up to the conventions of the International Labour Organisation, and applies to all their business units, managed internally.' But it has not published a copy of this code. None of the other companies have revealed if they have a supplier code of conduct.

Tricky issues

One major concern about the cocoa industry is how many chemical fertilisers and pesticides the farmers use. The best protection for the cocoa trees is for farmers to do mixed planting, which also enables the farmers to provide their own food, as well as using the income from cocoa to pay for health-care, education and other costs. Although their chocolate is not certified organic, the Day Chocolate Company says that it is very unusual for its farmers to use chemicals.

The pesticide lindane has been banned for agricultural and horticultural use in the EU, on the grounds that it is a hormone disrupter linked with health problems such as breast cancer, but it is still used on cocoa plantations, exposing the workers to potential health risks. Chocolate companies say they have no way of knowing whether their cocoa is sprayed with lindane, as they don't buy direct from the growers. They should be encouraged to do their own tests.

Until recently, EU regulations did not permit British milk chocolate to be labelled as chocolate on the continent, because of its 5 per cent vegetable fat content. Bowing to pressure from British companies, the EU has now agreed that it can be labelled as 'family milk chocolate' rather than as 'vegelate'. The lower cocoa content can mean less money for the cocoa farmers. Cadbury's Dairy Milk, for example, only contains around 20 per cent cocoa solids.

- Divine
- Green & Blacks
- Plamil
- Traidcraft

- Kinder Egg
- Lindt
- Ritter Sport
- Thornton's

- Dairy Milk
- Chocolate Orange
- KitKat
- Mars Bar

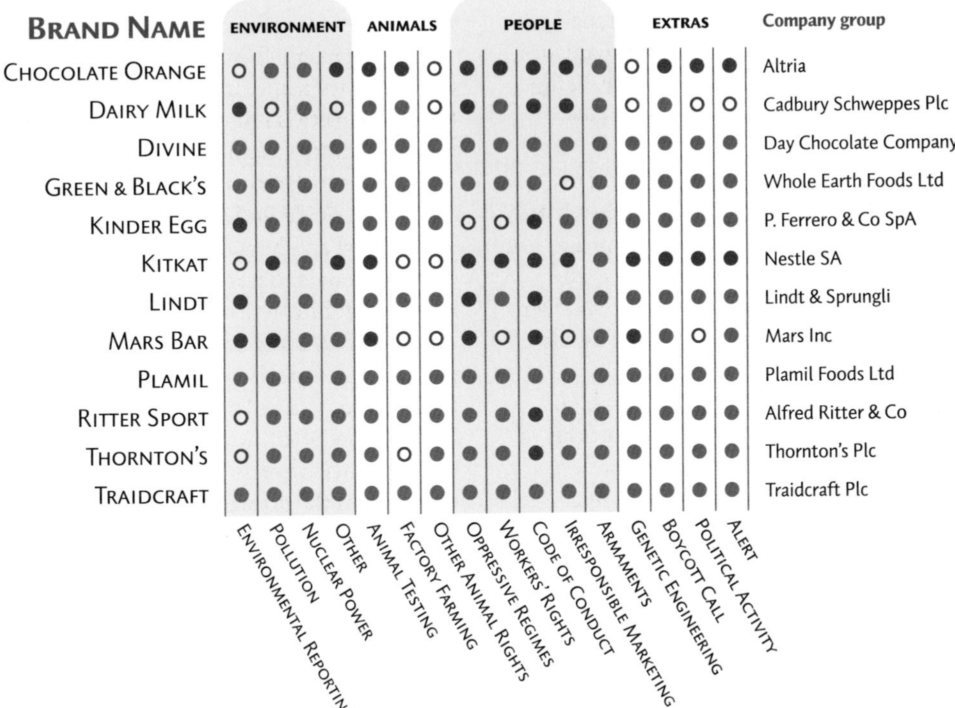

Brand Name	Environment				Animals			People					Extras				Company group
	Environmental Reporting	Pollution	Nuclear Power	Other	Animal Testing	Factory Farming	Other Animal Rights	Oppressive Regimes	Workers' Rights	Code of Conduct	Irresponsible Marketing	Armaments	Genetic Engineering	Boycott Call	Political Activity	Alert	
Chocolate Orange	Middle	Top	Top	Bottom	Bottom	Bottom	Middle	Bottom	Bottom	Bottom	Bottom	Top	Middle	Bottom	Bottom	Bottom	Altria
Dairy Milk	Bottom	Middle	Top	Middle	Top	Top	Middle	Bottom	Top	Bottom	Bottom	Top	Middle	Top	Middle	Middle	Cadbury Schweppes Plc
Divine	Top	Top	Top	Top	Top	Top	Top	Top	Top	Top	Top	Top	Top	Top	Top	Top	Day Chocolate Company
Green & Black's	Top	Top	Top	Top	Top	Top	Top	Top	Top	Top	Middle	Top	Top	Top	Top	Top	Whole Earth Foods Ltd
Kinder Egg	Bottom	Top	Top	Top	Top	Top	Top	Middle	Middle	Bottom	Top	Top	Top	Top	Top	Top	P. Ferrero & Co SpA
KitKat	Middle	Bottom	Top	Bottom	Bottom	Middle	Middle	Bottom	Bottom	Bottom	Bottom	Top	Bottom	Bottom	Bottom	Bottom	Nestle SA
Lindt	Bottom	Top	Top	Top	Top	Top	Top	Bottom	Top	Bottom	Top	Top	Top	Top	Top	Top	Lindt & Sprungli
Mars Bar	Bottom	Bottom	Top	Top	Bottom	Middle	Middle	Bottom	Middle	Bottom	Middle	Top	Bottom	Top	Middle	Top	Mars Inc
Plamil	Top	Top	Top	Top	Top	Top	Top	Top	Top	Top	Top	Top	Top	Top	Top	Top	Plamil Foods Ltd
Ritter Sport	Middle	Top	Top	Top	Top	Top	Top	Top	Top	Bottom	Top	Top	Top	Top	Top	Top	Alfred Ritter & Co
Thornton's	Middle	Top	Top	Top	Top	Middle	Top	Top	Top	Bottom	Top	Top	Top	Top	Top	Top	Thornton's Plc
Traidcraft	Top	Top	Top	Top	Top	Top	Top	Top	Top	Top	Top	Top	Top	Top	Top	Top	Traidcraft Plc

Key

- Top rating (no criticisms found)
- Middle rating
- Bottom rating
- A related company has a bottom rating and the company itself has a middle rating
- A related company has a middle rating
- A related company has a bottom rating

Source: ECRA-See page 14 for full key to symbols.

Cooking oil

With olive oil being touted as an antidote to ageing, there's little wonder that nearly every granny now pours it over her salads. But we should be aware that the great rush to expand production in Mediterranean countries is threatening the local ecology and causing serious soil erosion. So it's best to buy organic if you can, it's even more delicious and better for the environment. Here, we look at the major branded cooking oils, including supermarket own-brands.

Trouble in Spain

An important advantage of most olive oil is that it is almost certain to be GM-free, but the food and development organisation Sustain reports that over-intensification of olive oil production in Spain has resulted in erosion and other agronomic and environmental problems, causing irreversible damage in over 40 per cent of Andalucia. The new methods of production have also involved increasing the use of herbicides, pesticides and fungicides. Sustain recommends that consumers choose organic olive oil wherever possible.

Purity at a cost

Most of the UK's oilseed rape is grown as a winter crop, which Sustain argues has had a detrimental effect on Britain's environment, causing biodiversity to suffer and bird populations to decline. Winter crops have also at times provided an excuse for mass shooting of wood pigeons.

Although British farmers are not likely to be introducing GM crops yet, the whole GM issue remains important with cooking oils, simply because much of our oil is imported and because most of the major oil seeds have already been the targets of experimentation. Worryingly for consumers concerned with GM issues, vegetable oil produced from GM plants does not have to be labelled as GM – this is because the processing of oils means that neither protein nor DNA is thought to be present. Those who want to avoid any GM link should opt for sunflower oil, olive oil or organic oils. We should be aware that maize oil, soya oil and canola (rapeseed) oils may be processed from GM plants, especially if they originate from Canada. Some companies are trying to source their vegetable oils from GM-free crops, but progress has been patchy. Consumers can ask their stores for their policy on GM oil.

Own-brand oils

Most supermarkets refuse to say which companies produce their own-brand cooking oils. Pressure from consumers may change this policy eventually, but until we can be certain of the identity of the own-brand suppliers, the brands will continue to be rated with the supermarket. Unlike other companies, supermarkets are rated according to their stocking policies.

60-second green guide

- Buy glass bottles in preference to plastic ones
- There is little risk of active GM materials being present in any oil
- For the least risk of GM 'contamination', use olive oil
- Most vegetable oils are equally good for you

Packaging

More expensive oils are likely to be in glass bottles, which are easy to recycle. But products in the lower price range are almost always packaged in plastic bottles, some of which may be made from PVC (which is identifiable by a '3' inside a recycling symbol on the base of the bottle). Plastic recycling in the UK is still very poorly developed, with about 95 per cent of it still being landfilled or incinerated.

- Filippo Berio
- Pura
- Suma

- Marks & Spencer
- Meridian
- Princes
- Safeway
- Sainsbury

- Asda
- Crisp & Dry
- Flora
- Mazola
- Olivio
- Tesco

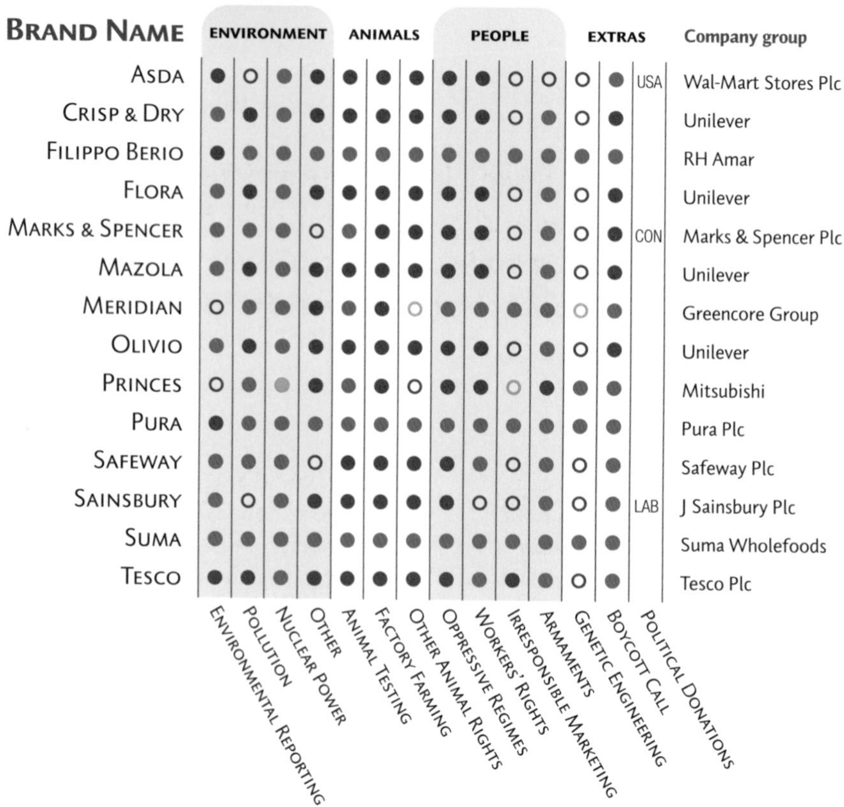

Key

- Top rating (no criticisms found)
- Middle rating
- Bottom rating
- A related company has a bottom rating and the company itself has a middle rating
- A related company has a middle rating
- A related company has a bottom rating

Source: ECRA-See page 14 for full key to symbols.

Crisps

The big crisp manufacturers make a lot of noise and fuss in their efforts to make kids fall in love with their crisps but they prefer to only whisper about what their products are made of, what additives they put in and the more general health risks. Probably the best way for us to reduce these risks is to look for organic crisps.

Keeping kids healthy

Recently, the Food Commission sharply criticised snacks promoted by footballers and accused the food marketing firms of undermining children's nutrition. A supermarket survey had failed to find any healthy children's food promoted with football imagery, Walkers' being the main culprit with its tartrazine-laced Footballs, promotions in association with Gary Lineker and David Seaman and a FA Premier League sticker-offer in its other brands. 'It would be better if children were shown that the way to emulate their sporting heroes is to eat and drink healthily,' said one mother on the Food Commission's Parents' Jury.

Crisps can be healthier than a lot of junk foods, but they should be eaten in moderation. A recent study by Baby Organix found that children are consuming more than twice as much salt in their diet as the government recommends. The UK Asthma & Allergy Research Centre says that 'significant changes in children's hyperactive behaviour could be produced by the removal of colourings and additives from their diet.' It is recommended that brilliant blue (E133), tartrazine (E102), quinoline yellow (E104) and sunset yellow (E110), colours which appear most commonly in kiddie snacks like Monster Munch, should be eliminated from kids' diets. Monosodium glutamate (E621) is another controversial additive present in many crisps, despite being banned for use in baby foods.

Some crisp manufacturers are also moving into the wholesale use of artificial sweeteners because they cost a fraction of the price of sugar. Many are then ignoring their legal obligation to state directly under the brand name that a product contains sweeteners, consigning it instead to the small print.

Natural and organic

Tra'fo, Kettle, Cape Cod and Jonathan Crisp products contain only 'natural' ingredients.

Companies have a small circle in the GE column on the table if not all of their products can be guaranteed not to contain GM-derived ingredients. Although companies in Britain have made considerable progress in sourcing non-GM derivatives, many on the 'red list', including Golden Wonder, are there because of lack of assurances that dairy ingredients like whey are from non-GM fed cows.

Certified organic products are always totally GM-free. Many supermarkets are now selling own-brand organic crisps, which are being manufactured for them by companies such as Stour Valley Foods. Jonathan Crisp and Tra'fo crisps are all organic, and Kettle has one organic variety.

Monsanto is currently developing a 'higher-solids' potato, which will absorb less oil during processing, as well as bruise-free potatoes. It remains to be seen whether they will fare better than its Bt potatoes, which companies such as McDonalds, P&G and Pepsi subsidiary Frito-Lay are now refusing to use, even in the US, due to the high level of public concern about the technology.

Packaging

Old-fashioned polypropylene packets as used by Seabrooks, and a lot of the '10p snacks', are in theory easier to recycle than the plasticated foils which most manufacturers now use.

Pringles cartons are the ultimate packaging excess. They contain six different materials, including steel, aluminium, PET and polyethylene, some of them in composite form. As Pringles now make up at least ten per cent of the entire UK 'bagged snacks' market, they are becoming a significant contributor to landfill waste.

- Highlander Snacks
- Jonathan Crisp
- Kettle Chips
- Red Mill
- Stour Valley
- Tra'Fo

- Bensons
- Cape Cod
- Golden Wonder
- Mission Foods
- Seabrook

- Brannigans
- KP
- Phileas Fogg
- Pringles
- Walkers

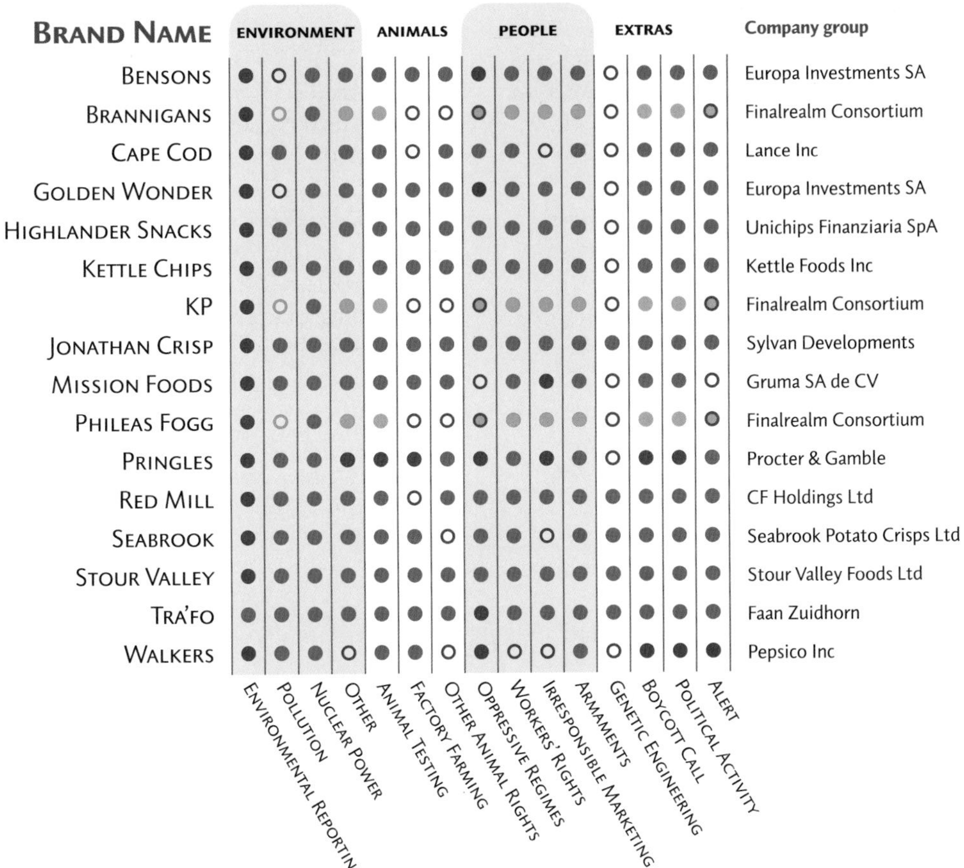

BRAND NAME
ENVIRONMENT
ANIMALS
PEOPLE
EXTRAS
Company group
BENSONS
BRANNIGANS
CAPE COD
GOLDEN WONDER
HIGHLANDER SNACKS
KETTLE CHIPS
KP
JONATHAN CRISP
MISSION FOODS
PHILEAS FOGG
PRINGLES
RED MILL
SEABROOK
STOUR VALLEY
TRA'FO
WALKERS
Europa Investments SA
Finalrealm Consortium
Lance Inc
Europa Investments SA
Unichips Finanziaria SpA
Kettle Foods Inc
Finalrealm Consortium
Sylvan Developments
Gruma SA de CV
Finalrealm Consortium
Procter & Gamble
CF Holdings Ltd
Seabrook Potato Crisps Ltd
Stour Valley Foods Ltd
Faan Zuidhorn
Pepsico Inc
ENVIRONMENTAL REPORTING
POLLUTION
NUCLEAR POWER
OTHER
ANIMAL TESTING
FACTORY FARMING
OTHER ANIMAL RIGHTS
OPPRESSIVE REGIMES
WORKERS' RIGHTS
IRRESPONSIBLE MARKETING
ARMAMENTS
GENETIC ENGINEERING
BOYCOTT CALL
POLITICAL ACTIVITY
ALERT

Key

- Top rating (no criticisms found)
- Middle rating
- Bottom rating
- A related company has a bottom rating and the company itself has a middle rating
- A related company has a middle rating
- A related company has a bottom rating

Source: ECRA-See page 14 for full key to symbols.

Sustainable fishing

It was once thought that the sea was an inexhaustible source of fish. Yet over-exploitation of this natural resource has resulted in depleted fish stocks and damaged marine eco-systems. Overfishing is one of the world's most pressing environmental issues. The social and economic impacts are severe too. Billions of people depend upon seafood as a major food staple and hundreds of thousands depend on the seafood industry for employment. The need to reverse this trend is paramount to the survival of the industry, those who depend on it and the natural marine environment.

THE ISSUE

A fishery is an area of the sea where the target fish species is caught by net, line or another fishing method. Fisheries that are ecologically balanced and are not depleted of natural resource are becoming increasingly rare. According to the Food and Agriculture Organisation (FAO 2002), only one quarter of the worlds fish stocks are within safe environmental levels. The remaining fish stocks are either partly or fully overfished or in a serious stage of depletion. This means that the majority of the world's fisheries are in need of management reviews if they are not to be lost forever.

The consequences of overfishing are occurring already. In 1992, one of the world's richest natural resources, the cod stocks off the Canadian Grand Banks, Newfoundland, disappeared virtually overnight as a result of poor fisheries management with devastating consequences for the marine environment and the local community. About 40,000 jobs were lost and the fishery still remains closed today.

There are numerous reasons for the collapse of fisheries and the depletion of fish stocks. Technological advances have enabled the fishing industry to target the resource more precisely and take more from our seas than is sustainable. Bigger boats, more powerful engines, developments in radar and sophisticated refrigeration systems mean that fishermen can stay out at sea for longer, travel further and locate fish more easily. Catching fish, therefore, is no longer a lottery and as a result more fish are being caught then ever before. Another reason for the collapse of fisheries is the marketplace, which sanctions overfishing by allowing the sale of endangered fish for profit. The problem is that the market is about today and tomorrow and maybe next week but certainly not about ten years' time.

People and food

In the developed world, seafood is regularly enjoyed by billions of people for taste and health reasons. However, the current unsustainable fishing climate is more of a threat to developing countries, where 3.5 billion people currently depend upon the ocean for their primary source of food (UNEP 2004). If fish stocks continue to deplete, then demand for fish in these coastal areas may outstrip the supply.

Livelihood and empoyment

As a major renewable resource, fisheries provide a livelihood for hundreds of thousands of people around the world, sustaining coastal communities and representing a valuable source of income to the global community. The role of fishermen is crucial in the lives of many a community who fish for local needs. 90% operate on a small-scale, accounting for over half of the global fish catch (UNEP 2004). These are the fishermen who increasingly will be squeezed by the large operators who come in search of new stocks as they exhaust the old. It is the greed of the rich world that has produced the shortages and it will be the wealth of the rich world which will buy what fish are left even though it is essential to the very existence of the poor.

Fishermen around the world need to be assured of the future of the fishing industry for the sake of their livelihoods, whether they fish on a local scale or on a much larger scale. Unsustainable fishing affects fishermen in both developed and developing countries alike.

Call to action

Raising awareness of overfishing is the first step to tackling the problem.

Ethical consumers can demand fish from sustainable and well-managed stocks to help safeguard the world's seafood supply. This will put pressure on retailers to stock sustainably harvested seafood products. This in turn will help to provide incentives for the seafood industry to fish in a responsible way.

One solution – Marine Stewardship Council (MSC)

In the mid 1990s conservationists and industrialists alike saw that they had a common interest in changing the marketplace in terms of its operation. This lead to the creation of the Marine Stewardship Council (MSC) an international charity dedicated to saving the world's fish stocks. The MSC created an environmental standard to reward well-managed and sustainable fisheries. Fisheries of any size, scale, type or location can voluntarily apply to assessed against the MSC Standard by independent certification bodies.
The MSC Standard considers the condition of the fish stock, the impact of fishing on the marine ecosystem and the management of the fishery. If they pass, products from certified fisheries win the right to use the MSC blue eco-label, harnessing consumer preference for sustainable seafood. It is possible to protect fish stocks and marine ecosystems whilst continuing to fish, if the fishing is conducted in a responsible manner.

Examples of responsible fishing include building escape hatches into lobster creel pots, as in the Western Australian Rock Lobster fishery, the first in the world to receive the MSC environmental standard. These hatches will enable small lobsters to escape and reproduce whilst the adults remain within the creel. Another example from the Scottish Loch Torridon and Nephrops fishery, certified to the MSC Standard, is fisherman throwing juvenile fish back into the sea to allow them to reproduce, ensuring that the fish stock remains healthy. Measures to reducing by-catch are also being adopted in order to maintain healthy ecosystems. By-catch, such as fish, marine mammals and seabirds, can be caught accidentally by fishing gear and then thrown dead back into the ocean, disrupting the natural balance of the marine ecosystem. The New Zealand hoki fishery, certified to the MSC Standard, is implementing various measures to the fishery to reduce by-catch.

There are currently 10 fisheries certified to the MSC Standard and over 40 fisheries are at some stage of the fishery assessment process, which equates to approximately 4% of the total wild global fish supply.

The MSC provides a solution to the global problem of overfishing and is a market driven programme. Today there are over 200 seafood products carrying the MSC label in seventeen countries. New products are appearing every week. The consumer is empowered to make the best environmental choice in seafood, which is needed to complete the circle of influence that uses market forces to ensure the future of sustainable fisheries.

For information on where to buy MSC labelled products please visit www.msc.org Through our specific buying habits we can all help place a global industry back on a path to stability and long-term sustainability.

For more information, visit *www.mcsuk.org* or see relevant links from *www.gooshing.co.uk*

Ice cream

Pure ice cream should be made like an egg custard, churned and frozen, but the purer it is the more expensive it is. The cheaper ice creams on the market are combinations of skimmed milk or milk powders, with lots of sugar and sweeteners, and things like hardened vegetable fats, emulsifiers, colourings, flavourings, acidity regulators and other artificial processing aids, whipped up with lots of air. If we want to avoid all these phoney things, we should look for organic dairy ice creams or, if we can find them, organic non-dairy ones. All the dairy ice creams in this report are organic, although it also includes a few non-organic (non-dairy) ice creams and sorbets.

Ingredients to avoid

A quick look at the ingredients list should be enough to know what level of additives the product contains. We should look out for the worse E-numbers, such as annatto (E160b), sunset yellow (E110) and carmoisine (E122) as they have been linked to health problems such as asthma, rashes and hyperactivity; some have also been linked to cancer in test animals. Particular concern has been raised about E110, a coal-tar dye which is a by-product of the petrochemical industry; because of its toxic risks, manufacturers have been persuaded not to use it in baby food.

The growth hormone bovine somatotropin (commonly called rBST here, or BGH in the US) was designed to be given daily to cows to increase their milk yield. Because of serious health concerns for cows and for humans, the EU introduced a moratorium on the drug which is still in effect, meaning the use of rBST is not currently legal in the EU. The Soil Association says that their organic standards prohibit the use of rBST in the production of milk. All the non-dairy alternatives naturally do not contain this hormone. The Organic Consumers Association in the US has an ongoing boycott of Häagen-Dazs in protest of its use of milk from cows injected with rBST.

Organic options

Manufacturers of organic ice cream generally have a good awareness of the benefits of natural ingredients. All the smaller producers of ice cream covered in this report state their commitment to minimising the use of artificial ingredients.

Some larger retailers are also reducing the amount of artificial additives in some ranges and selling more organic goods, which by their nature are likely to contain a high proportion of natural ingredients.

Of the non-dairy alternatives, First Foods' First Glacé appears to contain the least additives. First Foods states that its products contain 'no artificial additives, colouring or flavouring.' Neither Mother Hemp nor Fayrefield Foods (Swedish Glacé) list the ingredients for their products on their websites, or make a statement regarding additives, although both claim to be cholesterol-free.

Taste tests

The UK Consumers' Association recently held taste tests for a range of ice creams and frozen desserts. Green & Blacks' chocolate ice cream came out as a favourite, and its vanilla range went down well too. Rocombe Farm's chocolate and vanilla flavours also tingled the taste buds, both coming out with an 'above average' rating. The Swedish Glacé vanilla flavour came up trumps, although Tofutti's equivalent didn't fare so well, scoring an 'average' rating, as did its chocolate dessert.

Organic
- Cream O'Galloway
- Green & Blacks
- Little Big Food Co
- Rocombe Farm

Non-Dairy Desserts
- Mother Hemp
- Rocombe Farm

Organic
- Safeway
- Waitrose

Non-Dairy Desserts
- First Glace
- Swedish Glace
- Tofutti

Organic
- Sainsbury's
- Tesco

Non-Dairy Desserts
- Carte D'Or
- Haagen-Dazs

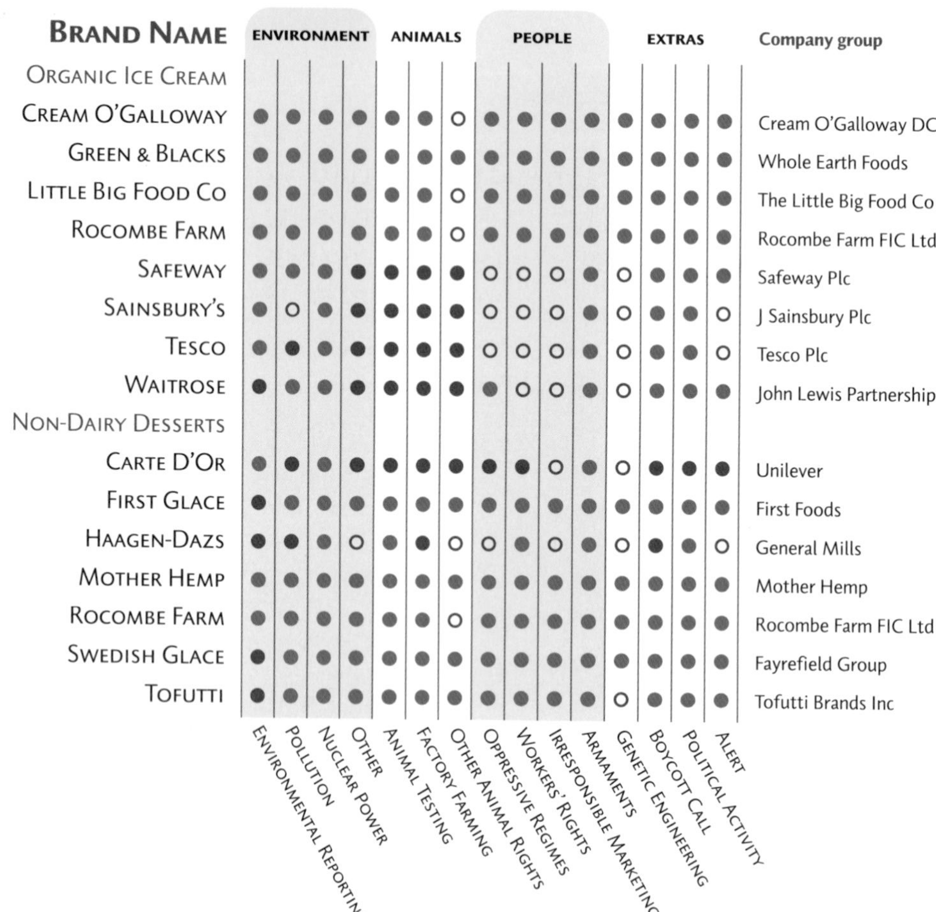

Brand Name	Environment: Environmental Reporting	Environment: Pollution	Environment: Nuclear Power	Environment: Other	Animals: Animal Testing	Animals: Factory Farming	Animals: Other Animal Rights	People: Oppressive Regimes	People: Workers' Rights	People: Irresponsible Marketing	People: Armaments	Extras: Genetic Engineering	Extras: Boycott Call	Extras: Political Activity	Extras: Alert	Company group
Organic Ice Cream																
Cream O'Galloway	Top	Top	Top	Top	Top	Top	Middle	Top	Top	Top	Top	Top	Top	Top	Top	Cream O'Galloway DC
Green & Blacks	Top	Top	Top	Top	Top	Top	Top	Top	Top	Top	Top	Top	Top	Top	Top	Whole Earth Foods
Little Big Food Co	Top	Top	Top	Top	Top	Top	Middle	Top	Top	Top	Top	Top	Top	Top	Top	The Little Big Food Co
Rocombe Farm	Top	Top	Top	Top	Top	Top	Middle	Top	Top	Top	Top	Top	Top	Top	Top	Rocombe Farm FIC Ltd
Safeway	Top	Top	Top	Bottom	Bottom	Bottom	Bottom	Middle	Middle	Middle	Top	Middle	Top	Top	Top	Safeway Plc
Sainsbury's	Top	Middle	Top	Bottom	Bottom	Bottom	Bottom	Middle	Middle	Middle	Top	Middle	Top	Top	Middle	J Sainsbury Plc
Tesco	Top	Bottom	Top	Bottom	Bottom	Bottom	Bottom	Middle	Middle	Middle	Top	Middle	Top	Top	Middle	Tesco Plc
Waitrose	Bottom	Top	Top	Bottom	Bottom	Bottom	Bottom	Top	Middle	Middle	Top	Middle	Top	Top	Top	John Lewis Partnership
Non-Dairy Desserts																
Carte D'Or	Top	Bottom	Top	Bottom	Bottom	Bottom	Bottom	Bottom	Bottom	Middle	Top	Middle	Bottom	Bottom	Bottom	Unilever
First Glace	Bottom	Top	Top	Top	Top	Top	Top	Top	Top	Top	Top	Top	Top	Top	Top	First Foods
Haagen-Dazs	Bottom	Bottom	Top	Middle	Top	Bottom	Middle	Middle	Top	Middle	Top	Middle	Bottom	Top	Middle	General Mills
Mother Hemp	Top	Top	Top	Top	Top	Top	Top	Top	Top	Top	Top	Top	Top	Top	Top	Mother Hemp
Rocombe Farm	Top	Top	Top	Top	Top	Top	Middle	Top	Top	Top	Top	Top	Top	Top	Top	Rocombe Farm FIC Ltd
Swedish Glace	Bottom	Top	Top	Top	Top	Top	Top	Top	Top	Top	Top	Top	Top	Top	Top	Fayrefield Group
Tofutti	Bottom	Top	Top	Top	Top	Top	Top	Top	Top	Top	Top	Middle	Top	Top	Top	Tofutti Brands Inc

Key

- Top rating (no criticisms found)
- Middle rating
- Bottom rating
- A related company has a bottom rating and the company itself has a middle rating
- A related company has a middle rating
- A related company has a bottom rating

Source: ECRA-See page 14 for full key to symbols.

Jams & spreads

Although home-made jams, marmalade, lemon curd and other spreads usually have much better ingredients than those on the supermarket shelves, few of us have the time or opportunity to make the stuff. So if you want to have the healthiest spreads for breakfast and tea-time you need first to have a look at what goes into the shop varieties. The volume leaders are Robertsons and Chivers-Hartley, while Chivers-Hartley is also the largest own-brand maker. Baxters and Duerrs make own-brands too.

Fruit levels

To be called jam, a preserve needs only to have a minimum of 35 per cent fruit content, while marmalade can have as little as 20 per cent fruit. We should be aware that in many commercial jams some of the fruit can be from frozen or concentrate sources. Also the fruit and sugar is heavily boiled, which reduces the nutritional value.

Extra jam has 45g of fruit per 100g. Compôtes are preserves with very high fruit levels, so they do not set in the same way as traditional jam, but they retain much more of the nutritional value of the fruit.

Other ingredients

To be called jam or marmalade, a preserve has to have at least 60g of sugar per 100g of product – even for the extra-fruit varieties. Reduced-sugar jams have 30-55g, but will often have added colour, emulsifier, preservative and stabiliser. Fruit spreads are usually purely derived from fruit, relying on a fruit juice such as apple for sweetness. This means they are best kept in the fridge as they do not keep as long as sugar-rich jam or marmalade.

Artificial sweeteners may be used in 'diet' products, under a variety of guises such as aspartame, saccharin or xylitol. In higher fruit-content products, preservatives may be used. Preservatives such as potassium sorbate (E200-213) are suspected of causing allergic reactions, gastric irritations and problems with conception in some people. Manufacturers could avoid using them by noting a shorter shelf life and recommending refrigeration.

Lemon curd contains eggs, which are likely to be battery-produced except in the case of organic products. Some jellies and jams may contain gelatine, an animal by-product, to aid with setting.

No genetically engineered fruit is permitted in the UK but the enzymes used to process the fruit, gelatine or added sweeteners could have involved GM. Choosing organic products allows us to avoid all these additives. The only brand that is exclusively organic is Bionova. Other companies, such as Meridian, Whole Earth, Hartleys (Wm P Hartley brand) and Baxters, make some organic jams. The Herb Stall was the only organic lemon curd producer found at the time of the survey.

Packaging

Although most fruit preserves are packed in glass jars, there has been some use of squeezy plastic bottles or pouches by companies like Hartleys and Robertsons. Some honey manufacturers are starting to pack their products in rigid plastic jars, and this could happen in the jam market too.

- Bionova
- The Herb Stall
- Whole Earth

- Baxters
- Bonne Maman
- Duerr's
- Stute
- Tiptree

- Chivers
- Frank Cooper
- Hartley's
- Meridian
- Robertsons

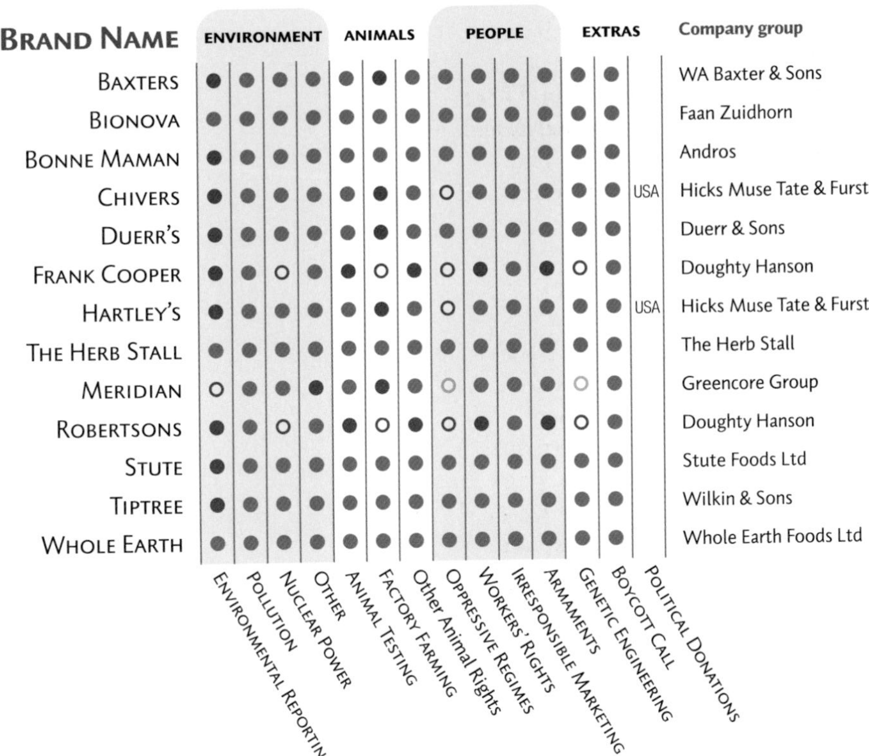

Brand Name	Environment: Environmental Reporting	Environment: Pollution	Environment: Nuclear Power	Environment: Other	Animals: Animal Testing	Animals: Factory Farming	Animals: Other Animal Rights	People: Oppressive Regimes	People: Workers' Rights	People: Irresponsible Marketing	People: Armaments	Extras: Genetic Engineering	Extras: Boycott Call	Extras: Political Donations	Company group
Baxters	Bottom	Top	Top	Top	Top	Bottom	Top	Top	Top	Top	Top	Top	Top		WA Baxter & Sons
Bionova	Top	Top	Top	Top	Top	Top	Top	Top	Top	Top	Top	Top	Top		Faan Zuidhorn
Bonne Maman	Bottom	Top	Top	Top	Top	Top	Top	Top	Top	Top	Top	Top	Top		Andros
Chivers	Bottom	Top	Top	Top	Top	Bottom	Top	Middle	Top	Top	Top	Top	Top	USA	Hicks Muse Tate & Furst
Duerr's	Bottom	Top	Top	Top	Top	Bottom	Top	Top	Top	Top	Top	Top	Top		Duerr & Sons
Frank Cooper	Bottom	Top	Middle	Top	Bottom	Middle	Bottom	Middle	Bottom	Top	Bottom	Middle	Top		Doughty Hanson
Hartley's	Bottom	Top	Top	Top	Top	Bottom	Top	Middle	Top	Top	Top	Top	Top	USA	Hicks Muse Tate & Furst
The Herb Stall	Top	Top	Top	Top	Top	Top	Top	Top	Top	Top	Top	Top	Top		The Herb Stall
Meridian	Middle	Top	Top	Bottom	Top	Bottom	Top	Related company middle	Top	Top	Top	Related company middle	Top		Greencore Group
Robertsons	Bottom	Top	Middle	Top	Bottom	Middle	Bottom	Middle	Bottom	Top	Bottom	Middle	Top		Doughty Hanson
Stute	Bottom	Top	Top	Top	Top	Top	Top	Top	Top	Top	Top	Top	Top		Stute Foods Ltd
Tiptree	Bottom	Top	Top	Top	Top	Top	Top	Top	Top	Top	Top	Top	Top		Wilkin & Sons
Whole Earth	Top	Top	Top	Top	Top	Top	Top	Top	Top	Top	Top	Top	Top		Whole Earth Foods Ltd

Key

- Top rating (no criticisms found)
- Middle rating
- Bottom rating
- A related company has a bottom rating and the company itself has a middle rating
- A related company has a middle rating
- A related company has a bottom rating

Source: ECRA-See page 14 for full key to symbols.

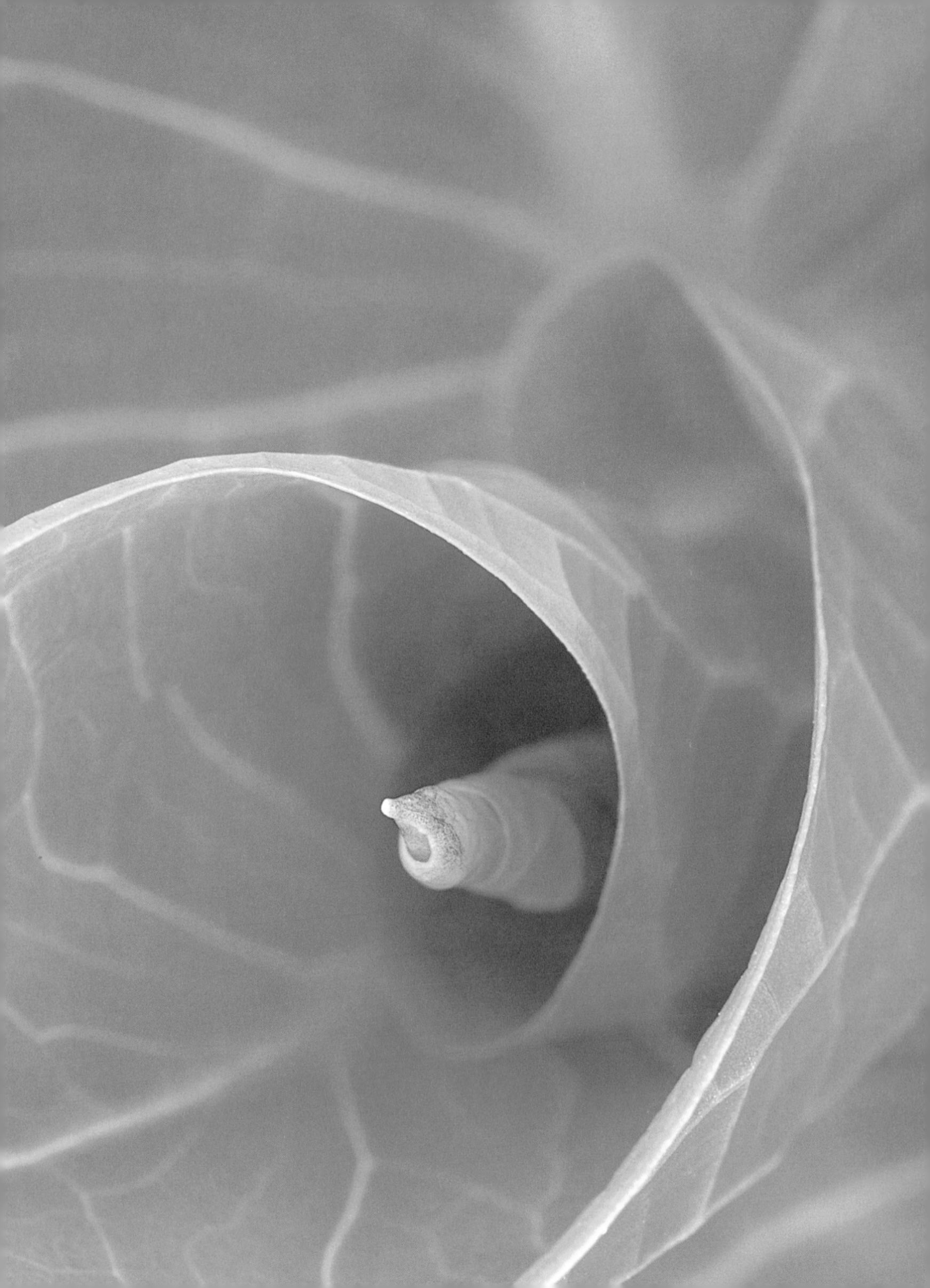

Pasta

Tagliatelli, linguine, fusilli, or just good old spaghetti, whichever kind you fancy, the artistic shapes of pasta are always popular whether in salads or as the basis of delicious and varied main dishes – with tomato, seafood or meat sauces. Although most of the different kinds of pasta available are equally healthy, we can always go one better and look for organic and/or fresh varieties. With some practice, you can even try to make your own.

Pure wheat

Traditional quality pasta should be made with 100 per cent durum wheat, in wholewheat or semolina form. However, with the growth in the own-brand market pushing prices down, many of the cheaper pastas now contain 'soft wheat' substitutes, which can result in a slightly sticky or slimy texture.

A richer pasta is produced with the addition of egg, which vegans inevitably avoid. Tomato or spinach is added to produce the distinctive red or green pastas, and some pasta-makers are fond of ingredients like nettles, beetroot and chilli.

Fresh pasta

In Italy, fresh pasta is available in over a hundred variations of shape and filling, and it is sold in specialist shops to be eaten on the day of purchase. In the UK, most of the fresh pasta available is not quite that fresh, as preservation in a modified environment is usual to extend the shelf life. Some from specialist shops is very good, but at the same time many of the fully-prepared fresh pasta meals on the supermarket shelves are rather over-stodgy with not many authentic ingredients.

Fresh pasta most often contains egg, which again is not good news for vegans, and if the pasta is from a non-organic company the eggs will probably be from battery farms. All brands certified as organic by the Soil Association will contain only free-range eggs.

Organic, whole wheat and GM

As the supermarket own-brands are responsible for more than three quarters of all UK pasta sales, the introduction of organic own-brand pasta ranges is a positive step towards sustainable agriculture.

We need to be wary of wholewheat pasta varieties (unless they are clearly marked as organic) because they are far more likely to contain chemical residues, as the husk or bran of the wheat absorbs more of the pesticides and fertilisers than the semolina used alone in white varieties.

As there are no GM varieties cleared for sale within the EU, dry pasta in its standard form should be GM-free, with the possible exception of the red, tomato pasta which could contain GM tomato paste. All the pasta certified as organic by the Soil Association is sure to be GM-free.

Packaging

Most pasta is packaged in polypropylene, which although recyclable will usually end up in landfill. Given the expansion of the dried product during cooking and the need for thicker packaging for fresh pasta (in order to maintain the seal around the modified environment), far greater volumes of plastic are needed for the fresh product.

Alternatives

For those with wheat or gluten intolerances, Orgran produces a rice pasta which has been produced in isolation from all other foodstuffs. Another possible alternative may be one of the speciality pastas produced by Terra e Cielo, which are made from farro wheat or 'spelt' (an ancient forerunner to modern wheat), which contains considerably less gluten and which the company claims may be suitable for people with a mild wheat intolerance.

An alternative to expensive fresh pasta is to make your own, starting with lasagne, which can be made by rolling out flour and water in the right quantities.

- Barilla
- Dellugo
- Fiorucci
- La Terra e Cielo
- Organico
- Orgran
- Pastificio Rana
- Puglisi

- Meridian
- Morrisons
- Safeway

- Asda
- Buitoni
- Marks & Spencer
- Marshalls
- Sainsbury
- Seeds of Change
- Sitoni
- Tesco

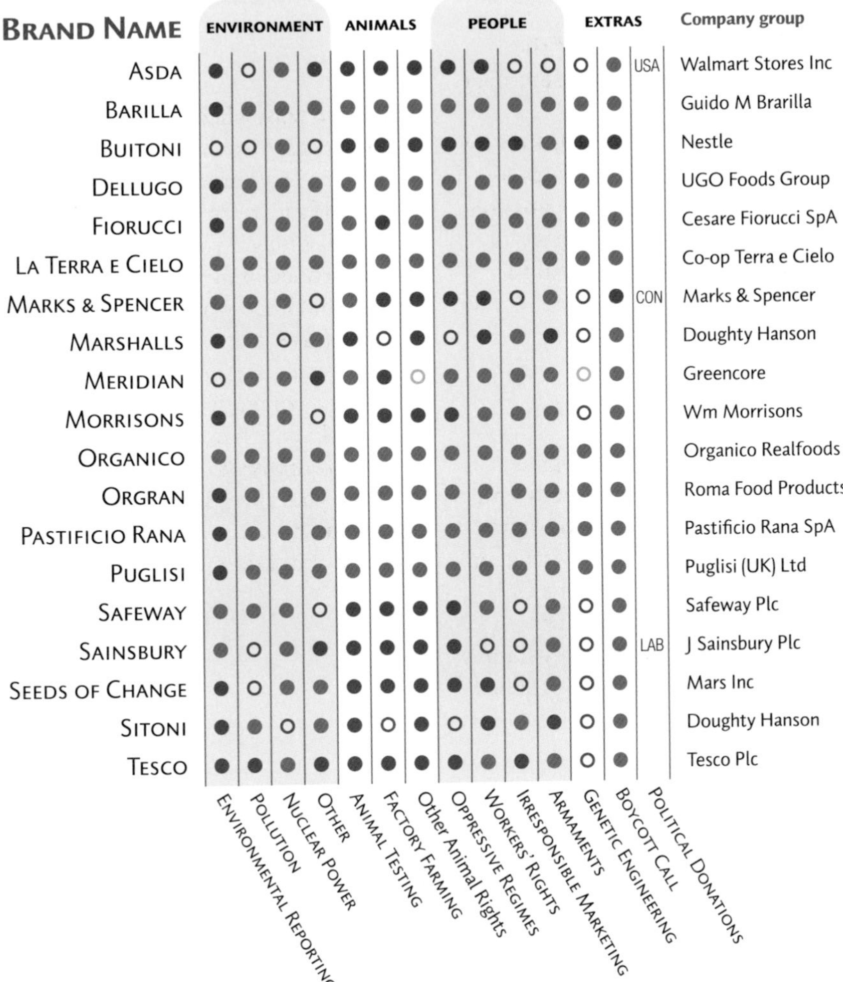

Key

- Top rating (no criticisms found)
- Middle rating
- Bottom rating
- A related company has a bottom rating and the company itself has a middle rating
- A related company has a middle rating
- A related company has a bottom rating

Source: ECRA-See page 14 for full key to symbols.

Soft drinks

Kids just love fizzy drinks and most of us seem to be happy to buy it for them – but it's hardly a necessity of life! There's simply too much sugar, while ingredients like acids and caffeine are potentially harmful if taken in excess. We need to think about alternatives and, while we're at it, try to stop ourselves buying yet more plastic bottles that end up in the landfill.

Sweet and damaging

The average person consumes four pints of liquid each day. In the UK, around 20 per cent of this is in the form of soft drinks, with the volume slowly rising. High consumption of soft drinks means that other healthier drinks are being replaced. Apart from the water, there is very little in soft drinks that is even vaguely beneficial.

Whether still or fizzy, off-the-shelf soft drinks can contain the equivalent of up to 15 cubes of sugar, well over half the recommended daily maximum. This can lead to dental cavities and other health problems associated with high intakes of sugar. The acids in many soft drinks (found in both ordinary and no-sugar varieties) can also cause tooth decay and erosion of the hard enamel on the surface of the tooth and do not require the presence of plaque for this to occur. In 1996, research found that dental erosion as a result of drinking acidic drinks and other sources affected 30 per cent of 13-year-olds. Even Ribena's 'tooth-kind' drink failed dental tests carried out in two different studies.

All soft drinks given to children should be diluted to avoid tooth decay, given with meals if possible and in cups rather than bottles, as sipping drinks causes greater damage.

Other nasties

It's not just the sugar in soft drinks which can cause health problems. Caffeine, found in many fizzy drinks in varying levels, is addictive and can cause hyperactivity, disrupted sleep and withdrawal symptoms in children and adults. In Glasgow, a survey found an unusually high level of orofacial granulomatosis – an oral version of Crohn's disease which has been linked to a sensitivity to preservatives and flavourings in carbonated soft drinks. Research in the US has also found links between cola consumption and kidney stones in men. Artificial sweeteners – such as those found in many diet and no-sugar drinks – have also been linked with a number of health problems, although research has yet to prove any conclusive links.

Confused identities

At the time of research the following is the case: in the UK, Pepsi's brands are licensed to Britvic, which itself is owned by Bass plc. Consequently, Pepsi-owned brands receive the combined marks of Bass plc and Pepsico Inc (an amber circle on the table). Although the Libby's brand is no longer actually produced by Nestlé, it still owns the brand name. Hanover Acceptances subsidiary, Gerber Foods – the new licensee of the brand – has an agreement with Nestlé for the Libby's name, so consequently Baby Milk Action still lists Libby's in its Nestlé boycott information, because Nestlé still profits from it. This licensing agreement also applies to other ex-Nestlé brands, Um Bongo, Libby's C and Jusante. The Nestlé logo is now absent from all packaging, meaning that consumers may have unwittingly been buying Libby's brands believing them to be dissociated from the Nestlé empire. On the table, the Nestlé marks are those which are amber.

Packaging

Soft drinks are likely to come in aluminium or steel; glass; plastic bottles or cartons. The volume of packaging used each year is staggering. We use around six billion aluminium cans, 225 million plastic containers – mostly plastic bottles – and six billion glass containers annually. Less than a third of steel and aluminium cans and only five per cent of plastics are recycled in the UK, the remainder being landfilled or incinerated. Glass is the best option, as it can be recycled indefinitely.

KEEPING HEALTHY – AND GREEN

- One soft drink in a day has usually more than an enough extra energy for one person
- Use glass bottles not plastic ones
- Recycle plastic bottles
- If you buy cans, make sure you crunch and recycle them

- Innocent
- Irn Bru
- Rio
- Rubicon
- Vimto
- Whole Earth

- Aqua Libra
- Britvic
- Purdey's
- Robinsons
- Virgin Cola

- Coca-Cola
- Libby's
- Pepsi
- Schweppes
- Sunny Delight
- Ribena

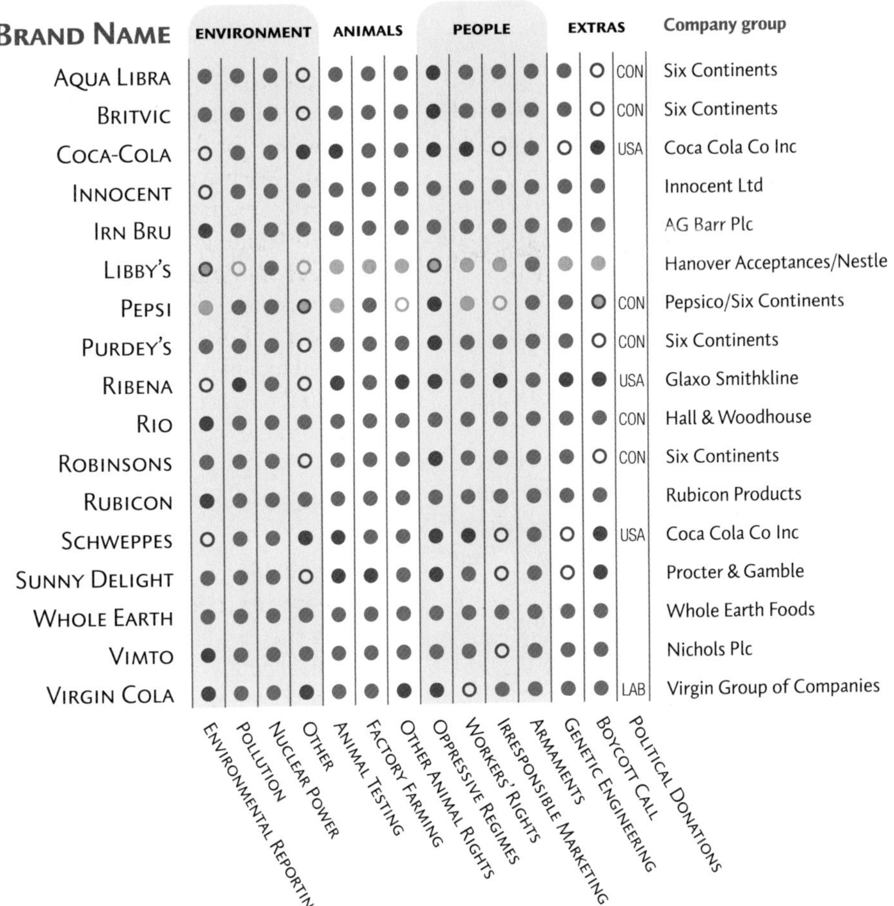

Key

- ● Top rating (no criticisms found)
- ○ Middle rating
- ● Bottom rating
- ◉ A related company has a bottom rating and the company itself has a middle rating
- ○ A related company has a middle rating
- ● A related company has a bottom rating

Source: ECRA-See page 14 for full key to symbols.

The Gr8

G8

Fair Trade text petition

TEXT now...

Text G8 followed by your name and country to 83070

The G8 summit of world leaders meet in July 2005 in Scotland. Join the first ever text petition to get Fair Trade on the agenda.

Target 1,000,000 names

World leaders are keen to expand the global economy through increased trade, but poorer countries are continually being dealt a crooked deal. Fundamental changes to trade rules are needed for a real change in global poverty.

For more information go to
www.newconsumer.org

Soup

Packet soups and canned soups may seem like a good and quick form of nutrition, but we should think again before buying. Their nutritional value varies and some of the companies making them have poor ethical records.

Healthy diets

Like many types of processed foods, ready-made soups have been criticised for often containing high levels of sugars, salt and artificial additives such as flavourings and thickeners. Packet soups have been most heavily condemned for containing little of nutritional value, while canned soups often use high levels of sugar and thickeners. Fresh carton soups are often a healthier option but many still have a high salt content.

Home-made soups made with organic vegetables and with sparing use of salt make healthy, filling and balanced meals. If made in large quantities, they can be easily refrigerated or frozen.

Companies

Consolidation in the food industry means that supermarket shoppers are faced with an array of companies with problematic ethical records, while the smaller companies and brands are being squeezed out of the mass markets.

Apart from the vegetarian companies Suma and Just Wholefoods, all of the companies included here have connections with factory farming.

Although the issue of the irresponsible marketing of baby foods and breastmilk substitutes usually focuses on the activities of Nestlé, Heinz has also been the subject of sustained and serious criticisms on the subject from campaigning organisations such as Baby Milk Action. It has been criticised for violations of the International Code of Marketing of Breastmilk Substitutes in countries including Pakistan, Uganda, Peru, Mexico, Ghana and Malaysia. Farleys, a Heinz subsidiary, was also cited back in 1994 as having produced marketing material which played on the insecurities of women by claiming that breastfeeding harmed the sex lives of many new mothers, and that 'modern women' regarded breasts as 'more than just feeding machines'. Fortunately, we have not found the same claims in recent Farley's marketing materials.

Organic issues

Suma and Just Wholefoods both sell only organic brands of soup, and the New Covent Garden Soup Company has brought out a range of organic choices. Other than these, all the products concerned are made from non-organic produce, which generally involves the use of pesticides and potentially environmentally-damaging growing systems.

Packaging is another issue, as ready-made soup comes either in packets, tins or cartons. None of the products examined had any indication that they were packaged in recycled materials.

- Just Wholefoods
- New Covent Garden
- Suma

- Batchelors
- Baxters
- Campbells
- Soup Sensations

- Heinz
- Knorr

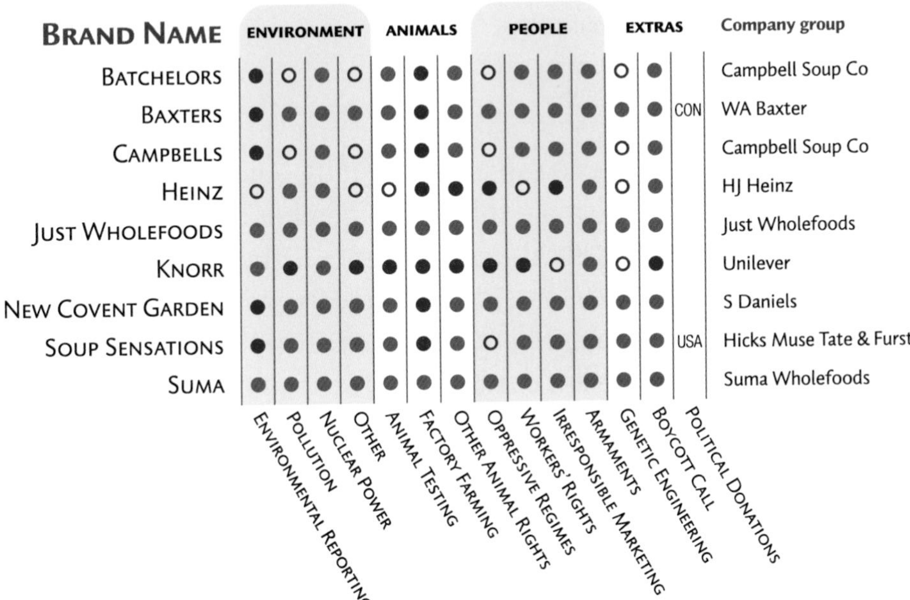

Brand Name	Environmental Reporting	Pollution	Nuclear Power	Other	Animal Testing	Factory Farming	Other Animal Rights	Oppressive Regimes	Workers' Rights	Irresponsible Marketing	Armaments	Genetic Engineering	Boycott Call	Political Donations	Company group
	ENVIRONMENT				ANIMALS			PEOPLE				EXTRAS			
Batchelors	Bottom	Middle	Top	Middle	Top	Bottom	Top	Middle	Top	Top	Top	Middle	Top		Campbell Soup Co
Baxters	Bottom	Top	Top	Top	Top	Bottom	Top	Top	Top	Top	Top	Top	Top	CON	WA Baxter
Campbells	Bottom	Middle	Top	Middle	Top	Bottom	Top	Middle	Top	Top	Top	Middle	Top		Campbell Soup Co
Heinz	Middle	Top	Top	Middle	Middle	Bottom	Bottom	Bottom	Middle	Bottom	Top	Middle	Top		HJ Heinz
Just Wholefoods	Top	Top	Top	Top	Top	Top	Top	Top	Top	Top	Top	Top	Top		Just Wholefoods
Knorr	Top	Bottom	Top	Bottom	Bottom	Bottom	Bottom	Bottom	Bottom	Middle	Top	Middle	Bottom		Unilever
New Covent Garden	Bottom	Top	Top	Top	Top	Bottom	Top	Top	Top	Top	Top	Top	Top		S Daniels
Soup Sensations	Bottom	Top	Top	Top	Top	Bottom	Top	Middle	Top	Top	Top	Top	Top	USA	Hicks Muse Tate & Furst
Suma	Top	Top	Top	Top	Top	Top	Top	Top	Top	Top	Top	Top	Top		Suma Wholefoods

Key

- Top rating (no criticisms found)
- Middle rating
- Bottom rating
- A related company has a bottom rating and the company itself has a middle rating
- A related company has a middle rating
- A related company has a bottom rating

Source: ECRA-See page 14 for full key to symbols.

Sugar

Most of us know that too much sugar is bad for us, but we would find it hard to live without it. The main thing to remember is that too much processing removes its most nutritious elements. Other factors to consider are the livelihoods of workers in fields and factories who have helped bring the sugar to our supermarkets, where our sugar comes from and who has been benefiting from the recent changes in the world trade rules.

Health factors

Processed white sugar supplies our bodies with little more than cheap calories. If we take too much we risk not only tooth decay but other long-term problems such as diabetes, dyspepsia and heart and liver disease. Too much sugar can even affect our concentration.

Some scientists argue that we are abusing the evolutionary role of our sweet tooth by consuming refined sugar. Our ancestors would have satisfied their cravings for sweetness by eating fruit and sweet vegetables, and in so doing would have obtained necessary nutrients like vitamin C. In places where sugar cane is eaten raw, people have healthy teeth because of the vitamins and minerals that occur naturally in the juice.

Unrefined or raw brown sugars have been processed to some degree but they retain more nutrients than white sugar. Any superior brown sugar will have been derived from cane. Brown sugar from beet has been coloured with caramel or molasses.

Free trade

Although we would normally argue in favour of locally-grown produce over imports, a special case can be made for sugar cane because of its importance to the poorer economies of the world. The movement towards free trade mapped out by the World Trade Organisation aims to eliminate the guaranteed quotas and prices for sugar producers in countries like Jamaica, the Philippines and Mauritius. A report published in 1999 stated that the economic situation for small and medium-sized sugar planters in the Philippines had seriously deteriorated over the last few years.

The Sugar Register of FLO (Fairtrade Labelling Organisations International) – which is used for the UK's Fair Trade Mark – has encountered difficulties in setting certification standards. Accepted criteria normally operate on the basis of the need of disadvantaged Third World farmers, which rules out poor-country sugar producers as they already get preferential treatment (higher prices) from the EU.

Most of the socially-conscious companies buy their sugar from Mauritius, which has a relatively progressive and equitable system in place. Its Sugar Syndicate pays the same pro rata rate whether the sugar comes from a large estate or from one of 30,000 smallholdings. As things stand at the moment, the existence of the Syndicate rules out schemes to benefit individual disadvantaged growers, which is another requirement for Fairtrade Mark certification, but the Sugar Register has been looking for a way round this problem.

Organic

The traditional practice of cold pressing sugar cane is being used by a German company called Rapunzel. It pays a premium to Brazilian farmers to produce an organic product it calls Rapadura, which has a mild caramel-like flavour and retains all the nutrients of the sugar cane. It is suitable for baking and has a powdery consistency. Sucanat and Syramena are two other brands, available through some wholefood stores, that have undergone minimal processing.

- Traidcraft
- Whitworths

- Billingtons

- Silver Spoon
- Tate & Lyle

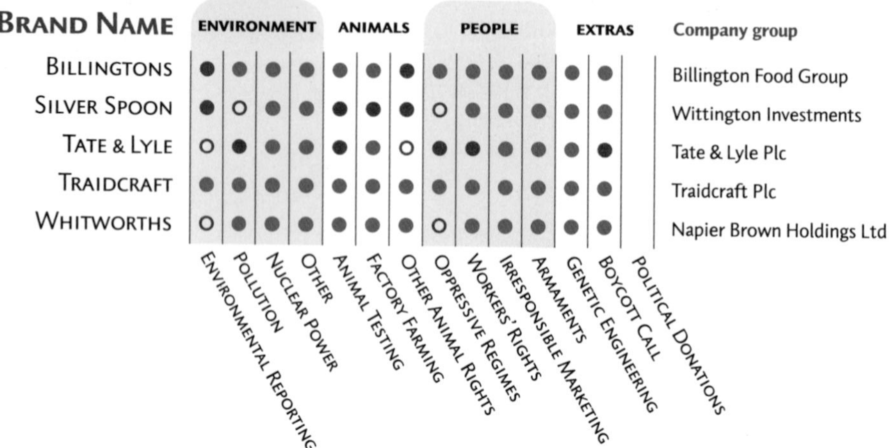

Brand Name	Environment: Environmental Reporting	Environment: Pollution	Environment: Nuclear Power	Environment: Other	Animals: Animal Testing	Animals: Factory Farming	Animals: Other Animal Rights	People: Oppressive Regimes	People: Workers' Rights	People: Irresponsible Marketing	People: Armaments	Extras: Genetic Engineering	Extras: Boycott Call	Extras: Political Donations	Company group
Billingtons	Bottom	Top	Top	Top	Top	Top	Bottom	Top	Top	Top	Top	Top	Top		Billington Food Group
Silver Spoon	Bottom	Middle	Top	Top	Bottom	Bottom	Bottom	Middle	Top	Top	Top	Top	Top		Wittington Investments
Tate & Lyle	Middle	Bottom	Top	Top	Bottom	Top	Middle	Bottom	Bottom	Top	Top	Top	Bottom		Tate & Lyle Plc
Traidcraft	Top	Top	Top	Top	Top	Top	Top	Top	Top	Top	Top	Top	Top		Traidcraft Plc
Whitworths	Middle	Top	Top	Top	Top	Top	Top	Middle	Top	Top	Top	Top	Top		Napier Brown Holdings Ltd

Key

- ● Top rating (no criticisms found)
- ○ Middle rating
- ● Bottom rating
- ● A related company has a bottom rating and the company itself has a middle rating
- ○ A related company has a middle rating
- ● A related company has a bottom rating

Source: ECRA-See page 14 for full key to symbols.

Tea & coffee

Tea and coffee were the first products used to spearhead the 'fair trade' campaign for a better deal for Third World farmers and plantation workers. Now, after years of perseverance, the campaign has begun to score real success; the supermarket groups are taking the issues of socially-responsible sourcing seriously. The brands are becoming increasingly high quality. At least one in five people now recognise the Fairtrade mark and know that it signifies a better deal for Third World producers.

Fair trading

The world of tea and coffee shows us how the more ethical markets of the future will evolve, although consumer vigilance will always be vital to maintain and improve upon the gains. Some of the big food companies are still peddling false claims about the fair trading of their goods when it is clear that they do nothing of the sort.

The key criteria that decide whether a brand deserves the Fairtrade Mark include the following: collective bargaining and representation for workers; good basic wages or purchase prices; welfare provisions; health and safety; good environmental practices; and long-term trading relationships based on continuity and mutual advantage.

Social conditions

Wages and conditions for tea plantation workers are often poor, with their living facilities below acceptable standards. The fair trade campaign hopes to have a long-term beneficial effect on improving their income and their overall living conditions.

As coffee is often grown by independent farmers, the everyday problems are more to do with the price they receive for their crop and the frequent delays they suffer in receiving payments. Again, the fair trade campaign is trying to address these procedural difficulties, even where they are a symptom of the difficult economic or political conditions of the countries where the crop is grown.

Environment

In most tea plantations, pesticides are often mixed in the fields without proper drainage and treatment. Workers say that protective masks, goggles or gloves are rarely provided. The same is true of the large coffee plantations in Brazil and Colombia, where the cultivation is also so intensive that natural nutrients are drained away and have to be replaced with fertilisers. In the long term, it is hoped that workers and farmers will become more aware of the dangers and hazards and that the plantation companies will adopt more responsible policies.

BRANDS ON THE SHELVES

Amongst the fairly-traded tea brands are Clipper's, Equal Exchange, Ridgways, Teadirect, Percol and Traidcraft. Teadirect was the fastest growing tea brand in the UK in the year to April 2003 – the Teadirect blend has been enhanced with tea from an new producer in Kenya.

The fairly-traded coffee brands include Cafédirect, Equal Exchange, Percol, and Traidcraft.

The great news in this sector is that some of these brands are really beginning to prove themselves to consumers on all fronts, including superb taste and quality. This is why Cafédirect expanded its turnover by over 30 per cent in 2003, enabling it to pay £2.8 million in premiums to its tea, coffee and cocoa producers.

The Fairtrade Foundation's website (*www.fairtrade.org.uk*) keeps up to date with the latest developments.

TEA
- Clipper
- Equal Exchange
- Percol
- Teadirect
- TopQualiTea
- Traidcraft

COFFEE
- Cafédirect
- Equal Exchange
- Percol
- Traidcraft

TEA
- Co-op 99
- Ridgways
- Typhoo
- Yorkshire Tea

COFFEE
- Douwe Egberts
- Lavazza
- Rombouts

TEA
- Jacksons of Piccadilly
- PG Tips
- Tetley
- Twinings

COFFEE
- Carte Noir
- Kenco
- Maxwell House
- Nescafé

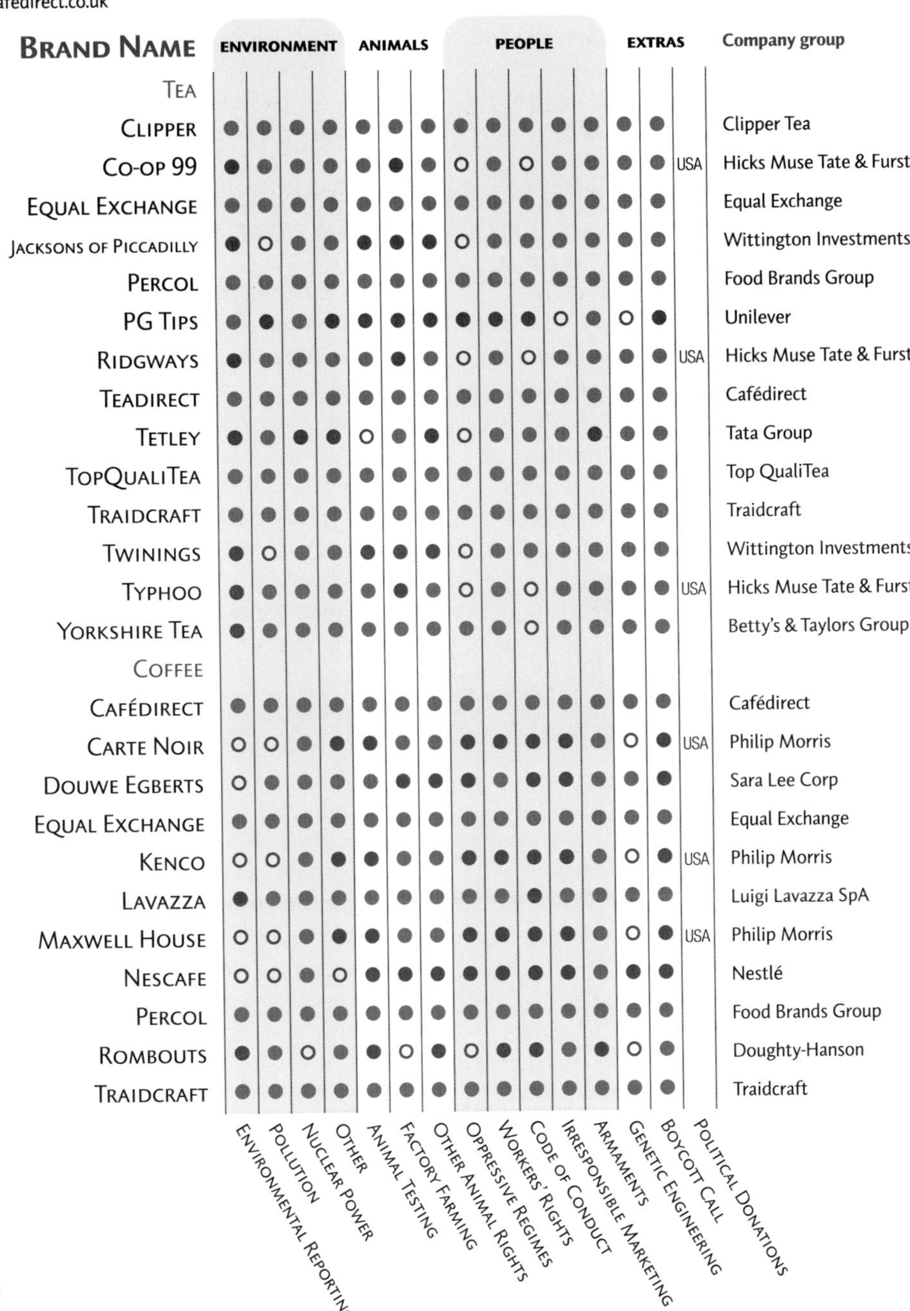

Brand Name	Environment				Animals			People					Extras			Company group
	Environmental Reporting	Pollution	Nuclear Power	Other	Animal Testing	Factory Farming	Other Animal Rights	Oppressive Regimes	Workers' Rights	Code of Conduct	Irresponsible Marketing	Armaments	Genetic Engineering	Boycott Call	Political Donations	
Tea																
Clipper	◍	◍	◍	◍	◍	◍	◍	◍	◍	◍	◍	◍	◍	◍		Clipper Tea
Co-op 99	●	◍	◍	◍	◍	●	◍	○	◍	○	◍	◍	◍	◍	USA	Hicks Muse Tate & Furst
Equal Exchange	◍	◍	◍	◍	◍	◍	◍	◍	◍	◍	◍	◍	◍	◍		Equal Exchange
Jacksons of Piccadilly	●	○	◍	◍	●	●	●	○	◍	◍	◍	◍	◍	◍		Wittington Investments
Percol	◍	◍	◍	◍	◍	◍	◍	◍	◍	◍	◍	◍	◍	◍		Food Brands Group
PG Tips	◍	●	◍	●	●	●	●	●	●	●	○	◍	○	●		Unilever
Ridgways	●	◍	◍	◍	◍	●	◍	○	◍	○	◍	◍	◍	◍	USA	Hicks Muse Tate & Furst
Teadirect	◍	◍	◍	◍	◍	◍	◍	◍	◍	◍	◍	◍	◍	◍		Cafédirect
Tetley	●	◍	●	●	○	◍	●	○	◍	◍	◍	●	◍	◍		Tata Group
TopQualiTea	◍	◍	◍	◍	◍	◍	◍	◍	◍	◍	◍	◍	◍	◍		Top QualiTea
Traidcraft	◍	◍	◍	◍	◍	◍	◍	◍	◍	◍	◍	◍	◍	◍		Traidcraft
Twinings	●	○	◍	◍	●	●	●	○	◍	◍	◍	◍	◍	◍		Wittington Investments
Typhoo	●	◍	◍	◍	◍	●	◍	○	◍	○	◍	◍	◍	◍	USA	Hicks Muse Tate & Furst
Yorkshire Tea	●	◍	◍	◍	◍	◍	◍	◍	◍	○	◍	◍	◍	◍		Betty's & Taylors Group
Coffee																
Cafédirect	◍	◍	◍	◍	◍	◍	◍	◍	◍	◍	◍	◍	◍	◍		Cafédirect
Carte Noir	○	○	◍	●	●	◍	◍	●	●	●	●	◍	○	●	USA	Philip Morris
Douwe Egberts	○	◍	◍	◍	◍	●	●	●	◍	●	●	◍	◍	●		Sara Lee Corp
Equal Exchange	◍	◍	◍	◍	◍	◍	◍	◍	◍	◍	◍	◍	◍	◍		Equal Exchange
Kenco	○	○	◍	●	●	◍	◍	●	●	●	●	◍	○	●	USA	Philip Morris
Lavazza	●	◍	◍	◍	◍	◍	◍	◍	◍	●	◍	◍	◍	◍		Luigi Lavazza SpA
Maxwell House	○	○	◍	●	●	◍	◍	●	●	●	●	◍	○	●	USA	Philip Morris
Nescafe	○	○	◍	○	●	●	●	●	●	●	●	◍	●	●		Nestlé
Percol	◍	◍	◍	◍	◍	◍	◍	◍	◍	◍	◍	◍	◍	◍		Food Brands Group
Rombouts	●	◍	○	◍	●	○	●	○	●	●	◍	●	○	◍		Doughty-Hanson
Traidcraft	◍	◍	◍	◍	◍	◍	◍	◍	◍	◍	◍	◍	◍	◍		Traidcraft

Key

See page 237

Whisky

Before we start on 'the hard stuff' it might be a good idea to try and get a few things straight, because once we're on our way we're sure to forget!

What's in it?

The name whisky comes from Irish Gaelic *usque baugh*, or Scottish Gaelic *uisge beatha*, meaning 'water of life'.

For no good reason, the spirit distilled in Scotland and Canada is spelt 'whisky' while in Ireland and America they spell it 'whiskey'. Wherever it's from, the stuff is distilled from the fermented mash of cereal grains. In Scotland the main grain used is barley. In Ireland, other grains may be used with barley. In Canada and America, the grains are usually rye and maize (the latter is known over there simply as 'corn').

Things distinguishing the flavour include the quality of the water, the drying of the grain (in many Scottish distilleries this is done over peat fires) and the oak casks in which the spirit is matured.

Different kinds

- 'Blended' whisky, which is the most commonly drunk in Britain, can be a combination of up to 50 different malt and grain whiskies.
- 'Malt' whisky is made from malted (or sprouted) grains. A whisky simply labelled as 'malt' may include malt whiskies from several different distilleries.
- To be labelled 'single malt', a whisky has to come from only one distillery.
- 'Grain' whisky is made from a mixture of malted barley and unmalted grains such as wheat or maize.
- Irish whiskey is distilled three times rather than twice, which is usual for Scotch, and is made from malted and unmalted barley as well as other grains such as maize.

The best overall scoring brands are Glenmorangie, owned by Glenmorangie Plc, and Grants, who are owned by William Grant and Sons. Next comes Famous Grouse, Jameson and Whyte & Mackay. Bells and Teachers fall into the lowest section of this relatively high scoring product category. Which ones taste best is up to you!

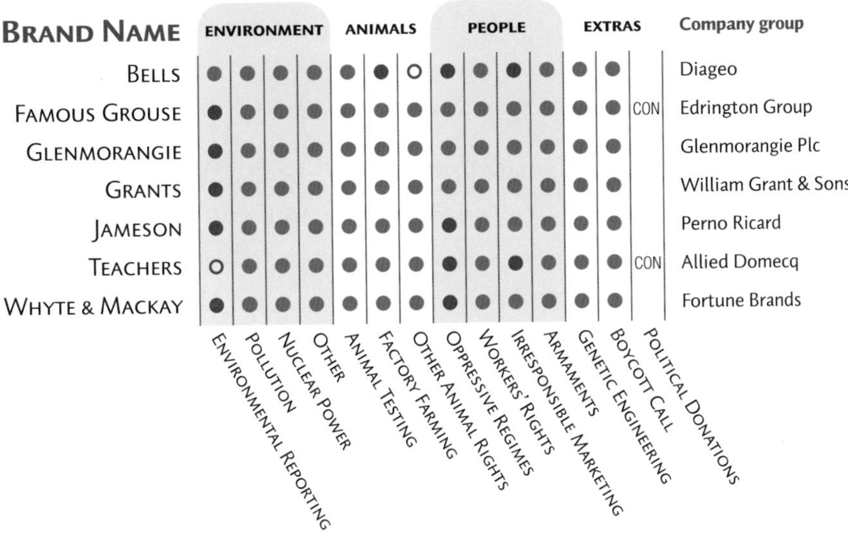

Brand Name	Environmental Reporting	Pollution	Nuclear Power	Other	Animal Testing	Factory Farming	Other Animal Rights	Oppressive Regimes	Workers' Rights	Irresponsible Marketing	Armaments	Genetic Engineering	Boycott Call	Political Donations	Company group
	Environment				**Animals**			**People**				**Extras**			
Bells	Top	Top	Top	Top	Top	Bottom	Middle	Bottom	Top	Bottom	Top	Top	Top		Diageo
Famous Grouse	Bottom	Top	Top	Top	Top	Top	Top	Top	Top	Top	Top	Top	Top	CON	Edrington Group
Glenmorangie	Bottom	Top	Top	Top	Top	Top	Top	Top	Top	Top	Top	Top	Top		Glenmorangie Plc
Grants	Bottom	Top	Top	Top	Top	Top	Top	Top	Top	Top	Top	Top	Top		William Grant & Sons
Jameson	Bottom	Top	Top	Top	Top	Top	Top	Bottom	Top	Top	Top	Top	Top		Perno Ricard
Teachers	Middle	Top	Top	Top	Top	Top	Top	Bottom	Top	Bottom	Top	Top	Top	CON	Allied Domecq
Whyte & Mackay	Bottom	Top	Top	Top	Top	Top	Top	Bottom	Top	Top	Top	Top	Top		Fortune Brands

Key

- Top rating (no criticisms found)
- Middle rating
- Bottom rating
- A related company has a bottom rating and the company itself has a middle rating
- A related company has a middle rating
- A related company has a bottom rating

Source: ECRA-See page 14 for full key to symbols.

- Glenmorangie
- Grants

- Famous Grouse
- Jameson
- Whyte & Mackay

- Bells
- Teachers

Yoghurt

With the ever-growing popularity of yoghurt it is good to keep asking questions about ingredients and the welfare of the animals producing the milk.

The case for organic

Organic-standard yoghurt is not only better for the consumer but better for the milk-producing cow. According to the Soil Association, calves on organic farms will have been suckled for around nine weeks, rather than separated from their mothers within a few days, and the disease rates of animals are lower because of better husbandry and a diet of mostly grass and clover. Organic cows are not kept permanently shut up indoors throughout the winter as non-organic herds often are.Goat and sheep yoghurt also comes from less intensive conditions as it is produced by smaller companies; it is also important for the ten per cent of the population who are lactose-intolerant.

Live yoghurt

Live yoghurts contain two species of bacteria naturally found in the human gut which can, unlike ordinary yoghurt bacteria, pass via the stomach into the intestines, with the claimed benefits of improving digestion and helping to prevent colon cancer. In fact, for people who are already fit, the benefits are probably marginal, but live yoghurt is almost certainly very beneficial for people who are recovering from a stomach bug or who are taking antibiotics.

Gelatine

Gelatine may be added to thicken fat-reduced yoghurts and so vegetarians should keep a careful eye on the ingredients list.

Non-dairy

Most non-dairy yoghurts are made from soya and as such will be highly processed and may contain salt, sugar and other additives, but they contain the same bacterial cultures as conventional yoghurt. As some soya is from GM sources, you may be best advised to look for organic products or those labelled as non-GM.

Alternatives

You can make your own yoghurt by buying a pot of live yoghurt, adding milk and leaving it in a warm place. It works equally well for soya yoghurts. The system can go on almost indefinitely, but consult a reliable recipe book for useful tips about storage and hygiene.

- Rachel's Dairy
- Yeo Valley Organic

- Muller
- Onken
- Provamel Yofu
- Total
- Woodlands Park

- Danone
- Ski
- St Ivel Shape
- Weight Watchers

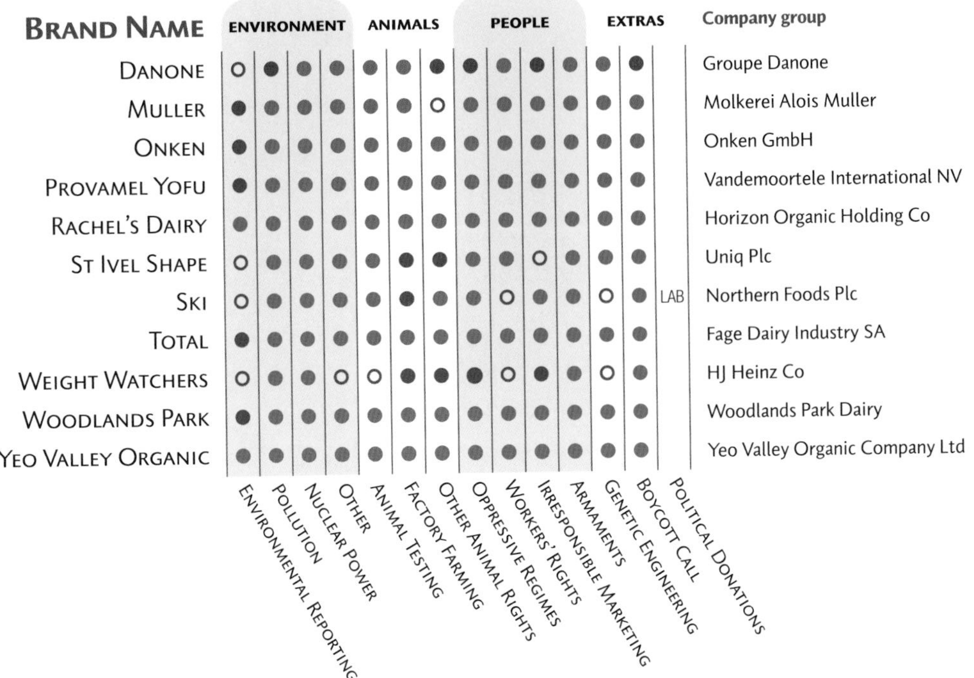

Brand Name	Environment				Animals			People				Extras			Company group
	Environmental Reporting	Pollution	Nuclear Power	Other	Animal Testing	Factory Farming	Other Animal Rights	Oppressive Regimes	Workers' Rights	Irresponsible Marketing	Armaments	Genetic Engineering	Boycott Call	Political Donations	
Danone	Middle	Bottom	Top	Top	Top	Top	Bottom	Bottom	Top	Bottom	Top	Top	Bottom		Groupe Danone
Muller	Bottom	Top	Top	Top	Top	Top	Middle	Top	Top	Top	Top	Top	Top		Molkerei Alois Muller
Onken	Bottom	Top	Top	Top	Top	Top	Top	Top	Top	Top	Top	Top	Top		Onken GmbH
Provamel Yofu	Bottom	Top	Top	Top	Top	Top	Top	Top	Top	Top	Top	Top	Top		Vandemoortele International NV
Rachel's Dairy	Top	Top	Top	Top	Top	Top	Top	Top	Top	Top	Top	Top	Top		Horizon Organic Holding Co
St Ivel Shape	Middle	Top	Top	Top	Top	Bottom	Bottom	Top	Top	Middle	Top	Top	Top		Uniq Plc
Ski	Middle	Top	Top	Top	Top	Bottom	Top	Top	Middle	Top	Top	Middle	Top	LAB	Northern Foods Plc
Total	Bottom	Top	Top	Top	Top	Top	Top	Top	Top	Top	Top	Top	Top		Fage Dairy Industry SA
Weight Watchers	Middle	Top	Top	Middle	Middle	Bottom	Bottom	Bottom	Middle	Bottom	Top	Middle	Top		HJ Heinz Co
Woodlands Park	Bottom	Top	Top	Top	Top	Top	Top	Top	Top	Top	Top	Top	Top		Woodlands Park Dairy
Yeo Valley Organic	Top	Top	Top	Top	Top	Top	Top	Top	Top	Top	Top	Top	Top		Yeo Valley Organic Company Ltd

Key

- Top rating (no criticisms found)
- Middle rating
- Bottom rating
- A related company has a bottom rating and the company itself has a middle rating
- A related company has a middle rating
- A related company has a bottom rating

Source: ECRA-See page 14 for full key to symbols.

Good Health & Beauty

- Cold remedies
- Essential oils
- Eye care products
- Holidays
- Jeans
- Nappies
- Outdoor equipment
- Pain remedies
- Perfumes & aftershaves
- Sanitary protection
- Shampoo
- Skincare
- Soap
- Sports shoes
- Suntan cream
- Toothpaste
- Vitamins
- Alternative clothing directory

Cold remedies

Cold remedies don't attempt to cure a cold but instead contain a combination of ingredients that target individual symptoms. There are more than 200 different cough and cold remedies and new or updated products are coming out all the time. This ethical report just looks at the cold remedies, rather than the cough medicines or decongestants for hay fever.

Atishoo, atishoo, we all fall down

The common cold is one of the most widespread infections, and it is caused by one of over 2,000 different viruses. Most of us suffer at least one cold a year. Instead of going to the doctor we seek out remedies at the chemists, where they are available without a prescription. Ingredients found amongst the most popular cold remedies often include a painkiller with a decongestant and caffeine.

Big pharma

The companies in the cold remedy business are mostly big players in the pharmaceutical industry. It is an industry often and rightly criticised for inflated prices, animal testing and the marketing of banned or less suitable drugs in the Third World.

The Consumer Association has complained that branded cough and cold remedies are sold at higher prices than the equivalent generic drug. Some researchers have claimed that the remedies have no strictly medical benefit.

Animals

According to UK law, a variety of medical experiments are specifically required before a pharmaceutical product can be licensed. Consequently almost all pharmaceutical companies conduct or fund a large proportion of animal experimentation. It is not just pharmaceutical products that are tested on animals. Companies such as Procter & Gamble are known to test cosmetic ingredients on animals, which is not a process required by law.

The arguments against animal testing of pharmaceuticals have been well documented. With the advent of new technologies, the alternatives to animal testing are also growing and include using tissue culture and computer modelling. Although testing may be required by law, and laws are made to regulate these practices, often animals have been found in appalling conditions.

Alternatives

A weak immune system will increase susceptibility to colds and other viruses. A balanced diet, including lots of fresh vegetables and fruit, will help maintain a healthy immune system. Garlic, echinacea and vitamin C are all popular cold-prevention measures. High stress levels have also been shown to weaken the immune system.

The best treatment of cold symptoms is a combination of painkillers and hot drinks with honey and lemon. Steam inhalations with oil vapour such as menthol or eucalyptus can be as effective as branded decongestants. Another popular remedy is to bathe with drops of lavender, tea-tree and eucalyptus essential oils.

- Cold-eeze
- Coldenza
- Olbas Oil

- Benylin 4 Flu
- Karvol
- Lemsip Original
- Nurofen Cold & Flu
- Sudafed

- Beecham's
- Day Nurse
- Vick's Vapour Rub

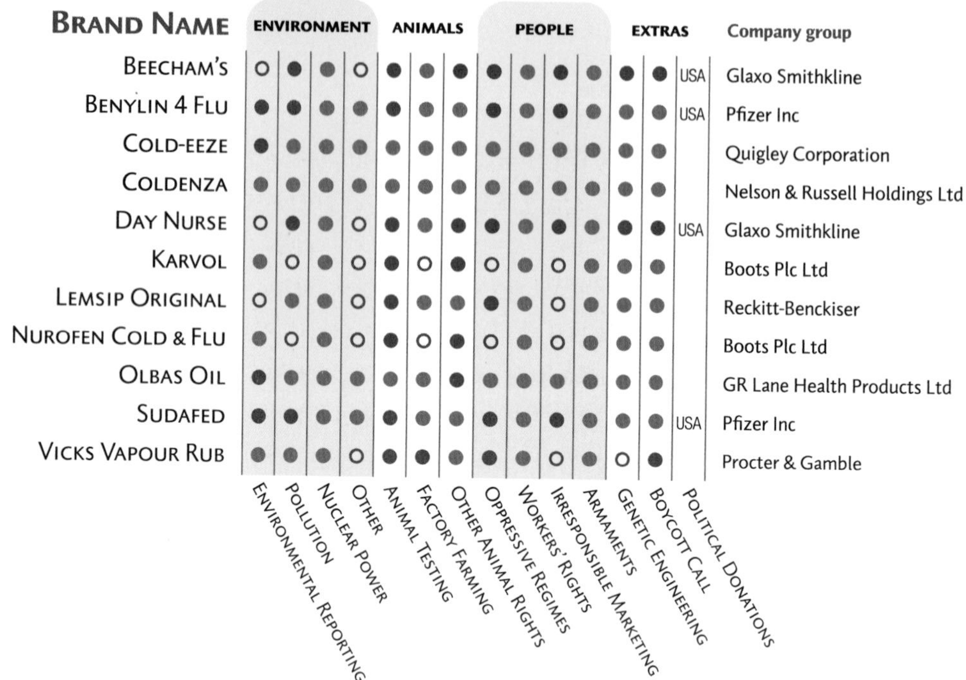

Brand Name	Environmental Reporting	Pollution	Nuclear Power	Other	Animal Testing	Factory Farming	Other Animal Rights	Oppressive Regimes	Workers' Rights	Irresponsible Marketing	Armaments	Genetic Engineering	Boycott Call	Political Donations	Company group
	ENVIRONMENT				ANIMALS			PEOPLE				EXTRAS			
Beecham's	Middle	Bottom	Top	Middle	Bottom	Top	Bottom	Bottom	Top	Bottom	Top	Bottom	Bottom	USA	Glaxo Smithkline
Benylin 4 Flu	Bottom	Bottom	Top	Top	Bottom	Top	Top	Bottom	Top	Bottom	Top	Top	Top	USA	Pfizer Inc
Cold-eeze	Bottom	Top	Top	Top	Top	Top	Top	Top	Top	Top	Top	Top	Top		Quigley Corporation
Coldenza	Top	Top	Top	Top	Top	Top	Top	Top	Top	Top	Top	Top	Top		Nelson & Russell Holdings Ltd
Day Nurse	Middle	Bottom	Top	Middle	Bottom	Top	Bottom	Bottom	Top	Bottom	Top	Bottom	Bottom	USA	Glaxo Smithkline
Karvol	Top	Middle	Top	Middle	Bottom	Middle	Bottom	Middle	Top	Middle	Top	Top	Top		Boots Plc Ltd
Lemsip Original	Middle	Top	Top	Middle	Bottom	Top	Top	Bottom	Top	Middle	Top	Top	Top		Reckitt-Benckiser
Nurofen Cold & Flu	Top	Middle	Top	Middle	Bottom	Middle	Bottom	Middle	Top	Middle	Top	Top	Top		Boots Plc Ltd
Olbas Oil	Bottom	Top	Top	Top	Top	Top	Bottom	Top	Top	Top	Top	Top	Top		GR Lane Health Products Ltd
Sudafed	Bottom	Bottom	Top	Top	Bottom	Top	Top	Bottom	Top	Bottom	Top	Top	Top	USA	Pfizer Inc
Vicks Vapour Rub	Top	Top	Top	Middle	Bottom	Bottom	Top	Bottom	Top	Middle	Top	Middle	Bottom		Procter & Gamble

Key

- Top rating (no criticisms found)
- Middle rating
- Bottom rating
- A related company has a bottom rating and the company itself has a middle rating
- A related company has a middle rating
- A related company has a bottom rating

Source: ECRA-See page 14 for full key to symbols.

Essential oils

The market for essential oils for personal relaxation and healing has grown rapidly in the last ten years. About 400 different kinds of essential oil are now available, each claims its own special fragrance and restorative or healing power. Before we start to use any oils, however, it is always good idea to get some guidance on the best uses for them and to know about some of the potential hazards of misuse. Because there are so many different brands of oils – with many of them distributed only through local networks – here we concentrate on the most common brand names.

Ancient remedies

Aromatherapy as we know it today was rediscovered and researched in the 1930s but some forms of it are as old as humanity itself. Tea-tree, for example, has long been used as an antiseptic by the Aboriginal people of Australia. In ancient Egypt, priestesses were said to have burned oils and gums, such as frankincense, to clear their minds. The ancient cultures using aromatherapy included those of Egypt, Greece, Rome, Arabia, India and China. Rosemary was revered in several cultures as regenerative, which is probably why traces of the herb have been found in Egyptian tombs. In fourteenth-century England, pomanders of oranges and cloves were used (presumably unsuccessfully) to ward off the Black Death.

Mind and body

Essential oils are usually used in the bath or in fragrancers (oil burners) or are blended with a carrier oil to produce a massage oil. Research into the oils – which can be extracted from herbs, spices, wood and flowers – suggests that they work on both the mental and physical levels. They are popular both for relieving stress and for helping to heal muscular, circulatory, respiratory, digestive and skin problems and disorders.

Most oils are obtained by distillation, whereby the plant material is placed in large vats and processed using steam, so that the cooled water can then be separated from the essential oil. No waste products occur, as both the oil and water can be used. Another process for producing essential oils is called 'expression'. (Essential oils should not be confused with those simply called 'aromatherapy oils', which are often a blend of oils and dilutants.)

Taking care

As all essential oils are extremely concentrated, they should be kept away from the eyes, they should not be taken internally, they should not be applied on the skin undiluted and the dilution should be done following the instructions carefully. All bottles should have leaflets with appropriate safety warnings and clear instructions on use. The Aromatherapy Trade Council (ATC), the main representative body issues guidelines on responsible marketing, product labelling and marketing. Leading members of the ATC are Tisserand, Nelson & Russell, Essentially Oils, Neal's Yard and Gerard House.

There is a growing range of organic oils guaranteeing that pesticides have not been used on the plants from which they are extracted.

- Body Shop
- Culpeper
- Neal's Yard
- Nelson & Russell

- Tisserand
- Essentially Oils

- Nature's Garden (Holland & Barrett)
- Gerard House
- Boots

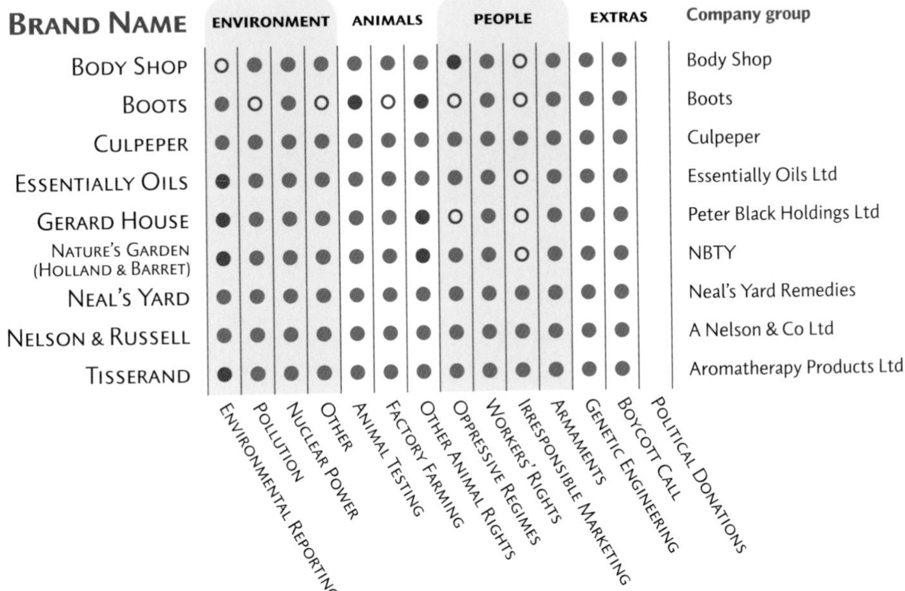

Brand Name	Environment: Environmental Reporting	Environment: Pollution	Environment: Nuclear Power	Environment: Other	Animals: Animal Testing	Animals: Factory Farming	Animals: Other Animal Rights	People: Oppressive Regimes	People: Workers' Rights	People: Irresponsible Marketing	People: Armaments	Extras: Genetic Engineering	Extras: Boycott Call	Extras: Political Donations	Company group
Body Shop	Middle	Top	Top	Top	Top	Top	Top	Bottom	Top	Middle	Top	Top	Top		Body Shop
Boots	Top	Middle	Top	Middle	Bottom	Middle	Bottom	Middle	Top	Middle	Top	Top	Top		Boots
Culpeper	Top	Top	Top	Top	Top	Top	Top	Top	Top	Top	Top	Top	Top		Culpeper
Essentially Oils	Bottom	Top	Top	Top	Top	Top	Top	Top	Top	Middle	Top	Top	Top		Essentially Oils Ltd
Gerard House	Bottom	Top	Top	Top	Top	Top	Bottom	Middle	Top	Middle	Top	Top	Top		Peter Black Holdings Ltd
Nature's Garden (Holland & Barret)	Bottom	Top	Top	Top	Top	Top	Bottom	Top	Top	Middle	Top	Top	Top		NBTY
Neal's Yard	Top	Top	Top	Top	Top	Top	Top	Top	Top	Top	Top	Top	Top		Neal's Yard Remedies
Nelson & Russell	Top	Top	Top	Top	Top	Top	Top	Top	Top	Top	Top	Top	Top		A Nelson & Co Ltd
Tisserand	Bottom	Top	Top	Top	Top	Top	Top	Top	Top	Top	Top	Top	Top		Aromatherapy Products Ltd

Key

- ● Top rating (no criticisms found)
- ○ Middle rating
- ● Bottom rating
- ◉ A related company has a bottom rating and the company itself has a middle rating
- ○ A related company has a middle rating
- ● A related company has a bottom rating

Source: ECRA-See page 14 for full key to symbols.

Eye care products

As spectacles and contact lenses become increasingly sophisticated they tend to use new materials that may have environmental impacts.

Spectacles

Chemicals are used to coat both contact lenses and spectacle lenses which may degrade into toxic materials when they are disposed of. However there are some more ecologically-aware companies attending to this problem by producing special lens coatings which degrade into harmless substances within seven days.

Many plastic spectacle lenses are made from 'CR39', a synthetic material that is kept in cold storage and cleaned with freon gas before coating. These may have an overall higher effect on the environment than glass lenses.

Frames with higher environmental impacts include those made of titanium or petroleum-based plastics.

The frames recommended by ECRA are those made from cellulose acetate, which are derived from plant cellulose and acetic acid, both of which are sustainable materials.

Scientific and military connections

Perhaps it's in the nature of precision engineering that some leading contact lens manufacturers are also involved in other activities which some of us may find distasteful – such as pursuing monopolies in human gene research or making accessories for the defence industry. Some of these involvements are shown on the table.

Solution mysteries

Although contact lens solutions may not appear to contain animal-derived ingredients, most brands are likely to have been tested on animals. The Vegan Society publishes a list of vegan-friendly contact lens solutions.

Alternatives

Laser treatment and the 'Bates method' of eyesight correction are possible alternatives to spectacles or contact lenses. Laser treatment is extremely expensive, however, while the Bates method – which involves exercises to retrain the eyes to relax and refocus – has not convinced a lot of people that it actually works!

Another 'ethical' idea is to buy a decent pair of spectacles to please oneself but make a donation to charities that provide opthalmic help to people in poor countries, such as Vision Aid Overseas.

- Allergan
- Sauflon

- Bausch & Lomb
- Chauvin Pharm

- Alcon
- Cibavision
- Johnson & Johnson
- Pilkington Barnes-Hind
- Wesley-Jessen

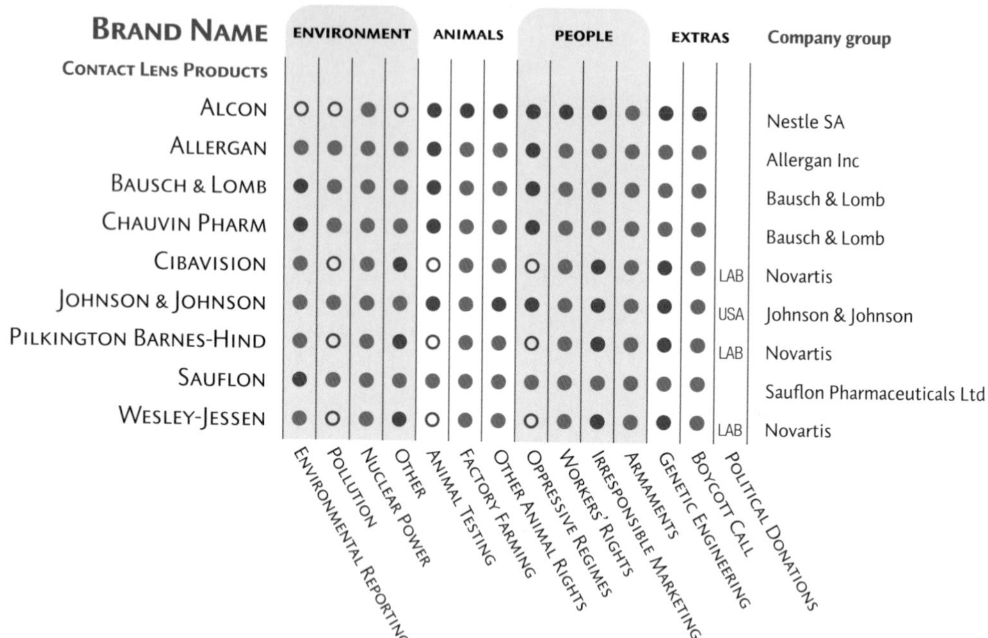

BRAND NAME	Environmental Reporting	Pollution	Nuclear Power	Other	Animal Testing	Factory Farming	Other Animal Rights	Oppressive Regimes	Workers' Rights	Irresponsible Marketing	Armaments	Genetic Engineering	Boycott Call	Political Donations	Company group
	ENVIRONMENT				ANIMALS			PEOPLE				EXTRAS			
CONTACT LENS PRODUCTS															
ALCON	○	○	◍	○	●	●	●	●	●	●	◍	●	●		Nestle SA
ALLERGAN	◍	◍	◍	◍	●	◍	◍	●	◍	◍	◍	◍	◍		Allergan Inc
BAUSCH & LOMB	●	◍	◍	◍	●	◍	◍	●	◍	◍	◍	◍	◍		Bausch & Lomb
CHAUVIN PHARM	●	◍	◍	◍	●	◍	◍	●	◍	◍	◍	◍	◍		Bausch & Lomb
CIBAVISION	◍	○	◍	●	○	◍	◍	○	◍	●	◍	●	◍	LAB	Novartis
JOHNSON & JOHNSON	◍	◍	◍	◍	●	◍	●	●	◍	●	◍	●	◍	USA	Johnson & Johnson
PILKINGTON BARNES-HIND	◍	○	◍	●	○	◍	◍	○	◍	●	◍	●	◍	LAB	Novartis
SAUFLON	●	◍	◍	◍	◍	◍	◍	◍	◍	◍	◍	◍	◍		Sauflon Pharmaceuticals Ltd
WESLEY-JESSEN	◍	○	◍	●	○	◍	◍	○	◍	●	◍	●	◍	LAB	Novartis

Key

- ◍ Top rating (no criticisms found)
- ○ Middle rating
- ● Bottom rating
- ◉ A related company has a bottom rating and the company itself has a middle rating
- ◌ A related company has a middle rating
- ◦ A related company has a bottom rating

Source: ECRA-See page 14 for full key to symbols.

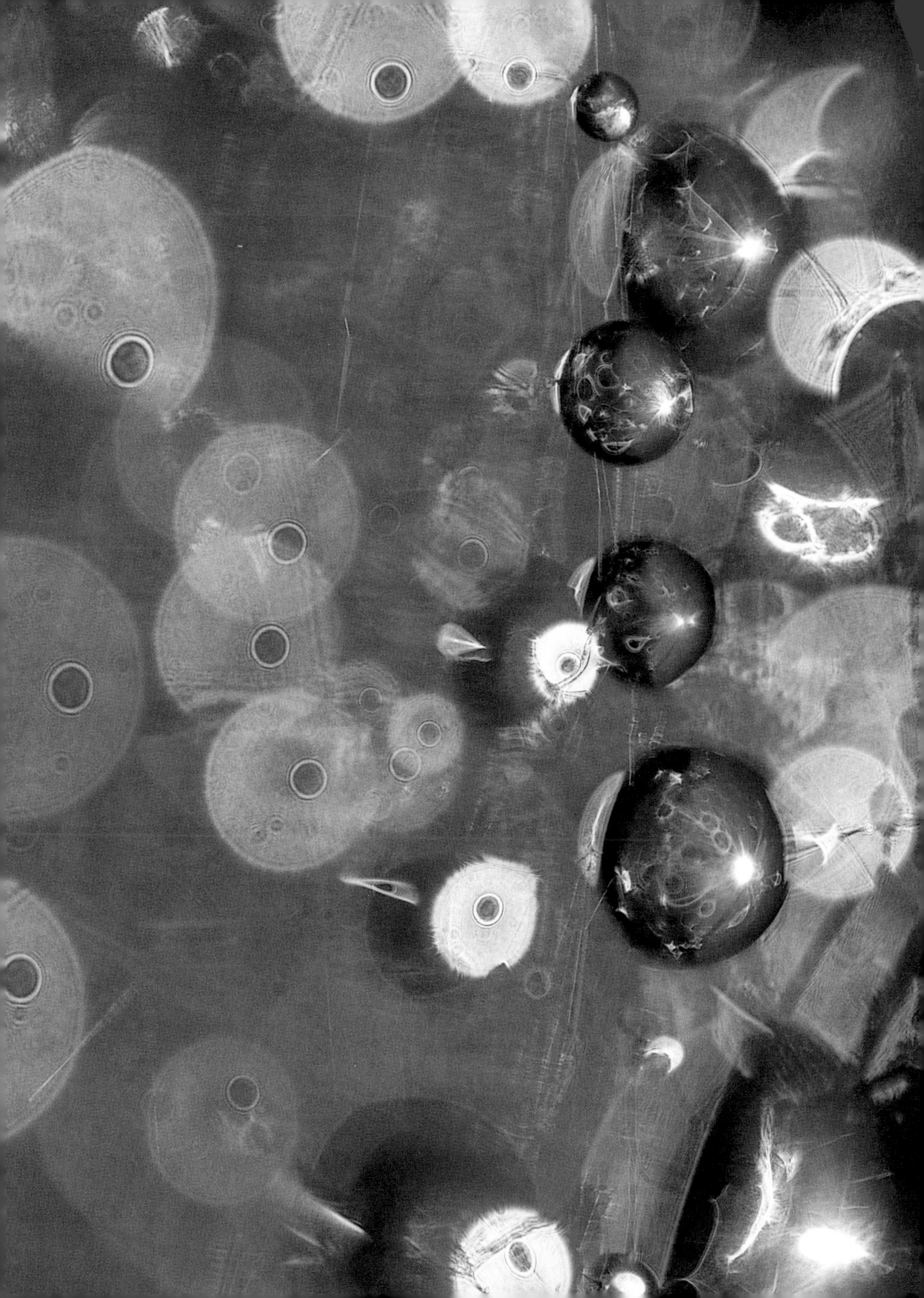

Holidays

Whether we take our holidays in the Caribbean or Croatia, Spain or the Seychelles, it's worth being aware of some potential negative costs to culture, economy and environment. The planes we fly in to get there consume thousands of gallons of fuel, with costs to us all, and the locals do not necessarily benefit from the places we chose to stay in. Not that we shouldn't be enjoying ourselves!

The cost of flying

As more planes do frequent short-haul flights, staying in the air most of the working day, the cost of flying is coming down. But the cost of flying is not just to our pockets. In fact it's a heavy load for the environment to bear. A London-New York return flight produces more carbon dioxide per passenger than the average British motorist produces in 12 months. And fuel emissions in the upper atmosphere hurt the ozone layer more directly than those on the ground. Scientists predict that by 2015 half the annual destruction of the ozone layer may be caused by aircraft.

Package holidays that include the cost of the flight, hotel and meals may also seem to be a great bargain these days. But here's another point to think about. The money we pay for a package benefits the tour operator much more than it does the people who provide the services when we get there.

More than half the foreign holidays taken by British people every year, are sold as packages by the few big companies that dominate the trade. Packages leave less chance for us to engage directly with the places we visit.

West is west

Tourism is predominantly a Western pastime. It can encourage us to respect different cultures, but it can also add to the difficulties of the faraway communities that we interact with.

Images of local and indigenous people are used in tourist marketing to sell different destinations. A brochure on Kenya nearly always features a Maasai warrior – it doesn't tell you that Maasai communities have been evicted from their land to make way for some of Kenya's famous national parks, including Amboseli.

In Goa, developers of a 5-star hotel forced farmers to hand over their farms for a golf course by shutting off irrigation to their fields. In Peru, communities of Yagua Indians have been coerced to move nearer the tourist lodges so that they can be photographed more conveniently. In Burma, the government forcibly moved local people so as to develop the site around the temples at Pagan.

In general, the poorer the local people are the easier it is for the tourism developers to push them aside and/or employ them for a new way of life, catering for international visitors.

Degradation

It is easy to see how tourism can encourage begging and hustling. It transforms traditions of hospitality into commercial transactions. Tourism can also reduce cultural traditions into meaningless sights and attractions, as when sacred dances are performed as after-dinner shows in luxury hotels.

The expansion of international travel is also a big factor in the growth of international prostitution, contributing to the negative images of great cities like Bangkok, but also occurring in much smaller and more vulnerable societies than Thailand, with distorting cultural and economic effects.

When tourism becomes a big factor in a small economy, it can change the traditional economic balance away from farming or hunting and it can lure away the brightest people in a community, who would otherwise be needed to educate the next generation and play a more productive role. The hustle of the tourist trade has come to have more importance than the survival of the old traditions and their positive development in the 21st century. As this goes on, there could soon be no 'exotic' people left.

HINTS FOR A GREENER TRAVELLER

- The 'darkest green' travellers may choose to take holidays close to home
- Other air travellers (with a green conscience) can make donations to environmental organisations like Future Forests *(www.futureforests.com)* and Climate Care *(www.climatecare.org)* or Carbon Storage Trust. You can pay a levy based on the length of each flight – they plant trees or find other ways to absorb carbon dioxide. Or make back the cost by switching your electricity to a 100% renewable electricity supplier
- You can become better informed about the effects of air travel *(see www.chooseclimate.org)*
- When you arrive in a strange country, make sure to learn at least some of the language
- Visit local cafés and restaurants and talk to local people away from the main tourist centres
- Choose an eco friendly holiday company – see Ethical Marketplace at the back of his book
- Find out more about these and other issues at *www.tourismconcern.org.uk* who we thank for helping us with this section
- See *www.gooshing.co.uk* for advice on the most ethical and best deal travel companies

Jeans

Jeans and other basic items of clothing are increasingly being made as cheaply as possible. This means that the clothing companies are always looking to find factories with really cheap labour costs. Companies subcontract their manufacturing to factories in the Far East, Central America or Eastern Europe, wherever the wages are lowest. These factories may in turn subcontract further to other companies which produce the goods at an even cheaper rate. This process may be repeated several times, sometimes spreading to countries elsewhere in the world – all of which makes it difficult to monitor the working conditions.

Sweatshop labour

The term 'sweatshop' is increasingly used to describe conditions throughout the global garment industry, where workers, often young women, work very long hours for wages that are often insufficient to live on. Reports of intimidation, forced overtime, strip-searching and child labour are also rife. In the US in January 1999, campaign groups and trade unions filed a federal lawsuit against 18 companies operating in the Pacific island of Saipan, which is part of the US Commonwealth of the Northern Mariana Islands. The lawsuit, which was filed on behalf of 35,000 Saipan garment workers, alleged that the companies had formed a 'racketeering conspiracy' to use indentured labour to produce clothing on the island; that contractors, manufacturers and retailers 'had engaged in and benefited from forced labour'; and that 'workers were forced into conditions constituting peonage and involuntary servitude, in violation of human rights laws'.

Since then, companies like Levi Strauss, Calvin Klein and Donna Karan have reportedly settled claims and have agreed to independent monitoring of Saipan contractors in future contracts – but other big names have carried on regardless.

Jeans found on sale in the UK are increasingly likely to have been manufactured in central and eastern Europe or in north Africa. Shop searches carried out by ECRA indicated that Poland has become a popular manufacturing location, as have Tunisia (which is on ECRA's list of oppressive regimes) and Morocco. Working practices in such countries often leave much to be desired. Labour Behind the Label have reported that Gap factory workers in Russia had allegedly been paid just 11 cents per hour and were being kept in 'slave-like' conditions.

In Bulgaria, a factory manufacturing

clothing for Levi Strauss stores in the UK was reported to be allegedly strip-searching female workers at the end of their shifts on a regular basis, ostensibly to check they had not stolen anything. One worker, interviewed by the Sunday Times, reported that she had been sacked after refusing to be strip-searched. In addition the factory allegedly failed to pay sufficient wages for workers to feed and house a family properly.

Codes of conduct

Documents are sometimes produced by the clothing companies setting down minimum standards for working conditions. They cover issues such as working hours, freedom of association, child labour and health and safety. On the table, no companies have the top rating, which requires a code of conduct with independent monitoring by outside agencies. Those with codes but failing to ensure independent monitoring receive a middle rating. Those with a bottom rating either do not have a code of conduct or did not respond to ECRA's request for a copy. Furthermore, just because a company's code of conduct appears on its corporate website, this does not mean that it applies on the factory floor. When codes do exist, they frequently fall short of demands made by labour rights campaigners; for example, the Clean Clothes Campaign criticised Levi Strauss's code of conduct for designating a standard work week of 60 hours, above the internationally recognised standard workweek of 48 hours, and for not insisting that workers were paid a living wage.

Growing the cotton

In 1999, it was estimated that 45 per cent of all cotton planted was genetically modified. All the companies profiled are likely to use GM cotton in their jeans since separation of GM and non-GM cotton is not always undertaken. No mainstream jeans company appears to have taken a stance on this issue.

- Amazing Jeans
- Diesel
- Easy
- Falmer
- French Connection
- Lee Cooper

- Burton
- Lee
- New Look
- Next
- Trader (Debenhams)
- Wrangler

- Calvin Klein
- DKNY
- Gap
- Levi
- Marks & Spencer
- Moto (Top Shop)

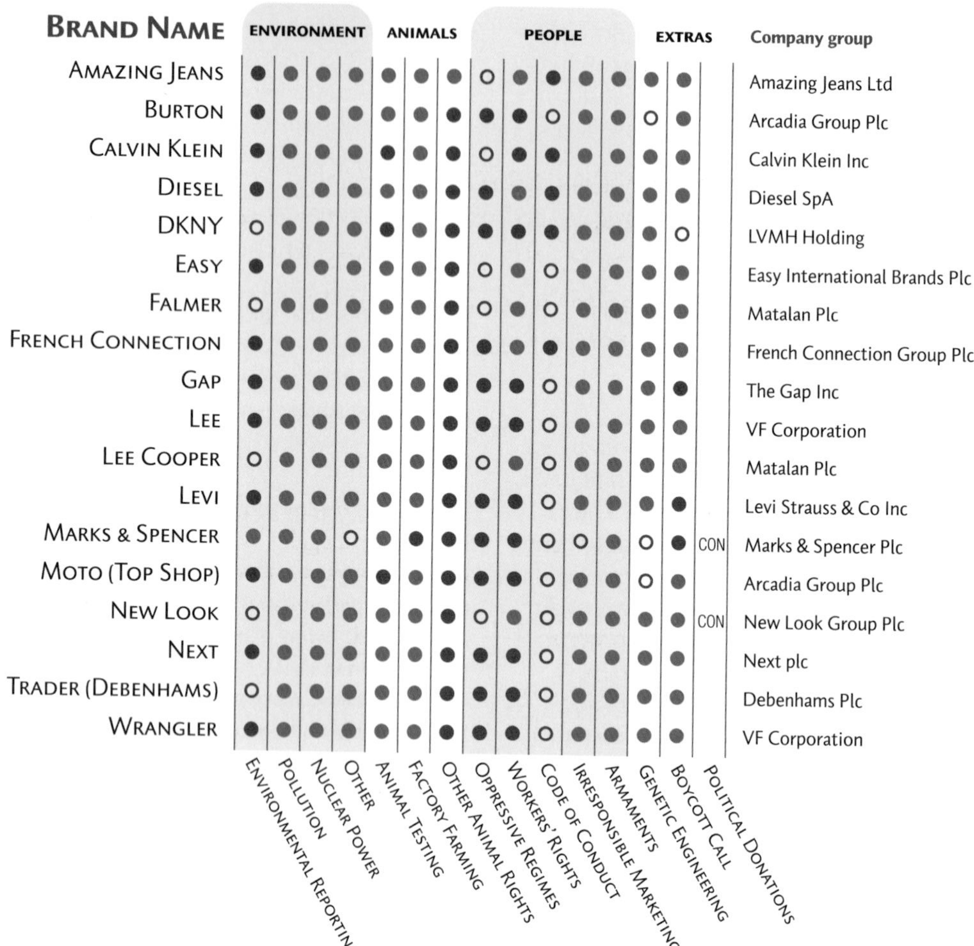

Key

- ● Top rating (no criticisms found)
- ○ Middle rating
- ● Bottom rating
- ● A related company has a bottom rating and the company itself has a middle rating
- ○ A related company has a middle rating
- ● A related company has a bottom rating

Source: ECRA-See page 14 for full key to symbols.

Nappies

Three billion disposable nappies are thrown away every year in the UK. As quick as spending a penny, or a pound, they're thrown in the bin and end up in our ever-expanding landfill sites. Disposable nappies contribute about four per cent to all landfilled domestic waste, at an estimated cost of disposal of £40 million. What a waste!

Bum fluff

The main disposable nappies are Procter & Gamble's Pampers and Kimberly-Clark's Huggies.

The bulkiest component of disposable nappies (or diapers, as they are known in the US) is paper pulp fluff, for which the rising demand is beginning to threaten old-growth forests in Canada, Scandinavia and the Baltic states. Valuable wetlands, moors and meadows risk being destroyed in the quest for new plantations.

Other components include plastics and chemicals derived from non-renewable sources. There is controversy about the safety of some commonly-used chemicals such as the absorbing agent sodium polyacrylate. Babies with sensitive skin may react to absorbent gels.

Hygiene

The average baby gets through about 5,000 nappies on its way to being potty trained. Disposables are commonly binned or, much worse, flushed away. Putting them in the bin without first cleaning off waste is unhygienic and, though few people know it, actually illegal. Chucking them down the toilet happens far too commonly, and they can cause serious maintenance problems in sewers and sewage farms. Many of them also end up in the sea – a Marine Conservation Society report found an average of between one and two washed up disposable nappies per kilometre of shoreline surveyed.

Re-usables

Re-usable 'terry' nappies really do offer a viable alternative to disposables. Only a small percentage of UK parents use them, but there is much higher use of re-useables in North America and Australia.

Terries used to be seen as hard work but washing machines have reduced this and there are plenty of nappy washing services available around the country, some run by local authorities. There are also plenty of new varieties, with specially fitted shapes and pin-free fastening systems, and re-usable overpants for added safety and comfort. The Real Nappy Association advocates the use of thin liners placed inside a terry, allowing solid waste to be peeled away and safely disposed of. These are biodegradable.

Real nappies help to counter nappy rash as they are breathable. But perhaps the best argument for them is the saving in cash terms – total nappy expenditure has been estimated at £250 for re-usables compared with as much as £700-£1,000 per baby for disposables.

There are several nappy brands which we have not yet fully audited but appear to be truly progressive (for example Nature Boy and Girl, and Greenfibres own brand).

You can order a range of 'green fibred' goods and garments by calling 0845 330 3440 or visiting *www.greenfibres.com*.

• Svenska Own-Brands

• Pampers

• Huggies

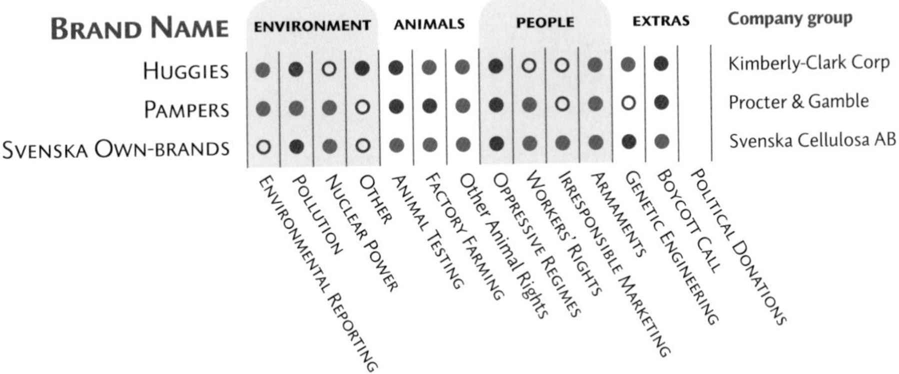

Key

- Top rating (no criticisms found)
- Middle rating
- Bottom rating
- A related company has a bottom rating and the company itself has a middle rating
- A related company has a middle rating
- A related company has a bottom rating

Source: ECRA-See page 14 for full key to symbols.

Outdoor clothing

For at least ten years now, the outdoor clothing market – especially for items like waterproof jackets, walking boots and rucksacks – has become a highly branded and expensive affair, rather like sports clothing for teenagers only aimed at generally older and better-off customers. Whatever age we are, we need to be aware that what helps keep us healthy (and maybe alive!) could be hurtful to others. Just as with sportswear and jeans, some of these products are increasingly outsourced from countries with poor labour conditions.

The cheap labour issue

Some firms have been accused of workers' rights violations in the past five years. For example, the working conditions in certain factories in China and Indonesia are said to be hazardous. In China, staff working in factories subcontracted by one company were apparently forced to work overtime, 12-14 hours a day, seven days a week with as little as one day off a month, and had no unions to represent them. Campaigners argue that companies subcontracting to factories in the developing world should be held responsible for any workers' rights violations that may occur there.

ECRA wrote to all the companies in this report to request a copy of any code of conduct for workers' rights that they may have. Hi-Tec, Blacks and Peter Storm replied but made no mention of independent monitoring – which is a key element required for ECRA's best rating in this column. Pentland (Berghaus) is a member of the UK government sponsored Ethical Trading Initiative (ETI) – a multi-stakeholder project designed to address global workers' rights issues but still some way from offering consumer guarantees.

For those who want to buy products from countries that do not have repressive regimes, Zamberlan boots are made in Italy, Ethical Wares boots are made in the UK, while Patagonia's waterproofs and rucksacks are made in Portugal.

What materials?

Ironically, some production processes for outdoor equipment can actually damage outdoor environments, and others may cause debilitating effects on humans as well. ECRA wrote to all the companies in the report to request an environmental report. Patagonia probably had the best environmental policy with claims to have eliminated PVC, chlorine bleach and azo dyes and to use 100 per cent organic cotton and to have reduced formaldehyde levels. (Adidas was probably next best with a calendar for the elimination of PVC, and mentions of a number of other substances it avoids.)

There is an ongoing boycott of Adidas-Salomon AG, organised by the Australian Wildlife Protection Council (www.awpc.org.au). It concerns Adidas' use of kangaroo skin for some of its football boots. According to the AWPC, 6.9 million kangaroos are shot every year, and 'skins come from the large red males who take ten years to reach alpha status and are being continually massacred so few survive to pass on their superior genes to the next generation. This means that smaller, weaker and younger males are left to breed with the females, producing offspring who are less likely to survive a major drought or other natural disasters.'

- Ethical Wares
- Karrimor
- Lowe Alpine
- Patagonia
- Sprayway
- Vango

- Blacks
- Hi-Tec
- Peter Storm
- Zamberlan

- Berghaus
- Gelert
- Salomon
- The North Face

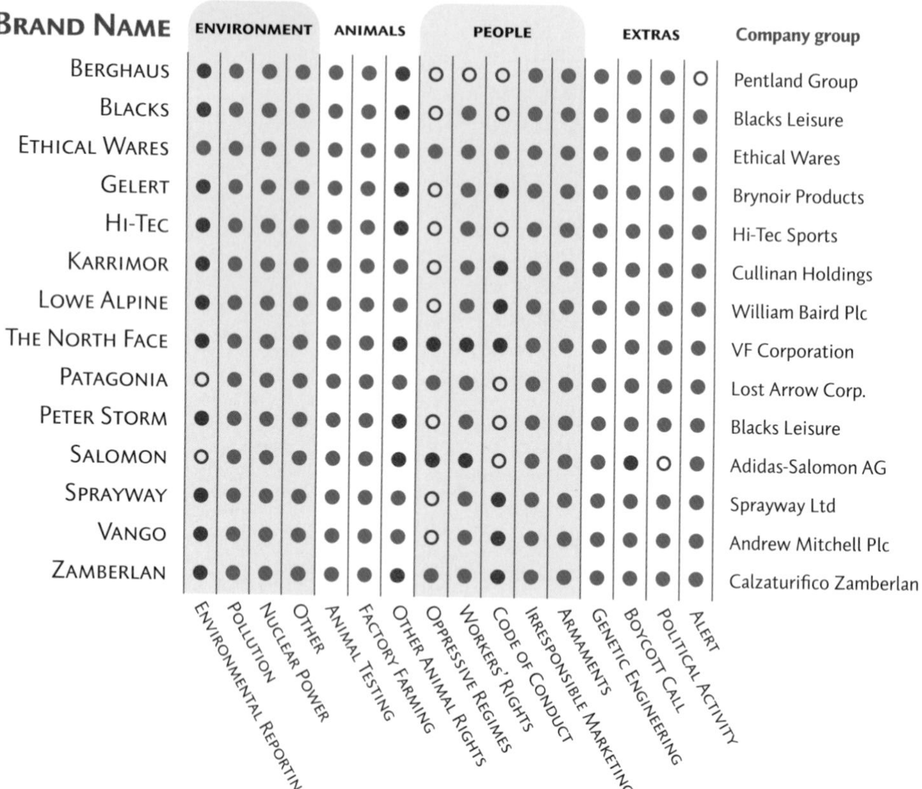

Brand Name	Environment				Animals			People					Extras				Company group
	Environmental Reporting	Pollution	Nuclear Power	Other	Animal Testing	Factory Farming	Other Animal Rights	Oppressive Regimes	Workers' Rights	Code of Conduct	Irresponsible Marketing	Armaments	Genetic Engineering	Boycott Call	Political Activity	Alert	
Berghaus	Bottom	Top	Top	Top	Top	Top	Bottom	Middle	Middle	Middle	Top	Top	Top	Top	Top	Middle	Pentland Group
Blacks	Bottom	Top	Top	Top	Top	Top	Bottom	Middle	Top	Middle	Top	Top	Top	Top	Top	Top	Blacks Leisure
Ethical Wares	Top	Top	Top	Top	Top	Top	Top	Top	Top	Top	Top	Top	Top	Top	Top	Top	Ethical Wares
Gelert	Bottom	Top	Top	Top	Top	Top	Bottom	Middle	Top	Bottom	Top	Top	Top	Top	Top	Top	Brynoir Products
Hi-Tec	Bottom	Top	Top	Top	Top	Top	Bottom	Middle	Top	Middle	Top	Top	Top	Top	Top	Top	Hi-Tec Sports
Karrimor	Bottom	Top	Top	Top	Top	Top	Top	Middle	Top	Bottom	Top	Top	Top	Top	Top	Top	Cullinan Holdings
Lowe Alpine	Bottom	Top	Top	Top	Top	Top	Top	Middle	Top	Bottom	Top	Top	Top	Top	Top	Top	William Baird Plc
The North Face	Bottom	Top	Top	Top	Top	Top	Bottom	Bottom	Bottom	Bottom	Top	Top	Top	Top	Top	Top	VF Corporation
Patagonia	Middle	Top	Top	Top	Top	Top	Top	Top	Top	Middle	Top	Top	Top	Top	Top	Top	Lost Arrow Corp.
Peter Storm	Bottom	Top	Top	Top	Top	Top	Bottom	Middle	Top	Middle	Top	Top	Top	Top	Top	Top	Blacks Leisure
Salomon	Middle	Top	Top	Top	Top	Top	Bottom	Bottom	Bottom	Middle	Top	Top	Top	Bottom	Middle	Top	Adidas-Salomon AG
Sprayway	Bottom	Top	Top	Top	Top	Top	Top	Middle	Top	Bottom	Top	Top	Top	Top	Top	Top	Sprayway Ltd
Vango	Bottom	Top	Top	Top	Top	Top	Top	Middle	Top	Bottom	Top	Top	Top	Top	Top	Top	Andrew Mitchell Plc
Zamberlan	Bottom	Top	Top	Top	Top	Top	Bottom	Top	Top	Bottom	Top	Top	Top	Top	Top	Top	Calzaturifico Zamberlan

Key

- Top rating (no criticisms found)
- Middle rating
- Bottom rating
- A related company has a bottom rating and the company itself has a middle rating
- A related company has a middle rating
- A related company has a bottom rating

Source: ECRA-See page 14 for full key to symbols.

Pain remedies

Most of us do not bother our doctors when we suffer from headaches and instead look for a painkiller or analgesic such as paracetamol, aspirin or ibuprofen. Ethics may not be top of your list when you reach for emergency pain relief, but ethical alternatives *are* available.

Brands and generics

Like nearly every other consumer product, there is an abundance of different pain remedy brands available, with a choice of between 30 and 50 different analgesics in the shops. The main active ingredients are paracetamol (acetaminophen in the US), aspirin and ibuprofen.

Formulations may contain one of these or a combination and may also include codeine and other ingredients, such as caffeine. There are more brands available than there are formulations, many being identical but for the brand name. Branded painkillers are a good income for the pharmaceutical companies, as simply by branding a well-established drug – such as aspirin – they can sell it at an inflated price, sometimes as much as six times the price of a 'generic' (the term referring to the scientific name for a drug such as aspirin). Only drugs for which the patent has expired are available as generics and may be produced by any company. For example, since January 1998, it has been possible to purchase ibuprofen, whereas before this it was only available as a brand such as Nurofen. Painkillers come in a range of formats – capsules, tablets, caplets and soluble tablets. Vegetarians would probably do better to avoid capsules as they often contain gelatine.

Animal testing

Most of the companies included in this report were known to be involved in animal testing. Although companies are obliged in most countries to test pharmaceutical products on animals, some are involved in testing not for medical use. Companies producing generics may be less likely to be involved in animal testing as they simply produce drugs that were developed by others.

Alternatives

Dealing with the causes of stress is usually preferable to having to deal with the symptoms such as pain. Regular exercise and relaxation techniques like yoga, meditation and massage can be good stress-busters. Aromatherapy can also be useful, and lavender is often recommended.

It has been suggested that migraines may be triggered by certain food and drink. The most common triggers are thought to be red wine, chocolate, cheese and citrus fruit. Avoiding these may limit the chances of an attack.

- Codis
- Disprin
- Disprol
- LloydsPharmacy
- Superdrug

- Aspro Clear
- Boots
- Feminax
- Neurofen
- Veganin

- Anadin
- Hedex
- Panadol
- Solpadeine

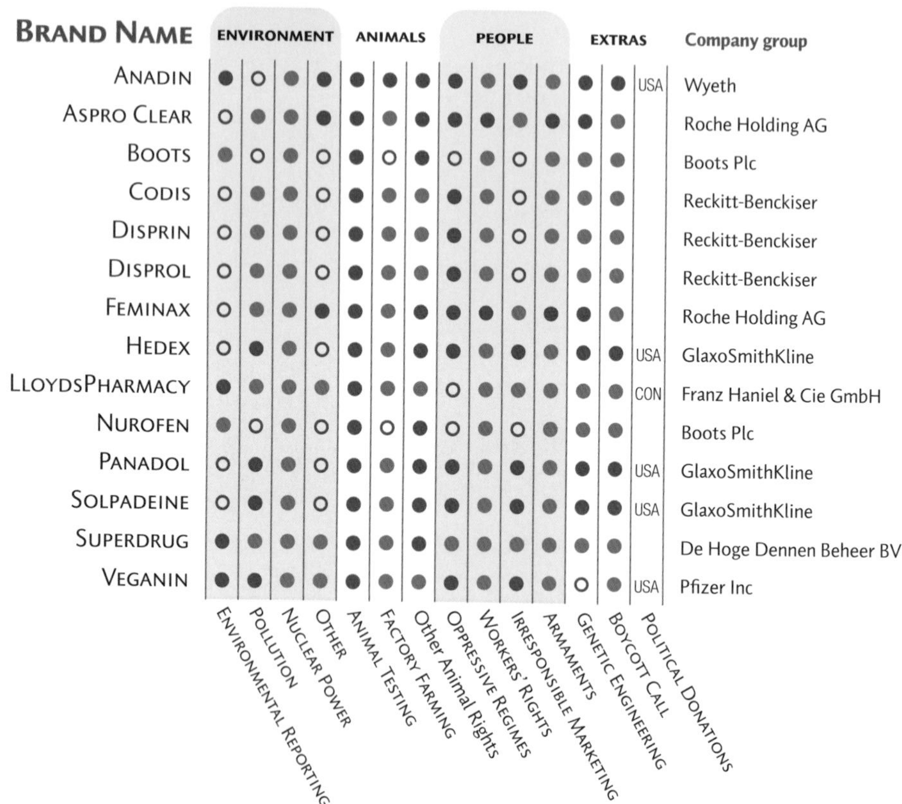

Brand Name	Environment: Environmental Reporting	Environment: Pollution	Environment: Nuclear Power	Environment: Other	Animals: Animal Testing	Animals: Factory Farming	Animals: Other Animal Rights	People: Oppressive Regimes	People: Workers' Rights	People: Irresponsible Marketing	People: Armaments	Extras: Genetic Engineering	Extras: Boycott Call	Extras: Political Donations	Company group
Anadin	●	○	◍	●	●	●	●	●	◍	●	◍	●	●	USA	Wyeth
Aspro Clear	○	◍	◍	●	●	◍	●	●	●	◍	●	●	◍		Roche Holding AG
Boots	◍	○	◍	○	●	○	●	○	◍	○	◍	◍	◍		Boots Plc
Codis	○	◍	◍	○	●	◍	◍	●	◍	○	◍	◍	◍		Reckitt-Benckiser
Disprin	○	◍	◍	○	●	◍	◍	●	◍	○	◍	◍	◍		Reckitt-Benckiser
Disprol	○	◍	◍	○	●	◍	◍	●	◍	○	◍	◍	◍		Reckitt-Benckiser
Feminax	○	◍	◍	●	●	◍	●	●	●	◍	●	●	◍		Roche Holding AG
Hedex	○	●	◍	○	●	◍	●	●	◍	●	◍	●	●	USA	GlaxoSmithKline
LloydsPharmacy	●	◍	◍	◍	●	◍	◍	○	◍	◍	◍	◍	◍	CON	Franz Haniel & Cie GmbH
Nurofen	◍	○	◍	○	●	○	●	○	◍	○	◍	◍	◍		Boots Plc
Panadol	○	●	◍	○	●	◍	●	●	◍	●	◍	●	●	USA	GlaxoSmithKline
Solpadeine	○	●	◍	○	●	◍	●	●	◍	●	◍	●	●	USA	GlaxoSmithKline
Superdrug	●	◍	◍	◍	●	◍	●	◍	◍	◍	◍	◍	◍		De Hoge Dennen Beheer BV
Veganin	●	●	◍	◍	●	◍	◍	●	◍	●	◍	○	◍	USA	Pfizer Inc

Key

- ◍ Top rating (no criticisms found)
- ○ Middle rating
- ● Bottom rating
- A related company has a bottom rating and the company itself has a middle rating
- A related company has a middle rating
- A related company has a bottom rating

Source: ECRA-See page 14 for full key to symbols.

Perfumes & aftershaves

Perfumes make up one of the ultimate consumer luxuries. Driven by huge advertising campaigns and promotional activities, the fragrance industry is locked onto the 'aspirational' and escapist part of human nature.

Secret ingredients

Apart from the dream and a briefly lingering scent, what we are really being sold in our bottle of perfume is nothing more than a container of unnamed and unspecified chemicals, or if we're lucky, a phial full of essential oils.

Perfume recipes have so far been protected from compulsory labelling as a result of highly-effective multinational company lobbying. Perfume was recently excluded from EU laws aimed at full ingredient listings because most perfumes had 'too many ingredients' to list. The cosmetics and toiletries industry has around 6,000–8,000 ingredients to play with, although it is hardly likely that any single perfume uses more than 20 or so of these. Only about half of the thousands of ingredients available are the fragrances themselves.

Allergies & animal cruelty

Since a third of all allergies are caused by fragrance, the elixir in the bottle might give you headaches, rashes or make you sneeze.

In addition to fragrance, perfumes sometimes contain cruelly-derived ingredients and fixatives like musk ('a dried secretion from the preputial follicles of the musk deer'), civet (taken from the scent glands of the Ethiopian civet cat), ambergris (taken from sperm whales) and castor (from follicles near the genitals of beavers).

The perfume may also have been made from flowers picked in the Third World (where many of the cheaper essential oils are sourced), often using child labour.

Unfortunately, since the manufacturers are not obliged to list their ingredients, there is no easy way of finding out quite what your favourite perfume does contain.

Targeting the kids

Recently, child protection authorities and watchdog groups have criticised the perfume industry for the marketing of scents for children.

Since 1995, Versace, Agnes B, Nina Ricci, Givenchy and Guerlain have all introduced children's perfumes for children aged between 4 and 15.

Some watchdog groups have expressed the fear that the premature sexualisation of children in certain advertisements runs the risk of legitimising and encouraging sexual interest in children

WOMEN'S

- Amethyst Mist
- Aurelia
- Chanel Nº 5
- White Musk

MEN'S

- Activist
- Aurelius
- Ginger FM
- Sirius

WOMEN'S

- Beautiful
- Joop
- Opium
- Youth Dew

MEN'S

- Aramis
- Jazz

WOMEN'S

- Anais Anais
- Charlie
- CK One (Unisex)
- Dune

MEN'S

- Farenheit
- Lynx
- Old Spice
- Safari for Men

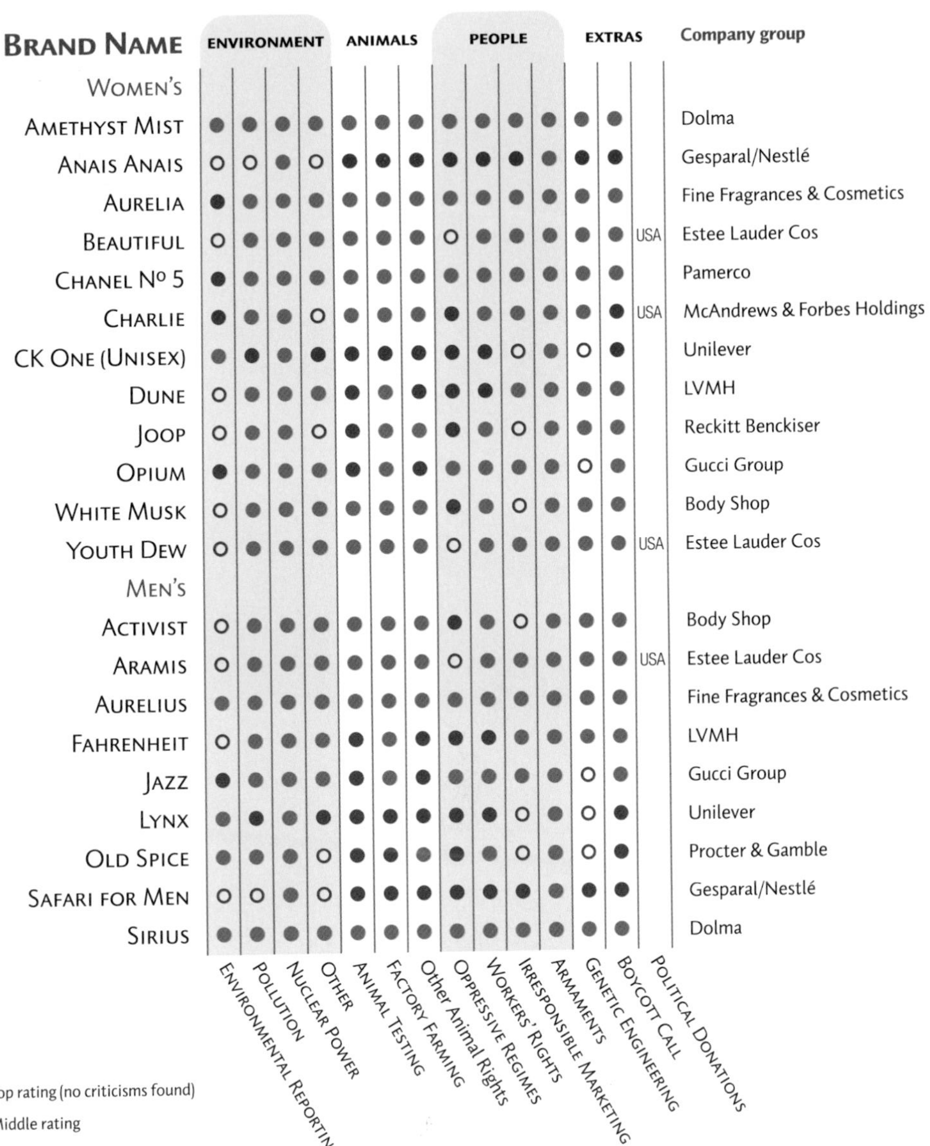

Key

- Top rating (no criticisms found)
- Middle rating
- Bottom rating
- A related company has a bottom rating and the company itself has a middle rating
- A related company has a middle rating
- A related company has a bottom rating

Source: ECRA-See page 14 for full key to symbols.

Sanitary protection

Women in the UK typically spend more than £300 a year on sanitary protection, mostly on the Always, Allday and Tampax brands, which are all produced by one company, Procter & Gamble. They have been able to cash in on the fact that girls now start to menstruate much earlier than they used to (typically at between 10 and 13 years old). A new high-growth area is 'every-day panty liners', which have controversially been touted as intrinsic to 'daily freshness'. There are important health and environmental issues to consider, but alternatives are available.

Health

Manufacturers estimate that ten per cent of women have permanently deserted the tampon due to fears of the blood infection Toxic Shock Syndrome (TSS). This is a rare, but painful and occasionally fatal, disease. Ninety-nine per cent of TSS cases are found in women wearing rayon-blend tampons, the most common kind. Natracare does 100 per cent cotton tampons, which may therefore be safer.

The superabsorbent polyacrylate gel AGM was banned from tampons in 1995 because of links to TSS, but it is still used in some towels. The main safety issue arises from the temptation to change gel-filled towels less frequently, causing a build up of bacteria. Additionally, a recent Canadian study on babies' nappies also found that when dry, AGM powder can travel up the urethra to the kidneys and cause scarring.

Women's Environmental Network (WEN) has campaigned on the issue of GM cotton in tampons and towels. Aside from the environmental objections to modification of the cotton crop, the organisation is concerned about potential alterations in absorbency levels increasing the risk of TSS, and about the potential transfer of antibiotic resistance marker genes. Using disposable sanitary products risks putting toxins next to your skin or vaginal tissue. Some residues, such as pesticides and dioxins from the bleaching process, have been linked to birth defects, reproductive disorders, depressed immunity and cancer.

The environment

Casual flushing of sanitary protection waste means that much of it ends up in rivers and sewage outfills, acting as a breeding ground for diseases and potentially being mistaken by sea mammals for prey. Otherwise, it festers in landfill sites, where it takes six months for a tampon to degrade. Plastic packaging and applicators may persist indefinitely in the environment. Reusable sanitary protection, such as the Keeper, washable sanitary towels, and sponges are the best environmental option as there are no disposal issues to consider.

The percentage of waste paper pulp in tampons and towels has increased during the last ten years, but it has recently taken a dive again due to a move away from recycled products to a focus on premium ones. Manufacturers are playing to the fact that around half of women declare themselves prepared to pay more if they sense a higher quality and comfort level – hence the extra wings, gels and gauzy layers that keep appearing.

- Keeper
- Lotus Pads
- Luna Sponges
- Many Moons
- Natracare
- Soft-Tampons

- Bodyform
- Helen Harper
- Libresse
- Lil-lets

- Alldays
- Always
- Carefree
- Kotex
- Tampax

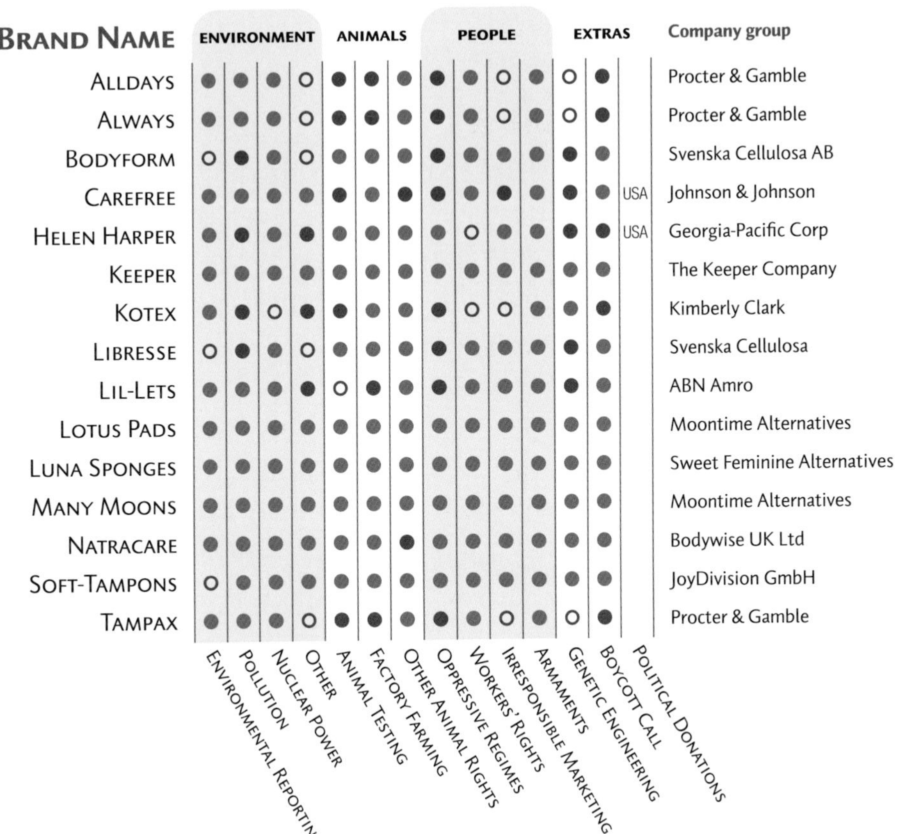

Brand Name	Environmental Reporting	Pollution	Nuclear Power	Other	Animal Testing	Factory Farming	Other Animal Rights	Oppressive Regimes	Workers' Rights	Irresponsible Marketing	Armaments	Genetic Engineering	Boycott Call	Political Donations	Company group
Alldays	grey	grey	grey	open	black	black	grey	black	grey	open	grey	open	black		Procter & Gamble
Always	grey	grey	grey	open	black	black	grey	black	grey	open	grey	open	black		Procter & Gamble
Bodyform	open	black	grey	open	grey	grey	grey	black	grey	grey	grey	black	grey		Svenska Cellulosa AB
Carefree	grey	grey	grey	grey	black	grey	black	black	grey	black	grey	black	grey	USA	Johnson & Johnson
Helen Harper	grey	black	grey	black	grey	grey	grey	grey	open	grey	grey	black	black	USA	Georgia-Pacific Corp
Keeper	grey	grey	grey	grey	grey	grey	grey	grey	grey	grey	grey	grey	grey		The Keeper Company
Kotex	grey	black	open	black	black	grey	grey	black	open	open	grey	grey	black		Kimberly Clark
Libresse	open	black	grey	open	grey	grey	grey	black	grey	grey	grey	black	grey		Svenska Cellulosa
Lil-Lets	grey	grey	grey	black	open	black	grey	black	grey	grey	grey	black	grey		ABN Amro
Lotus Pads	grey	grey	grey	grey	grey	grey	grey	grey	grey	grey	grey	grey	grey		Moontime Alternatives
Luna Sponges	grey	grey	grey	grey	grey	grey	grey	grey	grey	grey	grey	grey	grey		Sweet Feminine Alternatives
Many Moons	grey	grey	grey	grey	grey	grey	grey	grey	grey	grey	grey	grey	grey		Moontime Alternatives
Natracare	grey	grey	grey	grey	grey	grey	black	grey	grey	grey	grey	grey	grey		Bodywise UK Ltd
Soft-Tampons	open	grey	grey	grey	grey	grey	grey	grey	grey	grey	grey	grey	grey		JoyDivision GmbH
Tampax	grey	grey	grey	open	black	black	grey	black	grey	open	grey	open	black		Procter & Gamble

Column groups: ENVIRONMENT (Environmental Reporting, Pollution, Nuclear Power, Other); ANIMALS (Animal Testing, Factory Farming, Other Animal Rights); PEOPLE (Oppressive Regimes, Workers' Rights, Irresponsible Marketing, Armaments); EXTRAS (Genetic Engineering, Boycott Call, Political Donations).

Key

- Top rating (no criticisms found)
- Middle rating
- Bottom rating
- A related company has a bottom rating and the company itself has a middle rating
- A related company has a middle rating
- A related company has a bottom rating

Source: ECRA-See page 14 for full key to symbols.

Shampoo

Hair care is intrinsic to our desire to present a pleasing image in the increasingly fashion-conscious world we live in. Even those with a concern for nature and the environment can be seduced by the apparently 'natural' or even 'organic' kinds of shampoo and conditioner that now litter the shelves of supermarkets and chemists' stores.

The natural look

Over the past few years, booming interest in organic produce has caused the mainstream cosmetic companies to flirt heavily, and successfully, with the natural image in launching their new product lines. This corporate romance with nature can be criticised as a cheap attempt to appear ecologically sound, as the few token 'natural' ingredients invariably mask the usual chemical cocktail. Alternative groups, including ECRA, have called for Elida Fabergé to withdraw or rename its Organics line until all ingredients are certified organic. Of course, alternative producers have long been proclaiming the benefits of natural ingredients, with product lines true to their principles.

Suds law

The long list of ingredients on the back of a shampoo bottle can be hard to decipher without specialist chemical knowledge. A commonly-used shampoo ingredient due to its propensity to foam is Sodium Laurel Sulphate, or its milder form Sodium Laureth Sulphate. Claims about the former's damaging health effects point to it being an allergen, with symptoms including skin and eye irritation. Industry replies to such concerns emphasise that these chemicals are used in measured amounts that have been legally decreed as safe for use.

Dandruff is a problem that many people are tackling with medicated shampoos. Anti-dandruff shampoos again can contain potentially toxic chemicals and can even aggravate the problem. Eating foods that contain the right fats – such as raw nuts and cold-pressed vegetable oils – is one way to address the imbalance.

Alternatives

In the days before shampoo, people resorted to more imaginative methods of achieving glossy locks. Soap was used as an all-round cleanser for hair and body, but as water has become more alkaline (hard) its effectiveness has declined, leaving hair rough and tangled. In areas with a soft water supply, using a plain soap with conditioner is an option. Otherwise adding something acidic along with soap, such as vinegar or lemon juice, can neutralise the hard water. If you follow up with conditioner, your hair should be left healthy. It is possible to dispense with shampoo completely. However, people may find the transitional period unpleasant as the scalp's naturally-produced oils (washed out by shampooing) kick back into action.

Animal testing

Some companies skirt round the issue of animal testing, at the same time keeping themselves open to new ingredients, by adhering to the 'five-year rolling rule' which means five years must have elapsed since the ingredient was tested on animals. Naturewatch and BUAV support use of the 'fixed cut off date', whereby companies refuse to use ingredients tested on animals after a certain date. In the table, a full red circle indicates the company has no written animal testing policy statement, or did not reply to ECRA's request for one, or sent a policy with standards less stringent than those required for an empty red circle (middle rating). An empty red circle indicates that the company does not have a fixed cut-off date, but has a policy of not testing products or ingredients on animals, and of not commissioning such tests.
A green circle indicates that the company does not sell animal tested products or ingredients, and upholds a fixed cut-off date. (For details as to which companies did and did not provide animal testing policy statements, please see the relevant ECRA Research Supplement).

- Body Shop
- Faith in Nature
- Green People
- Hemp Garden
- Honesty
- Natura Organics
- Neem Care
- Weleda

- Botanics
- Henara
- Original Source
- Superdrug
- VO5

- Aussie
- Head & Shoulders
- L'Oréal
- Organics
- Pantene Pro-V

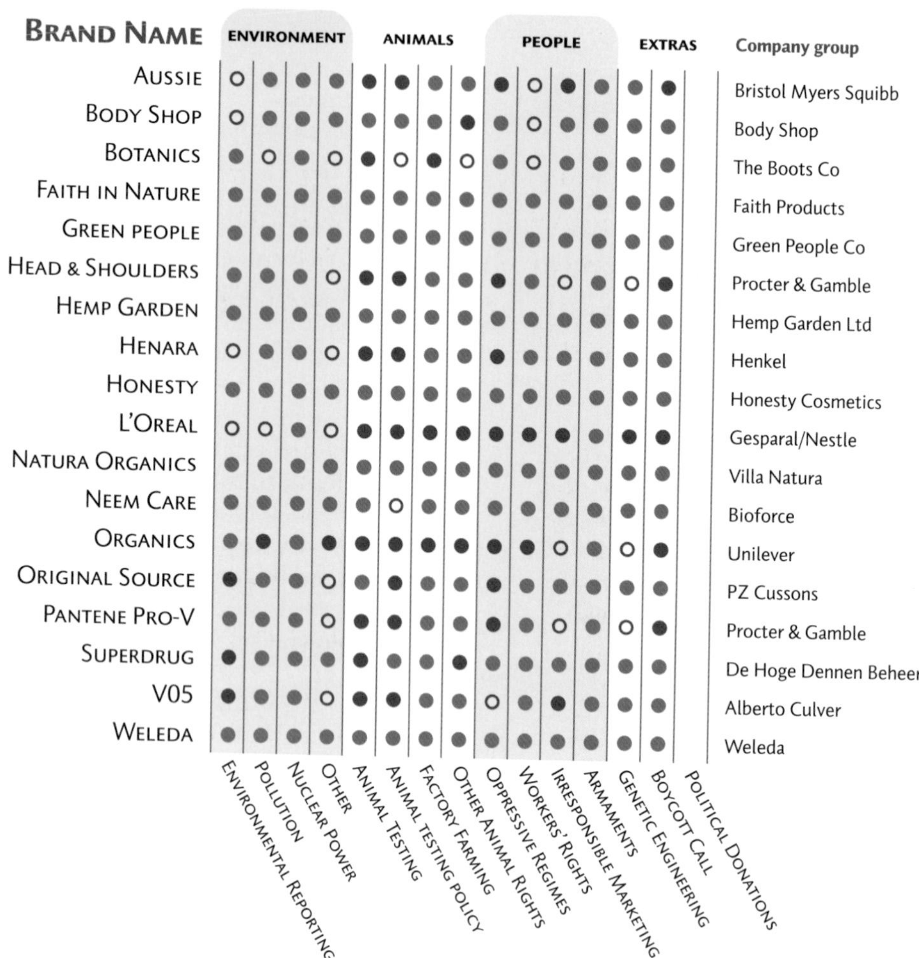

Brand Name	Environmental Reporting	Pollution	Nuclear Power	Other	Animal Testing	Animal Testing Policy	Factory Farming	Other Animal Rights	Oppressive Regimes	Workers' Rights	Irresponsible Marketing	Armaments	Genetic Engineering	Boycott Call	Political Donations	Company group
	ENVIRONMENT				ANIMALS				PEOPLE				EXTRAS			
Aussie	○	◍	◍	◍	●	●	◍	◍	●	○	●	◍	◍	●		Bristol Myers Squibb
Body Shop	○	◍	◍	◍	◍	◍	◍	●	◍	○	◍	◍	◍	◍		Body Shop
Botanics	◍	○	◍	○	●	○	●	○	◍	○	◍	◍	◍	◍		The Boots Co
Faith in Nature	◍	◍	◍	◍	◍	◍	◍	◍	◍	◍	◍	◍	◍	◍		Faith Products
Green people	◍	◍	◍	◍	◍	◍	◍	◍	◍	◍	◍	◍	◍	◍		Green People Co
Head & Shoulders	◍	◍	◍	○	●	●	◍	◍	●	◍	○	◍	○	●		Procter & Gamble
Hemp Garden	◍	◍	◍	◍	◍	◍	◍	◍	◍	◍	◍	◍	◍	◍		Hemp Garden Ltd
Henara	○	◍	◍	○	●	●	◍	◍	●	◍	◍	◍	◍	◍		Henkel
Honesty	◍	◍	◍	◍	◍	◍	◍	◍	◍	◍	◍	◍	◍	◍		Honesty Cosmetics
L'Oreal	○	○	◍	○	●	●	●	●	●	●	●	◍	●	●		Gesparal/Nestle
Natura Organics	◍	◍	◍	◍	◍	◍	◍	◍	◍	◍	◍	◍	◍	◍		Villa Natura
Neem Care	◍	◍	◍	◍	◍	○	◍	◍	◍	◍	◍	◍	◍	◍		Bioforce
Organics	◍	●	◍	●	●	●	●	●	●	●	○	◍	○	●		Unilever
Original Source	●	◍	◍	○	◍	●	◍	◍	●	◍	◍	◍	◍	◍		PZ Cussons
Pantene Pro-V	◍	◍	◍	○	●	●	◍	◍	●	◍	○	◍	○	●		Procter & Gamble
Superdrug	●	◍	◍	◍	●	◍	◍	●	◍	◍	◍	◍	◍	◍		De Hoge Dennen Beheer
V05	●	◍	◍	○	●	●	◍	◍	○	◍	●	◍	◍	◍		Alberto Culver
Weleda	◍	◍	◍	◍	◍	◍	◍	◍	◍	◍	◍	◍	◍	◍		Weleda

Key

- ◍ Top rating (no criticisms found)
- ○ Middle rating
- ● Bottom rating
- A related company has a bottom rating and the company itself has a middle rating
- A related company has a middle rating
- A related company has a bottom rating

Source: ECRA-See page 14 for full key to symbols.

Skincare

Even though the big cosmetics firms love to use the word 'natural' on their products, they don't really mean what they say. Most skincare products use man-made chemicals, some of which may be potentially toxic. If we want to be sure that something is really natural we have to look behind the marketing slogans and read the small print.

How natural?

Lack of proper industry regulation means that a product can be called 'natural' even it contains as little as 1 per cent of natural ingredients!

Specific ingredients that we should try to avoid include: propylene glycol, formaldehyde, ammonia derivatives – (diethanolamine, triethanolamine and monoethanolamine), isopropyl, alpha hydroxy acid and benzoic acid. Friends of the Earth focuses its campaigns on chemicals which interfere with our body's hormones and those which 'bio-accumulate' (aren't broken down by the body). It says these chemicals should be phased out and replaced by safer alternatives. The long-term effects of these chemicals are so far unknown and, more worryingly, even if they were found to be harmful, our bodies would be unable to eliminate them. Friends of the Earth is also concerned about the potential for similar damage from artificial musks.

Good Shopping Guide Ethically Certified companies like Green People Company and Honesty try to avoid some of the most worrying chemicals – and produce excellent products.

The OK list

Of the brands/companies on this table, Friends of the Earth recommends the following as being free from alkylphenols, artificial musks, bisphenol A and phthalates:

- Boots Skin Kindly Rich Moisturising Cream, Fragrance Free Moisturising Cream, No. 7 Essential Moisturising Cream
- Crookes Healthcare E45 range (E45 Moisturising Cream)
- Estée Lauder's Clinique dramatically Different Moisturising Lotion, Clarifying Lotions – Mild, 2, 3, and 4

Not OK

And Friends of the Earth says that these contained one or more of the worrying ingredients (at time of ECRA report, April 2002):

- Beiersdorf Nivea
- Boots Oil of Evening Primrose Moisture Cream
- Elida Faberge Vaseline Intensive Care products
- Procter & Gamble Oil of Olay, Secret Products

Others

L'Oreal and Johnson & Johnson did not provide Friends of the Earth with any information on individual products, so it recommends that we avoid their products as well. Even the Body Shop was named as containing one or more of the chemicals in its products, although it is also in Friends of the Earth recent research listed as top in a league of cosmetic companies working toward removing risky chemicals from their products.

Packaging

A particular problem with moisturisers is the amount of packaging they create. Most brands use plastic packaging, which is most likely to end up in landfill, with only a small amount being recycled or incinerated. Plastic recycling is expensive and the value of recycled plastic is low, so it can cost more to recycle plastic than to landfill it. Of the brands covered here, Culpeper is the only one using glass to package its skincare products. The Body Shop used to refill old bottles, although these days not every shop offers this facility; but its shops will still accept the used bottle for recycling and offer consumers a replacement with a 10 per cent discount.

Sources to check

- *www.greenpeople.co.uk/info.asp* an excellent company.
- Honesty Cosmetics is a highly progressive company also.
- The authors of Cosmetics Unmasked (published by Thorsons), Gina & Steve Antczak, have their own website: *http://www.gina.antczak.btinternet.co.uk*
- The Ecologist, 22 April 2001, "Home Sickness" *(www.theecologist.org)* has a good general article on chemicals
- For more details on the above Friends of the Earth report, see the relevant ECRA research supplement – order it at *www.ethicalconsumer.org*

- Body Shop
- Culpeper
- Green People
- Hemp Garden
- Honesty
- Lush
- Natura Organics
- Weleda

- Aveda
- Clarins
- Neutrogena
- Nivea
- Origins

- Boots
- E45
- L'Oreal
- Oil of Olay
- Ponds

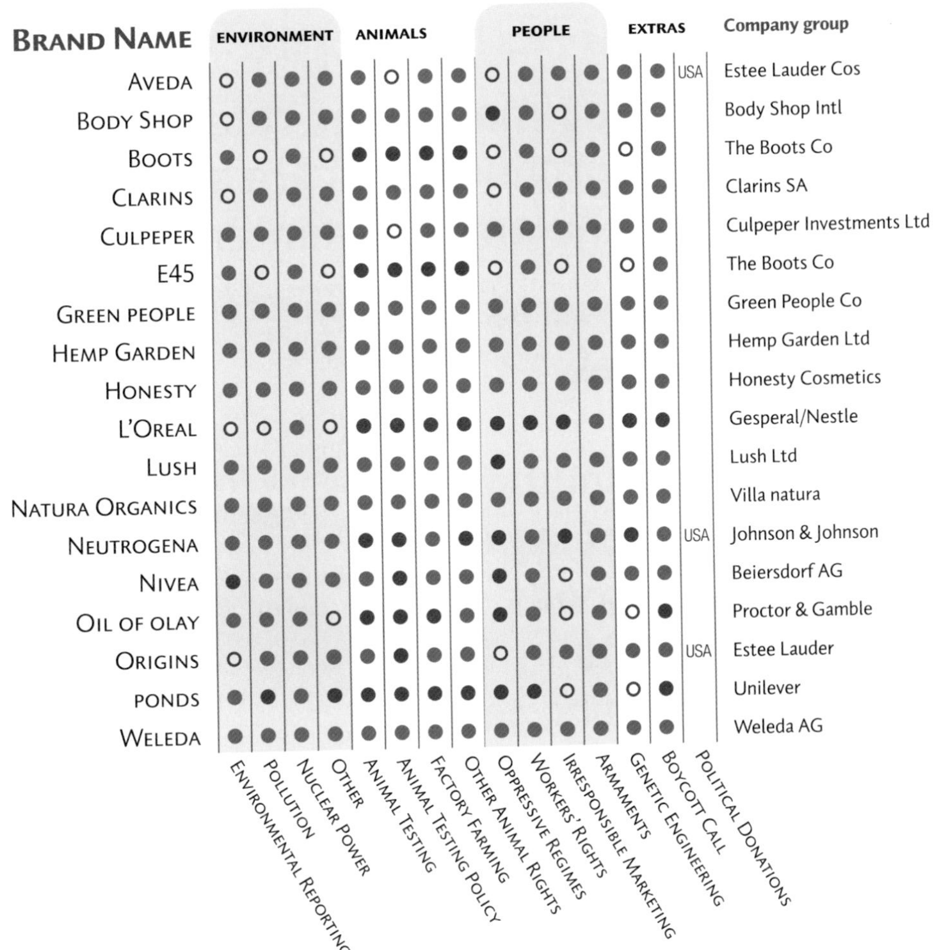

Brand Name	Environmental Reporting	Pollution	Nuclear Power	Other	Animal Testing	Animal Testing Policy	Factory Farming	Other Animal Rights	Oppressive Regimes	Workers' Rights	Irresponsible Marketing	Armaments	Genetic Engineering	Boycott Call	Political Donations	Company group
	Environment				**Animals**				**People**				**Extras**			
Aveda	○	●	●	●	●	○	●	●	○	●	●	●	●	●	USA	Estee Lauder Cos
Body Shop	○	●	●	●	●	●	●	●	⬤	●	○	●	●	●		Body Shop Intl
Boots	●	○	●	○	⬤	⬤	⬤	⬤	○	●	○	●	○	●		The Boots Co
Clarins	○	●	●	●	●	●	●	●	○	●	●	●	●	●		Clarins SA
Culpeper	●	●	●	●	●	○	●	●	●	●	●	●	●	●		Culpeper Investments Ltd
E45	●	○	●	○	⬤	⬤	⬤	⬤	○	●	○	●	○	●		The Boots Co
Green People	●	●	●	●	●	●	●	●	●	●	●	●	●	●		Green People Co
Hemp Garden	●	●	●	●	●	●	●	●	●	●	●	●	●	●		Hemp Garden Ltd
Honesty	●	●	●	●	●	●	●	●	●	●	●	●	●	●		Honesty Cosmetics
L'Oreal	○	○	●	○	⬤	⬤	⬤	⬤	⬤	⬤	⬤	●	⬤	⬤		Gesperal/Nestle
Lush	●	●	●	●	●	●	●	●	⬤	●	●	●	●	●		Lush Ltd
Natura Organics	●	●	●	●	●	●	●	●	●	●	●	●	●	●		Villa natura
Neutrogena	●	●	●	●	⬤	⬤	●	⬤	⬤	●	⬤	●	⬤	●	USA	Johnson & Johnson
Nivea	⬤	●	●	●	●	⬤	●	●	⬤	●	○	●	●	●		Beiersdorf AG
Oil of Olay	●	●	●	○	⬤	⬤	⬤	●	⬤	●	○	●	○	⬤		Proctor & Gamble
Origins	○	●	●	●	●	⬤	●	●	○	●	●	●	●	●	USA	Estee Lauder
Ponds	●	⬤	●	⬤	⬤	⬤	⬤	⬤	⬤	⬤	○	●	○	⬤		Unilever
Weleda	●	●	●	●	●	●	●	●	●	●	●	●	●	●		Weleda AG

Key

- ● Top rating (no criticisms found)
- ○ Middle rating
- ⬤ Bottom rating
- A related company has a bottom rating and the company itself has a middle rating
- A related company has a middle rating
- A related company has a bottom rating

Source: ECRA-See page 14 for full key to symbols.

Soap

Few of us take much interest in the ingredients of the soap we use. A single bar may contain a huge variety, and perhaps we should consider whether they are really necessary. Natural and hand-made products are much more 'friendly'.

Ingredients

Made from animal or vegetable fats, oils or grease, soap is formed when the fats interact with an alkali. Preservatives, salts, colours, perfumes, moisturisers and emulsifiers may then be added, with the more adventurous brands including fruits, spices and essential oils. Traditionally, soaps were produced from animal fats such as fish oils or tallow, listed in the ingredients as 'sodium tallowate'. The Vegan Society describes tallow as 'hard animal fat, especially that obtained from the parts about the kidneys of ruminating animals.' Although there are vegetable alternatives, many of the major soap brands still contain animal fats and consequently are not suitable for vegetarians or vegans.

Vegetable soaps may also contain added ingredients such as honey, lanolin and milk, preventing them from being suitable for vegans. Lush, Caurnie, Suma, Faith and Body Shop soaps are all suitable for vegetarians. Caurnie and Faith soaps are all vegan, while all except Suma's honey soaps are suitable for vegans. Body Shop produces a list of its 'vegan non-friendly' products and Lush soaps clearly labels those which are suitable for vegans.

Making soap cleanly

Most of the bigger brand soaps are made from a common soap bar, manufactured by large commercial producers who sell it on in the form of dried soap nodules to individual soap makers for reprocessing.

Soaps made by the 'alternative' producers, such as Caurnie, Faith and Suma are hand-made, which, if nothing else, keeps more people employed. According to information from Suma, the cold saponification process used by Suma and Caurnie is more energy-efficient as 'all the ingredients remain in the mix, with only such heat input as is required to raise the temperature of the mix to body heat.'

A commercial processor may use a boiling process which could consume up to 65kw hours of electricity and 15 tonnes of water in producing 1 tonne of soap. The alternative soap makers claim that commercial producers extract the glycerine, selling it as a by-product, instead of leaving it in the soap. Since glycerine is a natural moisturiser, it explains why many soaps can dry the skin.

Synthetics and packaging

Most of the major soaps contain synthetic (petrochemical-based) ingredients, while Suma, Faith and Caurnie use natural ingredients and instead of adding an artificial fragrance use essential oils or fruits to scent their soaps. The synthetic ingredients used by the larger companies are often irritants for sensitive skin.

The packaging by the major brands is often excessive, with Imperial Leather – the UK's best-selling soap – using three wrappers, including a box. In comparison, Suma's soap is sold completely loose and just wrapped in a brown envelope. Lush products also have little or no packaging and Faith and Caurnie soaps also have minimal packaging.

Those small bits of soap that are too small to wash with can be kept in a soap jar which can be used in hot water as a soft jelly to use for washing-up.

- Body Shop
- Caurnie Soaps
- Faith in Nature
- Hemp Garden
- Lush
- Organic Soaps
- Suma

- Imperial Leather
- Nivea
- Pearl
- Simple

- Camay
- Dove
- Fairy
- Palmolive
- Pears

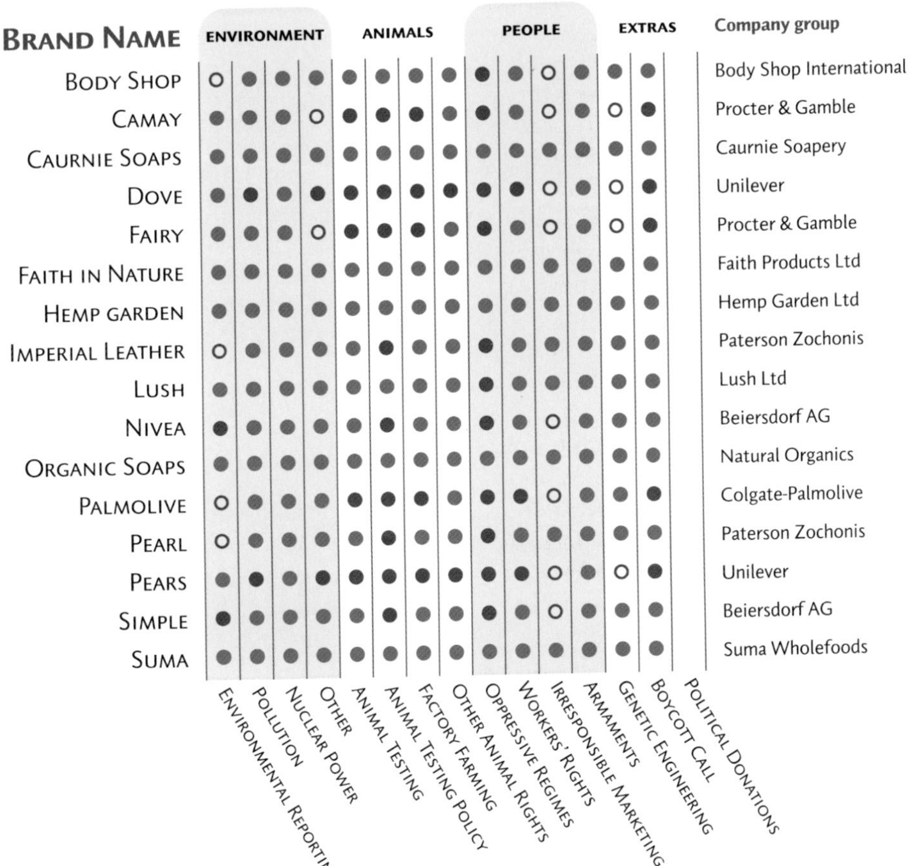

Brand Name	Environment: Environmental Reporting	Environment: Pollution	Environment: Nuclear Power	Environment: Other	Animals: Animal Testing	Animals: Animal Testing Policy	Animals: Factory Farming	Animals: Other Animal Rights	People: Oppressive Regimes	People: Workers' Rights	People: Irresponsible Marketing	People: Armaments	Extras: Genetic Engineering	Extras: Boycott Call	Extras: Political Donations	Company group
Body Shop	Middle	Top	Top	Top	Top	Top	Top	Top	Bottom	Top	Middle	Top	Top	Top		Body Shop International
Camay	Top	Top	Top	Middle	Bottom	Bottom	Bottom	Top	Bottom	Top	Middle	Top	Middle	Bottom		Procter & Gamble
Caurnie Soaps	Top	Top	Top	Top	Top	Top	Top	Top	Top	Top	Top	Top	Top	Top		Caurnie Soapery
Dove	Top	Bottom	Top	Bottom	Bottom	Bottom	Bottom	Bottom	Bottom	Bottom	Middle	Top	Middle	Bottom		Unilever
Fairy	Top	Top	Top	Middle	Bottom	Bottom	Bottom	Top	Bottom	Top	Middle	Top	Middle	Bottom		Procter & Gamble
Faith in Nature	Top	Top	Top	Top	Top	Top	Top	Top	Top	Top	Top	Top	Top	Top		Faith Products Ltd
Hemp Garden	Top	Top	Top	Top	Top	Top	Top	Top	Top	Top	Top	Top	Top	Top		Hemp Garden Ltd
Imperial Leather	Middle	Top	Top	Top	Top	Bottom	Top	Top	Bottom	Top	Top	Top	Top	Top		Paterson Zochonis
Lush	Top	Top	Top	Top	Top	Top	Top	Top	Bottom	Top	Top	Top	Top	Top		Lush Ltd
Nivea	Bottom	Top	Top	Top	Top	Bottom	Top	Top	Bottom	Top	Middle	Top	Top	Top		Beiersdorf AG
Organic Soaps	Top	Top	Top	Top	Top	Top	Top	Top	Top	Top	Top	Top	Top	Top		Natural Organics
Palmolive	Middle	Top	Top	Top	Bottom	Bottom	Bottom	Top	Bottom	Bottom	Middle	Top	Top	Bottom		Colgate-Palmolive
Pearl	Middle	Top	Top	Top	Top	Bottom	Top	Top	Bottom	Top	Top	Top	Top	Top		Paterson Zochonis
Pears	Top	Bottom	Top	Bottom	Bottom	Bottom	Bottom	Bottom	Bottom	Bottom	Middle	Top	Middle	Bottom		Unilever
Simple	Bottom	Top	Top	Top	Top	Bottom	Top	Top	Bottom	Top	Middle	Top	Top	Top		Beiersdorf AG
Suma	Top	Top	Top	Top	Top	Top	Top	Top	Top	Top	Top	Top	Top	Top		Suma Wholefoods

Key

- Top rating (no criticisms found)
- Middle rating
- Bottom rating
- A related company has a bottom rating and the company itself has a middle rating
- A related company has a middle rating
- A related company has a bottom rating

Source: ECRA-See page 14 for full key to symbols.

Sports shoes

The big names, like Adidas, Reebok, Nike and Puma, have for some years been receiving flak for their use of 'sweatshop' labour and so most now produce 'corporate responsibility' reports to allay our fears. The smaller firms seem to be less interested in the issue, but it hasn't gone away. We should also take a look at the kinds of materials being used in any shoes we buy.

Material matters

- Polyvinyl chloride (PVC) may be the most damaging plastic to human health and the environment. According to Greenpeace, Adidas, Asics, Nike and Puma are now phasing it out. New Balance has eliminated some PVC but set no start-date for phase-out; Fila, Reebok and Saucony made no commitments
- Nike has signed up to a Climate Savers pact and aims to reduce greenhouse gas emissions across its operations, replacing sulphur hexafluoride (a greenhouse gas nearly 35,000 times more potent than an equivalent weight of carbon dioxide) in its 'air' trainers
- Sports shoes comprise dozens of mostly synthetic materials. Leather uppers are tanned via a 20-step process using strong chemicals. In countries without much environmental protection, tannery wastes can be discharged untreated into the water systems, making tap water undrinkable

ECRA labour principles

Someone recently worked out that a Thai worker would have to work for 26.5 million days or 72,000 years to receive what Tiger Woods gets during his five year contract with Nike and that Nike spends the equivalent of 14,000 workers' daily wages to pay Tiger Woods for a day.

Campaigners are trying to persuade companies to agree to:

- No use of forced labour or child labour
- Freedom of association and collective bargaining
- Payment of a living wage
- A 48-hour week maximum
- Safe working conditions
- No race or gender discrimination

To achieve ECRA's top rating, a company's labour code would have to promise systematic monitoring by fully-independent inspection teams, something no multinational has ever agreed to. It would also need to ensure enforcement of workers' right to organise and bargain collectively. But even these become problematic in countries like China, where authentic trade union activity is illegal and there are no NGOs. Most sports footwear companies still site their production in countries with authoritarian governments which forbid and repress independent trade union organising.

A recent Oxfam report on conditions in four Indonesian factories demonstrated that positive change in response to international pressure is possible. However, the interviewees were still living in extreme poverty, subjected to verbal abuse, intrusive physical examinations and dangerous conditions. 'Those improvements which have occurred are commendable,' said the report. 'Unfortunately they fall well short of ensuring that Nike and Adidas workers are able to live with dignity.'

A couple of years ago, Nike claimed that it had dramatically increased wages at its Indonesian factories, but failed to point out that the increases fell below what was needed to keep up with massive inflation in the country. Companies continue to treat the sweatshop issue as a public relations inconvenience rather than as a serious human rights matter.

- Asics
- Brooks
- Cheatah
- Hi-Tec
- Le Coq Sportif
- Mizuno
- Puma
- Saucony

- Adidas
- Ellesse
- New Balance
- Reebok

- Fila
- Gola
- Nike
- Umbro

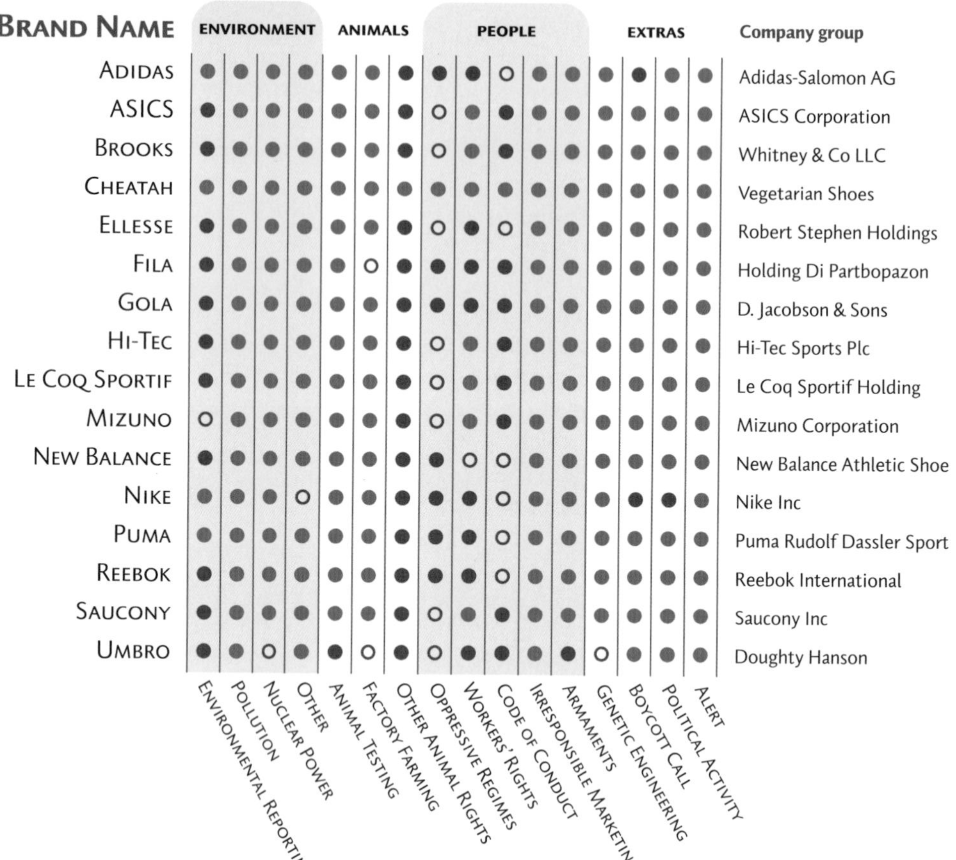

Brand Name	Environment				Animals			People					Extras				Company group
	Environmental Reporting	Pollution	Nuclear Power	Other	Animal Testing	Factory Farming	Other Animal Rights	Oppressive Regimes	Workers' Rights	Code of Conduct	Irresponsible Marketing	Armaments	Genetic Engineering	Boycott Call	Political Activity	Alert	
Adidas	◍	◍	◍	◍	◍	◍	●	●	●	○	◍	◍	◍	●	◍	◍	Adidas-Salomon AG
ASICS	●	◍	◍	◍	◍	◍	●	○	◍	●	◍	◍	◍	◍	◍	◍	ASICS Corporation
Brooks	●	◍	◍	◍	◍	◍	●	○	◍	●	◍	◍	◍	◍	◍	◍	Whitney & Co LLC
Cheatah	◍	◍	◍	◍	◍	◍	◍	◍	◍	◍	◍	◍	◍	◍	◍	◍	Vegetarian Shoes
Ellesse	●	◍	◍	◍	◍	◍	●	○	●	○	◍	◍	◍	◍	◍	◍	Robert Stephen Holdings
Fila	●	◍	◍	◍	◍	○	●	●	●	●	◍	◍	◍	◍	◍	◍	Holding Di Partbopazon
Gola	●	◍	◍	◍	◍	◍	●	●	●	●	◍	◍	◍	◍	◍	◍	D. Jacobson & Sons
Hi-Tec	●	◍	◍	◍	◍	◍	●	○	◍	●	◍	◍	◍	◍	◍	◍	Hi-Tec Sports Plc
Le Coq Sportif	●	◍	◍	◍	◍	◍	●	○	◍	●	◍	◍	◍	◍	◍	◍	Le Coq Sportif Holding
Mizuno	○	◍	◍	◍	◍	◍	●	○	◍	●	◍	◍	◍	◍	◍	◍	Mizuno Corporation
New Balance	●	◍	◍	◍	◍	◍	●	●	○	○	◍	◍	◍	◍	◍	◍	New Balance Athletic Shoe
Nike	◍	◍	◍	○	◍	◍	●	●	●	○	◍	◍	◍	●	●	◍	Nike Inc
Puma	◍	◍	◍	◍	◍	◍	●	●	●	○	◍	◍	◍	◍	◍	◍	Puma Rudolf Dassler Sport
Reebok	●	◍	◍	◍	◍	◍	●	●	●	○	◍	◍	◍	◍	◍	◍	Reebok International
Saucony	●	◍	◍	◍	◍	◍	●	○	◍	●	◍	◍	◍	◍	◍	◍	Saucony Inc
Umbro	●	◍	○	◍	●	○	●	○	●	●	◍	●	○	◍	◍	◍	Doughty Hanson

Key

- ◍ Top rating (no criticisms found)
- ○ Middle rating
- ● Bottom rating
- A related company has a bottom rating and the company itself has a middle rating
- A related company has a middle rating
- A related company has a bottom rating

Source: ECRA-See page 14 for full key to symbols.

Sun protection

Experts point out that we don't need to use the most expensive formulations of sunscreens if we want to avoid excessive exposure to the sun's harmful rays. They also say that sunscreens don't necessarily prevent skin cancer, and that the best way to minimise risks is to seek the shade and simply not go out in the sun too much.

Screens and blocks

The British Department of Health and the US Food and Drug Administration claim that, although sunscreen prevents sunburn, there is no proof that it actually prevents cancer. They also warn that the main danger of sunscreen is that people increase their risk of skin cancer by increasing the length of time they spend in the sun. They warn against the use of expensive and very high sun protection factor (SPF) lotions as the 'benefits are minimal'. A study by the Consumers' Association in 2001 found that cheap sunscreens can provide as much sun protection as those at the more pricey end of the market.

Sunscreen only works when it's slapped on thick and at least half an hour before we go outside, as it doesn't start working immediately. The Department of Health recommends that we use a sunscreen with a minimum rating of SPF 15. Unfortunately, many alternative cosmetic companies only produce low factor sunscreens. For example, Weleda uses a filter based on the vegetable extract camphor to produce SPF 8 in its highest-rated product. Honesty Cosmetics, a Good Shopping Guide Approved Brand, has an SPF 15 product.

Studies suggest that sunscreens with SPF 15–20 are generally acceptable, but that those above this level increase their ratings by increasing concentrations of key chemical components, which can cause irritation. Meanwhile, the EU is abolishing the term 'sunblock' because it is potentially misleading to customers.

What chemicals?

Sunscreens may contain one or more of a number of different active compounds to block out the sun's rays, such as OMC (octyl methoxycinnamate), benzophenone, benzophenone 3 (oxybenzone), titanium dioxide, zinc oxide and talc, all of which should be listed on the packaging. Unfortunately, despite the potential risks of some of these, it isn't possible to find a sunscreen with a high SPF which doesn't use at least one of them.

Animal testing

Sunscreens are currently classed as cosmetics, which means that animal testing is not required by law. Every year 35,000 animals in the EU are subjected to unnecessary experiments to test cosmetic products. The UK introduced a total ban on the testing of cosmetics products and ingredients on animals in November 1998, but because there is no worldwide ban, many cosmetics sold in the UK will simply have had their tests carried out elsewhere. Until a clear deadline is set, there is little regulatory incentive for widespread industry change

The only companies which have fixed cut-off dates for their animal testing policies are the Body Shop, Estee Lauder, Honesty, Green People and Weleda. Vegans and vegetarians will be pleased to know that sunscreens by Honesty contain no animal-derived ingredients, but they will have to watch out for beeswax, chitin, collagen, elastin, lanolin and stearin, which may be found in other companies' products.

REMEMBER

- Skin cancer can be caused by excessive exposure to the sun
- Skin cancer rates in the UK have doubled in the last 20 years and skin cancer is now the second most common cancer in the UK
- Wear a hat, sunglasses and tightly woven clothes
- Pale clothes let more sun through than darker ones
- On holidays in the hottest weather, have a long lunch and a siesta!

Packaging

The majority of sun lotions come in plastic bottles (usually polyethylene, PE or HDPE) and can only be recycled where such facilities exist. However, Weleda's sun cream is packaged in an aluminium tube to enable it to be easily recycled. None of the surveyed sunscreens came in packaging which was recycled or refillable.

- Banana Boat
- Body Shop
- Delph
- Green People
- Honesty
- Malibu
- Weleda

- Calypso
- Clarins
- Estee Lauder
- Nivea Sun

- Ambre Solaire
- Coppertone
- Piz Buin
- Simple
- Soltan

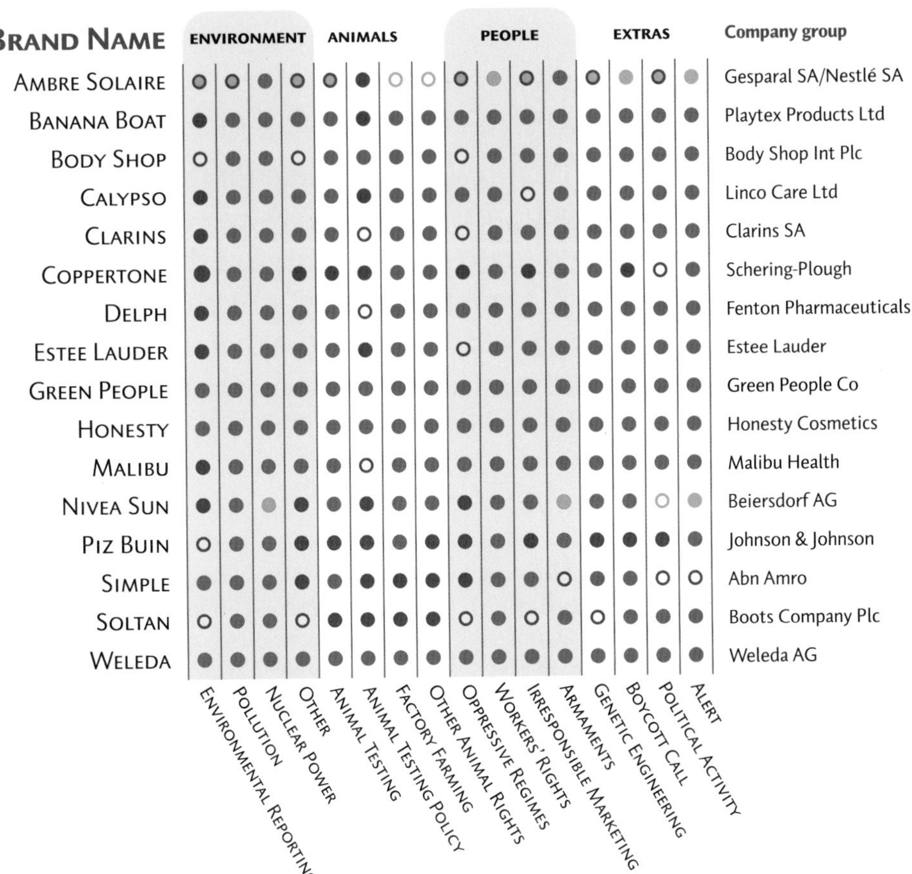

BRAND NAME
ENVIRONMENT
ANIMALS
PEOPLE
EXTRAS
Company group
AMBRE SOLAIRE
Gesparal SA/Nestlé SA
BANANA BOAT
Playtex Products Ltd
BODY SHOP
Body Shop Int Plc
CALYPSO
Linco Care Ltd
CLARINS
Clarins SA
COPPERTONE
Schering-Plough
DELPH
Fenton Pharmaceuticals
ESTEE LAUDER
Estee Lauder
GREEN PEOPLE
Green People Co
HONESTY
Honesty Cosmetics
MALIBU
Malibu Health
NIVEA SUN
Beiersdorf AG
PIZ BUIN
Johnson & Johnson
SIMPLE
Abn Amro
SOLTAN
Boots Company Plc
WELEDA
Weleda AG
ENVIRONMENTAL REPORTING
POLLUTION
NUCLEAR POWER
OTHER
ANIMAL TESTING
ANIMAL TESTING POLICY
FACTORY FARMING
OTHER ANIMAL RIGHTS
OPPRESSIVE REGIMES
WORKERS' RIGHTS
IRRESPONSIBLE MARKETING
ARMAMENTS
GENETIC ENGINEERING
BOYCOTT CALL
POLITICAL ACTIVITY
ALERT

Key

- Top rating (no criticisms found)
- Middle rating
- Bottom rating
- A related company has a bottom rating and the company itself has a middle rating
- A related company has a middle rating
- A related company has a bottom rating

Source: ECRA-See page 14 for full key to symbols.

Toothpaste

It's much more important for us to clean our teeth for the sake of our dental health than for cosmetic reasons. This is why we should hesitate before buying whitening and smokers' toothpastes, as these often contain abrasives. There are plenty of kinds to choose from with all the necessary information on ingredients to help us avoid those things that we don't really want to put in our mouths. This report covers the nine biggest manufacturers and seven alternative brands.

Labelling

The British Dental Health Foundation and the British Dental Association both run labelling schemes which allow oral health and hygiene products to carry the BDHF or BDA logo. Companies have to pay for the initial checks on the products and then pay an annual fee to the relevant body in order to carry the logo. The Consumers' Association has concerns over accreditation schemes arguing that toothpastes without a logo are not necessarily any worse.

Fluoride

Some claim that fluoride is necessary for healthy teeth and that tooth decay rates have fallen by 75 per cent since fluoride toothpaste came onto the market in the 1970s. Concerns exist about adding fluoride to water supplies, and readers wishing to know more about this debate can contact: Safe Water Information Service, Eye Manor Cottage, Eye, Leominster HR6 0DT (*http://members.aol.com/forgood/swis/*). Readers worried about this issue can choose fluoride-free toothpastes such as Green People, Kingfisher, Tom's of Maine or the appropriate Weleda brand.

Other ingredients

Many toothpastes contain sodium lauryl sulphate (SLS), a synthetic foaming agent. Some experts have raised concerns about this ingredient, saying that it is a suspected gastro-intestinal or liver toxicant. Other concerns point to the fact that it has been associated with recurrent mouth ulcers. It is nevertheless an industrial-strength detergent, so many people may want to think twice before putting it in their mouths. However a small application for a short period followed by a thorough rinsing should be harmless for most people. For those with a recurring mouth ulcer problem, Green People and Weleda toothpastes are SLS-free.

Triclosan (which may also be listed under CH 3635, Irgasan Ch 3635 or Ster-Zac) is an antibacterial agent which has also been controversial because it may increase the groth of superbugs. It has not been shown to be dangerous for human health however.

All toothpastes list the active ingredients, so amounts of triclosan and fluoride salts present in the paste should always be found on the packet. Toothpaste brands which contain triclosan include Colgate, Crest, Mentadent P, Sensodyne F and Macleans. Other brands marketing themselves as 'antibacterial' may also contain triclosan.

Packaging

Most toothpastes now come in plastic tubes, and several in pump dispensers. Some still come in the traditional aluminium tube. Tom's of Maine says that its aluminium tube, lined with food-grade plastic, can be recycled along with aluminium cans. Kingfisher Natural Toothpaste is packed in boxes manufactured from recycled cardboard and its tubes are made from biodegradable cellulose.

Alternatives

Dabur is an ayurvedic brand and made according to ancient Hindu principles.

If you wish to join the six per cent of the population who don't use toothpaste at all, experiment with sea salt, soot, chalk or bicarbonate of soda. The flavour of these can always be improved by adding a bit of mint essential oil.

- Green People
- Kingfisher
- Nelson
- Pearl Drops
- Sarakan
- Thursday Plantation
- Tom's of Maine
- Weleda

- Arm & Hammer
- Crest
- Dabur
- Oral B

- Aquafresh
- Colgate
- Euthymol
- Mentadent P

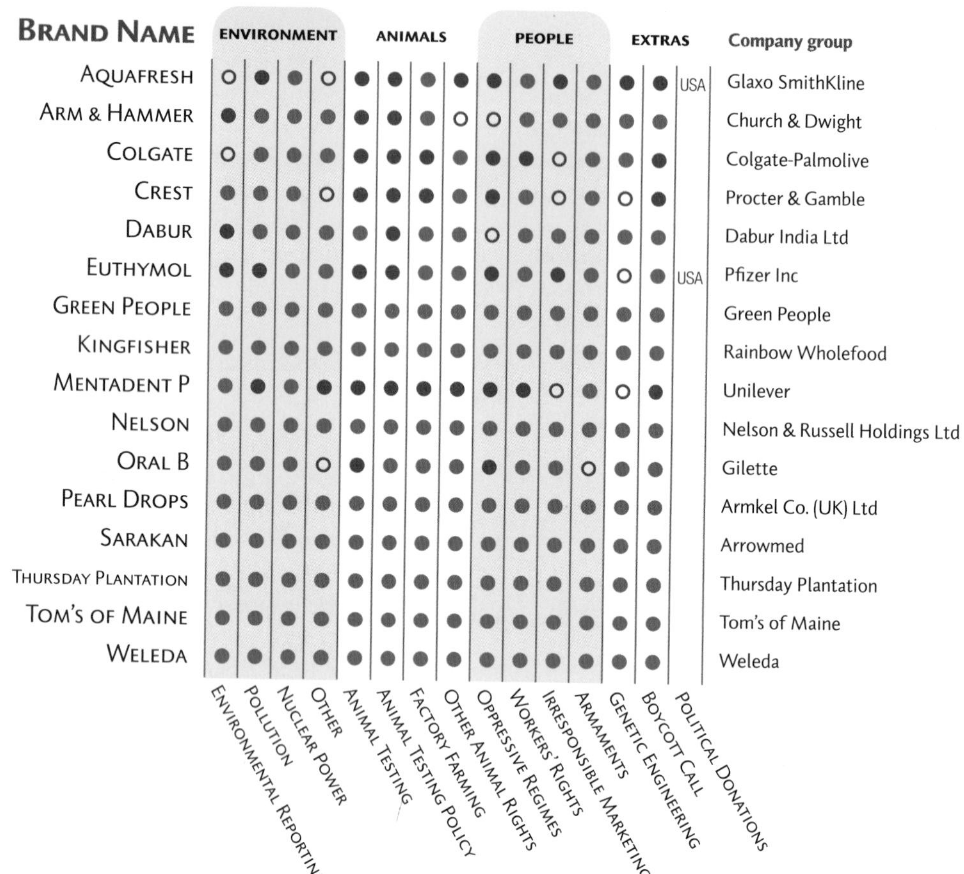

Key

- Top rating (no criticisms found)
- Middle rating
- Bottom rating
- A related company has a bottom rating and the company itself has a middle rating
- A related company has a middle rating
- A related company has a bottom rating

Source: ECRA-See page 14 for full key to symbols.

Vitamins

Vitamin supplement pills have become popular as a way of boosting diets or fighting off infections, but most of the accompanying marketing is just a load of hype. The makers are keen to prey on our insecurities about inadequate diets. Healthy eating is definitely the best way to get all the vitamins we need, but there are several exceptions to this rule.

Good in their way

Vitamins are chemically-produced pills, and debates have arisen whether they are effective or not. A leading official of the Food Commission has argued that they are oversold and has expressed concerns over the health claims of many of the vitamins. So far, most research into vitamins has focused on the effects of vitamins in food, rather than those in pills. In Toronto, scientists found that carotenoids and nutrients such as vitamin E are 'more beneficial if eaten in foods rather than taken as supplements.' The micro-nutrients in food may also 'play an important role in the prevention of disease' and may not be found in pills or capsules.

One of the most convincing justifications for taking vitamin pills is that our busy lifestyles and the abundance of low-nutrient convenience foods mean that vitamin and mineral tablets may be needed to supplement a less-than-ideal diet. Pre-pregnant, or pregnant women are also advised to take folic acid supplements.

Research shows that people who take vitamins are in fact those who are less likely to need them, and that they already eat healthily. Advertisements and health editorials commonly target vegetarians and vegans as those who are most in need of supplements. However, both the Vegan and Vegetarian Societies argue that a healthy, mixed diet should provide us with all the nutrients we need. Meanwhile the vitamin industry argues that there will always be some people who are either deficient in one or more nutrients or who have special nutritional or medical needs for particular nutrients at certain times in their lives - these include young children and adolescents; immobile, housebound or institutionalised elderly people; vegans and some vegetarians; smokers; heavy drinkers; people who are chronically ill, and anybody on a restrictive diet, including long term slimmers.

Ingredients

When the Food Commission conducted a survey into additives it was shocked by the numbers contained in supplements, as well as by the lack of clear labelling of ingredients.

Its survey found a colouring in Redoxon which is banned in virtually all foods. Artificial sweeteners, aspartame and sorbitol, as well as talcum powder, silicon dioxide and anti-caking agents were found in some other supplements. More worryingly, a government survey in 1998 discovered higher-than-permitted levels of lead and arsenic in a number of supplements. Although the government did not at the time conclude that the products posed a significant risk, manufacturers were required to change formulations.

Companies

At the time of our research, American Home Products (AHP) owned Solgar, one of the major vitamin brands. AHP and Numico have each been criticised by UNICEF for violating the WHO Code of Marketing, relating to the marketing of breast milk substitutes. (See ECRA background materials for more details).

Packaging

Many vitamin pills are vastly overpackaged. Some products – such as Seven Seas – are packaged in an outer box as well as the vitamin bottle, while Perfectil vitamins go even further by packaging each individual pill in its own bubble pack. The majority of vitamin bottles are also made from plastic, although a few brands use glass. Viridian was the only company offering recycling of its bottles. Consumers can return their empty Viridian glass bottle to the place of purchase, receive a 25p refund, and the bottle gets recycled – the company also makes a charity donation for every sale.

- Holland & Barrett
- Perfectil
- Quest
- Red Kooga
- Viridian

- Boots
- FSC
- GNC
- Seven Seas

- Centrum
- Redoxon
- Sanatogen
- Solgar

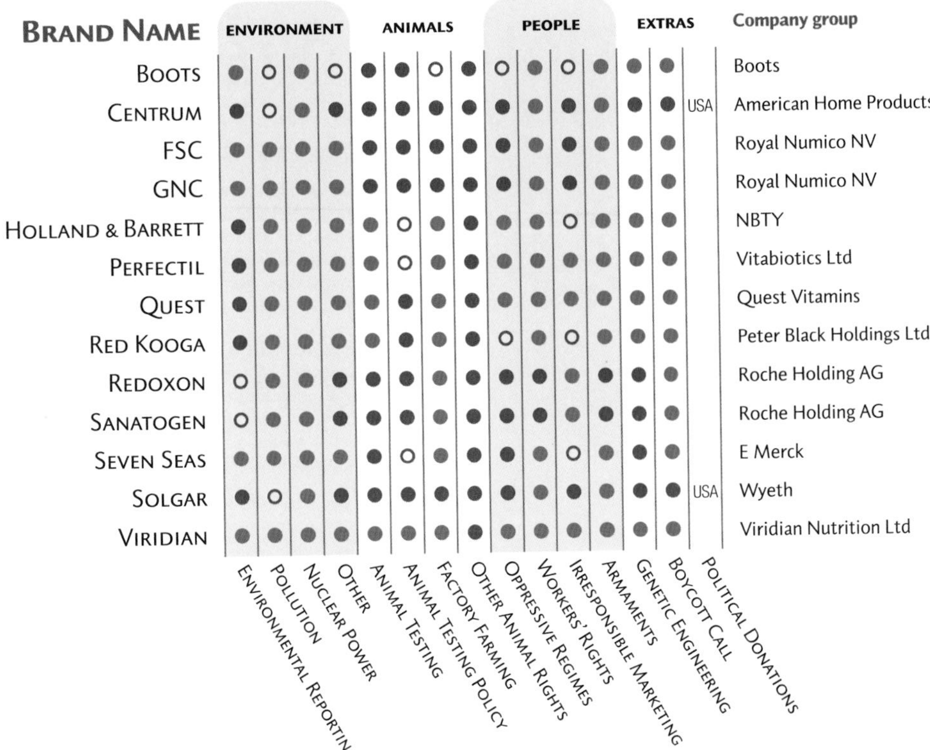

Key

- Top rating (no criticisms found)
- Middle rating
- Bottom rating
- A related company has a bottom rating and the company itself has a middle rating
- A related company has a middle rating
- A related company has a bottom rating

Source: ECRA-See page 14 for full key to symbols.

Alternative clothing directory

Major suppliers

Bishopston Trading Company
A workers' co-operative which has grown out of the linking of the southern Indian village of KV Kuppam with Bishopston in Bristol. Supplying through five shops and via mail order, the company sells organic cotton clothes for both children and adults. *www.bishopstontrading.co.uk*
33 Silver Street, Bradford-on-Avon
BA15 2LB Tel: 01225 867 485
8a High Street, Glastonbury BA6 8SU.
Tel: 0145 883 5386
33 High Street, Stroud GL5 1AJ
Tel: 0145 376 6355
193 Gloucester Road, Bishopston, Bristol BS7 8BG
Tel: 0117 924 5598
79 High Street, Totnes TQ9 5PB
Tel: 0180 386 8488

Chandni Chowk
Supplier of clothes made with hand-spun natural fibres and coloured using vegetable dyes.
www.chandnichowk.co.uk
102 Boutport Street, Barnstaple
EX31 1SY Tel: 01225 483 541
6 New Bond Street Place, Bath BA1 1BH
Tel: 01271 374 714
66 Park Street, Bristol BS1 5JN.
1 Harlequins, Paul Street, Exeter EX4 3TT
14a, The Bridge, Riverside Place,Taunton TA1 1UG
Tel: 01823 327 377

Siesta
Fairly traded 'ethnic' style clothes from Latin America.
www.siestacrafts.co.uk
1 Palace Street, Canterbury CT1 2DY
Tel: 01227 464 614

Traidcraft PLC
A range of menswear and womenswear, available mail order and on-line.
www.traidcraft.co.uk
Kingsway North, Gateshead, Tyne & Wear NE11 0NE
Tel: 0191 491 1001

Mail Order or online ordering

Clothworks
Range of fashionable classic womens' clothing and a modern range of childrens' clothes. All materials used including fastenings, are natural and organic.
www.clothworks.co.uk
PO Box 3233, Bradford on Avon
BA15 2WB Tel: 01225 309218

Garthenor Organic Pure Wool
Hand knitted garments, from certified organic British sheep – spun locally and not died nor bleached. Range includes adult, children and baby clothing.
www.organicpurewool.co.uk
Llanio Raod, Tregaron, Ceredigion, Wales
Tel: 01570 493 347

Gossypium
Simple modern organic cotton clothing, including underwear and pyjamas. Men's, women's and children's ranges available.
www.gossypium.co.uk
Gossypium House, Abinger Place, Lewes BN7 2QA
Tel: 01273 897 509

Greenfibres
Mail-order supplier of organic clothing (including jeans and sportswear).
www.greenfibres.com
99 High Street Totnes, Devon TQ9 5PF
Tel: 01803 868001

Hemp Union
Sells a small range of hemp clothing, trousers, jeans and tops.
www.hemp-union.karoo.net
24 Anlaby Rd, Hull HU1 2PA Tel: 01482 225328

HUG
Organic fairly traded modern fashions from Peru. Men's, women's and children's ranges.
www.hug.co.uk

Marlo Clothing
Contemporary organic cotton and hemp clothing, using natural dyes.
www.marlo.co.uk Tel: 01736 753254

Natural Collection
Hemp clothing, organic exercise gear, organic t-shirts, organic wool socks, hemp socks, vests, underwear.
www.naturalcollection.com Tel: 01225 442288

One World is Enough
Handmade non-organic clothing for women, men and children, from Fair Trade suppliers.
www.one-world-is-enough.net
1 The Broadway, Mill Road, Cambridge CB1 3AH
Tel: 01223 500167

People Tree Ltd
UK arm of the Japan-based Fair Trade Company, selling organic, fair-trade clothes. Aimed at the fashion conscious.
www.ptree.co.uk Tel: 020 7808 7060

RE-VIV
A range of clothing made entirely from recycled materials.
16 Alma Rd, Retford DN22 6LW
Tel: 01777 705557

SE Clothing
Hemp clothing hand made to order in the UK. The Grange, All Saints, St Elmham, Halesworth IP19 0NX
Tel: 01986 782476

Spirit Of Nature
Organic cotton clothes, including men's workshirts.
www.spiritofnature.co.uk Tel: 0870 725 988

Schmidt Natural Clothing
Organic cotton clothing for children and underwear for adults, mail order.
www.naturalclothing.co.uk Tel: 01342 822 169

Smart Tart
Individual designer bags and clothing made from recycled materials, hemp and vegetarian 'leather'.
www.smarttart.co.uk Tel: 01736 787091

Other shops

Patagonia
Outdoor clothing made from organic cotton and hemp, including fleeces made from recycled plastic.
www.patagonia.com
Unit 705, 50 Westminster Bridge Road, London SE1 7QY Tel: 020 7721 8717

Natural Fact
Large collection of organic cotton and hemp clothing for men and women, and children up to two years old.
192 Kings Road, London SW3 5XP Tel: 020 7352 4283

Textiles from Nature
Organic cotton, hemp, jute and recycled fabrics by the metre, for those who fancy making their own.
www.textilesfromnature.com
84 Stoke Newington Church Street, London N16 0AP
Tel: 020 7241 0990

Tumi
Fairly traded clothes from Latin America.
www.tumicrafts.com
8/9 New Bond Street Place, Bath
BA1 1BH Tel: 01225 446025
1/2 Little Clarendon Street, Oxford OX1 2HJ
Tel: 01865 512 307

Tucano
Organic cotton and hemp clothing, including beach wear.
Pound House, Pound Rd, West Wittering, West Sussex
PO20 8AJ Tel: 01243 513 757

Second-hand clothes

Second-hand or 'recycled' clothes are one of the best environmental options and can be obtained throughout the country from a variety of charity shops. As well as being a low-cost alternative to high street retailers, the money paid for clothing can also go to a good cause. Second-hand clothing can also be found in retro shops, car boot sales and from friends and relatives.

Fair Trade shops selling Traidcraft clothes:

A World of Difference
13 Narrowgate, Alnwick NE66 1JH
Chester Fairtrading, Westly Methodist Church, St. Johns St. Chester CH1 1DA Tel: 07790 655526
Fairer World, 84 Gillygate, York YO31 7EQ Tel: 01904 655 116
Gateway World Shop, Market Place, Durham DH1 3NJ Tel: 0191 384 7173
Just Fair Trade, 10 Bishop Street, Town Hall Square, Leicester LE1 6AF Tel: 0116 255 9123 *www.justfairtrade.com*
Just Trading, 7 Fountain Street, Nailsworth, Stroud, GL6 0BL Tel: 01453 833 002
Liverpool World Shop, 64 Bold Street, Liverpool L1 4EA Tel: 0151 708 7328
One World Shop, St John's Church, Princes St, Edinburgh EH2 4BJ
www.oneworldshop.co.uk Tel: 0131 229 4541
The Green Shop, 30 Bridge Street, Berwick Upon Tweed TD15 1AQ Tel: 01289 305566
Traders Fair World Shop, Portal Precinct, Sr Isaac's Walk, Colchester CO1 1JJ Tel: 01206 763 380
Traid Links, 20 Market Place, Wirksworth DE4 4ET Tel: 01629 824393
World of Difference, 20 High Street, Rugby CV21 3BG Tel: 01788 579 191

Cited organisations

86 Ltd (see *www.86.co.uk*) is the media consultancy behind *The Good Shopping Guide*, responsible for public relations, digital strategy and advertising. 86 specialises in raising the profile of progressive and ethical companies. Call them on 0207 229 1894 for a presentation.

BUAV The British Union for the Abolition of Vivisection

ECRA The Ethical Consumer Research Association

EIRIS The Ethical Investment Research Service

The Ethical Marketing Group publishes *The Good Shopping Guide*. A group set up to bring high level media expertise to cause-related projects.

Fairtrade Foundation exists to ensure a better deal for marginalised and disadvantaged Third World producers.

FLO Fairtrade Labelling Organisations International

FOE Friends of the Earth is the largest network of environmental organisations, represented in 68 countries

GM Genetically manipulated (modified)

Labour Behind the Label is a UK network of organisations supporting garment workers' rights

National Food Alliance is now called Sustain and campaigns for 'better food and growing'

Naturewatch is an animal welfare campaigning organisation

Soil Association campaigns for organic food and growing and sustainable forestry

Sustain Previously called the National Food Alliance, it campaigns for better food and growing.

WHO The World Health Organisation

www.thegoodshoppingguide.co.uk Stay up to date with the latest developments and purchase discounted copies of *The GOOD Shopping Guide* direct.

www.gooshing.co.uk The UK's leading online ethical shopping facility. Compares ethics of 250,000 products and searches 350 online shops to find you the cheapest price.

ECRA

The vast majority of the research featured in *The Good Shopping Guide* comes from ECRA. Their gold-standard research combined with a fierce independence add to their growing reputation.

What is ECRA?

The Ethical Consumer Research Association (ECRA) is the UK's only alternative consumer organisation looking at the social and environmental records of the companies behind the brand names.
ECRA exists to promote:

- universal human rights
- environmental sustainability
- animal welfare...

...by providing information on consumer issues which empowers individuals and organisations to act ethically in the market place.
ECRA therefore

- produces a magazine *Ethical Consumer*,
- maintains a publicly accessible database of ethically-related corporate information – Corporate Critic,
- and conducts research for campaign groups and ethically minded organisations.

ECRA was founded in June 1987 and is a not-for-profit, voluntary organisation owned and managed by its staff as a workers' co-operative. Proud to have maintained its independence, ECRA is funded almost entirely by readers' subscriptions and by adverts from ethically-vetted companies.

Why ethical consumerism?

ECRA believes that the global economic system should be able to pursue ethical as well as financial goals – a belief which is gaining increasingly wider acceptance. In a world where people feel politically disempowered, and where governments are perceived as being less powerful than corporations, citizens are beginning to realise that their economic vote may have as much influence as their political vote. This is true both for individuals and for institutional purchasers and investors.

Ethical Consumerism is not a replacement for other forms of political action, but it is an important additional way for anyone to exert their influence. In 2001 'The ECRA Manifesto for Change' was published. It outlines policy recommendations for the UK Government in its second term of office. A copy of this article is available on their website at *www.ethicalconsumer.org/aboutec/manifesto.htm* or in issue 72 of *Ethical Consumer*.

WHAT IS *ETHICAL CONSUMER* MAGAZINE?

Ethical Consumer was launched in March 1989 and is the UK's leading alternative consumer magazine. Each issue contains four product reports, looking in depth at the ethical issues raised by campaigners. It also has news pages and features covering the latest ideas in the fields of ethical investment, organic food, consumer boycotts and corporate campaigning.

Product tables present a summary of the information held on ECRA's database (see below) and written details appear in separate 'Research Supplements' available from ECRA. Information is presented in a way that allows readers to make decisions based upon their own beliefs and priorities. There are more than 200 product reports in print covering everything from Petrol to Pickles...and a full list of reports appears on the website or is available free from ECRA's office.

Ethical Consumer magazine is available by subscription and costs £19.00 for six issues. They also sell individual back issues of the magazine, Research Supplements and campaign postcards to send to companies. Subscriptions and reports can be bought by post, by credit card over the phone, or from their website. Contact details appear below, or see the subscription advert on page 309.

WHAT IS CORPORATE CRITIC DATABASE?

For over a decade ECRA has been creating a database of information in the public domain on potentially unethical corporate behaviour. There are now around 50,000 abstracts on nearly 20,000 companies. The information sources are international, and include reference publications from campaign groups like Friends of the Earth, commercial directories on the defence and nuclear industries and public records on pollution prosecutions and emission levels. Increasingly, information is requested directly from companies on issues such as environmental reporting, animal testing policy and codes of conduct. In 2001 ECRA created a separate subsidiary company called ECIS to manage and develop the database and company rating side of its work.

Guest users can access an on-line version of this database free, to see the type of data held on specific companies. To access more detailed information, users need to pay and charges start at around £50 for pay as you go, or £420 a year for a years unlimited access. For more information see *www.ethicalconsumer.org/corp_critic.htm*

WHAT OTHER RESEARCH DOES ECRA DO?

For people or groups wanting more information about the ethical record of a particular company group, ECRA provides a research service and costs start at £35 per company. ECRA also conducts independent research into the comparative environmental impacts of different products, and has researched the Green Building Handbook Volumes I and II (E&FN Spon 1997/2000).

ECRA has also produced detailed research on ethical issues in specific industry sectors and markets for campaign groups such Friends of the Earth and Oxfam. ECRA provides consultancy services for companies like the Co-operative Bank which have programmes of ethical policy development.

CONTACT ECRA:
ECRA Publishing Ltd
Unit 21, 41 Old Birley Street,
Manchester
M15 5RF

Tel: 0161 226 2929 (12noon-6pm)
Fax: 0161 226 6277
mail@ethicalconsumer.org
www.ethicalconsumer.org

Original publication dates and issue numbers:

All-in-ones (Commissioned Jan 2004)
Baby Food 63 (Feb/Mar 2000)
Bananas 61 (Oct/Nov 1999)
Banks & Building Socs 72 (Aug/Sept n 2001)
Batteries 46 (Apr/May 1997)
Bedtime Drinks (commissioned July 2003)
Beer, lager, cider 72 (Feb/Mar 2002)
Biscuits 77 (June/July 2002)
Bread 56 (Dec/Jan 1998-99)
Boilers 78 (Aug/Sept 2003)
Bottled Water 72 (Feb/Mar 2002)
Butter & Marg 62 (Dec 1999/Jan 2000)
Cat & Dog food 66 (Aug/Sept 2000)
Cereal 63 (Feb/Mar 2000)
Chocolate 79 (Oct/Nov 2002)
Cleaners 81 (Feb/Mar 2003)
Cold Remedies 49 (Oct/Nov 1997))
Computers 65 (June/July 2000)
Cookers 76 (Apr/May 2002)
Cooking Oil 67 (Nov 2000)
Credit Cards 68 (Dec 2000/Jan2001)
Crisps 80 (Dec 2002/Jan 2003)
Essential Oils 51 (Feb/Mar 1998)
Eye Care 42 (July/Aug 1996)
Fax Machines 55 (Oct/Nov 1998)
Fridges 69 (Feb/Mar 2001)
Ice Cream 78 (Aug/Sept 2002)
Insurance 80 (Dec 2002/Jan 2003)
Jams & Spreads 68 (Dec 2000/Jan2001)
Jeans 76 (Apr/May 2002)
Kettles 77 (June/July 2002)
Kitchen Appliances 62 (Dec 1999/Jan 2000)
Laundry Detergents 57 (Feb/Mar 1999)
Mortgages 70 (Apr/May 2001)
Nappies 57 (Feb/Mar 1999)
Outdoor Equipment 82 (Apr/May 2003)
Painkillers 55 (Oct/Nov 1998)
Paint 79 (Oct/Nov 2002)
Pasta 64 (April/May 2000)
Perfumes & Aftershaves 47 (June/July 1997)
Printers (Commissioned Jan 2004)
Sanitary Protection 71 (June/July 2001)
Shampoo 74 (Dec 2001/Jan 2002)
Skincare 76 (Apr/May 2002)
Soap 61 (Oct/Nov 1999)
Soft Drinks 65 (June/July 2000)
Soup 66 (Aug/Sept 2000)
Sports Shoes 98 (Aug/Sept 2002)
Sugar 62 (Dec 1999/Jan 2000)
Suntan 82 (Apr/May 2003)
Tea & Coffee 73 (Oct/Nov2001)
Toothpaste 69 (Feb/March 2001)
Toys 79 (Oct/Nov 2002)
TV & Video 56 (Dec 1998/Jan1999)
Vacuum Cleaners 59 (June/July 1999)
Vitamins 64 (April/May 2000)
Washing Machines 82 (Apr/May 2003)
Washing up Liquid 63 (Feb/Mar 2000)
Whisky 49 (Oct/Nov 1997)
Yoghurt 54 (Aug/Sept 1998)

Contact ECRA for a full index of previous reports.
[All table ratings have been updated by ECRA at least to May 2002]

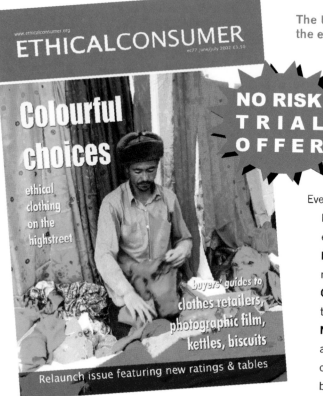

Good Network

- Good NGOs
- Green events
- Ethical internet

Good NGOs

Thanks to all the NGOs listed below (and a great many others not listed here) for giving a voice, help and love to some of the world's most important issues concerning different peoples, animals and environments. The great news is that memberships of many NGOs are soaring as they emerge as the key component to a genuine 21st century debate. Free from the chains of political and corporate expediency they continue to present a genuinely independent view to fellow man. We urge you to join them in helping make the world a better place.

You can make easy tax-free donations to many of these NGOs at *www.gooshing.co.uk*.

AMNESTY INTERNATIONAL

Amnesty International (AI) is among the leading human rights organisations in the world, untainted by political, economic or religious bias. Amnesty aims to enshrine universal entitlement to "physical and mental integrity, freedom of conscience and expression, and freedom from discrimination." *www.amnesty.org.uk* Tel: 0044 (0)20 7814 6200

BARNARDOS

Barnardos aims to help young people in grave need of assistance, its 357 centers around Britain helping children and teenagers from unfortunate backgrounds. Barnardos provides fostering and adoption services, and combats a plethora of problems, including sexual abuse and homelessness. *www.barnardos.org.uk* Tel: 08457 697967.

THE BLUE CROSS

The Blue Cross offers guidance, advice and support for pet and horse owners, and, through several animal adoption centers, re-homes thousands of animals each year. Its network of hospitals offers free veterinary care for animals whose owners cannot afford private vets' fees. *www.bluecross.org.uk*
Tel: 0044 (0)20 7932 4060

BRITISH RED CROSS

The British Red Cross is part of the largest independent humanitarian network in the world, offering impartial assistance to those in need. The Red Cross assists the victims of armed conflict, and works against disease and human suffering in the British Islands and around the world. *www.redcross.org.uk* Tel: 0044 (0)20 7235 5454

BROCKWOOD PARK SCHOOL

Brockwood Park School is a residential school for students aged 14 - 19 from around the world. Students gain a good academic education and one that nurtures in them human qualities and encourages enquiry about all aspects of life and relationship. *www.brockwood.org.uk* Tel: 0044 (0)1962 771744

BUAV

The BUAV is the world's leading anti-vivisection organisation campaigning peacefully to end all animal testing nationally and internationally - through campaigning, political lobbying, legal challenges, lab animal rescue and groundbreaking undercover investigations. The BUAV runs 'no animal testing' Standards for beauty, household and petfood products. *www.buav.org* Tel: 44 (0)20 7700 4888

CAFOD

CAFOD (Catholic Agency for Overseas Development) aims to alleviate poverty and create a more just world. CAFOD has bases in over 60 countries, attempting to help the poor in each country without racial or religious bias. CAFOD's other aims include campaigning for a fairer world and putting faith into action. *www.cafod.org.uk* Tel: 00 44 (0)20 7733 7900

Cancer Research UK

Aiming to find a cure for cancer through world-class research, Cancer Research UK is the pre-eminent cancer charity in the UK. With an annual scientific spend of around £191 million, raised almost entirely through voluntary contributions, Cancer Research UK is backed by a dedicated team of 3,000 scientists. *www.cancerresearchuk.org* Tel: 0044 (0)20 7242 0200

Christian Aid

Christian Aid works in some of the world's poorest communities in more than 50 countries. It works where the need is greatest, regardless of religion, supporting local organisations which are best-placed to understand their communities. To find out more about Christian Aid's work visit: *www.christianaid.org.uk* or *www.christian-aid.ie* for the Republic of Ireland
Tel: 0044 (0)20 7523 2041 or 01 611 0801 (Dublin)

CIWF

Compassion in World Farming is the leading international organisation actively campaigning to improve the lives of all farmed animals by abolishing factory farming and long distance animal transport. Based in the UK, CIWF has offices and representatives across the world. *www.ciwf.org*
Tel: 00 44 (0) 1730 264 208

Comic Relief

Having attracted over 2050 celebrities to its cause over the years, Comic Relief aims to redress serious issues through comedy and laughter. As well as raising money, the Comic Relief show televised once a year aims to inform and educate the public and promote social change. *www.comicrelief.org.uk*
Tel: 0044 (0)20 7820 5555

Environmental Investigation Agency (EIA)

"One of Britain's most effective conservation groups" – BBC Wildlife Magazine. This year the Environmental Investigation Agency (EIA) celebrates twenty years of protecting wildlife, people and planet. EIA is an independent, international campaigning organisation committed to investigating and exposing environmental crime. *www.eia-international.org*
Tel: 0044 (0)20 7354 7960

The Fairtrade Foundation

The Fairtrade Foundation awards the FAIRTRADE Mark – the only consumer guarantee that products are independently certified to meet international Fairtrade standards – available on over 250 products in most major retail outlets. The Foundation raises public awareness about Fairtrade and organizes the nationwide Fairtrade Fortnight in March each year. It is also the UK member of the international Fairtrade Labelling Organisations (FLO), which unites 18 national Fairtrade initiatives across Europe, North America and Mexico. Latest information about products and activities on their website. *www.faritrade.org.uk* Tel: 0044 (0)20 7405 5942

Friends of the Earth

Friends of the Earth is the largest international network of environmental groups in the world, represented in 68 countries. It is one of the leading environmental pressure groups in the UK and has a unique network of campaigning local groups, working in more than 200 communities in England, Wales & Northern Ireland. *www.foe.co.uk*
Tel: 0044 (0)7490 1555

Forest Stewardship Council (FSC)

FSC is an international, non-governmental organisation dedicated to promoting responsible management of the world's forests. It was founded in 1993 in response to public concern about deforestation and demand for a trustworthy wood-labelling scheme. There are national working groups in 28 countries including the UK.
www.fsc-uk.info Tel: 0044 (0)1686 413916

Greenpeace

Active in 40 countries worldwide, Greenpeace is a non-profit organisation with several environmental aims, including curbing climate change and preserving our oceans and ancient forests. To maintain independence, Greenpeace only accepts donations from individual supporters and foundation grants.
www.greenpeace.org.uk Tel: 0044 (0)20 7865 8100

Global Action Plan

Global Action Plan is an independent charity committed to encouraging the public to be more environmentally sustainable. Working with business, schools and local communities we believe that every little helps to make a real difference. To see how green you are visit www.greenscore.org.uk and *www.carboncalculator.com*
www.globalactionplan.org.uk / *www.ergo-living.com*
Tel: 0044 (0)207 405 5633

Guide Dogs for the Blind

The Guide Dogs for the Blind Association supplies guide dogs and other mobility services to blind and partially sighted people in the UK, and attempts to educate people on the need to care for their eyes.
www.guidedogs.org.uk Tel: 0870 600 2323

Help the Aged

Help the Aged aims to enrich the lives of older people by reinforcing their social status. Of the money the charity spends, 28 per cent goes to combating elderly poverty, 30 per cent to reducing isolation, 13 per cent to defeating ageism and 29 per cent to promoting quality in care. *www.helptheaged.org.uk*
Tel: 0044 (0)20 7278 1114

International Tree Foundation

The International Tree Foundation (ITF) is 80 years old and works towards a world richer in trees, by planting, preserving and educating people on the value of trees worldwide. In the UK, ITF members work in their local communities. On a global scale, ITF tree planting grants help the world's poorest environments and societies. *www.internationaltreefoundation.org*
Tel: 0870 7744269

League Against Cruel Sports

Founded in 1924, the League Against Cruel Sports maintains a unique approach to the protection of wildlife - combining campaigning with conservation. The League has always been at the forefront of the campaign to ban hunting with dogs. To achieve their goal, they liaise closely with politicians in pressing for government action. *www.league.uk.com*
Tel: 0845 330 8486

Macmillan Cancer Relief

Offering expert care, practical and emotional support for those who have been diagnosed with cancer, Macmillan Cancer Relief uses specialist nurses and doctors. These specialists are recruited to provide quality cancer care, treatment centers, financial help and information. *www.macmillan.org.uk*
Tel: 0808 808 2020

Marie Curie Cancer Care

Marie Curie Cancer Care offers high quality nursing free of charge, and allows terminally ill people to spend their last days in the comfort and privacy of their own home. The organisation's team of scientists is investigating the cancer disease in an attempt to find a cure. *www.mariecurie.org.uk* Tel: 0044 (0)20 7599 7777

The Marine Stewardship Council

The Marine Stewardship Council (MSC) is an international, non-profit organisation, working to prevent the collapse of fish stocks. It has developed an environmental standard for well-managed and sustainable fisheries. Fisheries that meet this standard are awarded with a blue eco-label enabling consumers to identify sustainable seafood products and make the best environmental choice in seafood.
www.msc.org Tel: 0044 (0)20 7350 4000

National Trust
The National Trust was founded in 1895 and set up to act as a guardian for the nation in the acquisition and protection of threatened coastline, countryside and buildings. The National Trust now cares for over 612,000 acres of beautiful countryside in England, Wales and Northern Ireland, plus almost 600 miles of coastline and more than 200 buildings and gardens of outstanding interest and importance.
www.nationaltrust.org.uk Tel: 0870 458 4000

Nicaragua Solidarity Campaign (NSC)
NSC sell fair-trade Nicaraguan coffee, Mexican & Guatemalan crafts, books, solidarity t-shirts etc. They also organise fair-trade tours to Nicaragua and campaign around trade justice so get in touch. Free world music CD if you join! Email: *nsc@nicaraguasc.org.uk* *www.nicaraguasc.org.uk*
Tel: 0044 (0)20 7272 9619

NSPCC
The NSPCC (National Society for the Prevention of Cruelty to Children) is the leading UK charity in the field of child protection, and is currently the only children's charity with statutory powers. This power enables to act decisively to alleviate cruelty to children. *www.nspcc.org.uk*
Tel: 0044 (0)20 7825 2500

One World Action
One World Action aims to defeat poverty and promote democracy in the less developed world, One World Action works with partner organizations on the ground to inculcate respect for human freedoms in Africa, Asia and America. The organisation also liaises with senior policymakers in both Britain and the EU.
www.oneworldaction.org Tel: 0044 (0)20 7833 4075

Oxfam
Oxfam is a development, relief and campaigning organisation Oxfam works to combat poverty and suffering, by addressing important issues such as fair trade, conflict, education, debt, aid and employment conditions in developing countries.
www.oxfam.org.uk Tel: 0870 333 2700

Pesticide Action Network
Pesticide Action Network UK (PAN UK) promotes healthy food, agriculture and an environment which will provide food and meet public health needs without dependence on toxic chemicals, and without harm to food producers and agricultural workers.
www.pan-uk.org Tel: 0044 (0)20 7274 8895

PDSA
Every working day, PDSA caters for 4,500 sick and injured pets of less fortunate people. With 46 PetAid hospitals and hundreds of associated private practices, PDSA has established itself as Britain's leading veterinary charity. *www.pdsa.org.uk*
Tel: 0044 (0)1952 290999

Prince's Trust
The Prince's Trust is a UK charity that supports young people who face more obstacles than most, helping them overcome barriers and get their lives working. The Trust provides practical support such as training, mentoring and financial assistance, including for young entrepreneurs. Since 1983 they've helped more than 60,000 young people start in business. The Prince's Trust website has a directory of nearly 1,500 Trust-supported businesses in 100 categories, across the UK. Visit *www.princes-trust.org.uk/finder*
Tel: 0800 842 842

The Rainforest Foundation
The Rainforest Foundation provides valuable support for the efforts of native inhabitants of the world's rainforests to protect their environment. The Foundation assists such peoples in securing their rights and natural resources, and obtaining essential services from the relevant state.
www.rainforestfoundationuk.org
Tel: 0044 (0)20 7251 6345

The Ramblers Association
The Ramblers' Association is the biggest organisation in Britain to support walkers, and has a membership of 139,000. The organisation protects Britain's unique network of public paths, provides information allowing people to plan their walk, and offers a variety of other functions. *www.ramblers.org.uk*
Tel: 0044 (0)20 7339 8500

Royal National Institute for the Blind

Royal National Institute for the Blind (RNIB) offers practical support and information for the two million British people with sight problems. RNIB offers help for such people through the development of Braille, Talking Books and computer training.
www.rnib.org.uk Tel: 0845 766 9999

Royal National Institute for Deaf People

Through the use of campaigning, education and training courses, the Royal National Institute for Deaf People (RNID) purports to represent the 8.7 million people with hearing disabilities in the UK. It is the largest charity in this field in Britain.
www.rnid.org.uk Tel: 0808 808 0123

Royal National Lifeboat Institution

The Royal National Lifeboat Institution (RNLI) saves lives at sea through a supply of the provision of a 24-search and rescue service around British and Irish coasts using volunteer crews. Relying on voluntary contributions, RNLI crews rescue an average of 19 people every day. *www.rnli.org.uk*
Tel: 0800 543210

RSPB

The Royal Society for the Protection of Birds (RSPB) aims to create a healthy environment for birds and wildlife, and even offers volunteers the chance to watch and observe some of the rarest species of bird in Britain. *www.rspb.org.uk* Tel: 0044 (0)1767 680551

RSPCA

(Royal Society for the Prevention of Cruelty to Animals) By promoting responsible pet ownership, the RSPCA attempts to promote kindness and prevent cruelty to animals. The RSPCA also aims to prevent unnecessary suffering and find new, responsible owners for unwanted animals. *www.rspca.org.uk*
Tel: 0044 (0)1895 231435

Save the Children

Save the Children works in the UK and across the world. Emergency relief runs alongside long-term development and prevention work to help children, their families and communities to be self-sufficient. Save the Children learn from the reality of children's lives and campaign for solutions to the problems they face. *www.savethechildren.org.uk*
Tel: 0044 (0)20 7012 6400

Scope

Scope is a natural disability organisation which concentrates on cerebral palsy, and aims to achieve equality and respect for disabled people. Scope also works toward the idea that disabled people should have the same human and civil rights as everyone else.
www.scope.org.uk Tel: 0808 800 3333

Spinal Research

Spinal Research is a pioneering charity which is making progress in its aim to find ways to repair spinal cord injury and to reverse the paralysis that results from it.
www.spinal-research.org Tel: 0044 (0)1483 898 786

Sport Relief

Affiliated to Comic Relief, Sport Relief funds projects which use sport to alleviate violence in tense communities, and provide the confidence of group activity to hundreds of less fortunate people. Sport Relief also sends celebrities abroad to spread the group's message in disadvantaged areas.
www.sportrelief.com Tel: 0044 (0)20 7820 5555

Surfers Against Sewage

Surfers Against Sewage campaign for clean, safe recreational waters, free from sewage effluents, toxic chemicals and nuclear waste. Using a solution based argument of viable and sustainable alternatives, SAS highlight the inherent flaws in current practises, attitudes and legislation, challenging industry, legislators and politicians to end their 'pump and dump' policies. *www.sas.org.uk* Tel: 0845 4583001

Survival

Survival International is a worldwide organisation supporting tribal peoples. It stands for their right to decide their own future and helps them protect their lives, lands and human rights. Survival has supporters in 82 countries and is the only organisation to make use of public opinion and public action to secure long-term improvement for tribal peoples. *www.survival-international.org* Tel: 0044 (0)20 7687 8700

Tear Fund

Tearfund is active throughout the world, with numerous regional strategies. These include providing support for communities in managing healthcare; focusing on children at serious risk in disadvantaged areas; and augmenting food and housing security in poorer regions. *www.tearfund.org* Tel: 0044 (0)20 8977 9144

Tourism Concern

Tourism Concern works with communities in countries which are popular tourist destinations, with the aim of curbing the amount of poverty tourism causes. Through the use of advocacy and publicity, Tourism Concern attempts to find way of increasing the benefits of tourism to destination countries. *www.tourismconcern.org.uk* Tel: 0044 (0)20 7133 3330

Trees for Cities

Trees for Cities is an independent charity that plants trees and re-landscapes public spaces in urban areas of greatest need; our aim is to stimulate a greening renaissance in cities around the world. The public can get involved by sponsoring trees or volunteering at our events. *www.treesforcities.org* Tel: 0044 (0)20 7587 1320

Unicef

UNICEF, the United Nations Children's Fund, is a global champion for children's rights which makes a lasting difference by working in partnership with others, from governments and teachers to youth groups and mothers. UNICEF is a driving force for people throughout the world working to ensure a better future for children *www.unicef.org.uk* Tel: 0044 (0)207 405 5592

Women's Environmental Network (WEN)

Women's Environmental Network (WEN) campaigns on issues which link women and the environment, and is particularly ardent on issues concerning women's health and reproductive systems. WEN's approach emphasises the belief that women have the right to information to enable them to make fair choices. *www.wen.org.uk* Tel: 0044 (0)20 7481 9004

World Development Movement (WDM)

The World Development Movement tackles the underlying causes of poverty. They lobby decision makers to change the policies that keep people poor. WDM research and promote positive alternatives. They work alongside people in the developing world who are standing up to injustice. *www.wdm.org.uk* Tel: 0044 (0)20 7737 6215

World Vision

World Vision is a Christian charity and one of the world's leading relief and development agencies, currently helping over 100 million people in nearly 100 countries in their struggle against poverty, hunger and injustice, irrespective of their religious beliefs. *www.worldvision.org.uk* Tel: 0044 (0)1908 841000

WSPA

WSPA (World Society for the Protection of Animals) interacts with over 460 member organisations to improve global standards of animal welfare. WSPA envisages a world in which the welfare of animals is understood and respected by everyone, and enshrined in effective legislation. *www.wspa.org.uk* Tel: 0044 (0)20 7793 0208

WWF (World Wildlife Fund)

The World Wildlife Fund (WWF) is working around the world to protect endangered wildlife, and preserve wild lands and address global threats and challenges. Working with dedicated members and conservation partners, WWF protects endangered wildlife and habitats on a global scale. *www.wwf-uk.org* Tel: 0044 (0)1483 426444

(You can make easy tax-free donations to many of these NGOs at *www.gooshing.co.uk*. Here you will also find 250,000 products for sale – with ethical ratings and a price-search mechanism that will find you the cheapest purchase point from over 350 online shops)

Green events

A note on the year's Green Events, by Peter McCaig.

It used to be that being an environmentalist was something that went against the grain. With the majority of people cheerfully chewing up the planet's resources it was easy at times to feel isolated and disheartened if you were the only one you knew making conscious choices. Whenever I got like this, feeling I was bucking the trend instead of going with the flow, I would look for events such as a protest march or festival to participate in where I knew I would be in the company of like minded spirits who cared as much about environmental and social issues as I did. Inevitably I would come away feeling revived and re-empowered to go on trying to make a difference. Rubbing shoulders with other activists made me feel I wasn't on my own, and that my efforts were not wasted. The positive effect of making a stand and demonstrating one's solidarity was even widely publicised in the press after the huge demonstration against the upcoming invasion of Iraq in January 2003. Even though it didn't achieve the desired effect of averting the war and subsequent bloodshed, thousands of people later surveyed reported a 'feel good' factor though having taken a stand and demonstrated their solidarity.

More recently, it begins to feel that those taking an active part in social or environmental issues, whether it's buying fair traded goods or participating in recycling initiatives or human rights campaigns, are more the rule rather than the exception. If, at any point, however, you feel your spirits flagging here are a few events for you to attend and give your resolve a boost.

Green Events is a free magazine which provides comprehensivealternative listings for London and elsewhere. You can visit their website at www.greenevents.fsnet.co.uk

Kingston Green Fair
London's biggest & best green fair on the banks of the Thames, which traditionally kicks off the festival season.

Bank Holiday Monday 30th May 2005, 11 am - 8 pm

Canbury Gardens, Kingston Upon Thames 020 8974 8608, *www.kingstongreenfair.org*

Camden Green Fair & Bikefest
North London's biggest Green Fair and bicyclists' rally is scheduled to take place on a Sunday in late June or early July

Call the Info hotline: 020 7974 2192 or 07963 818016 nearer the date for precise information.

The Big Green Gathering 2005
All the participants from Green Fields of the Glastonbury festival traditionally decamp to Cheddar in Somerset for what is Britain's biggest solar and wind powered event at the end of July.

For enquiries and further information, email: *info@big-green-gathering.co.*
Tel: 01458 834629.
www.big-green-gathering.com

Ambient GreenPicnic
A one day eco-friendly event promoting environmental issues, arts and music. Usually on the first Sunday in August at Shalford Park, Guildford.

Contact Craig Hills 07956-319692,
info@ambientpicnic.co.uk
www.ambientpicnic.co.uk

Carshalton Environmental Fair
Demonstrating the best environmental initiatives south of the river.

For more information or to book a stall call 020 8647 9201 or email: *environmentalfair@hotmail.com*

Bank holiday Monday 29th August, 11 am - 8 pm Carshalton Park, Ruskin Road, Carshalton, (near Sutton)

Northampton Green Festival
Free - Northampton's Green Festival aims to promote ecological balance, social justice, and sustainability in a friendly and relaxing environment.

Abington Park, Northampton 1st Sunday in September

info@greenfestival.org.uk www.greenfestival.org.uk

Car Free Day
If you're feeling guilty about using up your carbon allowance attending every Green Event in 2005 then maybe 22nd September is the day for you to compensate by staying at home, turning off every appliance in the house, defrosting the fridge, and participate wholeheartedly in European Car Free Day.

For more info see www.22september.org

For monthly updates on all kinds of green events taking place through 2005 see *www.greenevents.fsnet.co.uk*

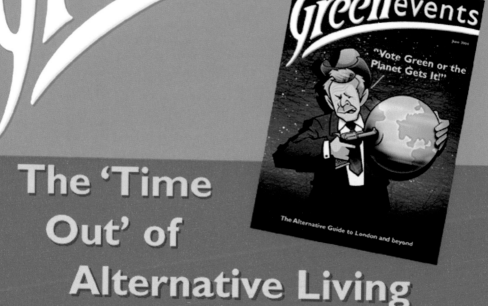

Ethical internet

The Internet has always been fertile ground for ethically-minded and socially conscious organisations and individuals. Since its inception it's been a place for forward thinkers and early adopters, and ethical shoppers can now have a field day! And by its nature the World Wide Web is environmentally sound, an endless library of information yet no tree has ever been cut down in its name! But the web can be a monster too, full of mind polluting words and images. The following URLs fall under the best possible category, representing an enlightened approach to living, shopping, surfing...

www.gooshing.co.uk
"Google for searching: Gooshing for shopping!" This is the new website from the people who each year brings you the ethical shopping bible, *The Good Shopping Guide*. It compares prices and ethical ratings on over 250,000 products from over 350 online sales points. Gooshing really is the best one stop shop for every price-sensitive ethical shopper. Read more about it on page 324.

www.ethicalconsumer.org
This is the website for the pioneering Manchester-based organisation which examines the social and environmental records of the companies behind the brand names. The Ethical Consumer Organisation was the first of its kind in the UK.

www.adbusters.org
Adbusters organise International Buy Nothing Day and TV Turn-Off Week. Adored by academics and switched-on consumers, the Adbusters website is a joy to surf through, exposing many multi nationals and their hidden agendas with the powerful weapons of knowledge and humour. Adbusters is launching its own brand not for profit trainers, taking on arch rivals like Nike head-to-head!

www.naturalcollection.co.uk
Natural collection sell a range of eclectic, unusual, useful and interesting products carefully chosen to inspire ideas towards a sustainable future. Shoppers can donate a percentage of their purchase to worthwhile organisations including Friends of the Earth and Greenpeace.

www.planetark.org
By far the biggest archive for all environmental-related news issues. It also supplies a daily email package of all World Environment News headlines.

www.ethicalexchange.co.uk
Offers news both online and by email as well as providing a directory of ethical organisations.

www.ethicaljunction.co.uk
A one-stop shop for ethical advice and information.

www.getethical.com
The Big Issue's online ethical resource is a trustworthy resource for companies dedicated to social and environmental justice. It is an excellent shopping site as well as a portal to the wider world of ethical news.

www.greenguide.co.uk
This website is run by the publishers of Pure Magazine and The Green Guide. It's good for news updates and shopping too.

www.good-energy.co.uk
Switch to the UK's only 100% green electricity supplier here. Good Energy is recommended by Friends of the Earth and other independent organisations.

www.foe.co.uk and www.greenpeace.org
The online homes of arguably the most important non government organisations in the environmental field.

www.thegoodshoppingguide.co.uk
This is where you can buy direct copies of *The Good Shopping Guide* for your friends with free packaging and postage.

www.ethical-company-organisation.org
The online home of the Ethical Company Organisation and its company accreditation scheme.

www.surefish.co.uk
This is a website and ISP that works to change lives. 100% of its profits support Christian Aid's work to reduce poverty world-wide.

Website accessibility

Websites should be accessible to a wide range of people with disabilities. It not only makes good business sense for companies to allow as many people to view their sites as possible, but is essential to fulfil their obligations under new UK anti-discrimination laws. So why do the majority of companies get it so badly wrong?

There are 37 million people with disabilities in the European Union and contrary to what many companies would have you believe, the Internet is a huge part of disabled peoples' lives. They want to be able to buy tickets to see a concert, carry out online banking and do just about anything else.

Architects who design buildings and shops have a duty to provide equal access for all. Unfortunately web designers, the "architects of the Web", have been slow to understand Web accessibility issues.

People with a wide range of visual, hearing, motor and cognitive impairments often use special assistive devices to access a computer or the Internet, such as voice recognition software, various keyboard adaptations and speech output systems. Unfortunately design faults in many websites mean that access is often limited.

In a bid to highlight the issue, we commissioned the accessibility experts at Enable Interactive to survey the websites of 50 of the UK's 100 most ethical companies (as published by the Ethical Company Organisation in 2004).

Enable Interactive

(*www.enableinteractive.co.uk*) tested each site for accessibility, usability (how user-friendly the site is) and compliance against the Web Content Accessibility Guidelines (which define websites' legal obligation under European legislation).

THE 10 BEST-PERFORMING WEBSITES WERE...

1 Rachel's Organic Dairy

2 Bradford & Bingley

3 Highland Spring

4 Cafédirect

5 Green & Blacks

6 Percol

7 Alliance & Leicester

8 Jonathan Crisp

9 Neal's Yard

10 The Redwood Wholefood Company

Source – Enable Interactive 2004

Enable Interactive stated that although the companies in *The Good Shopping Guide's* Top 100 must be congratulated on their general ethical standards, there is plenty of room for improvement in the way their websites cater for the disabled."

One of Enable Interactive's accessibility experts, Matt Connolly, said 'Improving accessibility has become really important. It's not just about being seen to be doing the socially responsible thing - companies need to consider the bigger picture. An inaccessible website is the online equivalent of painting your product black and putting it on a high shelf where your customers can't reach it."

Traditionally many companies have seen accessibility as a drain on resources or simply a legal hurdle to be overcome. What they are ignoring is the frustration or negative feelings a customer will have toward the company if they have an unsuccessful interaction with a product or service.

A properly implemented web accessibility strategy will not only avoid possible prosecution under the Disability Discrimination Act but genuinely helps a very large number of people.

About Gooshing

Saving you money. Saving the planet. Gooshing is set to become the world's favourite shop!

The Ethical Company Organisation started *The Good Shopping Guide* just 3 years ago and, have now launched www.gooshing.co.uk – to make online ethical shopping easier and cheaper. This way ethical shopping will become an even more powerful movement, worldwide.

The secret of Gooshing's growing popularity among green, animal welfare and human rights supporters is that it is a genuine one-stop-shop. It features thousands of different products – providing ethical comparisons and a price-search mechanism which guarantees to deliver you the lowest price on your product of choice from over 350 retailers.

Gooshing uses the ethical rating research system of The Ethical Company Organisation's Research Department. This uses significantly less ethical criteria than those found in *The Good Shopping Guide* – focusing on those that are most relevant to the products that are most commonly bought online. Because of the differing methodology, ethical ratings will occasionally differ slightly from those found in *The Good Shopping Guide*.

In total, Gooshing features over 250,000 products – everything from cds, dvds, home appliances, computer gear, electronics, home office, energy etc etc.

Whatever you want to buy, Gooshing will direct you to the most ethical brand choices – and then the very cheapest place to buy that product.

And you can buy securely using a credit or switch card - the goods will be delivered direct to your door.

Gooshing aims to save you money and put even more ethical consumer pressure on the world's worst offending companies – to be more respectful to the peoples and the animals and the environment of the world we live in. Now that's gooshingly good shopping!

save money · save the planet
gooshing
world shopping revolution
shop at gooshing.co.uk

We highly recommend you use *www.gooshing.co.uk* for all your online shopping needs.

The Ethical Marketplace

I USED TO BE A PLASTIC CUP...
I USED TO BE A PLASTIC CUP...
...that's Remarkable
Pencils made from recycled plastic cups & other recycled products...
Remarkable
Remarkable Pencils Ltd
56 Glentham Road London UK SW13 9JJ
Tel: 020 8741 1234 Fax: 020 8741 7615
www.remarkable.co.uk
Turning junk into something Remarkable

What more could we want?
The League Against Cruel Sports has long campaigned for a ban on bloodsports, but the end of the hunt will not bring an end to the abuse and suffering of thousands of other animals in the name of sport.
For information on the hunt bill, our new campaigns and ways to help, visit:
www.league.uk.com
83/87 Union St, London, SE1 1SG
020 7403 6155 gsg@league.uk.com

Infinityfoods
The Organic & Natural food Wholesaler
Over 4,000 lines mostly Organic.
Full range of commodities & branded goods.
An extensive & expanding range of "Infinity" own label products & commodities.
National delivery service.
www.Infinityfoods.co.uk
Franklin Road, Portslade, East Sussex, BN41 1AF.
Tel : 01273 424060. Fax : 01273 417739

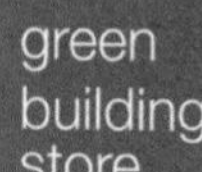
green
building
store

RUGMARK®

RUGMARK
International Trade Mark

w.greenfibres.com
eco goods and garments
• organic bedding, pillows, & mattresses
• organic clothes, cosmetics, & cleaners
• free mail order brochure
0845 330 3440
GREENFIBRES
freepost LON7805 gsg
totnes TQ9 5ZZ

Siesta
1 Palace Street
Canterbury Kent CT1 2DY
Tel: (01227) 464614
Fax: (01227) 832241
Email: siesta.uk@virgin.net
www.siestacrafts.co.uk
A Recognised Fair Trade Supplier of Ethnic Musical Instruments, Gifts & Clothing
Please contact us for a catalogue or see the website

green people
organic lifestyle
3 layers of protection!
natural anti-oxidants
natural UVA & UVB filters
natural suntan accelerator
100% gentle
100% vegetarian
100% cruelty-free
handmade with certified
organic ingredients
Vegan
we don't use Sodium Lauryl/Laureth Sulphate, Parabens, Synthetic Fragrances, Colourants, Petrochemicals, Ethyl Alcohol, PABA-sunscreen, Urea, PEG's, DEA, TEA, irritating emulsifiers or any unnecessary synthetic additives common in many of today's health and beauty products
tel. 08702 401444 www.greenpeople.co.uk

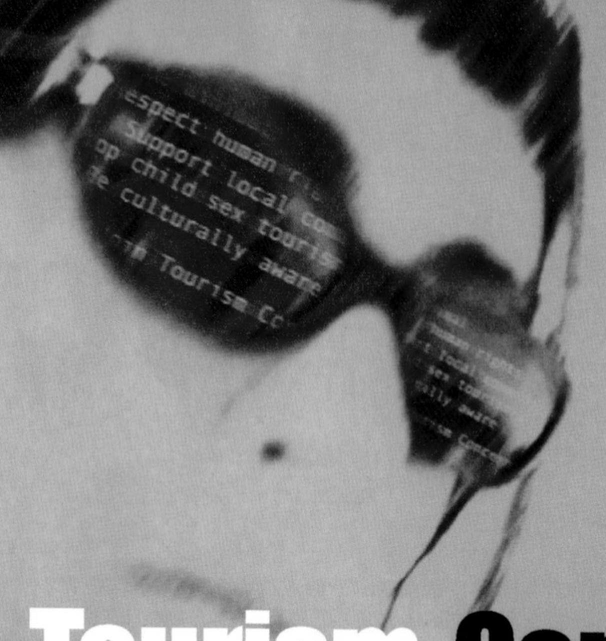

next stop: fair trade tourism